TOP HAT, GREY WOLF AND CRESCENT

HUGH POULTON

Top Hat, Grey Wolf and Crescent

Turkish Nationalism and the Turkish Republic

NEW YORK UNIVERSITY PRESS
Washington Square, New York

First published in the U.S.A. by
NEW YORK UNIVERSITY PRESS
Washington Square
New York, N.Y. 10003

Library of Congress Cataloging-in-Publication Data

Poulton, Hugh.
    Top Hat, Grey Wolf, and Crescent: Turkish nationalism and
the Turkish Republic / Hugh Poulton.
          p.   cm.
    Includes bibliographical references (p.   ) and index.
    ISBN 0-8147-6648-X
    1. Nationalism—Turkey.   2. Pan-Turanianism.   3. Islam—Turkey.
4. Minorities—Turkey—Politics and government.   I. Title.
DR432.P68   1997
320.5′4′09561—dc20   96-41941
                                                                    CIP

Printed in England

For Matt, Zak and Joe

ACKNOWLEDGEMENTS

The writing of this book would not have been possible without the help and support of a large number of people. I especially thank John Norton, Andrew Mango, all those at the School of Oriental and African Studies, London University, who helped in a variety of ways, and all those at Turkey Briefing when it was still operational (especially Patricia, Susannah, Amelia, Adrian and Libby). Special thanks go to Aydin for his hospitality and help, and above all to Bill Hale for all his guidance and comments. I also wish to thank Christopher Hurst and Michael Dwyer for their role in the editing and production of the book. I of course accept full responsibility for the opinions expressed, and for any errors.

April 1997   H. P.

CONTENTS

1

NATIONALISM

This chapter looks at nationalism as a political ideology. It will examine its birth in Europe and its subsequent spread around the globe. The different varieties of nationalism will be analysed as will some of the main theories about it. The chapter will conclude with an attempted synthesis of the main theories which will be used in subsequent chapters as a framework for the analysis of Turkish nationalism.

Nationalism is primarily about belonging. It is about one form of group identity and the loyalties of the individual. Some, like Eric Hobsbawm,[1] tended, till recently at least, to see nationalism as a political force on the wane. This was perhaps due to the traditional Marxist antipathy to it as a rival to international class solidarity, its discrediting due to the horrors produced by Nazism and the Second World War, and the seeming emergence in Western Europe of a pan-national political structure – the European Community. However, events during the 1990s in Eastern Europe and the former Soviet Union demonstrate that nationalism remains as potent a force as ever. The rise of Jean-Marie Le Pen in France and the recent anti-immigrant riots in Germany have also shown that nationalism, chauvinism and racialism can be as virulent as it has ever been, even in the heartland of Western Europe. Another illustration of nationalism in contemporary Europe is the strength of opposition to the European Union in countries like Britain, Denmark and even the EU's 'core' countries like Germany and France. It seems that nationalism is destined to continue as a prime mobiliser.

[1] Eric Hobsbawm, *Nations and Nationalism since 1870: Programme, Myth, Reality* (Cambridge University Press, 1990) p. 192.

The French Revolution and 'the Nation'

Anthony Smith defines nationalism as 'an ideological movement for the attainment and maintenance of autonomy, cohesion and individuality for a social group deemed by some of its members to constitute an actual or potential nation. In other words, nationalism is both an ideology and a movement'.[2] Although others like Ernest Gellner approach the definition of nationalism from different angles, which will be discussed below, this seems a useful starting-point.

Most observers see nationalism as a modern phenomenon which originated in Europe at the end of the eighteenth or beginning of the nineteenth century. The events of the French Revolution and the ensuing wars revealed fully, perhaps for the first time, the enormous latent power of 'the nation' and 'nationalism' as a means of mass mobilisation, as well as spreading the idea of popular sovereignty as the foundation of ruling legitimacy. Whether one sees nationalism as a reaction to the power of revolutionary France which first occurred in Eastern Europe, primarily among German-speaking peoples divided among a patchwork of states – as Kedourie and others do[3] – or sees its origins in revolutionary France itself with such crucial events as the 'Declaration of the Rights of Man and the Citizen' and the *levée en masse* of 1793 serving to release its latent power, is perhaps a matter of choice. The two different starting-points are reflected in the contrast between 'civic' and 'ethnic' nationalism as discussed below. However, there is wide consensus that nationalism as a political doctrine originates in this period. For example, whereas before the French revolution it was common for wars to be fought with much assistance from foreign – often Swiss – mercenaries, henceforth national armies became the norm. Similarly, whereas before the revolution it was not seen as odd that the ruler of one country might be the titular head of another, such situations came to be seen as increasingly anachronistic.

Clearly, some understanding of what constitutes 'a nation' is

[2] Anthony Smith, 'The Formation of Nationalist Movements', in Anthony Smith (ed.), *Nationalist Movements* (London: Macmillan, 1976), p. 1.

[3] Elie Kedourie, *Nationalism* (London: Hutchinson, 1966), *passim*, and *Nationalism in Asia and Africa* (New York: Meridian, 1970), *passim*; Tom Nairn, *The Break-up of Britain* (London: Verso, 1981), *passim*.

of critical importance in any discussion of nationalism. What then is a nation? The 'Declaration of the Rights of Man and the Citizen' stated:

> The principle of sovereignty resides essentially in the Nation; no body of men, no individual, can exercise authority that does not emanate expressly from it.[4]

However, as Kedourie points out, the meaning of the word 'nation' has changed in the course of time. For example, medieval universities were divided into 'nations' – the University of Paris had four: *'la nation de France'* included all speakers of Romance languages while *'la nation de Germanie'* included English speakers.[5] However, while 'nation' did not historically have the connotations which it later gained in the Declaration, it certainly referred to a wider section of society than royalty and the aristocracy. Thus, in the French case, the 'nation' was a concept of internal politics relating to the division of power. It was later, with the Napoleonic Wars, that it came to mean the French people rather than other peoples –Germans, Russians, etc. In this case, French nationalism became identified with Bonapartism and even became distinguished from republicanism.

Sieyès answered the question 'what is a nation' with the answer 'a body of associates living under one common law and represented by the same legislature.'[6] However, this takes no account of differences, real or imaginary, of religion, language or culture, nor the revolutionary and destructive impact of nationalism (an ideology and movement which looks to the 'nation' for legitimacy) on, for example, heterogeneous empires. The subjects of such empires may well live 'under one common law' and be 'represented by the same legislature' but are perceived as 'multi-national' by nationalists. Ernest Renan in his 1882 lecture *'Qu'est-ce qu'une Nation?'* looked at the different criteria for distinguishing nations –language, culture and so on–and found them all wanting as definitive markers. He concluded that the will of the individual must ultimately indicate whether a nation exists or not, and his own description of the nation is that it is a 'daily pleb-

---

[4] Quoted in Elie Kedourie, *Nationalism*, p. 12.

[5] *Ibid.*, p. 13.

[6] Quoted in *Ibid.*, p. 15.

iscite'.[7] This element of will is also reflected in Mazzini's definition
of a nation being 'a fellowship of free and equal men bound
together in a brotherly concord', with the primary bond being
language.[8] The element of 'will' will be further looked at later
in connection with the question of whether states create nations,
or vice-versa, or both.

Mazzini's definition has similarities to Anthony Smith's of a
nation as

> ....a large, vertically integrated and territorially mobile group
> featuring common citizenship rights and collective sentiment
> together with one (or more) common characteristic(s) which
> differentiate its members from those of similar groups with
> whom they stand in relations of alliance or conflict.[9]

However, common citizenship rights are not a requisite. Indeed,
much nationalist activity is based precisely on the idea that the
perceived nation does not have common rights, due to its being
divided between different states. Smith's inclusion of 'large' in
his definition is also interesting. How large is 'large'? Large enough
to be able to realise a sustainable economy within the idealised
nation state framework? This question has acquired European
significance with the fragmentation of the former Yugoslavia and
the ironic spectacle of a minister from Luxembourg, speaking in
the name of the European Community, telling the Slovenes and
the Croats that they were too small to secede from the Yugoslav
federation.[10] Despite these reservations, Smith's definition would
seem a reasonable starting-point. Although 'the nation' is of crucial
importance to 'nationalism', Smith rightly points out that there
are many 'nations' (as defined) without nationalism and vice versa.[11]

[7] Ernest Renan, 'What is a Nation?' in A. Zimmern (ed.), *Modern Political Doctrines* (Oxford University Press, 1939), pp. 186-205.

[8] G. Mazzini, *The Duties of Man and other Essays* (Everyman's Library, repr. 1966) pp. 55-8.

[9] Anthony Smith, *Theories of Nationalism* (London: Duckworth, 1971), p. 175.

[10] Laura Silber and Allan Little, *The Death of Yugoslavia* (London: Penguin, 1995), pp. 175.

[11] Anthony Smith, *Theories of Nationalism*, p. 175.

Minority intellectuals and upward mobility

Why would/should the individual want to be part of a nation in Renan's 'daily plebiscite' anyway? Given that there is a universal 'need to belong', and that all (or at least the vast majority) of human beings crave security and desire to belong to a human group of some kind,[12] why the nation as opposed to empire, guild, city or class? Kedourie, who, as noted above, sees nationalism as primarily a German invention, concentrates on the evolution of German thought from Kant to Fichte and Herder. Fichte posited a universal consciousness, with affinities to Rousseau's general will, which transcended all individuals, and that the universe is 'an organic whole, no part of which can exist without the existence of all the rest.'[13] In his *Foundations of Natural Law* in 1796, he states:

> Between the isolated man and the citizen, there is the same relation as between raw and organised matter ... In an organised body each part continuously maintains the whole, and in maintaining it, maintains itself also. Similarly the citizen with regard to the state.[14]

But the German society to which Fichte referred was divided between a patchwork of states, some very small indeed, and the above does not answer the question 'why the nation rather than the state'. Culture was the key, seen by Fichte as the process whereby a human being really becomes human.[15] He saw struggle between these small states as a good thing:

> One should not regret the decline of one's own country [state] in a struggle as our true Fatherland must always be that state which occupies the highest rank of culture.[16]

This 'ethnocentric' nationalism related directly to the situation of the German states at that time: they were often small, internally rigid, absolutist states within which upward mobility was very

---

[12] *Ibid.*, p. 28.

[13] Quoted in Kedourie, *Nationalism*, p. 37.

[14] *Ibid.*

[15] *Ibid.*, p. 38.

[16] Fichte, quoted in *ibid.*, p. 54.

difficult. As Kedourie points out, the harbingers of German nationalism were the new intelligentsia who found the routes to their advancement blocked despite their acquired intellectual knowledge.[17] Kedourie raises the crucial matter of trying to ascertain what sort of person becomes an active nationalist, and his picture of the intellectual whose route to advancement is blocked, like Johann Gottfried von Herder, who poured his resentments and frustrations into his diaries in 1769,[18] can be repeated in many other contexts of rising nationalisms, both in Eastern Europe in the late nineteenth century and the European colonies in the twentieth century.

Conversely, perhaps, in situations where minority intellectuals have ample opportunity for advancement, the appeal of radical nationalism is diminished. For example Britain, whose empire and role as the leading industrial power in the second half of the eighteenth and the nineteenth century gave ample opportunity to the Scots and Welsh for advancement within the existing order. The Scots especially took full advantage of the new opportunities, providing many of the household names of the industrial revolution.[19] This situation perhaps helps to explain the absence of Scottish nationalism in that period.[20]

While economic success can alleviate potential nationalisms, economic malaise can do the reverse. Intellectuals naturally react to decline within their societies by seeking possible remedies. Nationalism, with its powerful mobilisatory appeal, is unsurprisingly often seen as a way of remedying a decline – indeed many see economic and social collapse as an essential precondition for the growth of radical nationalism, which can degenerate into racism or fascism.[21] The situation of a society with a very low standard

---

[17] *Ibid.*, p. 43.

[18] *Ibid.*, p. 44.

[19] See Linda Colley, *Britons: Forging the Nation, 1707-1837* (London: Pimlico, 1994), pp. 117-32.

[20] See Nairn, *op. cit.*, pp. 94-125.

[21] Benedict Anderson, in *Imagined Communities: Reflections on the origin and Spread of Nationalism* (London: Verso, rev. edn 1991), p. 149, contends that fascism as a phenomenon is not such a close relative of nationalism, and is more to do with crises in capitalism, etc. However, I find his arguments on this unconvincing and follow others like Kedourie (*Nationalism, passim*) and Nairn (*op. cit.*, pp. 14-15) who see a close link between fascism and nationalism.

of living to begin with can serve as a similar impetus to that of an actual decline. In this case, the intellectual, often trained in the methods of a more 'advanced' society, can feel a sense of national shame at the backwardness of his or her own society. Nationalism holds strong appeal in such circumstances, with its promise that if the latent energies of 'the nation' could only be tapped, this humiliating backwardness would be overcome. Thus, nationalism is often used by élites as a method for attempting to overcome backwardness and achieve modernisation.

Mixed communities

Another environmental factor apparently conducive to breeding active nationalists is mixed communities and multi-ethnicity. As noted at the start, nationalism is about belonging, and a factor in this is that of contrast between the perceived group and one or a variety of 'others'. Where the group lives in close proximity or in mixed communities with these 'others', nationalism is often pronounced. Moreover, there is sometimes a 'knock-on' effect, with rival nationalisms in such areas becoming more defined in relation to each other. As one grows, so the other grows in reaction. As the Norwegian anthropologist Frederik Barth and others note, groups tend to define themselves not by reference to their own characteristics but by exclusion, that is by comparison to 'strangers'.[22] A good example of this tendency occurs in Canada, where, putting to one side the continuing crisis in Canadian national identity, due to problems between the French- and English-speaking groups, the vast majority of the population, most of whom live in close proximity to the border with the United States, when asked in public opinion polls to define what makes a Canadian, start with a negative definition – that is, not being a citizen of the United States.

It has often been noted that radical nationalists frequently come from border regions or regions where the group they champion is either a minority or faced with competing groups. For example Hitler, another frustrated and rejected would-be intellectual, came from Austria, Napoleon came from Corsica, and so on. As we

[22] See John Armstrong, *Nations Before Nationalism* (Chapel Hill: University of North Carolina Press, 1982), p. 5.

shall see later, in the Turkish context, initial leaders came from Russia or, like the Young Turk leaders, and Atatürk himself, from Macedonia; the present Turkish arch-nationalist, Alparslan Türkeş, was born in Cyprus. The current tragedy in Yugoslavia offers other examples of such nationalists from the 'periphery' like Radovan Karadžić, the leader of the Bosnian Serbs, who hails from a pleasant family in Montenegro and was looked down on by the Sarajevo élite. It seems that the 'periphery' is more conducive to creating nationalists than the 'centre'. Experience in Western Europe has also shown that the influx of large numbers of immigrants, especially those of a different colour who are more readily perceived as 'strangers', can give rise to virulent nationalism or racism in the centre itself. The key here is the presence of mixed communities.

War

Another important factor, which often combines with that of mixed communities, is war. We began with the French Revolution and the Napoleonic Wars as powerful stimulants to the new political creed of nationalism, and wars have continued to play this role. Indeed, one can see war as often playing a crucial part in determination of identity before the advent of modern nationalism. A case in point is that of England/Britain, which is problematic in terms of modern nationalism. What made the British? In a recent book,[23] Linda Colley, while beginning with the religious factor of Protestanism, points to war as an even stronger determinant of identity. The constant wars or threat of wars with France over an extended period are seen as crucial to the moulding of 'the British nation'. Here, France and the French were used as the 'other'. The actual hostilities played out on a world stage in India, Africa and North America merged with other forms of contest – notably trade, which, as noted above, allowed the potentially divergent elements like the Scots, the Welsh and even the Irish to merge into the whole without losing their distinctiveness.

Whether this patriotism in wartime can be equated with nationalism will be discussed below; the point here is the part war played in forging the group. For the British, success, both

[23] Linda Colley, *Britons*, pp. 283-320.

in war and trade, was perhaps crucial, and the steady post-empire and post-Second World War decline of Britain has seen a rising nationalism among the British 'minorities'. The importance of war to nationalism as an anvil for hammering out a national identity is also mirrored in the frequent use of military parades and military anniversaries in national celebrations in many countries. Armies and universal conscription (revealingly termed national service) are also used as a means of instilling unitary nationalistic values into a heterogeneous population, as well as aiding a general socialisation process. The role of the army as a primary educator in the state language is often marked – Israel and Turkey (see Chapter 4) being cases in point. War is a powerful delineator between different groups, and the combination of modern nationalism with war often leads to the terrible spectacle of whole populations being stigmatised with collective guilt and subjected to inhuman measures, purely for being perceived as belonging to the wrong group.

The German model and the importance of language

Having pointed to some factors – frustrated intellectuals, economic malaise, mixed communities and war – which aid the growth of nationalism, perhaps we should return to factors by which the group or 'nation' is differentiated from others, especially in mixed 'peripheral' areas. Kedourie points to all these factors in the nineteenth-century German situation. Here the populace was divided between a patchwork of states, some no more than a few square kilometres in area and with very small populations. Hence, radical German nationalists like Fichte and Herder looked to an amalgamation of these states which would possibly allow greater leeway for their talents; the criterion they used for the amalgamation was language. This raises problems about how to define a language as opposed to a dialect. In Western Europe, the decline of Latin as the universal language of scholarship, due to the advent of the printing press and a new wider public unwilling to learn a 'foreign' language, led to the emergence of state languages. In such cases, for instance in France, one dialect, *langue d'oïl*, became the official state and literary language (and thus the carrier of 'high' culture),[24] while others like Provençal remained mere dialects.[25]

The French Revolution had begun with the idea that the nation was a number of individuals who had signified their will as to the manner of government. Now according to Kedourie,[26] the Germans amplified this so that the nation was seen as the natural division of the human race endowed by God with its own character, which its citizens must, as a duty, preserve pure and inviolable. Thus, it follows that the best political arrangement was for each nation to form its own state – the 'Nation State'. Hence, multi-national states were 'unnatural' and doomed to decay, while, conversely, the small German states were destined to unite.

But what differentiated a German from his or her neighbours? The answer for German nationalists was language. As Herder in his *Treatise upon the Origin of Language* wrote in 1772, language was not a colourless medium but a repository of emotions and inner experience and the outcome of a particular history, the legacy of a distinctive tradition.[27] F. Schleiermacher asserted that 'only one language is firmly implanted in an individual.'[28] Fichte agreed with this and was very critical of the use of foreign loan words, calling instead for a 'purification' of German, which had to be 'cleansed' of foreign accretions and borrowings.[29] In this view, the language group becomes paramount and its borders are those of the 'nation'. Unlike some, Kedourie sees no clear-cut distinction between linguistic and racial nationalisms; language, according to the German model, was merely an outward sign, peculiar to a nation because that nation constituted a racial stock.[30] Whereas in nationalist doctrine language, race, culture and some-times religion constitute different aspects of the nation, Kedourie sees it as 'misplaced ingenuity to try and classify nationalisms

---

[24] The role of 'high' cultures *vis-à-vis* 'low' cultures is discussed below in relation to Gellner's ideas.

[25] Actually, Provençal had been a literary language in the Middle Ages, while *langue d'oïl* had a (more rare) literary form as well as the spoken form. The question of language/dialects in the Turkish case is looked at in Chapter 3.

[26] Kedourie, *Nationalism*, p. 58.

[27] Herder, quoted in *Ibid.*, p. 62.

[28] F. Schleiermacher, quoted in *Ibid.*, p. 63.

[29] Fichte, quoted in *Ibid.*, p. 66-7.

[30] *Ibid.*, p. 71.

according to the particular aspect which they choose to emphasise.'[31]

Where Kedourie does differentiate, however, is in the distinction
he perceives between nationalism, patriotism and xenophobia.
Patriotism is seen as affection for one's country and loyalty to its
institutions, which he regards as a universal phenomenon, in the
same way as xenophobia. However, nationalism is not a universal
phenomenon, he argues, but a product of recent history. In this
context Kedourie asserts that it is

> ....inexact to speak ... of a British or American nationalism
> [for those] who recommend loyalty to British or American
> political institutions. A British or American nationalist would
> have to define the British or American nation in terms of
> language, race or religion [and thus sort out the population
> by this criteria].[32]

Similarly, Kedourie suggests that nationalism is not equatable with
tribalism, as tribal custom is not due to the 'general will' or
reason and thus does not derive from self-determination.[33] While
his point about tribalism is perhaps valid, his refusal to allow for
the growth of a 'civic' nationalism – that is, one where loyalty
to the institutions and the state are paramount over those of the
language group – appears too restrictive; we will return to this
later.

Kedourie does, however, rightly point to the problems of his
model when applied to areas like Eastern Europe, where different
language groups are or were inextricably mixed. He points out
that if the language group equates to 'the nation state' then irredentism and conflict inevitably arise. He makes the valuable
point that nineteenth-century nationalism was for the main
espoused by 'literary men who had never exercised power and
thus not used to the necessities and obligations between states.'[34]
Whereas Fichte saw the linguistic boundary as the 'real' boundary,
in reality frontiers were 'established by power and maintained by
the constant and known readiness to defend them by arms not

---

[31] *Ibid.*, p. 73.
[32] *Ibid.*, p. 74.
[33] *Ibid.*
[34] *Ibid.*, pp. 69-71.

by professors and folklore experts.' Nor in Kedourie's view could boundaries be decided by plebiscites as these were not akin to elections which could be overturned at some future date[35] – a view mirrored in Renan's 'daily plebiscite' model. In addition, towns were often populated by people drawn from different language groups in the surrounding countryside. In many areas the countryside itself was a patchwork of differing language or dialect groups located in villages which, while in geographical proximity, were different from each other in nineteenth-century German nationalist terms.

The picture is further complicated in Asia, where often large centralised empires had no exact borders, leaving large areas nominally controlled by military centres where local powers were actually able to retain degrees of autonomy. To these observations, the nationalist could possibly reply that, certainly, historic boundaries were made by force, and that large centralised empires often had inexact boundary areas. Sometimes such areas were deliberately kept unmobilised as a means of preserving central control. However, the nationalist would argue, the new creed would tear up these 'artificial' and 'unjust' frontiers and establish 'true' ones based on the only criterion which really mattered – the 'real' nation. It is unclear how a nationalist would view the situation of an 'open' frontier as seen in the cases of both the United States and Russia, which expanded across continents they perceived as effectively empty (even though the lands were not entirely unpopulated).

This leads on to the sometimes fine line between nationalism and chauvinism – that is, between claiming an equal place for a particular group or nation and claiming a superior position. Nationalists naturally tend to emphasise the perceived positive aspects of their particular nation – especially when one or more group is claiming the same territory. It is a relatively small step from this to asserting one's claim by claiming superiority, often ransacking history for examples, real or imagined, to back up the claim. This can also lead to claiming 'historic' areas for a 'nation' even though these lands have been lived in (or 'occupied') by other peoples for long periods – for example Israel. The struggles in Central Europe in 1848, when the so-called (and self-claimed)

---

[35] *Ibid.*, p. 125.

historic nations such as the Germans and the Magyars claimed that their particular nationalisms were more justified than Romanian, Czech, Serb or Croat ones, are illustrations of this. In many cases extreme nationalists tend to claim that their particular nation is innately the most superior in the world. Thus, nationalism which sees each nation with its own particular character degenerates into chauvinism and racism, where the characteristics are graded so that one nation is seen as superior to another. In this, the study of history in particular assumes enormous significance for nationalists. Here, Smith makes the point that in Africa pre-colonial history is often scarce and that the trauma of colonialism and slavery, and the racial aspects of both, are often more potent in the consciousness than this more shadowy history. In such cases, Smith asserts, skin colour can play the same role as language did in the German case, and act as a substitute for history as well as language.[36]

An obvious weakness of Kedourie's views is that he uses the German experience as the model for all emergent nationalisms. As such his view of nationalisms in Asia and Africa is particularly scathing, as he sees them as complete inventions by unrepresentative Western-trained élites.[37] Moreover, due to his emphasis on 'organic' nationalism along the German model, and his denial of a 'civic' nationalism along the lines of Western as opposed to the Central or Eastern European variety (that is, where loyalty to institutions and the state tended to rule over loyalty to a language group), he tends to see all nationalism as a destructive force. While it is true that modern nationalism has perhaps been responsible for 'new and greater conflicts', as Kedourie suggests,[38] it has also been the engine for modernisation in many cases. Either way, it is a fact that nationalism remains a potent force and one which cannot be easily dismissed.

'Civic' and 'ethnic' nationalisms

The question of the growth of nationalism in the European colonies

[36] Anthony Smith, *Nationalism in the Twentieth Century* (Oxford University Press, 1979), p. 21.

[37] Elie Kedourie, *Nationalism in Asia and Africa, passim.*

[38] Elie Kedourie, *Nationalism*, p. 138.

of Asia and Africa in the twentieth century brings us back to the
concept of 'civic' nationalism. Smith rejects as too narrow
Kedourie's 'organic' basis for nationalism, and instead tries to
accommodate the German 'blood and soil' nationalism with the
'Whig' doctrine of Locke and Mill. The latter derives from Locke's
theories of individual rights, and leads to the notion that self-
government, that is 'national' government as opposed to 'foreign',
is likely to be 'good' government.[39] This theme also occurs strongly
in the American Revolution and the advent of American (US)
nationalism. Such an approach is seen in Hans Kohn's distinction
between 'Western' – that is, 'civic' – nationalisms and 'Eastern' (organic) nationalisms. The former emerged in England, the United
States, France, Holland and Switzerland, and he sees them as
predominantly an expression of the rising middle classes, harking
back to the Renaissance cultural models and as essentially rationalist,
optimistic and pluralist. The latter, which emerged in Eastern
Europe and Asia, he sees as movements of the lower aristocracy
and 'the masses'. These were essentially emotional but authoritarian
reactions against the perceived inferiority of the relevant ancient
organic *volk vis-à-vis* the West, combined with a messianic sense
of having been chosen for a mission for mankind.[40]

Smith points out that there have been manifestations of this
'organic' nationalism within the Western 'civic' sphere, and
manages to accommodate both models in his description of the
core nationalist doctrine, which appears to be fairly comprehensive.
This is that: humanity is naturally divided into nations; each nation
has its peculiar character; the source of all political power is the
nation, the whole collectivity; for freedom and self-realisation,
people must identify with a nation; nations can only be fulfilled
in their own state; loyalty to the nation state overrides other
loyalties; and the primary condition for global freedom and harmony
is the strengthening of the nation state.[41]

He also distinguishes between populations which have developed
into nations apparently 'without a major rupture involving a
developed nationalism', and the majority of present nations which

[39] Anthony Smith, *Theories of Nationalism*, p. 10.

[40] Hans Kohn, *The Idea of Nationalism: A Study in its Origins and Background*
(New York: Macmillan, 1967 [1994]), *passim.*

[41] Smith, *Theories*, p. 21.

did have such a rupture.[42] This appears to overemphasise the
revolutionary nature of nationalism in creating or forging nations,
by implying that the absence of a widespread radical nationalist
movement in the formation of the nation means that the population
has somehow managed to remain immune to radical nationalism
and, by implication, will continue to do so. The case he uses as
an illustration is England.[43] As we have seen, however, the particular
circumstances of British dominance on the world stage in the
late eighteenth and nineteenth centuries, combined with the gradual
extension of perceived mass participation in the decision-making
progress at a time when nationalism appeared as a political ideology,
can explain the unusual English (or British) case where a fully
fledged nationalist movement was not evident. It can be argued
that, given the fore-mentioned circumstances, there was no need
for it. However, this does not mean there was no trace of English
nationalism; writers such as John Wilkes could be held up as
examples.[44]

The retreat from world-power status, combined with elements
of post-industrial society visible in Western Europe – for instance
regionalism and decentralisation of power within a 'United Europe'
of regions – have seen a revival of nationalisms in Britain. This
combines with a growth on the ultra-right racist nationalist fringe
(albeit numerically small), and, for example, Scottish nationalism,
which may well further grow and destroy the traditional boundaries
of the British state. Nationalist movements are not restricted to
the formation of nations and can arise or revive at any time,
even within apparently well-established nations, if the circumstances
are advantageous; examples are Le Pen in France and the rise of
the current nationalist right in Germany.

'Ethnic' and 'territorial' nationalisms

Nevertheless, Smith's division of nationalist movements between
the 'ethnic' and 'territorial' categories[45] is still useful. Whereas

---

[42] Anthony Smith, 'The Formation of Nationalist Movements' in Anthony
Smith (ed.), *Nationalist Movements* (London: Macmillan, 1976), pp. 2-6.

[43] *Ibid.*, p. 3.

[44] Colley, *op. cit.*, pp. 105-17.

[45] Smith, *op. cit.*, *passim*.

the cases of 'ethnic' movements, especially the German one, have been the prime subject of Kedourie, the inclusion of 'territorial' nationalist movements as a separate category allows discussion of nationalist movements in the colonies, so castigated by Kedourie, along with cases of 'civic' nationalism. It also includes movements in states composed of different ethnic groups, like Switzerland, or composed of former members of nations – such as the 'melting pot' of the United States, as well as cases like Australia and other members of the British Commonwealth predominantly peopled by immigrants. As such, this distinction appears more useful than Kohn's East-West division, which would necessitate a third category for the post Second World War nationalisms in the colonies.

As Smith points out, these categories of 'ethnic' and 'territorial' are not necessarily mutually exclusive, and hybrids can and do occur – for instance, cases where the nationalist movements, while defining their aims on the territorial agenda of the ex-colonial territory, are clearly spearheaded by a particular ethnic group. Such situations would appear to be undermined following the collapse of the USSR and the end of bipolarity in the world. The bulk of colonial nationalist movements came to fruition after the Second World War. This was at a time when there was US-Soviet rivalry on the world stage, and an ultimate threat of global destruction if these two powers became involved in open conflict with each other. This helped 'freeze' the already existing boundaries. This rigidity of boundaries was further aided by the poor quality of almost all of them on ethnic terms, so that if a particular state opened a boundary issue then others could use the same arguments against it. Hence, by unwritten consent, the new rulers did not play the boundary revision card. The main exceptions to this were the establishment of the state of Israel, the partition of India and Pakistan along attempted religious lines immediately after the Second World War, and the later breaking away of Eastern Pakistan to form Bangladesh.

However, even before the ending of bipolarity, a rise of 'ethnic' nationalism in rivalry to the 'territorial' nationalism could be seen in some of these new states. The unsuccessful breakaway state of Biafra in the 1960s was one example. Other tendencies include the abandoning of the ex-colonial language in Malaya and other former colonies in favour of one 'dominant' native language. Here, the internal division of India along linguistic lines may yet prove to be of fundamental significance and aid tendencies at splitting the country into smaller units – a tendency already visible on religious lines with the Sikh independence movement. Of similar significance may be the ethnic persecution in countries like the Sudan and Burma of populations seen as alien to the rulers. In these cases, the leading ethnic group appears to be asserting overt hegemony, and the 'imagined' community – to use Benedict Anderson's term (see below) – encompassing more than one ethnic group, appears to be breaking down, with both majority nationalism (resulting in minority persecution) and minority nationalisms (both defensive and offensive) on the rise. The Horn of Africa is one area where new states formed more along 'ethnic' lines appear to have already emerged.

'*Imagined communities*' *and religion*

Anderson raises the point that the new creed of nationalism entailed new forms of allegiance for traditional societies, where the village community which had claimed the individual's loyalty was small enough for all members to know or come into contact with each other. In such societies, the pre-national state was not a body which overtly demanded active allegiance. Apart from periodic incursions by tax-collectors and recruitment officers – both invariably seen as alien and hostile by the community – traditional village societies were generally left alone. Indeed, in some cases they were deliberately left unmobilised. The new 'nation' nonetheless demanded allegiance to a larger body than the narrow local focus – one where it was not possible to know all the others and hence was an 'imagined community'.[46]

However, religious communities did form similar 'imagined communities' before the advent of nationalism. Such communities have had an ambivalent relationship with the creed of nationalism. Where the church became identified with the state, religion could be as important a vehicle for nationalism as other factors like language. This was especially true for Orthodox Christians, whose

---

[46] Anderson, *op. cit.*, p. 36, also points to the primary role of 'print capitalism' in forming a national consciousness, especially in the colonies. As such, he sees the role of the capitalist press as fulfilling that of the modern 20th-century state in Gellner's theories (see below).

church has traditionally been a 'state' church, in contrast to Roman Catholics, whose allegiance to Rome often proved problematic for emerging nationalist movements in Catholic countries. However, in cases where the believers were surrounded or threatened by other religious groups, Catholicism could also be used, as in the case of Poland. For Orthodox Christians, especially those in the Ottoman Empire, which was run on the *millet* principle whereby people were classified by belief rather than language or ethnicity, the formation of an autocephalous church was crucial for emerging nationalisms. This was shown by the Bulgarian case (and more recently and controversially the Macedonian one).

In the Islamic world, the community of believers also figured prominently as an 'imagined community', and the relationship between nationalism and Islam merits close attention. As the Ottoman Empire, despite its huge Christian and other populations, was a Muslim one, and modern Turkey is overwhelmingly Islamic in religious belief (as are the Turkic peoples outside the republic), this will be looked at in greater detail in Chapter 2.

Fragmentation and emergence of new states

The centrifugal forces in a number of countries leading to possible new states such as those in the Horn of Africa and elsewhere, have already been noted. More spectacular perhaps, has been the situation in the federal socialist states of the former USSR, Czechoslovakia and Yugoslavia. Here, the attempt at creating 'imagined communities' based on a 'Soviet', 'Czechoslovakian' or 'Yugoslav' citizen has failed completely and led to the break-up of the states and the formation of new ones based on a dominant nation or ethnic group. Moreover, many observers have noted that even in the more ethnically homogeneous states of the former Soviet block, the 'imagined' community based on class solidarity had long since been superseded; in practice, only lip-service was paid to it. As the modernisation of these societies slowed down or even reversed, due in no small part to the inherent political weaknesses of the command economies, the authorities often reverted to an overt nationalism, akin to classic 'ethnic' nationalism, as a form of legitimacy. This aided the extraordinary collapse of the communist systems in Eastern Europe in 1989 once the threat of Soviet intervention was removed. They were replaced by essentially nationalist regimes, often of a nakedly 'ethnic' character, which both alienated minorities within their borders and raised fears of irredentism among their neighbours.

In Western Europe, where well-developed and ancient states like France, Spain and Britain had moulded their populations into unified patriotic units, there has been a recent rise in regional nationalisms, so that even Spain and Britain may possibly cease to exist in their current form. Canada is another example. All this indicates that 'territorial' nationalism, while being a useful contrast to 'ethnic' nationalism, does not mean that the nations it produces cannot themselves come under attack from an 'ethnic' nationalism. Perhaps such 'territorial' nationalisms are often a preliminary stage, albeit of long duration in some cases. Unless they are wholly successful in creating the 'imagined' community which can survive the rigours of an economic turnaround, they may always be under threat from 'ethnic' nationalism; it must nonetheless be borne in mind that these 'ethnic' nationalisms are also 'imagined' (in Anderson's terms) and can themselves be created.

Even the classic case of the US 'melting pot' has recently come under pressure. Whereas in the past immigrant families from Europe and elsewhere were willing to submerge their previous national identity into the US one by learning English and giving allegiance to the institutions of the state, while at the same time retaining enough traditions to distinguish them from other sectors of society, there are signs that this is changing in places. The huge numbers of Spanish-speakers, who are also recent arrivals and are predominantly Catholic by religion, appear less willing to enter 'the pot', and insist on retaining their language. While some previous immigrant groups also preserved their language and whole way of life, these groups remained small idiosyncratic pockets in the social body. The new groups are larger and more problematic. Moreover, the colour problem in the inner cities was never adequately solved, and, in the current economic crisis, shows signs of becoming aggravated. Observers speak of a new 'tribalism' in the depressed US cities in which different ethnic groups are becoming more antagonistic to each other and to the concept of the United States, which is perceived as white, Anglo-Saxon and Protestant, and which thus does not include many of them. Perhaps the key factor here is again economic mobility. Where such mobility was available for immigrants, the 'melting pot' was able to function.

The recent economic malaise has aggravated the situation, with inner-city areas populated by black communities which are becoming increasingly depressed.

Global culture and reactions to it

Another recent aspect is the rise of so-called 'global culture' in which there appears to be a general tendency for differing states and cultures to resemble each other by copying a particular model of what is perceived as modern. This is seen in the apparently universal appeal of blue jeans and trainers in youth clothes, Western pop music, along with the penetration of domestic economies by multi-nationals so that even eating and drinking habits become homogenised. These 'cultural invasions' go hand in hand with a similar unification of modern architectural styles, regardless of indigenous cultures, so that, for example, all modern airports and hotels tend to resemble each other. Indeed some saw, and perhaps still see, the rise of this 'global culture', aided by the continuing revolution in electronics and the media, as signalling the end of classic nationalism as a driving force on the world stage.[47]

Such a view, often held by those who perceive nationalism as a universally negative feature, is perhaps too optimistic or utopian. While the 'communications revolution' has meant that a country like Bulgaria is no longer able to isolate itself from the outside world, or pursue policies of forced assimilation against minorities,[48] Chapter 9 also shows how satellite television from Turkey helps preserve and even expand Turkish culture among Muslims in Greece. A key factor here has been the growth of privatisation in the telecommunications industry which has seen the breaking

[47] Of course, satellite broadcasting and other 'high-tech' goods are available only to those who can afford them. Thus, the very poor are excluded from aspects of this 'global culture', and economic cleavages can become cultural ones.

[48] Zhivkov's Bulgaria attempted completely to seal off from outside influences the areas where Muslims and Turks lived during the infamous forced assimilation campaign of 1984-9. However, the advent of *glasnost* in the USSR made this policy unfeasible. The ethnic Turks were able to use the small opportunities afforded by the new climate – in particular the unjamming of foreign radio stations like Radio Free Europe – to defeat this policy. See H. Poulton, *The Balkans: Minorities and States in Conflict* (London: MRG Publications, 1991), p. 155. .

of the centralised state's monopoly.[49] This shows how the 'global revolution', far from creating the unified 'world culture' that some presage, can actually play a crucial role in preserving and strengthening cultural differences.[50]

Additionally, in many societies, the penetration of this 'global culture' has actually resulted in an essentially nationalist reaction, with attempts to stop what is perceived as a foreign cultural invasion. Even a nation as old and as seemingly secure as France

[49] This is also of relevance when we come to Gellner's concepts of 'high' and 'low' culture (see below). It can be argued that the 'global revolution' and the ending of the state monopoly on broadcasting have to some extent modified Gellner's model whereby the state propagated a single 'high' culture which superseded previous 'low' ones. In this new situation of greater opportunities for broadcasting 'minority interest' cultural programmes, it can perhaps be postulated that there is an emergence of 'medium' cultures, which while remaining minority ones *vis-à-vis* the dominant 'high' culture, can still retain their place in the modern set-up by using the new technological opportunities.

[50] Additionally, the world community has finally become aware of minority problems. The League of Nations, set up after the First World War, did have a number of provisions on the rights of minorities. However, these were largely ignored by states, with little or no sanction. The explosion of German nationalism under Hitler which led to the appalling destruction of the Second World War, led to revulsion against all forms of perceived nationalism which even included provisions for minorities. In the new post-war period, minority rights were ignored in favour of individual human rights. The dynamics of the Cold War led to a further emphasis on individual rights as both sides used different aspects of these rights in the ideological struggle – the Soviet camp stressing economic and social rights while the West stressed civil and political ones. In the late 1980s, minority rights once more came on the human rights agenda. Since then the international community has moved towards standardising and codifying minority rights, leading to the UN Declaration on the Rights of Persons belonging to National or Ethnic, Religious and Linguistic Minorities, adopted by UN General Assembly Resolution 47/135 of 18 December 1992. This has been followed by other regional declarations. While there remains little real sanction against offenders, and even European Union members like France – the classic model for 'territorial' nationalism – and Greece can seemingly continue with their denial of any ethnic minorities within their borders, no European country relishes being accused of trampling on minority rights by its peers. It seems probable that a country's minority record will come under increasing scrutiny and offenders will face increasing censure on the international stage. However, the 'right to national self-determination', as guaranteed in the international covenants, remains problematic. This 'right' was not originally intended to cover internal minorities, but rather cover whole populations in the colonies. The covenants also stress the territorial integrity of sovereign states. See Chapter 7 for how the inherent contradiction relates to Turkey's Kurdish population.

has tried to protect its culture by attempting to ban the incursion into the French language of such modern 'Anglo-Saxon' terms as *'le fast-food'* and *'le weekend'*. That this modern 'global culture' also has aspects of morality which at times are profoundly at odds with some traditional values – especially with reference to the role of women, and perceived pornography – further aids such a reaction. Indeed, some see the growth of so-called 'Islamic fundamentalism' as a desperate attempt at unity in Islamic societies which feel their entire way of life under threat from modernisation. As such, they see this ostensibly religious reaction as having similarities to a nationalist one.

This process can work both ways, since nationalists, as we have seen, are the very groups which have often emphasised this modernisation in the first place. They thus face a backlash from an alliance of traditional religious/conservative elements and those who see them as having 'sold out' to the West (especially to the US, the one remaining superpower and often used as a universal bogeyman). The fate of the Shah of Iran serves as a warning to those who attempt rapid modernisation of an essentially traditional culture along Western lines.[51] Although this 'global culture' is often perceived as being of US origin, even the United States itself is not immune from reaction against it. Some of the aspects of modern morality (or immorality as some perceive it) have profoundly shocked those in the United States who see such manifestations as running counter to perceived 'true American values'. The reaction has been used by such right-wing figures as Pat Buchanan, whose rhetoric of a moral crusade to 'cleanse' the United States bears striking similarity to revivalist movements in other cultures. It can be argued that these revivalist movements, with their emphasis on the national values under attack, are essentially nationalist, or at least have many similarities with nationalists. Thus, in some situations, two essentially nationalist movements can clash head on: a modernising nationalist movement led by Western-trained intellectuals attempting to radically modernise a traditional society, against a backlash of 'revivalist' nationalists in alliance with religious elements. This clash is not confined to the twentieth century, and can also be seen in examples like the differences between the 'West-ernisers' (those who wished to emulate the West) and the *'Narodniks'*

---

[51] In Turkey, Atatürk, as we see in subsequent chapters, also followed this path.

(those who looked for the essence and thus the salvation of the nation in the traditional values of the peasant) in nineteenth-century Russia. Both groups wanted to revive their nation, but by using very different means, and with very different aims.

Despite the above reservations, Smith's 'territorial' nationalism is very useful in discussing the original nationalist movements in the European colonies. In these cases, the nationalists, usually educated in the Western imperial centres, were resentful of the restrictions they faced on advancement within their societies due to the colonial powers' monopolisation of positions of real power. They were also resentful at the backwardness of their societies *vis-à-vis* the West, and almost invariably opted not for boundary revisions to accommodate more logically (according to the East European model) different language groups, but instead chose to work within the former colonial boundaries. After 'freeing' the territory from colonial rule, the new post-colonial nationalist leaders set about 'creating' the nation within these boundaries.[52] The state education system was the primary method of instilling the new 'national' values, often delving deep into history (into periods well before there was any concept of modern nationalism) for figures and myths to aid this process – as Kedourie puts it, using 'the past to subvert the present'.[53]

The mix of dialects and languages within the new unit was such that, in many cases, rather than base the new nationalism on a particular language group as in Eastern Europe, the language of the old colonial power remained the official state language. This retention of colonial boundaries made some see 'Third-World' nationalism as no more than anti-colonialism. Whereas East European nationalisms were based on groups with preexistent cultural ties, this 'Third-World' nationalism was actually anti-imperialism, pure and simple. Such a line was begun by the liberal J.A. Hobson at the turn of this century and taken up by Hilferding, and by Lenin and J.H. Kautsky among the Marxists. Others, like Hugh Seton-Watson, differentiated between these 'nation-building' nationalist movements and others based more

---

[52] The boundaries, it must be remembered, were often drawn by Western politicians to achieve a balance of power between the colonial forces and disregarded the ethnic differences of the local population.

[53] Kedourie, *Nationalism*, p. 75.

on the ethnic group, which he characterised as either 'independence' or 'irredentist' movements.[54]

Modernisation

Another angle has been taken by writers like Daniel Lerner, who
see three stages in the development of society from one based
on tradition to one in transition to the stage of modernity, and
stress the importance of urbanisation, exposure to the mass media
and political participation in voting.[55] Here, 'modern' societies
are ones which make use of science and technology and are
characterized by constant innovation and change. This leads to
a distinction between the nationalism of the peasant which is
seen as monocentric and closed – 'a kind of traditional solipsism'
–with that of the educated intelligentsia, which is outward looking.[56] In this approach, modernisation is the crucial point; it has
been developed by Smelser and Eisenstadt with the concept of
a 'religion of modernisation'.[57] The division of labour observed
by Durkheim in a modern society results in differentiation in the
transitory stage, and finally reintegration, with nationalism providing people with an overriding and easily acquired secular motive
– national strength – to overcome the painful process of dislocation
involved in modernisation. Thus, nationalism helps bridge the
gap between a preconstructural *Gemeinschaft*, and the *Gesellschaft*.[58]
The same point was made by Kedourie, who saw that modernisation
debilitated and destroyed tribalism and its social and political tradi-

---

[54] Anthony Smith, *Theories of Nationalism*, pp. 69, 70 and 201.

[55] Daniel Lerner, *The Passing of Traditional Society: Modernizing the Middle East*
(New York: Free Press, 1964) p. 46.

[56] Smith, *Theories of Nationalism*, p. 106.

[57] Neil J. Smelser, 'Towards a Theory of Modernization', in *Essays in Sociological
Behaviour* (Englewood Cliffs, NJ: Prentice-Hall, 1968), and N.S. Eisenstadt,
Modernization: Protest and Change (Englewood Cliffs, NJ: Prentice-Hall 1966),
passim.

[58] These two concepts were first expounded by the German sociologist F.
Tönnies, who contrasted the emotional warmth of structures like the family,
the clan, the village and friends (*Gemeinschaft*) with 'modern' impersonal structures
like the city, the state and industry (*Gesellschaft*). See F. Tönnies, *Community
and Association* (London: Routledge, 1955). This division has similarities to
Anderson's 'real' and 'imagined' communities.

tions, resulting in an atomised society which seeks in nationalism a substitute for the old order now irrevocably lost.[59] From this aspect of modernisation and atomised societies, we finally arrive at Ernest Gellner's proposals.

Gellner sees three processes as interdependent: the rise of nationalism; the pre-eminence of the intelligentsia; and modernisation. The scientific mode of thought it seen as the new standard: 'Science is the mode of cognition of industrial society, and industry is the ecology of science.'[60] Agricultural villages are too small to produce 'fully life-sized human beings'; only education and literary makes a complete human, and such education must be in some language, hence the importance of language, which reinforces cultural trends.[61] A large-scale education system alone ensures widespread citizenship. Why not a larger unit than the nation? In reply, Gellner argues that the unevenness of industrialisation working in larger units with urban working-class competition results in cultural appearances being used by privileged sections to increase their status at the expense of others. This leads to the reaction of workers from other groups following the appeal of their culturally similar intelligentsia. Thus, Gellner argues, people become nationalists not out of sentiment but out of objective and practical necessity. In this view, nationalism is a movement of nationalist secession, led by the intelligentsia and backed by the excluded mass of less skilled workers – both groups being uprooted, culturally mobile, and exposed to the dislocating effects of modernisation. Smith points out, however, that the urban working class was not always present in nationalist movements.[62] Here we can add that where there is a greater possibility of economic advancement by a particular 'national' group in a polity outside the national one – a kind of economic 'brain drain' – then many will opt for this rather than remain in the national backwater. A good example of this was the situation in the later part of the nineteenth century when Greeks from the independent but desperately impoverished initial Greek state migrated in large numbers to the Ottoman Empire to take advantage of the *Tanzimat*

[59] Kedourie, *Nationalism*, p. 112.
[60] Smith, *Theories of Nationalism*, pp. 109-10.
[61] *Ibid.*, p. 113.
[62] *Ibid.*, pp. 116-17.

reforms – so much so that it was only in the nineteenth century, after the foundation of modern Greece, that Greeks began to dominate the west coast of Anatolia.[63] Of course this depended on the 'host' state being relatively 'unnational' through not overtly favouring its 'own' people or discriminating against 'foreigners'. The Ottoman Empire during the *Tanzimat* reform movement apparently met these criteria.

'High' and 'low' culture and education

Despite this objection, Gellner further developed his thesis. In his *Nations and Nationalism* of 1983, he especially stresses the role of culture and education, and distinguishes between what he terms 'high' culture, which is the official culture of the state and its rulers, and 'low' cultures of the general population in pre-modern societies. These low cultures were often of a very local nature, with little uniformity between them. A modern economy depends on mobility and communication between individuals at a level that can only be achieved if these individuals have been socialised into a high culture – in fact, the same high culture – so as to be able to communicate properly. This can only be achieved by a fairly monolithic educational system. Thus, culture, not community, provides the inner sanctions. The requirements of a modern economy inevitably result in the new idea of the mutual relationship of modern culture and the state.[64]

Thus for Gellner, 'nationalism is essentially the general imposition of a high culture on society, where previously low cultures had taken up the lives of the majority, and in some cases the totality of the population.' This necessitates the 'generalised diffusion of a school-mediated, academy supervised idiom.'[65] As mobility of labour is essential in a modern society, with individuals required if necessary to move from one occupation to another within a single life-span due to constant innovation,[66] what is needed is:

---

[63] See Richard Clogg, 'The Greeks' in Benjamin Braude and Bernard Lewis (eds), *Christians and Jews in the Ottoman empire: that functioning of a plural society*, vol. 1 (New York: Holmes and Meier, 1982), pp. 195-7.

[64] Ernest Gellner, *Nations and Nationalism* (Oxford: Blackwell, 1983), p. 140.

[65] *Ibid.*, p. 57.

[66] *Ibid.*, p. 140.

.... [t]he establishment of an anonymous, impersonal society, with mutually substitutable atomised individuals held together by a shared culture of this [high] kind, in place of a previous complex structure of local groups, sustained by folk cultures reproduced locally and idiosyncratically by the micro-groups themselves.[67]

However, he points out that nationalists usually maintain the reverse by claiming to be acting in the name of a putative, often imaginary, folk culture – hence the ransacking of history which Kedourie so scorns. Indeed, Gellner does not seem to acknowledge an independent role for ethnicity, and tends to see the intelligentsia as the prime movers, often inventing the past completely to fit nationalist requirements. In this context, it should be noted that such 'inventions' and distortions are not the prerogative of nationalists, as shown by Hobsbawm and others in *The Invention of Tradition*. This demonstrated how similar methods have been used by a variety of people and interest groups to help forge or strengthen a common identity or allegiance.[68] Also of note is Gellner's view of the atomisation of modern society. This tends to reverse the view of Kedourie and others, who see nationalism as the result of atomised individuals seeking a substitute for old customs, rather than the cause of the atomisation. Gellner views high cultures of the agrarian age as minority accomplishments of privileged specialists, differentiated from fragmented, uncodified majority folk-cultures. The former tended and indeed aimed to be trans-ethnic and trans-political, frequently employing a dead or archaic idiom with no interest whatever in ensuring continuity between its mode of communication and that of the majority. The majority food producers were excluded from power and from the high culture, and were tied to a faith and a church rather than to a state and a pervasive culture.[69] By contrast, an industrial high culture is no longer linked – whatever its history –to a faith or a church, and requires 'the resources of a state co-extensive with society rather than merely those of a church superimposed on it.'[70]

---

[67] *Ibid.*, p. 57.

[68] Eric Hobsbawm *The Invention of Tradition* (Cambridge University Press, 1983), and T. Ranger (eds), *passim*.

[69] Gellner, *op. cit.*, p. 141.

[70] *Ibid.*

In Gellner's picture, culture needs to supersede religion:

A growth-bound economy dependent on cognitive renovation [i.e. a modern one] cannot seriously link its cultural machinery (which it needs unconditionally) to some doctrinal faith which [due to scientific advancement] rapidly becomes obsolete and often ridiculous.[71]

Hence, culture needs to be sustained *as culture*, not as an accomplishment to faith.[72] Although religion can in many cases be a useful contributor to nationalism, for Gellner culture comes before religion. Although Catholicism, for example, can be seen as a crucial component of being Polish, being Polish is the end rather than being a Catholic. Here, Gellner contradicts Durkheim's view that society worships itself through the opaque medium of religion, asserting that society can and does worship itself or its own culture directly. It can nonetheless be argued that in many cultures, especially Islamic ones, this new form of worship is not an adequate replacement for the emotional warmth and security of the old faith.

Gellner uses the example of Protestantism to back up his argument. Protestantism, he asserts, helped the emergence of the modern world due to its stress on literacy and scripturalism, its priestless unitarianism which abolished the monopoly of the sacred, and its emphasis on individualism. This led to the individual being dependent on his own conscience rather than on the ritual of others, and 'foreshadowed an anonymous, individualistic fairly unstructured mass society in which equal access to a shared culture prevailed and was publicly accessible in writing to all rather than the preserve of a privileged elite.' Equal access to a scripturalist God led to equal access to a high culture. In such a society, Gellner states, 'one's prime loyalty is to the medium of our literacy and to its political protector' – that is, the state.[73]

With his training as an anthropologist working in Islamic societies, Gellner has some interesting points to make about culture and Islam, especially with reference to the endemic tension between the *ulema* – led 'legalistic' Islam of the towns, and that of the Sufi

---

[71] *Ibid.*
[72] *Ibid.*, p. 142.
[73] *Ibid.*

tarikats in the more pluralistic countryside. He sees Islamic civilisation in the agrarian age as a good example of how agrarian societies are not prone to use culture to define political units and thus not given to being nationalistic. In the Islamic world, high culture is equated with the *ulema* and is trans-political and trans-ethnic. Low culture, on the other hand, is the *tarikat* 'folk' Islam of local shrines and holy lineages and is sub-ethnic and sub-political, reinforcing the vigorous local self-defence units (that is tribes). Thus, Islam already had a high and a low culture. If they became the idiom of the entire nation, agrarian high cultures usually became secularised, as the new basis of cognitive growth often put paid to absolutist pretensions. Islam however, is the most 'Protestant' of the great monotheisms and is ever prone to reformation. The emergence of 'the nation' and the victory of the reform movement can be seen as part of the same process:

> The dissolution of the vigorous old local and kin structures (which however survive as deadly shadows in the new centralised political structures) goes hand in hand with the elimination of the saint cults and their replacement by a reformed individualistic unitarian theology which leaves the individual believer to relate singly to one God and one large anonymous mediation free community – virtually the paradigm of the nationalist requirement.[74]

Whereas other high cultures in transition need to abandon their doctrinal underpinnings and support because the bulk of their doctrines appear indefensible and absurd in the light of modern science, this is not so for Islam, where the high culture dogma has already undertaken a purification in the name of freeing the true faith from ignorant rural superstition.[75]

Gellner's ideas have been studied here in depth since his ideas on Islamic societies and the relationship between nationalism and high and low Islamic culture have obvious relation to the study in hand. It must be borne in mind, however, that his field was primarily the Maghreb, and that he uses the case of Algeria as an example. He asserts that Islam in Algeria, with its reverence for holy lineages, was for all practical purposes co-extensive with

[74] *Ibid.*, pp. 75-9.
[75] *Ibid.*, p. 80.

the rural shrine and saint cults – that is low culture. In the twentieth century it repudiated all this and identified with a reformist scripturalism, denying the legitimacy of any saintly mediation between humans and God. Whereas 'the shrines had defined tribes and tribal boundaries, the scripturalism could and did define the nation.'[76] As he points out, in Algeria, in the liberation struggle and the 'birth of the nation', religion had fairly closely defined all the underprivileged, as against the privileged who were French and non-Islamic. This was not at all the case in Turkey. Nevertheless, his views do form an interesting backdrop to the study of nationalism in Turkey.

From this survey, we can see that there have been many different forms of nationalism and diverse analyses of it. While it is relatively easy to seek the exceptions that contradict a certain theory, it is perhaps more useful to attempt a synthesis of elements from different observers whose views are often complementary rather than in outright conflict. For the purposes of this study, nationalism will be defined as an activist political movement which aims to unite 'the nation' (however defined) on the basis of a putative shared culture, and which claims hegemony for its own vision of 'the nation'.

This somewhat loose definition allows the incorporation of the various nationalisms covered in the above discussion from 'modernisers' to religious 'reactionaries', 'organic' 'blood and soil' nationalisms to 'rational' ones. All claim to represent the whole collectivity, however defined, and are antagonistic to competing cultural claims on the totality or parts of this collectivity. Hence, there can often be different varieties of nationalism competing with each other for a particular claimed nation. These variants can be based on territory, ethnicity, religion or other factors. Smith's differentiation between 'ethnic' and 'territorial' nationalisms, while very useful, tends to negate other competing nationalist currents within a given polity. For example, while France is usually held up as the 'territorial' case *par excellence*, the Dreyfus affair and the rise of Le Pen clearly illustrate the competing strains of a more 'blood and soil' or 'ethnic' variety of nationalism.

[76] *Ibid.*, p. 73.

As we shall see later in the Turkish case, this competition between the different variants is based on different premises as to what constitutes 'the Turkish nation'.

Although there have been groups of people who can be seen as forming distinct 'nations' from antiquity onwards, nationalism is characterised as a modern movement dating from the time of the French Revolution. Its arrival on the political stage is closely linked to the advent of the modern state and the ensuing mass participation of all its adult members (at least in theory), as well as the needs of a modern economy with a literate, educated workforce. Whether modern nationalism appeared initially in revolutionary France with the mass mobilisation of the whole society in such measures as the *levée en masse* of 1793, or in Germany as a defensive reaction to the power of revolutionary France, is a matter of choice. One stresses the modernising aspect of the new creed, while the other stresses its aptitude for use as a cultural defence mechanism.

The question as to why certain groups living in multi-ethnic societies have negated an officially espoused nationalism, and instead have propagated their own rival brands, which have in some cases led to territorial disintegration, is perhaps more complicated. It would appear from the above discussion that a number of factors or potential factors need to be taken into account. These include problems of upward mobility and inter-ethnic rivalry among sections of the various communities, and how successful the dominant nationalism is in appealing to potentially secessionist groups. The sense of the 'Other' is crucial, and in mixed communities and border regions it appears particularly problematic.

If nationalism is seen as attempted cultural unity, then the means by which that culture is defined and propagated is crucial. Totally invented cultures with little or no underpinning in the societies in which they are operating have often proved, like the 'New Soviet Man', to be ephemeral. More successful have been those which have used facets of pre-existing cultural ties – predominantly language, but also religion and history (the latter often heavily doctored). However, this runs the risk of alienating groups whose linguistic, religious or historical sense is different. Many, especially in border regions, self-identify by defining what they are not – often using another group in close proximity as a negative pole. In such cases, attempts to unite all under one banner are inevitably problematic. In many developing countries, nationalism used anti-colonialism and anti-imperialism as major factors in cultural unity. While this has been relatively successful in the short-term and in the initial post-independence period, the basic problems of founding a more permanent cultural unity have emerged, later causing severe tensions and even the break-up of some states.

To summarise, while not attempting to be comprehensive, the following points have been raised in the above discussion: the make-up of people who become nationalists; the environments in which they operate and which are particularly conducive to nationalism; the distinction between 'ethnic' and 'territorial' nationalisms; the role of language, history, culture and religion in defining a nation; the use of nationalism by an intellectual élite to achieve modernisation; and the continuing nationalist pressures even after the 'creation of a nation'. These nationalist pressures can be both inter-ethnic, leading to possible break-up into smaller units, or a reactionary backlash in alliance with conservative religious elements, against new values which are seen as alien and contrary to 'national' traditions.

2

THE OTTOMAN EMPIRE, I: ISLAM, THE STATE AND THE PEOPLE

The following two chapters will look at group identity in the Ottoman Empire and the rise of nationalism within it up to the break-up of the empire and the Independence wars, resulting in the formation of the Turkish republic. This will include a brief analysis of Islam as an institution and as a competing ideology to nationalism, as well as the *millet* system and the rise of nationalism among the Christian populations of the empire. It will also look at the failed attempts of the *Tanzimat* reform movement to create an 'Ottoman' citizen, the reaction of the Young Ottomans, and the process by which Sultan Abdülhamid II used Islam to try to keep the empire from falling apart. The rise of a Turkish nationalism, inspired and in many ways led by *émigrés* from Russia, where Turkic minorities were subject to pan-Slavism in the form of Great Russian nationalism, will be analysed, as will the rise of nationalism among non-Turkish Muslim communities in the empire, especially the Arabs and the Albanians. The growth of Turkish and pan-Turkish nationalism in the Young Turk era, which escalated in the First World War, will also be assessed.

Islam

Islam, in its classical form, has strong aspects of a state incorporated within it. It encompasses a total way of life, a model for society, a culture and a civilisation. In effect it is the state, or should be if the rulers were true Muslims.[1] Whereas, for example, Christianity

---

[1] There are many standard books on Islam as a state religion, especially the works of H.A.R. Gibb and Guillaume. A useful synopsis is E. Mortimer, *Faith and Power: The Politics of Islam* (London: Faber and Faber, 1982).

was non-political from the start and there was thus the concept of 'church' as distinct from 'state', the community of believers founded by Mohammed was always virtually akin to a state. It claimed to be a divinely ordained political system. While Mohammed was alive the three powers of government were concentrated in his hands. He was the leader (the executive branch), the promulgator of divine and unchangeable legislation coming directly from God (the legislative), and the settler of disputes (the judicial).[2] After his death the divine link was finished. He was the last prophet and his revelation was final and relevant to all peoples for all time. The religious scholars elaborated the rules of the Koran and the Traditions about what Mohammed had said and done (the *Hadith*) into the *Shar'ia* (*Şeriat* in Turkish) – the divine law which was the basis of society. Thus, in the classic Islamic state there was a basic distinction between believers and non-believers. It was assumed that the law is the work of God and thus not open to change, with no differentiation between the sacred and the secular.

However, there were inevitably new situations which might and did arise, and to meet these there was some scope for *ijtihad* (interpretation) by the religious scholars. Additionally, the Seljuk state – the first Turkic Islamic empire – saw the incorporation of Turko-Iranian government practice of *urf*, or secular law-making. This resulted in the gradual secularisation of public law. The Mongols also regulated life by secular laws and introduced unquestionable and complete allegiance to the ruler.[3] The combination of these trends led to a body of public law known as *kanun*, with the *Şeriat* being effectively reduced to matters of private law such as inheritance and marriage. Nevertheless, the Şeyhülislam[4] retained the function of ensuring that state laws conformed with the *Şeriat* (even if the post became progressively controlled by the state bureaucracy in the nineteenth century, and thus in theory

---

[2] *Ibid.*, p. 38.

[3] Şerif Mardin, *The Genesis of Young Ottoman Thought* (Princeton University Press, 1962), p. 103.

[4] While Islam, especially Sunni Islam, does not have a religious hierarchy like that found in Christian churches, in the Ottoman system there was the post of the Şeyhulislam, who was the official leading religious scholar. The 'folk' Islam of the *tarikats* however did (and does) have hierarchies (see below).

– as well as in practice to some extent – the state was still based on religious law.

Mohammed was an Arab, the divine revelation as revealed to him by God was in Arabic and was transcribed in Arabic in the Koran, and the first Muslim state was an Arab one. Despite this legacy, which has been used by modern Arab nationalists,[5] the central idea of Islam was of a community of believers regardless of race or language. As noted above, the concept of the religious law was a powerful factor in binding the Islamic community into a single whole, reflected in the terminology of the *Dar-ül Islam* (the World of Islam) relating to the Islamic world, and the *Dar-ül Harb* (the World of War) relating to the rest of humankind. However, perhaps inevitably, after Mohammed's death significant differences emerged within the Islamic community. The main split was between Sunnis and Shias over the succession, with Shias following the claim of Ali, Mohammed's cousin and son-in-law. Ali's defeat in what was a quarrel over temporal power solidified into major doctrinal differences between Sunnis and Shias. This split was important in helping to produce a large degree of differentiation between the Ottoman and the Persian states, the Persian ruler Shah Ismail enforcing a Shiite homogeneity

[5] It is revealing that the sense of Islam as a trans-national community of believers which overrides national differences resulted in the initial Arab nationalists coming from the Christian Arab communities of Lebanon and Syria, who were less encumbered with the problems of reconciling universalist Islam with particularist nationalism. However, the secular nationalism of such people as Antun Saadeh, which was useful in claiming Arab independence from the Ottomans, fell victim to the overriding need to refer to the Arabic identity of the masses, which was firmly rooted in Islam and Islamic history. Later Arab nationalist ideologues like Sati al-Husri and Abd al-Rahman al-Bazzaz looked to Islam as an essential component of being Arab, with Mohammed viewed as the founder of the Arab nation – another typical case of modern nationalists transposing modern concepts backwards into history. An extreme version of this was propounded by Michel Aflaq, himself from a Christian background, who held that Islam *was* Arab nationalism. Thus Arab nationalism saw the redefinition of Islam as a national Arab religion. See Ernest Dawn, *From Ottomanism to Arabism* (University of Illinois Press, 1973); Sylvia Haim (ed.), *Arab Nationalism: an Anthology* (University of California Press, 1962); Bassam Tibi, *Arab Nationalism* (London: Macmillan, 2nd edn 1990); and Kemal H. Karpat (ed.), *Political and Social Thought in the Contemporary Middle East* (London: Pall Mall, 1968).

which became the basis of national sentiment.[6] The Ottomans were Sunni and adhered to the Hanafi school of law.[7]

The Sufi Tarikats

Alongside the mainstream legalistic Islam, which was rationalised and codified into a law and systematic theology guarded by the *ulema* (the religious experts, based in the cities),[8] existed the 'parallel'

---

[6] See John A. Armstrong, *Nations before Nationalism* (Chapel Hill NC: University of North Carolina Press, 1982). In central Anatolia large numbers of Shiites known as Alevis remained – at present their size is estimated at up to 20 per cent of the population of Turkey – despite the Ottoman authorities reacting to Ismail's repression of Sunnis by enforcing Sunni orthodoxy with the execution of thousands of Anatolian Alevis. Many others fled to Persia. The brunt of this repression fell on the Kızılbaş Shiite dervishes in rural areas whom Ismail hoped to use as a 'fifth column'. Urban Shiites in Anatolia were less receptive to Safavid propaganda and were generally tolerated, if discouraged.

[7] The majority of Muslims were and are Sunnis. Their name is derived from the *Sunna*, or words and deeds of Mohammed as recorded in the *Hadith* – they thus claim to be following the example of the Prophet. They believe the succession to Mohammed passed to the Caliphs. Despite the above description of Islamic law as attempting to be both all-encompassing and unchangeable, in the early period after Mohammed's death, Sunni Muslims saw the 'gates of *ijtihad*' as wider than became permissible later in Islamic doctrine. Each Sunni was obliged to adhere to one of the schools of 'law' – i.e. of religious norms. The four recognised schools, Hanafi, Malakite, Hanbali and Shafi, dating from the ninth century were named after their founding scholars (three other schools having died out by 1300). In theory a Muslim could decide which school to adhere to, but in practice, with some exceptions, a specific school predominated in a specific area. The Ottomans preferred the Hanafi school, which gave greater flexibility to political rulers, and this school was 'established' throughout the Ottoman Empire. Other schools were tolerated in Egypt. However, only in the Maghreb portions of the Ottoman Empire – i.e. Tunisia and Algeria, as the Ottomans did not control Morroco – where indigenous Muslims clung to the Malikite school, did this lead to anything approaching ethnic cleavages. In the main, the different schools in Sunni Islam did not a play a part in forming separate group identities in the sense of proto-nations; *Ibid.*, p. 234.

[8] As Armstrong points out, despite the crucial role played by nomadic warriors from both the Arabian deserts and the Turkic steppes in spreading the faith and the policy, orthodox Islam was essentially an urban religion and the city played a crucial role in Islamic consciousness as the idea. The sacred centre (Mecca, the vestigial city) along with the symbolic language of Arabic (often hardly more than a sacred alphabet) and the scriptures encoded in it are indispensable symbols; *ibid.*, p. 293.

or 'folk' Islam of the Sufis. Along with the legalistic and formalistic aspects of Sunnism, as embodied in the 'Five Pillars'-monotheism, praying five times daily, keeping the fast, making the pilgrimage to Mecca, and the giving of alms to the poor – there has from early times been this parallel Islam of the Sufis. A Sufi, so called after the distinctive woollen dress they traditionally wore, is anyone who believes in direct experience of God and is prepared to dedicate time and effort to achieve it. As such, Sufism caters to the mystic impulses of individuals. In practice it consists of feeling and unveiling a *ma'rifa* (gnosis) reached through a passage of ecstatic states which cannot be learned but only attained by direct experience, ecstasy and inward transformation.[9]

While the Seljuk Turks vigorously upheld orthodox Sunnism against any perceived Shiite or other heterodox tendencies, a change came about with Saladin. Henceforth, there was in Sunni Islam a qualified acceptance and respectability of Sufism,[10] which was not seen as a threat to, or a replacement of, formal Islam. Neither was there overt hostility between the different *tarikats* (ways); each viewed the others as equally valid routes to the end-product of mystic communion. Sufis accepted the law and formal requirements, but formed inner coteries and introduced hierarchical structures in the various *tarikats* due to their systems of relationships between a master and a disciple to achieve the desired mystic communion. Sufi orders thus helped fill the gap left by the suppression of Shiite sectarianism, as well as aiding conversion of non-Islamic peoples by allowing a certain symbiosis between Islamic and other religious beliefs and practices. As Trimingham points out, Sufi organisations tended to absorb popular movements, with Shiites particularly forced to seek asylum within Sufi groups, of whom the heterodox Bektaşi order allowed them fullest expression.[11]

This also held true for Christian communities in the Balkans who adopted Islam and the Bektaşi order. This was especially prominent in Albania. The Ottoman state was originally serviced

[9] J. Spencer Trimingham, *The Sufi Orders of Islam* (Oxford : Clarendon Press, 1971), pp. 1-3.

[10] *Ibid.*, p. 11.

[11] *Ibid.* p. 69. For more on the Alevis, the Bektaşis, and the Kızılbaşıs ee Chapters 4 and 8.

by a 'slave elite' of Christian boys taken from their homes by the *devşirme* system. This obliged Christian families to supply at intervals a proportion of their most able sons to be educated and raised as Muslims to run the empire in both civilian and military capacities.[12] The civilians often assumed the highest positions in the empire, while the military units, the Janissaries, were the elite units of the empire until their dissolution by Mahmud II in 1826. They were also, perhaps due in part to their Christian roots, overwhelmingly Bektaşi.

While there has been a symbiosis of *tarikats* with nationalist movements in some places,[13] this combination of Sufism and incipient nationalism – or at least the preserving of a group identity – appears to have been confined largely to the Caucasus. As such, it can perhaps be seen as a local defence mechanism of predominantly mountainous and thus compartmentalised Islamic communities against attack by an outside non-Muslim enemy. Elsewhere, the Sufi movements tended to be, like orthodox Islam itself, trans-ethnic and trans-national. Indeed Sufism encouraged direct contact be-

---

[12] This levy, unsurprisingly deeply unpopular with the Christian communities despite the opportunities of advancement it afforded to those taken, fell into abeyance in the seventeenth century and had completely disappeared by the eighteenth.

[13] This is especially evident in the resistance of Muslim minorities in Russia and even more so in the USSR. Faced with acute hostility from the atheist communist state, Sufism proved to be a powerful method of resistance. The Sufi orders are closed orders which could remain outside the system and, for example in the USSR, managed to run their own courts, financial systems based on the compulsory levy, and their own secret schools. Their dynamism and organisation proved invaluable in such a hostile climate. In the Caucasus particularly, a symbiosis of Sufi *tarikats* and tribal clans became perceptible in the nineteenth century, with the Shamil rebellion the most evident expression of this. This trend continued in the Soviet era and was especially strong in tribal areas of northern Daghestan. Sufi orders, especially the Nakşibendi and Kadiri *tarikats*, became heavily involved in the continuing resistance first to Russian and later to Soviet rule in the Caucasus. Indeed the very survival of the Chechen and Ingush peoples as distinct nations after their populations were deported *en masse* to Eastern Siberia and Kazakhstan in 1944 for alleged collaboration with the Nazis, can be seen as partly due to the activities of the Kadiri offshoot, the Uis Haji group, in the places of exile. See Alexandre Benningsen and S. Enders Wimbush, *Mustics and Commissars: Sufism in the Soviet Union* (London: Hurst, 1985), *passim*, and Marie Benningsen Broxup *et al.*, *The North Caucasus Barrier: The Russian Advance towards the Muslim World* (London: Hurst, 1992), *passim*.

tween Bosnia, Albania, Kosovo, parts of Bulgaria and Thrace, the Arab World, Iran and Central Asia.[14] Thus the very universality of the various Sufi movements helped bring about contacts between geographically distant and ethnically distinct parts of the Muslim community, thereby helping to promote and strengthen unity in the 'imagined' (in Benedict Anderson's usage) Islamic community.

Ottoman society

The majority of the population, whether Muslim or Christian, lived in rural communities. The village, along with religious loyalty, provided the primary focus of loyalty and identification (and still does to a large extent). Whereas the religious community was an 'imagined' one, the village was a 'real' one in the sense that the individual knew and was known by virtually all others in the group.[15] As the Ottoman state, up to the reforms of Mahmud II and the rule of Abdülhamid II (see below), was non-penetrative of the periphery, it seems fair to conclude that the village, along

---

[14] Harry T. Norris, *Islam in the Balkans: Religion and Society between Europe and the Arab World* (London: Hurst, 1993), *passim*.

[15] Anthropologists such as Carol Delaney continue to record the intense solidarity of the village, even today in the modern Turkish state, with all the new forms of communication and mobility. Delaney notes that the use of *yabana* (foreigner) is still used by villagers in central Anatolia for all outsiders (i.e. all non-villagers). The sense of strong village community is further illustrated by her observation that the arrival into the village she was studying of immigrant families from the Balkans was not accepted by other villagers. Eventually these new arrivals were resettled in their own village nearby. The fact that these immigrants were fellow Turkish-speaking Muslims but were still rejected shows the strength of the village community. Men who left the village to find work elsewhere still returned to the village for brides. As Delaney writes; 'If one leaves the village, one is still identified not just as a villager (*köylü*) but as a particular kind of villager [relating to the particular village]... If one is working or living outside one's natal village, one must return there for marriage papers, and most people are returned to be buried there, including even those who have migrated to Europe. One cannot adopt a different village or country any more than one can truly adopt a child. At best, residence outside of the village is seen as a matter of convenience and mutual accommodation; at worst it is felt as exile, the unenviable condition of *gurbet*.' See Carol Delaney, *The Seed and the Soil: Gender and Cosmology in Turkish Village Society* (Berkeley: University of California Press, 1991), p. 271.

with ties of kinship, was one of the primary sources of identification in the Ottoman period for settled rural communities.

For the tribal nomadic and semi-nomadic areas of southeast Anatolia particularly, the tribe played a similar role to that of the village in terms of identification. In these often largely Kurdish areas between the Ottoman and Persian Empires, tribesmen distinguished themselves from non-tribal people and saw themselves as a kind of military aristocracy. There was a strong but not complete correlation between tribalism and pastoral nomadism and semi-nomadism. As van Bruinessen points out, for the Kurds (although tribal and quasi-tribal structures have also survived among Turkic groups in Anatolia like the Yörüks),[16] the characteristic structural trait of southeastern Anatolian tribal peoples was segmentary organisation directly related to an ideology of the common descent of the tribe, enhanced by endogomy to the lowest level of segmentation (i.e. marriage to father's brother's daughter).[17] There was a sharp distinction between non-tribal peasants and tribal groups in the southeast, with tribesmen warriors seeing two castes: masters and servants, or rulers and ruled. Tribesmen were warriors who did not toil. Non-tribal Kurds were unfit to fight and were seen as being akin to sheep owned by the tribal chieftain – 'flock' being the primary meaning of Kurdish *reyet* (Arabic *ra'yah*).[18] (This term, *raya* in Turkish, meaning 'subjects', was also

---

[16] See Daniel G. Bates, *Nomads and Farmers* (Ann Arbor: University of Michigan Press, 1973), and 'Differential access to pasture in a nomadic society: the Yörük of southeastern Turkey' in W. Irons and N. Dyson-Hudson (eds), *Perspectives on Nomadism*, (Leiden: E.J. Brill, 1972).

[17] Martin M. van Bruinessen, *Agha, Shaikh and State* (Utrecht: Rijswijk University, 1978), pp. 146-7.

[18] *Ibid.*, p. 117. This division between nomadic tribal people and settled communities is common to many different societies and was also a major factor in Central Asia. There, until the advent of first Russian and then Soviet rule, the populations can be seen as divided between the nomadic semi-nomadic steppe-dwellers and the settled urban communities along the great rivers – see Elizabeth Bacon, *Central Asia under Russian Rule: A Study in Culture Change* (Ithaca, NY: Cornell University Press, 1966). Between the nomad and the settler there was and remains to some degree a natural hostility which is illustrated in the saying of a Yomut Turkoman: 'I do not have a mill with willow trees. I have a horse and a whip. I will kill you and go', and the Bedouin proverb 'raids are our agriculture' – Bruce Chatwin, *The Songlines* (London: Picador, 1988), pp. 221 and 224. Any nomad tribe can be seen as a potential or actual fighting force whose impulse, if not to fight other nomads, is to raid or threaten

used to denote the non-Muslim subjects of the Ottoman Empire, reflecting their second-class status – see below).

The Ottoman state began with the conquest by nomadic tribes, but eventually the settled Byzantine tradition became incorporated with (or even incorporated) the nomadic steppe values. The dichotomy between the two value systems was still very evident in late Ottoman times (and even today). Nomadic tribal values were still prevalent in the southeast of Anatolia, as well as in large parts of Bedouin/Arab lands, while Western Anatolia remained essentially sedentary.

As Bernard Lewis points out, although Islam was essentially an urban civilisation, there is no concept of the state, only the ruler; no court, only judges and helpers; and no city, only conglomerations of families, quarters and guilds, each with its own leader. No corporate persons were recognised under Islamic law and the *Şeriat* has no municipal code. Towns were not seen as legal or political entities.[19] The Islamic requisite of protecting male honour by keeping post-menstrual females within the family and away from contact with other males also led to the distinctive architecture of the Islamic city with its dead-end streets and high walls surrounding enclosed compounds. Within the Ottoman city, the smallest operative unit was the *mahalle*, or quarter, which played an analogous role to the village in terms of group identity. The term *hemşehri*, to denote a non-kin fellow member of such a grouping, referred to someone from the same village for rural communities, or someone from the same quarter for urban dwellers.[20] The big towns and cities were also the seats of government and centres of religious learning in areas like the southeast.

'the city'. They have often been recruited as mercenaries by settlers, e.g. the Cossacks who became the Tsar's state cavalry.

[19] Bernard Lewis, *The Emergence of Modern Turkey* (Oxford University Press, 1961), p. 387.

[20] As Mardin states, the *mahalle* was more of a compact *Gemeinschaft*, with its boundaries protected by tough young men and faithful dogs trained, like village dogs, to attack strangers. The mosque, again as in the Sunni village, was the social institution of instruction, and the café the communications centre. (Alevi villages were/are less compact and without a mosque.) Rules were flexible (more so than in the village), but inflexible regarding the mixing of sexes. *Mahalle* virtues were linked to the preservation of small groups. Şerif Mardin, 'Religion and Secularism in Turkey', in Kazancıgil and Özbudun (eds), *Atatürk: Founder of a Modern State* (London: Hurst, 1981), p. 214.

Here, while the rural population was often predominantly Kurdish, the towns would be mainly non-Kurdish,[21] consisting of Turkish-speaking and various Christian or Jewish groups.

The above gives some illustration of the complexity of late Ottoman society in terms of group identification. For example, Mardin describes the situation in Bitlis *Vilayet* at the start of the third quarter of the nineteenth century as 'still a crazy-quilt pattern of tribes, loose tribal federation, ethnic units and religious groups.'[22] The primary cleavage between nomads and settlers remained, but true nomads had already become a small group by that time, numbering some 40,000 out of a total population for the area of 398,000 in 1891. The process of settlement of tribes had been going on since shortly before the establishment of direct Ottoman rule. After 1842, a new pattern emerged of strictly Kurdish villages side by side with Armenian ones, replacing the earlier symbiotic arrangement of local tribes wintering in Armenian villages.[23] In that area, the Turkish-speakers who lived in the towns made up part of the notable class and virtually all the bureaucracy. Armenians were both town notables and villagers, while Kurdish speakers were minorities in the towns but made up the tribal and many village populations. Thus ethnic and religious groups lived side by side with widely divergent cultures. A French traveller on a fact-finding mission for the French government at the time reported:

> All these hamlets are made up of families of the same religious sect grouped together and forming a unit entirely distinct from the neighbouring hamlet in terms of mores, types and language: Armenians, Chaldeans, Kurds, Nestorians have each a completely different way of life.[24]

This picture of highly fragmented inward-looking local *Gemeinschafts* can be seen to be repeated throughout the Ottoman Empire, especially in Anatolia and the Balkans. As such, it appears

[21] Van Bruinessen, *op cit.*, p. 26.

[22] Serif Mardin, *Religion and Social Change in Modern Turkey: The Case of Bediüzzaman Said Nursi* (Albany: SUNY Press, 1989) p. 43.

[23] *Ibid.*, p. 44.

[24] Harry Binder, *Au Kurdistan. En Mesopotamie et en Perse* (Paris, 1887), p. 152, quoted in *ibid.*, p. 45.

to fit Gellner's paradigm of the pre-modern state, which is made up of a mass of local 'low cultures' with little uniformity between them. Given the sense of unity within Islam of the community of believers, why was the Ottoman Empire so fragmented in group identity? The non-penetrative aspect of the Ottoman state has been mentioned, as has the strong attachment to village, tribe or *mahalle*. These groups can be seen as being 'real' communities in Anderson's usage. The 'imagined' community remained the religious group, and for non-Muslims, the Ottoman *millet* system was crucial.

The millet system and the Muslims

The conquest of Byzantium and the advancement of the Ottomans almost to Vienna brought large Christian communities under Ottoman rule. Although there were inevitably some people who accepted the religion of the new rulers – the majority of Albanians, the Torbeşi of Macedonia, the Pomaks of the Rhodope mountains, and many Bosnians – the Ottoman rulers were non-assimilative and multi-national, without the technological and institutional facilities for integrating and unifying the subject peoples. Additionally, the Balkan peninsula is very mountainous and communications are difficult. This helped to produce communities that tended to be compartmentalised rather than unified. The Christian and Jewish populations were accepted, in accordance with the Islamic tradition, as 'people of the book'. The common ancestry of the three religions helped this tolerance – a tolerance illustrated by the acceptance of large numbers of Jews, especially Ladino-speaking Sephardim expelled from Spain in the late fifteenth century. Many of these people settled in Salonika, which subsequently became predominantly Jewish.

For Muslims, there was no official differentiation by language or race. Until the end of the nineteenth century, the concept of being a 'Turk', as used in modern parlance, was alien to the Ottoman elites, who saw themselves as Ottomans (*Osmanlı*) rather than 'Turks'; the latter seems to have implied 'uneducated peasants'. The importance of language in group identity has been noted in all studies of nationalism; so we should look at the Ottoman state language. A requirement of high office in the Ottoman Empire was first to be a Muslim,[25] and second to know Ottoman Turkish.[26] Ethnicity was not a factor *per se*, and many Grand Vezirs and high officials were originally from Albanian, Muslim Slav or other Ottoman Muslim populations. In fact, the whole concept of the 'slave élite' and the *devşirme* system worked against an 'ethnically pure' governing class. Ottoman Turkish was a requisite, but this was by no means the same as everyday spoken Turkish. It was a mixture of Turkish, Arabic and Persian and reflected the importance in Islamic society of men of the sword, men of the pen, and men of religion. Turkish terms predominated in military usage, while Persian words and forms were prevalent in the literary arts. Arabic – the language of Mohammed and of the holy Koran – naturally featured strongly in religious matters.[27]

As well as the large number of Arabic and Persian words in its vocabulary, Ottoman Turkish also required that when such words were used it should be with the relevant Arabic or Persian grammatical structures. Thus, a knowledge of all three languages was needed. In addition the Arabic script was used, although it was not suited for writing Turkish with its different vowels and was difficult to learn. All this made the official state language a privileged mystery to the mass of 'common people'. The problem of the script, which did not sign vowels, also resulted in frequent misunderstandings. To cap all this, by the late eighteenth and early nineteenth centuries, Ottoman Turkish had degenerated into bombast, with inelastic and tortuous embellished phrases and constructions.[28] Thus, the Ottoman Empire appears to fit Gellner's

---

[25] Although a number of officials such as ambassadors were non-Muslim, the top posts were reserved for Muslims.

[26] Modern scholars give credit for the first establishment of Turkish as the base of the official language, at least as far as Anatolia is concerned, to the Karamanids, who created a strong polity on the ruins of the Seljuk Sultanate in the thirteenth century. See M. Önder, 'Türk Diline Ferman...' in 'Türkçenin "Devlet Dili" Olarak İlânının, p. 684. Yildönümü, *Türk Dili*, vol. 10, (1961), pp. 599-601, quoted in David Kushner, *The Rise of Turkish Nationalism, 1876-1908* (London: Frank Cass, 1977) ff to p. 90. However, as shown below, this was not synonymous with demotic Turkish as spoken by the mass of the population.

[27] As far as one can tell, everyday language also contained a large number of Arabic and Persian Words. This is shown by the way Atatürk's language reformers (see Chapter 4) were unable to remove all the Arabic and Persian words, and often had to 'invent' Turkish words to replace them.

[28] B. Lewis, *op. cit.*, p. 420.

paradigm of a trans-ethnic and trans-political élite employing an archaic idiom with no interest in ensuring continuity between its mode of communication and that of the majority.

In 1859, large numbers of Muslims fled from the Caucasus to the Ottoman Empire to escape Russian rule. A further 5,000 left in 1865. Justin McCarthy estimates that approximately 1.2 million Caucasians emigrated from Russian-conquered territories in this period and some 800,000 of them moved to the Ottoman Empire.[29] Interestingly, the Hamidian regime, although pursuing a policy of pan-Islamism to try to keep the empire together, viewed such arrivals with suspicion. Despite the common bond of Islam and the shared linguistic attributes of those from the Turkic-speaking areas of Russia, they were viewed as foreigners, very much in the modern national usage.[30]

[29] Those who settled in Anatolia have largely become Turkified under the impact of Kemalist integral nationalism (see Chapter 3) – a process repeated with later Muslim immigrants from the Balkans. Those who settled in Arab lands of the empire were less easily assimilated however – see Paul B. Henze, 'Circassian Resistance to Russia', footnote 93 in Broxup *et al.*, *op. cit.*, who also cites Justin McCarthy, *The Fate of the Muslims* (forthcoming). Despite this apparent ease of assimilating non-Turkish-speaking Muslims (apart from the Kurds, as we shall see later) Henze notes that: [c]onsciousness of Circassian origin is nevertheless widespread among their descendants in modern Turkey.' See also P. Alford Andrews, *Ethnic Groups in the Republic of Turkey*, (Wiesbaden; Dr Ludwig Reichert Verlag, 1989). In the Balkans these groups progressively became peacefully assimilated into the relevant majority Islamic national community – i.e. the Turkish one in Bulgaria and Northern Greece, the Albanian one is Albania and the Albanian-dominated surrounds of Kosovo and Western Macedonia, and the Muslim Slav community in Bosnia and Eastern Sandžak; see H. Poulton, *The Balkans: Minorities and States in Conflict* (London: MRG Publications, 1993), *passim*.

[30] Selim Deringil, 'The Ottoman Empire and Pan-Islam in Turkic Russia' (paper delivered at conference on 'Change in Modern Turkey: Politics, Society, Economy', University of Manchester, 5-6 May 1993). Deringil points out that in the Russification campaigns from the 1880s onwards there is evidence that many Central Asian *ulema*, collaborated with the Russian regime, portraying the Tsar as the 'White Sultan' and calling for obedience to the temporal authority, as did the Ottomans in the Arab lands. Russia also began to portray itself as the protector of Muslims from Russia who had moved to the Ottoman Empire, which reinforced the idea that they were 'foreigners'. In 1897 there was a ban on the publication of the Koran by Russian subjects in Turkic Kashgar, with the Council for the Inspection of Holy Texts stating: 'If we allow the Koran to be published by any Muslim – this can have serious problems for the divine state.' There was also a ban on acquisition of property by non-Ottoman Muslims,

An interesting case is that of the Roma (Gypsies) of the Ottoman Empire. The Roma originated in India and moved through Anatolia to Europe.[31] Some groups became Muslim – in the Ottoman Empire most did so – while others became Christian. As such, many became assimilated into the Turkish-speaking mass – as illustrated by the second half of the Bulgarian proverb 'Save us O Lord ... from the Gypsy who becomes a Turk.' However, they have been subjected to racism and discrimination from all groups. This discrimination still continues in many places.[32]

· *The Christian millets*

While Christians and Jews were tolerated, until the *Tanzimat* reform movement they were not seen as first-class citizens, as the Muslims were. (In practice this continued even after the *Tanzimat*.) They were forbidden to carry arms or ride horses. They were not eligible for the army, apart from those young Christian boys taken by the *devşirme* system.[33] While certain avenues of

---

especially in Hejaz and Medina. The governor of Hejaz, Osman Nuri Paşa, blamed 'foreigners' for the bad situation there, as they did not pay taxes, and he especially mentioned 'Indians, Javanese and Turks' (!). Even when they came as immigrants they were treated with suspicion and closely watched – for example, the Kazan Kurban Tatars who were forcibly settled by the Ottoman authorities in carefully chosen places. Whether this points to a 'proto-nationalism' as Deringil asserts, or is more to do with allegiance to a particular state and Abdülhamid's fear of foreign claims over his citizens (which was justified given the prevailing situation in the empire) is debatable. The issue of property in the holy places of Mecca and Medina was understandably a thorny one. See also S. Deringil, 'The Invention of Tradition as Public Image in the late Ottoman Empire', in *Comparative Studies in Society and History*, vol. 35, no. 1, 1993.

[31] Donald Kenrick, *Gypsies: from India to the Mediterranean* (Toulouse: Gypsy Research Centre, CRDP Midi Pyrénées, 1993), *passim*.

[32] See Chapter 8.

[33] Although Christians did fight in the very early Ottoman armies, this quickly ended and the army became the Muslim army of a Muslim state; see Bernard Lewis, *Emergence*, p. 331. There was some Christian recruitment after 1908 but this was very small. The navy, however, was a different matter. For some time it was a faithful copy of the Venetian and Genoese navies, crewed mainly by Greeks, Dalmatians and Albanians. Attempts to replace these by the more dependable elements which made up the land army were not successful and there remained a dearth of skilled crews. Until the time of Mahmud I (1730-54) this necessitated hiring skilled crewmen from merchant ships who plied Ottoman

advancement were closed to them as non-Muslims, others, like commerce, were open to them. However, Mardin points out that the widely held belief that such commercial activity in the Ottoman Empire was always a monopoly of non-Muslims is something of a myth, and that the classic non-Muslim 'comprador' type only really appeared after the Crimean War.[34] Nevertheless, in the first half of the nineteenth century the Muslim Ottoman traders (*Hayriye Tüccarı*) all but vanished at the expense of the minority traders (*Avrupa Tüccarı*) protected by Western powers. The British also took advantage of the empire's weakness in the 1820s and 1830s to force free trade agreements on it. The Greek Phanariots had, by the late seventeenth century, acquired a monopoly on providing interpreters for the state – a monopoly that would last until the last Greek *dragoman* at the Porte was executed for treason at the time of the Greek revolt and the decision taken to use only Muslims thenceforward for such positions.[35]

Thus, the Ottoman state was an Islamic one and the population was divided by religious affiliation. The whole political and social system preceding the *Tanzimat* was based on the separation of groups – even down to regulations as to the colour and type of clothing each religious group could wear.[36] As noted above, all

---

ports in exchange for remission of customs duty. The navy remained dependent on Greek provincial pilots for navigation as well as Greeks and Arabic-speaking Muslims from North Africa. Thus it was not an indigenous Ottoman product. See H.A.R. Gibb and H. Bowen, *Islamic Society and the West*, vol. 2 (Oxford University Press, 1950), pp. 88-107.

[34] Şerif Mardin, *op. cit.*, p. 167.

[35] Bernard Lewis, *op. cit.*, pp. 60 and 86.

[36] Sultan Mahmud II took the first steps towards changing this, and towards ending the centuries-old institutionalised separation of his subjects by religious affiliation, by ordering government and army officials to stop wearing the habitual turban and flowing robes. These garments, by their shape and colours marked both the religion and the status of the wearer. For example, only Muslims were supposed to wear yellow shoes and green garments. Henceforth, by a decree of 1829, all officials, except those in the religious class were to wear the simple fez and European frock-coat, regardless of their status in life. Outside government service, changes in the hitherto rigid dress codes began, with the fez becoming universal (despite initial revolts against its imposition – revolts which were to be repeated when Atatürk, a century later, outlawed it in favour of the European brimmed hat or cap). The change in dress codes was particularly accelerated by the Crimean War and the corresponding large influx of foreign soldiers and merchants, who helped spread European ways and dress codes to all elements

Muslims were officially recognised as equal first-class citizens in the Muslim *millet.* Other 'peoples of the book' were organised into separate *millets* – Jews in one, members of the Armenian Church in another, etc. Faith, not ethnicity or language, was the differentiator.

There remains uncertainty over the origins of the *millet* system. Many trace the system back to the presumed appointment by Mehmed II, the conqueror of Istanbul, of Patriarch Gennadias, Bishop Yovakim of Bursa and Rabbi Capsali as hereditary leaders of the Greek, Armenian and Jewish communities. However, others, like Benjamin Braude, suggest that the term '*millet*' was really a set of mostly local arrangements which varied from place to place, and that there is much evidence to show that the authority vested in the leaders was personal rather than hereditary or institutionalised, and varied in its territorial extent.[37]

Despite their origins, perceived or real, the *millets* became accepted. The leaders had wide jurisdiction over their flocks, who were bound by their own regulations rather than Şeriat. The different *millets* were treated like corporate bodies and allowed their own internal structures and hierarchies; indeed the Ottoman state encouraged this by dealing exclusively with their heads rather than individual members. Included within these structures were the educational systems for the different religious communities. Thus, the religious community was the prime focus of identity outside of family and locality. For the Christian minorities especially, the *millet* system proved ideally suited to the transmission of the new creed of nationalism penetrating from the West. However,

---

of Istanbul's population. Women's clothing, however, changed much more slowly. See Stanford J. Shaw, *The Jews of the Ottoman Empire and the Turkish Republic* (London: Macmillan, 1991) pp. 149 and 169; and Bernard Lewis, *op. cit.*, p. 100.

[37] E.g., the Greek patriarchates of Jerusalem, Alexandria and Antioch retained their autonomy, at least in canon law, while for the Armenians, the see of Istanbul became 'over the centuries ... a sort of *de facto* patriarchate, but its ecclesiastical legitimacy was grudgingly recognized, if at all.' See Benjamin Braude and Bernard Lewis (eds), *Christians and Jews in the Ottoman Empire* (New York: Holmes and Meier, 1982), pp. 72-82, and the review article 'Remembering the Minorities' by Andrew Mango in *Middle Eastern Studies*, vol. 21, 1985, pp. 118-40. The Jews never had a single patriarchal leader for the whole community; see Shaw, *op. cit.*, p. 42.

as is shown in the next chapter, there was often tension between the traditional *millet* leaders and the new nationalist radicals.

The *millet* system also allowed the subject Christian peoples to retain their separate identities and cultures, rooted in their respective churches. Indeed the monophysite churches with Syrian, Armenian and Coptic adherents, as well as the Nestorians, survived mainly in the Muslim lands, while vanishing in the more intolerant Christian West. Along with the Jews expelled from England, France, Spain and Portugal, a variety of heterodox Christians including Protestants, Unitarians, and Russian Molokans received refuge in the Ottoman Empire.

3

THE OTTOMAN EMPIRE, II: THE PENETRATION OF NATIONALISM

The Tanzimat reform movement

By the end of the eighteenth century, sections of the ruling Ottoman elite had finally become aware of the extent to which the empire had fallen behind its rivals in Europe. Successive military defeats at the hands of the Russian Empire rammed the point home. In response, the empire attempted to replace old institutions with new and modern ones. The key reform was the abolition of the Janissaries, who had repeatedly proved themselves to be incompetent in fighting external enemies, and who were unable to settle internal revolts like those of the Serbs and Greeks. The objective was to replace them with a modern army.

The great reforms, initially attempted unsuccessfully by Selim III, began during the reign of Mahmud II, who firmly reasserted the control of the centre over the periphery. Mustafa Reşid Paşa, who served as Grand Vezir six times, led the way in introducing the reforms. At this time the weakness of the empire was plain to see. Without the help of foreign powers, notably Britain, it was hard pressed with the threat from Russia or from Mohammed Ali in Egypt. The latter was the prototypal reformer, and one whose success threatened to take over the empire itself. The price for British support was acceptance of free trade, and thus opening the empire to British commercial penetration, as well as paying at least lip-service to the principle of ending the formal inequality between Muslims and non-Muslims. Some tend to see the reform movement as due mainly to this Western (predominantly British) pressure. Perhaps some aspects, like the Imperial Rescript of 1856, were introduced primarily for foreign consumption (in this case due to the Crimean War). However, there is consensus that by attempting to copy institutions and methods from the West, the reform movement was mainly a genuine attempt to modernise the empire and try to ensure its survival.[1]

The *Tanzimat* embodied a whole series of reforms, dealing with virtually all aspects of interaction between the state and the individual. For the purposes of this study, we will examine the aspects dealing with differentiation between the various groups within the empire, especially those between Muslims and non-Muslims. As we have seen, Muslims were seen as first-class citizens; other religious groups, Christians or Jews, were tolerated but not treated as equals. The *Tanzimat*, introduced by Reşid and carried on by the modernist bureaucrats like Ali Paşa and Fuad Paşa who succeeded him, essentially undercut the entire system.

The reforms entailed a gradual and partial secularisation of the state machinery, the judiciary and education. From the start, with the 'Proclamation of the Rose Garden' in November 1839, the concepts of security of life and property, fair and public trial and – most shocking to devout Muslims – religious equality in the courts were clearly stated.[2] In May 1840, the new penal code emphasised the equality of all Ottoman subjects. While this was relatively ineffective, it was another step in the same direction. In May 1855 the poll-tax for non-Muslims was abolished and henceforth all could bear arms. The Imperial Rescript of February 1856 again emphasised full equality for all subjects. Sultan Abdülmecid (1839-61) clearly expressed the ideas of the reform movement to Albert Cohn, a Rothschild agent, during his visit to Istanbul in 1854 by telling him:

> My heart knows no difference among the *rayas* [peoples, literally 'flock'] of my empire; all rights and privileges will be given to all *rayas* without distinction.[3]

---

[1] See F.E. Bailey, *British Policy and the Turkish Reform Movement: A Study in Anglo-Turkish relations, 1826-1853*, (New York: Howard Fertig, 1970), and R.H. Davison, *Reform in the Ottoman Empire, 1856-1876* (Princeton University Press, 1963), *passim*.

[2] B. Lewis, *The Emergence of Modern Turkey* (Oxford University Press, 1961), p. 105.

[3] S. Shaw, *The Jews of the Ottoman Empire and the Turkish Republic* (London: Macmillan, 1991), p. 156. Individuals could pay a special tax in lieu of conscription, known as *bedel*. Most non-Muslims did so (as did some Muslims): hence the *bedel* effectively replaced the old tax on non-Muslims (known as *cizye*).

In practice, this meant that Christians, Jews and Muslims were admitted on an equal basis to government schools and positions in the administration (but not the army). The Greeks and Armenians, in particular, took advantage of the new openings in government service.

In the new system, the *millet* had become more of a purely religious organisation, rather than one dealing with all aspects of the relations between the individual and the state. In line with the gradual bureaucratisation of the Muslim offices of the Şeyhülislam, the 1856 rescript proposed giving fixed salaries to the clergies in Christian *millets* in place of the previous method of raising dues from the parishes. This would both raise the level of the lower clergy and help end the corruption resulting from the sale of religious office. It was aimed at providing relief for Slav Macedonian and Bulgarian villagers who previously had to support the Greek clergy. Unsurprisingly, the measure was opposed by the latter and, therefore, the rescript simultaneously proposed commissions for each *millet* to change their administrations to be more in tune with the new system. After a short resistance by the upper echelons of the Istanbul Patriarchate, a new constitution for the Greek (as it was now called) Orthodox *millet* was passed in 1862 which saw power within the *millet* pass from the previous all-powerful metropolitans to the lay constituency of the developing urban groups.[4]

New *millets* were created, mostly through outside pressure from the Great Powers, for Catholics and Protestants. Crucially, the monopoly of the Greek Patriarchate was broken with the creation of the Serbian Orthodox Church in 1557, the Bulgarian Exarchate Church in 1870, and the Romanian Orthodox Church in 1885. By 1875 there were nine recognised *millets*, of which six were fairly large; by 1914 there were seventeen.[5] As Shaw points out, the *Tanzimat* reforms took the first steps to ending the *millets'* monopolistic control over the lives of their followers by creating secular institutions of education, law and justice side by side with

---

[4] Kemal H. Karpat, *An Inquiry into the Social Foundation of Nationalism in the Ottoman States: From Social Estates to Classes, from Millets to Nations* (Princeton University Press, 1973), pp. 88-9.

[5] *Ibid.*.

the traditional ones.[6]

The Jews

Jews from Western and Central Europe – Ashkenazi Jews from Germany, France and Hungary, Italian Jews from Sicily, Otranto and Calabria, as well as Sephardic Jews from Spain and Portugal – were already fleeing persecution and emigrating to the Ottoman Empire in large numbers before the expulsion of all of Spain's Jewish population in 1492. They continued to arrive after then. As a result, by the early seventeenth century the Ottoman Jews formed both the largest and wealthiest Jewish community in the world. They settled in all parts of the empire but mostly concentrated in Istanbul, in eastern Thrace at Edirne, along the shores of the Aegean at Salonika and in Palestine.[7]

However, what Shaw calls 'the golden age of Ottoman Jewry' of the sixteenth and early seventeenth century, faded with the general Ottoman decline. Salonika's Jews became subject to repeated attacks in the eighteenth century by unruly Janissaries as well as the local Greek population.[8] Throughout southeastern Europe, the growing anarchy as the state declined led to increased blood-libel attacks[9] on Jews by Christians, and rampages by the

---

[6] The modern schools were also supplemented by the introduction of a large number of foreign Christian missionary schools, both Protestant and Catholic. These schools were intended for Muslims and Jews as well as Christians, with the aim of conversion to the particular brand of Christianity propounded. In the main, however, Muslims and Jews were forbidden to attend, so that only Christian Greeks and Armenians used them. Many of these converted and thus escaped traditional *millet* control. A result was that they often fell prone to violent revolutionary activities, using the missionary schools as active bases against the empire; Shaw, *op. cit.*, p. 157. This highlights an interesting point. Despite the suitability of the *millet* system for propagating nationalist ideas due to its preservation of separate group identity, in practice the *millets* were usually governed by conservative traditional leaders who preferred the continuation of Ottoman rule, and hence of their own absolute power within their communities, rather than radical change. By undermining their authority, the *Tanzimat* unintentionally helped the more radical nationalists.

[7] *Ibid.*, pp. 33-6.

[8] *Ibid.*, pp. 136-7. Some of them were later to play leading roles in the Young Turk and Kemalist revolutions.

[9] *Ibid.*, pp. 122-3.

Janissaries and other troops. The general decline in their situation saw the escape into religion of most Ottoman Jews, who turned their backs on rationalism and enlightenment.[10]

Because of this, the Jews initially lagged behind in the new opportunities afforded by the *Tanzimat* in the nineteenth century. The conservative elements in their *millet* leadership viewed the new educational opportunities with distrust. However, by the end of the century they had caught up in the educational stakes.[11] Indeed, by the time of Abdülhamid, the Jews were seen as the only loyal minority subjects of the empire, as they correctly saw repression by Christians as the main threat.[12]

Despite such loyalty, the failure of the *Tanzimat* reform movement to create an Ottoman citizen is amply illustrated by education statistics for the Jews. Late in the nineteenth century, when the Jewish community had come to accept the new opportunities made available by the *Tanzimat*, it was reported that of some 300,000 Jews then in the empire, as many as 100,000 knew French but only 1,000 understood Turkish. Hence, Shaw suggests, just as the traditional schools had cut young Jews off from Ottoman society by teaching only Hebrew, the modern schools were doing the same by emphasising French rather than Turkish.[13]

The Young Ottomans

Thus the *Tanzimat* did not succeed in making non-Muslims loyal to the empire. How did the *Tanzimat* ideas affect the Muslim

[10] *Ibid.*, pp. 129-31.

[11] *Ibid.*

[12] The newly-emerging national Orthodox Christian movements in the Balkans were often hostile to both Muslims and Jews and repeatedly slaughtered them together. The exception to this solidarity between Muslim and Jew in the face of Christian hostility came over the movement by Theodore Herzl and his supporters for a Jewish national state in Palestine. This movement, which many Ottoman Jews initially opposed, had many similarities with the Christian national movements in that it aimed at independence for a portion – and for the Muslims an historical and religiously important portion – of the empire. This movement tended to be fuelled by Jews who came to the Ottoman Empire fleeing from persecution in Europe and Russia. The numbers settling in Palestine quickly grew from 24,000 in 1882; 47,000 in 1890; 80,000 in 1908 to 85,000 in 1914; *Ibid.*, p. 217.

[13] *Ibid.*, p. 165.

Turkish-speaking population? The first reaction was that of the Young Ottomans, who came to prominence in the late *Tanzimat* period of 1867-78. They were the first organised opposition group from the Ottoman intelligentsia to use the ideas of the Enlightenment and attempt to synthesize modernisation with Islam. They were also the first Ottoman group to use the media as means of spreading their ideology.[14]

In many ways, they shared similar outlooks to the ruling elites they criticised so strongly. The Young Ottoman mentor Şinasi was intellectually closer to their sworn enemy Ali Paşa than he was to them. Şinasi typically embodied the eighteenth-century attitude of the eventual triumph of reason, while Namık Kemal, their main ideologue, embodied the typically modern reaction of militancy and the cult of national values – aspects which were even more pronounced in Ali Suavi and which were to become the hallmark of twentieth-century nationalism.[15] Most, like Namık Kemal, were from the translators office of the Foreign Ministry and thus were from that small segment of society who were in close contact with ideas from the West. However, in their actions and writings a sense of frustration at their inability to rise up the bureaucratic ladder is evident. Some, like Ziya Paşa, appear to have been blatantly opportunistic. The two main Young Ottoman thinkers for the purposes of this study are Namık Kemal and Ali Suavi. The crucial difference between their views and those of the great bureaucrats, like their arch-enemy, Ali Paşa, was their re-emphasis on Islam as an essential component of Ottoman society.

For Namık Kemal, the ideological vacuum resulting from the pushing back of religion from the public to the private sphere was one of the main weaknesses of the *Tanzimat.* He attempted to produce a synthesis between modernisation and Islam and looked for Islamic references for parliaments and representative government. He was opposed to the *Tanzimat* secularisation of law and looked to the *Şeriat* as the basis for much of society. He believed that when the *Şeriat* was not observed the empire declined and

---

[14] For the Young Ottomans see Şerif Mardin, *The Genesis of Young Ottoman Thought* (Princeton University Press, 1962), which has a full account of Young Ottoman thought. Also useful are R. Davison, *op. cit.*, and R. Devereux, *The First Ottoman Constitutional Period: a study of the Midhat Constitution and Parliament* (Baltimore: Johns Hopkins University Press, 1963).

[15] Mardin, *Genesis*, p. 117.

tyranny and injustice reigned.[16] He followed in Şinasi's steps by using simple direct speech in his writings – some of which are still used today in Turkish schools for imbibing the sense of 'fatherland'. He was also very successful in appealing to patriotism and is credited with first using the term *hürriyet* (freedom) and the first extensive use of *vatan* (fatherland), both of which he popularised. For Namık, *vatan* was an emotional bond containing memories of ancestors, recollections of one's own youth and earliest experiences.[17] The nationalist overtones of such usage are obvious. However, he did not really distinguish between different competing components of group loyalty to the *vatan*, and never satisfactorily distinguished between Ottoman and Islamic identities. For example, in the *Hürriyet* newspaper in 1868 he included Arab and Persian Muslims and the Arabian Caliphate in his appeal to 'Ottoman' pride.[18] As Bernard Lewis points out, he saw nothing incongruous in including Arabs and Persians in an appeal to Turkish *amour propre*.[19]

The confusion over what he actually meant by *vatan* is also shown by his interchangeable use of other key words like *ümmet* (religious community), *millet* (both as nation and religious group), *Türk* (Turk), *kavim* (tribe) and *mezheb* (denomination or sect). Despite the confusion, Namık Kemal's contribution was to replace the previous Ottoman concept of different peoples living harmoniously side by side but still separate, with that of a union of the population, i.e. a change from 'equal but separate status' to becoming fully integrated Ottoman citizens. Given his emphasis on Islam and the *Şeriat*, it is hard to fully comprehend how this was to come about in the Ottoman Empire unless all embraced Islam. Either way, with the rise of pan-Slavism and the Ottoman retreat in the Balkans, he gave up the idea of an Ottoman nation of different nationalities and religious groups, and showed himself more concerned during the exile of his last years in looking back to the glorious past of the Turks. More consistently with his Islamic leanings perhaps, he ended by looking to the possible

---

[16] *Ibid.*, p. 315.

[17] *Ibid.*, p. 327.

[18] Bernard Lewis, *Emergence*, p. 330.

[19] Bernard Lewis, 'History-writing and National Revival in Turkey', *Middle Eastern Affairs*, vol. 4 (1953), pp. 218-27.

reunion of all Muslims with the help of the Ottoman 'elder brothers'.[20] His last writings show a pronounced emphasis on the Turkish language as a means of uniting Muslims of the empire.[21] Essentially, his attempted synthesis of Islam and modern Western institutions failed, and he came to realise that his concept of an Ottoman nation embracing all the Ottoman peoples regardless of religion was diametrically at odds with his own emphasis on Islam.

More Islamic and as fiercely patriotic was Ali Suavi (1839-78) – 'a turbanned revolutionary'[22] and a radical zealot whose particular brand of religious demagoguery now appears to be extremely prevalent in the late 20th century. He was an advocate of 'direct Islamic democracy' with no real trace of the mechanisms of representation, parliamentarianism or popular sovereignty,[23] that is an Islamic state where all had equal access to the ruler, and all were ruled by the *Şeriat* alone. Along with his militant Islamism, he was fiercely patriotic. He repeatedly used the term 'Turk' and looked to Turks in Central Asia as 'brothers'. Furthermore, he called for the codification of Islamic laws in Turkish, and for Ottoman schools to adopt Turkish as the single language of instruction. Because of this some see Suavi as the first 'Turkist'. However, as Mardin points out, he was too much the Islamic purist to be a real adherent of Turkism.[24] Suavi's frequent use of the term 'Turk' is relevant. Most of the Ottoman elite still viewed the term as referring to ignorant Anatolian peasants rather than to themselves. Here again the impact of the West is significant,

---

[20] Mardin, *Genesis*, p. 332.

[21] In letters from his exile on the island of Lesbos to Menemenli Rifat in 1878 he makes this clear. On 30 August he wrote: 'While we must try to annihilate all languages in our country except Turkish, shall we give Albanians, Lazes and Kurds a spiritual weapon by adopting their own characters? ... Language ... may be the firmest barrier – perhaps firmer than religion – against national unity'; and on 13 September: 'Certainly it is impossible to encourage the spread of our language among Greeks or Bulgarians, but it is surely possible among Albanians and Lazes, namely Muslims. If we set up regular schools in their countries and carry out the programmes which are now not fulfilled, the Laz and Albanian languages will be utterly forgotten in 20 Years.' Fevziye Abdullah (ed.), *Namık Kemal'ın Hususi Mektupları*, vol. 2 (Ankara: 1969), quoted in Masami Arai, Turkish Nationalism in the Young Turk Era (Leiden: E.J. Brill, 1992), p. 3.

[22] B. Lewis, *Emergence*, p. 171.

[23] Mardin, *Genesis*, p. 383.

[24] *Ibid.*, p. 371.

as both the terms 'Turk' and 'Turkey' were in common use in Europe.[25]

Abdülhamid II and Pan-Islamism

A change in policy from the *Tanzimat* period was evident after Abdülhamid took power. He eschewed all thoughts of territorial expansion and turned his back on the previous reliance on the British to defend the empire against the Russians. He was an authoritarian and a centraliser who attempted to use Islam and pan-Islamism to hold the empire together in the face of external and internal threats. Article 3 of the 1876 Constitution specifically referred to the 'high Islamic Caliphate' of the House of Osman, and the Sultan, unlike his predecessors, greatly stressed this, expanding on it to make pan-Islamism official policy.[26] The new emphasis on Sultan as Caliph and protector of all Muslims throughout the world, while having some limited bearing on Muslims outside the empire, was really a foreign affairs bluff by Abdülhamid.[27] The main thrust of the new emphasis on religion

[25] Both terms were used by Ali Paşa himself in 1862, when he was Ottoman Foreign Minister, in a letter to the Ottoman ambassador in Paris. The letter was written in French by Ali's own hand. As M. Cavid Baysun suggests, it was probably sent in this form to be shown to the French Foreign Minister. The letter clearly calls for the retention of the Ottoman Empire, prophetically pointing to the alternatives of bloodshed and civil war continuing for a century in the Balkans, and uses the terms 'Turks' and 'Turkey'. See Bernard Lewis, 'Ali Pasha on Nationalism', *Middle Eastern Studies*, vol 10, 1974, pp. 77-9.

[26] Bernard Lewis, *Emergence*, p. 336.

[27] The new emphasis on the Sultan as Caliph did have some limited bearing on Muslims outside the empire. Abdülhamid's claims as Caliph were rejected in Morocco and northwest Africa due to the more successful competing claims of the Sultan of Morocco, who claimed descent from Mohammed's daughter Fatima. Abdülhamid was also not recognised by the various Dervish communities of Africa, including the powerful Senussi confraternity – see Sir Charles Eliot, *Turkey in Europe* (London: Frank Cass, reprinted 1965), p. 123. However, before the Russian conquest, the rulers of Central Asia did accept the supreme authority of the Sultan as Caliph, although the practical consequences were slight (*ibid.*). The policy did have an initial effect on the numerous Muslims under British control in India, but again the practical consequences were slight, as shown in the pathetic intervention of Indian Muslims in support of the Caliphate in 1923 (Bernard Lewis, *op. cit.*, p. 336). The policy was really a bluff, but however slight the practical effects, it was a bonus to have some potential, if not actual,

and the role of the Sultan as figure-head was internal.[28]

It was propagated to combat outside (Western) influence both on the heartlands of the empire and on the fringes such as Egypt where the Sultan was only nominally in control. One method of Western penetration was by economic and cultural means: by using trade, religion (where there were Christian minorities like the Armenians or the Christian Arabs of the Lebanon) and cultural methods such as opening schools, the foreign powers were attempting to make direct contact with the population through Western institutions. This was aided by the Capitulations and by the bankruptcy of the empire in 1875, with the resulting control of 25 per cent of its revenues by the Public Debt Administration, a kind of internal parallel government of taxation run by the Western powers. The British were also influencing Shiites in southern Iraq and to some extent in Arabia. Russian and Austro-Hungarian influence in the Balkans was growing, as was French influence in Syria and the Lebanon. Moreover, Italy was attempting to join in by similar methods in Albania and Tripoli. Thus, Abdülhamid was faced by the threat of the empire gradually being subverted, with sections of the population looking to Western consuls for support and services rather than to the official Ottoman structures.

To combat this, he embarked on a kind of *Kulturkampf* of enhancing Ottoman culture in Muslim areas by promoting religious loyalty to the empire and his own person. To propagate this he vastly improved the internal communications – especially the telegraph and the railways – and also increased education in the provinces. Centralisation was the key here, with railways to Baghdad, Syria and the Hejaz greatly aiding this process. The crucial aspect of the telegraph was seen at the time by Sir Charles Eliot, who noted that before the advent of telegraph communication, the Vali

---

hold over large numbers of Russian and British subjects. This bonus was not entirely unlooked for, as Abdülhamid sent emissaries for this purpose to Java, Iran, Turkestan, China, India and Africa; see Şerif Mardin, *Religion and Social Change in Modern Turkey: The Case of Bediüzzaman Said Nursi* (Albany: State University of New York Press), p. 126.

[28] See F.A.K. Yasamee, 'Abdülhamid II and the Ottoman Defence Problem', *Diplomacy and Statecraft*, vol. 4, no. 1 (1993), pp. 20-36.

.... had a proprietor's interest in his estate and was anxious to promote local interests and send as little money to Constantinople as possible. He was a centrifugal force and in his way promoted independence, whereas the modern Vali is entirely centripetal.[29]

In this *Kulturkampf,* Abdülhamid was successful in at least stemming the tide of this foreign penetration, although the struggle was not always bloodless.[30]

The use of pan-Islamism and the image of the Sultan as leader of all Muslims was especially used by Abdülhamid against incipient Arab nationalism. This was a particularly sensitive problem as Islam had of course originated with the Arabs and Arabic was the language of the Koran. Thus, any Arab opposition movement within the empire could possibly harness both nationalism and religion against the Ottoman system, with disastrous results for the empire.[31]

[29] Eliot, *op. cit.*, p. 149.

[30] The Armenian massacres of the 1890s can be seen at least in part as a result of this struggle with the Armenian community, once the *millet-i sadıka* (the loyal community) but now viewed as another potential Bulgaria and thus seen as treacherous. This and the new antagonistic inter-communal relations, accentuated by pan-Islam and the new emphasis on the Caliphate, helped create the climate for the massacres; *ibid.*, p. 401. See also Jeremy Salt, *Imperialism, Evangelism and the Ottoman Armenian, 1878-1896* (London: Frank Cass, 1993).

[31] Abdülhamid's policy of avoiding open confrontation and the use of Islam/pan-Islamism can be seen in his handling of the Egyptian crisis of 1881-2 and the rise of the Mahdi in Sudan. He was also wary of a cultural revival of Arabism in Syria, as well as the possibility of the spread of any form of successful Arab nationalism, as was threatened by Ahmed Urabi. As a counter, his position as the Caliph and leader of all Muslims was strongly emphasised. To get the point over to the Arab populations he used the Arab Şeyh Abulhuda as a leading state ideologue. Abulhuda was brought to Istanbul as an 'advisor', and between 1880 and 1908 he produced 212 books and brochures emphasising the duty of all Muslims to follow the Caliph – see S. Deringil, 'The Ottoman response to the Egyptian Crisis of 1881-1882', *Middle Eastern Studies*, vol. 24, 1988; Mardin, *Religion and Social Change*, p. 127; and F.A.K. Yasamee, 'The Ottoman Empire, the Sudan and the Red Sea Coast, 1883-1889' in S. Deringil and S. Kuneralp (eds), *Studies in Ottoman Diplomatic History* (Istanbul: İsis, 1990). Mardin sees this policy as being successful in defusing incipient nationalism in Syria, from where Abulhuda originated, and where he propagated the Rifai Sufi order to which he belonged; Mardin, *Religion and Social Change*, p. 127. The Arab nationalism espoused by Syrian Christians was not at this time popular with Syrian Muslim Arabs; C. Ernest Dawn, *From Ottomanism to Arabism* (Urbana:

Abdülhamid implemented strict centralisation, his personal dictatorship and Islam and pan-Islamism, along with his role as the Caliph, to create personal loyalty to himself and keep the Islamic elements in the empire unified. He also continued and expanded the *Tanzimat* education programme, with a considerable extension of the state schooling system.

Along with this came the attempt by his regime to make the empire more homogeneous by the compulsory use of demotic Turkish. This was established by a decree of 1894 requiring the use of Turkish in all the schools of the empire. The decree further stipulated the use of clear, simple language, devoid of Arabic and Persian words not commonly used, as well as the use of proper textbooks.[32] Language reform remained one of the main discussion points in the Hamidian period, with many press articles on what form this reform should take. This was compounded by a growing interest in Turks outside the empire – *Dış Türkler* – and the Turks' original homeland in Central Asia ('Turan'). Some writers wanted Ottoman Turkish to be reformed using more *Çağatay* – the Turkish of Central Asia. Others looked to different vocabularies, like those of Anatolia.[33] The press, within the limits imposed by the repressive Hamidian regime, also began discussing the notion of being a Turk and trying to reconcile this with the competing concepts of Ottomanism and Islamism.[34]

University of Illinois Press, 1973), p. 132.

[32] See Agâh Leverend, *Türk Dilinde Gelişme ve Sadeleşme Evreleri* (Ankara: Türk Dil Kurumu, 1949) pp. 143-5, and the circular to this effect to a high school in Monastir reproduced in M.F. Köprülü, *Milli Edebiyat Cerayanın İlk Mübessirleri* (Istanbul, 1928), quoted in David Kushner, *The Rise of Turkish Nationalism, 1876-1908* (London: Frank Cass, 1977), p. 79.

[33] See Kushner, *op. cit.*, pp. 56-80 for a full discussion of this debate. This has interesting parallells with the present debate over the relationship between Turkish and the Turkic languages of the newly independent Central Asian republics.

[34] It is noteworthy that the creators of climate for the acceptance of such new ideas as being a Turk through their articles in the leading newspapers (another novel feature of the Hamidian period) came from mixed communities. These, as shown in Chapter 1, are often the breeding ground of nationalists. For example, Şemseddin Sami – the editor from 1877 of *sabah* – and Ahmed Midhat Efendi were both from family backgrounds that were not wholly Turkish. Sami was from the prominent Albanian Frasheri family while Midhat had a Circassian mother. Necib Asım (Yazıksız) who wrote for Istanbul's then most popular daily, *Ikdam*, came from the mixed Arab province of Aleppo; *ibid.*, pp. 16-19.

There were now three apparently exclusive principles being articulated: Ottomanism, Islamism[35] and Turkism. How did Ottoman writers resolve the contradictions? Did the acceptance of these principles preclude harmony between Turks and non-Turks of the Empire? Ahmed Midhat attempted to square the circle by stating that Ottoman nationalism was unlike any other because, apart from Islam and the Caliphate, it rested on three separate bonds: first, on *Kayıhanlık*, which was the bond inherited from the Great Turkish tribe of Kayı Khan; second, on *Türklük*, founded on the pre-Ottoman Anatolian Turkish elements; and third, on the common homeland and state (*Osmanlılık*), which was shared by the whole population regardless of faith or nationality (*kavmiyet*).[36] This somewhat tortuous reasoning well illustrates the feelings of many Turkish intellectuals who saw that the Turks identified themselves with the Ottoman Empire more than other groups. At the same time, they upheld the *Tanzimat* concept of a multi-national empire living in peaceful harmony. This inherent contradiction – one which did not affect the Russian émigrés like Akçura (see below) – remained pronounced in Ottoman intellectuals right up to the end of the empire.

Despite this contradiction, in Abdülhamid's time the concept of being a Turk began to be popularised; even the Sultan viewed himself as a Turk.[37] However, the concept was closely connected with Abdülhamid's use of pan-Islam and any idea of Turkish unity propagated in Ottoman periodicals was cultural rather than political.

Anatolia

Until the second half of the nineteenth century, Anatolia as a geographical unit had not really figured in Ottoman consciousness as constituting the heartland of the empire. Although the Ottoman Empire had begun in the northwestern corner of Anatolia, the elite of the empire had always looked towards Europe, and Rumelia

---

[35] Islamism at this time can be seen as a reaction to perceived foreign cultural threat – here from the 'West' – with perceived alien cultural norms. This is akin to the current nationalist reaction in many parts of the world to the 'global culture' as described in Chapter 1.

[36] *Tercüman-ı Hakikat*, no. 5881, 13 September 1897, quoted in Kushner, *op. cit.*, p. 40.

[37] Kushner, *op. cit.*, p. 21.

was as important a focus of geographical loyalty as Anatolia. Whilst Anatolia had always been important for revenue and manpower for the army, it had no special distinction, and the Istanbul elites tended to view it as populated by ignorant peasants and nomads. Place of birth was the dominant focus of geographic loyalty. In the traditional Ottoman system, the ruling official class or 'slave elite' was raised in Istanbul from early childhood. Hence, they were cut off from their birthplaces – a process which helped to perpetuate the separation of centre and periphery.

This began to change with the *Tanzimat* period and the concept of *vatan* as popularised by Namık Kemal. However, while Namık Kemal's concept and use of the term '*vatan*' obviously struck a chord in Ottoman consciousness, it remained somewhat undefined and did not really correspond to the French notion of *patrie* with its distinct geographical connotations. To Namık Kemal, Islam remained the bond between the citizen and the '*vatan*'.[38] However, the concept of *vatan* as a geographic unit and the enhanced position of Anatolia within this came more to the fore as the nineteenth century wore on. In this process, the relentless loss of territory by the Ottomans in the Balkans throughout the century was naturally important. The drought of 1872 in Anatolia also raised a strong public reaction and helped focus public opinion in the capital on Anatolia as part of the heartland of the *vatan*.[39]

The growth and spread of Armenian and Greek nationalism in Anatolia, coming after the loss of most of the Balkans, also helped to raise this consciousness.[40] This once more illustrates how mixed communities and threats from other aggressive nationalisms are important factors in the growth of nationalist thought.[41]

[38] B. Lewis, *Emergence*, p. 333.

[39] The newspaper *Basiret* was especially active in this. In an article of 1874 it referred to the inhabitants of Anatolia: 'They are our homeland brothers who raise most of our soldiers and most of our labourers, and most of our necessary provisions are gained thanks to their effort and toil.' *Basiret*, no. 1,342, 24 Şaban 1290 (1874), quoted in Kushner, *op. cit.*, p. 51.

[40] For example *Tercüman-ı Hakikat*, no. 954, 24 August 1881, and no. 958, 31 August 1881, warned of the dangers of an Erministan (Armenia) appearing in eastern Anatolia, and also pointed to the declining position of the once strong and prosperous Muslim population of western Anatolia now under threat from growing Hellenisation. Quoted in Kushner, *op. cit.*, p. 52.

[41] Şemseddin Sami went further and in his 1901 dictionary emphasised the essentially Turkish – not just Muslim – character of Anatolia. In his view, with

Necib Asım followed on by pointing to the potential of Anatolia as a rich repository of Turkish peasant folklore and customs forgotten elsewhere. In his view, the rural and nomadic populations of Anatolia contained a treasure chest of words, phrases, songs, tales, proverbs, riddles, customs and manners peculiar to themselves, and he called for greater research into them. This view, which as shown below was repeated by Ziya Gökalp, is very reminiscent of East European 'ethnic' nationalism with its emphasis on 'the village' and 'the peasant' as the true repository of the attributes and virtues of 'the nation'. In contrast, 'the city' was seen by many nationalists as 'cosmopolitan', sometimes 'alien' and often suspect. Its reflection in early Turkish proto-nationalistic thought is especially relevant given the emphasis on 'the city' as the ideal in Islamic thought, and marks a distinct stage in the growth of nationalist thought among Muslim Turkish speakers of the Ottoman Empire. By the end of the Hamidian period, Anatolia had become closely identified with the concept of a Turkish homeland – Namık Kemal's concept of the *Vatan* had taken concrete geographical meaning.[42]

---

the exception of the Christian Greeks in large commercial ports like Izmir and on the Aegean islands, the population was essentially all of Turkish stock derived from mixing the indigenous populations with Turks and Turkmen. Even Lazes and Circassians were in a process of Turkification (*Türkleşmekte): Kamus-ül-A'lam*, I, pp. 396-7, quoted in Kushner, *op. cit.*, p. 52. See also Şükrü Hanioğlu, *Bir Siyasal örgüt olarak Osmanlı İttihad ve Terrakki Cemiyeti ve Jön Türklük*, vol. 1 (Istanbul: İletişim, 1985), pp. 626-41.

[42] This was clearly articulated by the poet Mehmed Emin, who wrote of the Anatolian peasant as a hero. In one of his most famous poems, 'A Voice from Anatolia, or Going into Battle', published in 1900, he writes: 'I am a Turk; my faith (*din*) and my race (*cins*) are mighty ... A man is the slave of his fatherland ... These lands are the home of my fathers.' Mehmed Emin, 'Anadolu dan bir Ses, yahut Cenge giderken', in *Türkçe Şiirler* (Istanbul: 1316 [1990]), p. 37, quoted in Kushner, op. cit., p. 54. This new emphasis on Anatolia was partly connected with one on Turkish as opposed to Islamic or Western culture. French influence among the literary elite was very strong and centred around *Servet-i Fünun* under the guidance of Tevfik Fikret, and the New Literature school. Turkists like Şemseddin Sami and Ahmad Midhat criticised the new school as being elitist, and viewed what they saw as the slavish imitation of the West as a threat to true Turkish culture. Instead, they looked to Mehmed Emin as the founder of a new nationalist school. Similar questions were raised concerning music; again Anatolia was held up by such people as Rauf Yekta, one of the most prominent contemporary musicologists, as a repository of flourishing Turkish music. 'In many places in Anatolia, and particularly in the regions of Urfa, Mosul and Erzerum ... Our music will greatly benefit if these

The rise of Albanian nationalism

It is worth looking more closely at the Albanians who, like the Turkish-speaking population of the empire, were predominantly Muslim but did not have the 'ethnic' link to Mohammed or the 'holy' language of the Koran as their mother tongue like the Arabs. Additionally, as we shall see, they played an important role in the early phase of the Committee for Union and Progress (CUP), which overthrew Abdülhamid.

The majority of Albanians were Muslim, with a large Orthodox minority in the south of the Albanian-inhabited lands, and a smaller Roman Catholic one in the more mountainous and tribal north, and had been regarded as especially loyal to the empire. Many senior Ottoman officials were of Albanian descent. However, the expansion of the Greek state to the south and the Serbian state to the north helped raise fears among the Muslim Albanian community that the Ottoman Empire might not prove strong enough to protect their interests against their rapacious neighbours. In 1878, a group of Albanian intellectuals founded the League of Prizren which aimed at asserting Albanian national consciousness by promoting the use of the Albanian language, and combating the threat of partition between Serbia and Greece, and possibly Bulgaria as well. In the early 1880s, under the guidance of intellectuals like Naim Frasheri, a number of schools were opened in southern Albania using the Albanian language as the medium of instruction. While this was as yet confined to a small intellectual circle and not a mass movement, it was nevertheless an important new factor.[43]

Abdülhamid clamped down on this and, as noted above, promoted pan-Islamic solidarity instead. Anyone in possession of written material in Albanian faced punishment. The Greek Patriarchate backed this up with the threat of excommunication of any Orthodox believer so convicted. The League of Prizren was banned and its leaders fled abroad. However, the pressure for greater cultural recognition continued within the empire. In 1896, Christian and Muslim Albanians combined[44] to send a joint appeal to

---

songs are collected, printed and disseminated with their notes. Our real national music is embodied in these pieces.' *Ikdam*, no. 1, 341, 6 April 1898, quoted in Kushner, *op. cit.*, p. 86.

[43] For more details on the Albanian movement see Stavro Skendi, *The Albanian National Awakening, 1878-1912* (Princeton University Press, 1967).

the Great Powers demanding a single administrative unit for the Albanian-inhabited lands with its capital in Monastir, as well as the establishment of Albanian schools. As a general rule, the Muslim Albanians in the north, faced with Serbian expansion, were the most prominent. The two clashed during the Greco-Turkish war, while the Orthodox Albanians to the south in Korçë and Kastoria regions remained faithful to the Greek cause.[45]

The first Albanian guerrilla movement with a political motivation (actually resistance against the activities of Bulgarian revolutionary groups) was founded in 1899 by Haji Mulla Zeka. By 1905, so-called Albanian Revolutionary Committees were being formed in numerous towns in Albania with the aim of staging an uprising against the Ottoman authorities. In the run-up to the 1908 Young Turk revolution, contacts had been established between some members of the Committee of Union and Progress (CUP – see below) in Macedonia and their opposite numbers in the Albanian Revolutionary Committees. In Debar the two actually amalgamated. In Skopje the CUP consisted largely of Albanians, and Midhat Frasheri in Salonika issued an appeal for all Albanians to support the revolution. Indeed, the Albanian Muslims were to the fore in the initial period of the Young Turk revolt, with Ahmad Niyazi Bey's flight from Resen into the mountains on 3 July 1908 with 200 men seen as the first real move. Under his influence, Albanian groups around Lake Ohrid all joined the movement, although in Korçë support was only forthcoming on the condition that he granted Albania autonomy after the revolution.

---

[44] This united nationalist action which cut across the great religious divides is something of a rarity in this period. Observers like Edith Durham writing in the early twentieth century (for example see her *High Albania* (London, 1909) point to this strength of Albanian nationalism and highlight the Albanian habit of switching faiths to suit temporary expediency, asserting that the only true religion of the Albanians is 'Albanianism'. This habit appears to have been more frequent in the rugged, often inaccessible mountains of the north. What is perhaps relevant is that the Bektaşi sect was especially pronounced among Albanian Muslims (see J.K. Birge, *The Bektashi Order of Dervishes* (London: Hartford, 1937). This sect was something of a halfway house between Christianity and Islam and often owed more to local folk culture than either, thus helping to bridge the great religious divide.

[45] See H. Poulton, *Who are the Macedonians?* (London: Hurst, 1995), Chapter 3, and Wayne S. Vucinich, *Serbia between East and West* Stanford University Press, 1968), p. 27.

Contrarily, the more conservative religious Albanian Muslims of Kosovo would only support the revolt if the Sultan remained on the throne – again illustrating the problems of nationalism in Islamic communities.

Thus, for a short period, the growing Albanian national movement was allied with, and essential for, the CUP. However, when it became apparent that the Young Turks' real agenda was to promote Turkish nationalism, this further stimulated Albanian nationalism culminating in the creation of an independent Albanian state in November 1912. In 1910-11 the Albanians came out in an open rebellion centred on Kosovo demanding their own educational facilities. A further rebellion broke out in May 1912, and before the outbreak of the Balkan Wars, the Albanian revolts were the biggest problem for the Young Turk governments. By the beginning of August the rebels had occupied as far east as Skopje and the government met many of their demands, granting an amnesty on 19 August 1912.[46] The change in consciousness brought about by the influence of Western nationalism on the Albanians is graphically illustrated by the major contemporary figure, Ismail Kemal Bey. In his memoirs it is clear that at first he saw himself mainly as an Ottoman and a Muslim, and later as an Albanian – a seemingly effortless change due in no small part to the emphasis by the CUP on Turkishness.[47]

The Turks and the Committee of Union and Progress (CUP)

As already noted, it was still too early to differentiate clearly between different Muslim groups and there was no real mass concept of being a Turk as opposed to a member of another Muslim community. Even the Albanian national movement was confined mostly to a small intellectual circle. All figures of the time group the Muslims together. However, Turkish sources state that of the 1.5 million Muslims in the three *vilayets* of Kosovo, Salonika and Monastir at the turn of the century, the majority were Turks, with the rest made up of Albanians and smaller numbers of Muslim Greeks, Slavs or Roma.[48]

[46] Sina Akşin, *Jön Türkler ve Ittihat ve Terakki* (Istanbul: Remzi Kitabevi, 1987), pp. 185-6, 198-9 and 210.

[47] Ismail Kemal Bey, *Memoirs* (London: Constable, 1920), *passim*.

[48] Akşin, *op. cit.*, p. 49.

However, all sources agree that the Muslims were the largest group, making up about half the total population. As the Ottomans progressively lost control of the Balkans, Muslims and Jews moved to Macedonia, swelling their respective populations. Additionally, a Greek source states that in 1904 the Porte decided to prevent soldiers who had finished their seven-year service in Macedonia from returning to Anatolia so as to bolster the Muslim element of the population.[49] The vast majority of the land was owned by Muslims, with the Slav or Greek populations mainly sharecroppers.[50]

As we have seen, Abdülhamid had undertaken an extensive expansion of the education programme. One result of this was a new breed of junior officials who both chafed at the constraints of his autocratic rule and looked for ways to defend what remained of the empire in the Balkans. The pressure from the Great Powers in the form of naval contingents despatched to force issues, and the presence of foreign officers in the country influenced the reforms and accelerated the growth of patriotism among young Ottoman officers and officials in Macedonia. The proximity of well-dressed and well-paid foreigners inevitably affected their Ottoman counterparts. In addition, these men could learn from the nationalism of the Christian groups.[51]

---

[49] P. Arjiropulus, 'O Makedonikos Agon – Apomnimoneumata' in *O Makedonikos Agonas Apomnimoneumata* (IMXA 199) (Salonika, 1984), quoted in V. Aarbakke, 'Ethnic Rivalry and the Quest for Macedonia' (unpubl. MA thesis, University of Copenhagen, 1992), footnote 21, p. 18.

[50] The Ottoman Empire in its classic form did not have a feudal class. After the conquest, private estates and most church lands were taken over by the state, which had divided the best lands into non-heritable fiefs, *timars*, usually under a Muslim military leader – the *askeri* class. However, many of the lower nobility were able to keep their earlier ownership and usually converted to Islam in the second generation. The tenure of the *askeri* class was subject to revocation at the whim of the centre. The peasants had the right to hereditary plots so long as they paid the tax-farming tithe. The system changed in the eighteenth century when weakness at the centre allowed the *timars* to change into *çiftliks* where landlords broke the non-hereditary right as well as the legal limits. The result was that the peasants' lot declined, which in many ways provided the real spur to the initial revolts which saw the establishment of the new Balkan states (see Aarbakke, *op. cit.*).

[51] In addition, Turkish Muslims in the new Bulgaria led the way in imbibing nationalist ideas. See ,Şerif Mardin, *Jön Türklerin Siyası Fikirleri, 1895-1905* (Ankara: İletişim, 1964), pp. 99-100. Such people were suddenly minorities whereas before they were majorities. Similarly, the leaders in propagating a

Macedonia became a school for nationalism for young officers from the war academy as well as members of the bureaucracy. In contrast to the Christian Balkan nationalists, who were often teachers and intellectuals, these harbingers of Turkish nationalism were army officers and junior officials. They formed the nucleus of the CUP, which overthrew Abdülhamid in 1908 and 1909.[52] Akşin gives the typical profile of a CUP cadre in Salonika in 1906 as being predominately Turkish (rather than from other Muslim groups – despite the above-mentioned closeness of the Albanians in the initial stages of the Young Turks period), young, connected with the administrative class, a product of Abdülhamid's schooling system, and of a 'bourgeois' mentality.[53] Thus, along with the inter-Christian struggles, Macedonia was the centre of the new breed of Young Turks.

The revolution began in Macedonia on 3 July 1908 when Niyazi took to the hills and appealed to Slavs living around Resen for support.[54] The Porte's countermeasures forced the CUP to act and Şemsi Paşa, sent to quell the rebellion, was assassinated on 7 July. His replacement, Osman Paşa, arrived in Monastir on 12 July, but by then his troops were in rebellion and the CUP was taking over. The Slavs sided with the rebellion from the start, and Muslims were also coming over. On 20 July, the Muslim population of Monastir rose in support and the 1876 Constitution, which Abdülhamid had replaced with his personal autocracy, was proclaimed there. Other towns quickly followed, and Salonika, the CUP centre but the last important place in Macedonia to

---

Turkish national consciousness were often Turks from Russia like Yusuf Akçura (see below) who, due to their position as members of a minority faced with strong nationalism from the majority, adopted Western ideas more quickly than the Ottoman Turks. Due to their power position within the empire the latter did not see themselves as being so immediately threatened.

[52] The whole Young Turk period is still fairly obscure due to a dearth of sources. By far the best account of the CUP is Akşin, *op. cit.* Mardin, *op. cit.*, is also good on the source of their ideology. For English readers the best is Feroz Ahmad's *The Young Turks: The Committee of Union and Progress in Turkish Politics, 1908-1914* (Oxford: Clarendon Press, date). Also useful is E.E. Ramsaur Jr., *The Young Turks – Prelude to the Revolution of 1908* (Princeton University Press, 1957).

[53] Akşin, *op. cit.*, p. 78.

[54] Ahmad, *op. cit.*, pp. 5-6.

move, finally declared for the Constitution on 25 July.[55] With
the Albanians in Kosovo threatening to march on Istanbul if the
Constitution was not reinstated, Abdülhamid conceded. A reaction
occurred in April 1909 with a counter-revolution in Istanbul,
but troops from Salonika including Mustafa Kemal (Atatürk) and
1,200 Macedonian revolutionaries under Sandanski[56] marched there
to restore the revolution. The revolution was initially greeted
with delight from almost all sections of the population, but the
new rulers' secret agenda of Turkicisation soon saw a return to
the old violent inter-ethnic rivalries.

Along with adopting nationalism from their Christian Balkan
counterparts, the Young Turks also adopted the blood-letting of
the Balkan bands. Henceforth, violence and assassination were to
be part of Ottoman governmental business. Their Turkish
nationalism was initially kept hidden in order not to antagonise
the other nationalities of the empire. However, the Turkish and
extreme centralising nature of their government quickly became
apparent and helped stimulate Albanian nationalism. This was
further aggravated by the Young Turk provisions for compulsory
Turkish in Albanian schools, along with the arrival of many Muslim
and Jewish emigrants from Bosnia-Hercegovina and Bulgaria who
were given land and settled in Albanian territories.[57]

On August 1909 the 'Law of Association' banned political
organisations based on an ethnic or national basis. This resulted
in the closing of Greek, Bulgarian and other minority clubs in
the capital and elsewhere.[58] The real aim of the Young Turks
was to modernise and Turkify the state.[59] As such, the old Ottoman
system of *millets* and populations classified by religion was to be abolished.

---

[55] *Ibid.*, p. 12.

[56] Macedonian or Bulgarian depending on one's viewpoint – see H. Poulton,
Who Are the Macedonians? (London: C. Hurst, 1995), *passim.*

[57] Akşin, *op. cit.*, pp. 206-7.

[58] B. Lewis, *Emergence*, p. 215.

[59] Here a distinction should be made between the main Young Turk factions,
which can be classified as Liberals and Unionists, the latter being supporters of
the CUP. The Liberals were decentralists and attracted support from non-
Muslims and non-Turks. For the purposes of our discussion, I will concentrate
on the Unionist faction and its Turkish nationalist agenda. However, it must
be borne in mind that prior to the First World War the Unionists were never
all-powerful, and were ousted by military coup in July 1912 before returning

The Russian Connection

Intellectuals from Russia played a crucial role in the birth and propagation of Turkish nationalism in the Ottoman Empire. Their experience of direct threat from the assimilatory power of Tsarist Russia in the second half of the nineteenth century galvanised them far more than the Ottoman Turks.[60] The latter were still fairly secure in their elite positions in the political apparatus, even if they had lost out to some extent in the rising commercial fields. The Turkic peoples from the Crimea were influential, as were those from Azerbaijan (which also enjoyed a cultural revival in the mid-nineteenth century)[61] again aided both by proximity

---

to power again by violence in January 1913. Some, like Feroz Ahmad, question whether Turkish nationalism was truly on the Unionist agenda and if it really did come to the fore in the period 1912-18, preferring to see the war-time regime as appealing to Ottoman/Muslim solidarity. As shown below, I tend to follow the 'conventional wisdom' which sees Turkish nationalism as growing in this period.

[60] The Turkic national awakening in Russia began as a modernisation movement – *Cadidism* – entailing a reform of the education system, with the attempt to elevate the vernaculars into modern literary languages. Its centre was Kazan and its leader was the Crimean Tatar Ismail Gasprinski (1851-1914). His main tool was the periodical *Tercüman*, established in the Crimea in 1883, which later carried the motto '*Dilde, Fikirde, İşte Birlik*' (Unity of language, ideas and action). This was often quoted by the Turkish press. See Kushner, *op. cit.*, p. 12.

[61] Azerbaijan's first Turkish newspaper was *Ekingi* (Cultivator). This appeared in Baku in 1875. The Azeri playwright, Mirza Fathali Ahundov (1812-78) gave the Ottoman government a plan for reform of the Turkish script which was considered by the Ottoman Scientific Society. Perhaps a greater influence was that of his friend Hüseyinzade Ali Bey (Turan) (1864-1941) who studied in St Petersburg, came to Istanbul in 1889 and began teaching at the Medical School. He spread pan-Turkic ideas of the unity of all Turks under Ottoman leadership to the students and helped from the Society of Union and Progress, returning to Azerbaijan at the turn of the century. Another Azeri pan-Turk was Ağaoğlu Ahmad (1869-1939) who studied in Paris, where he met Ahmed Riza and other Young Turk leaders. In 1894 he returned to the Caucasus and in 1906 started the newspaper *İrşad* (Guidance). After the 1908 Revolution he went to Istanbul and with Hüseyinzade and others published Türk Yurdu (see below). As noted above, the dervish communities helped maintain contacts between different parts of the Islamic world, and *tarikats* from Central Asia had for a long period maintained *tekkes* in Istanbul. One of the most important of these was the Uzbek *tekke* in Üsküdar, whose sheikh in the 1860s and 1870s was Buharalı Süleyman Efendi. In 1882 he published 'The Chagatay language and Ottoman Turkish', which introduced Chagatay to the Ottomans. Another *tekke*

and similar dialects, and Turkic Tatars from the Volga region.[62] However, the most influential, and one who will play a prominent role in this study, was Yusuf Akçura.

Yusuf Akçura was born in the town of Simbirsk (Ulyanovsk) in the Volga region and came to Istanbul in 1883. He attended a normal first and secondary school and then went to the War Academy, graduating in 1897. He soon got into trouble with the Hamidian regime due to his writings. Along with his close friend Ahmed Ferid (Tek) he was exiled to Tripoli in Libya. He escaped to Paris and then to Russia in 1902.[63] He began writing while a student at the War Academy in Istanbul and made contact with the Young Turks in Paris, writing articles on history for Ahmet Riza's gazette *Meşveret*.[64] His first important piece, and a pointer to the future, came out in 1903 entitled 'An Essay on the Historical Foundation of the Ottoman State.' In this he wrote: 'The Young Turks' attempts to found an Ottoman nation is cul-de-sac. Nationalism is the only road to take.'[65]

One year later in Cairo, his seminal work and key manifesto of Turkish nationalism, *Üç Tarz-i Siyaset* (Three Kinds of Politics), was published. In this pamphlet, Akçura detailed three political doctrines: first, the idea of an Ottoman nation – *Osmanlılık*; second, that of a state based on Islam as the criterion of citizenship, i.e., one of all the peoples of Islam – *İslamalık;* finally, a Turkish political nationalism based on the Turkish race – *Türkçülük*.

For Akçura, *Osmanlılık* was akin to trying to make the Ottoman Empire like the United States, where the concept of a fatherland (*vatan kavramı*) would lead to the forming of an Ottoman nation with freedom of religious belief.[66] This idea, which equates with

---

member, Mehmed Sadık, later published a Chagatay dictionary in Istanbul; *ibid.*, p. 13.)

[62] Sihabeddin Mergani (1808-88) – one of the greatest reformists among Russian Muslims – born near Kazan, came to Istanbul in 1881 and made contact with Cevdet and Münif Paşas – *ibid.*

[63] Enver Ziya Karal, 'Önsöz', in Yusuf Akçura, *Üç Tarz-i Siyaset* (Ankara: Türk Tarih Kurumu, 1976). For more details see Y. Akçura, *Türkçülük* (Istanbul: Toker, 1990), and François Georgeon, *Aux Origines du Nationalisme Turc: Yusuf Akçura* (1876-1935 (Paris: Institut d'Études Anatoliennes, 1980).

[64] Karal, *op. cit.*, p. 5.

[65] Quoted in *ibid.*, p. 6.

[66] Y. Akçura, *Üç Tarz-i Siyaset*, p. 19.

Smith's concept of a 'civic nationalism', he saw as a mistake which began with Mahmud II and reached its height at the time of Ali Paşa and Fuad Paşa – that is at the time of the *Tanzimat*. Akçura believed that the acceptance of the nationalist ideas of the French Revolution at the beginning of the nineteenth century in Europe was based on consciousness of race and ancestors. However, Mahmud and his successors were unable to understand this. Their faulty principles made them believe in the possibility of a single nation based on the mutual security and friendship of the state's different races and religion. Akçura parodies the arguments put forward: 'In truth, didn't the French nation come from a mixture of German, Celt, Latin, Greek and other assorted ancestors? Were not several Slav elements incorporated into the German nation?'[67] Similarly was not Switzerland composed of different races and religions? These examples, or so Akçura asserted, increased Mahmud's and others' confidence in the viability of creating an Ottoman nation. However, the success of the new Germany, with its model based more on race in the war with France of 1870-1, resulted in the decline of the perceived viability of an Ottoman nation.[68] In this, Akçura seems to be saying that the military victory of Germany, the archetypal state based on East European 'ethnic' nationalism, over France, the archetype of the 'West European' model of territorial nationalism, proves the superiority of the former over the latter – a rather crude 'might is right' attitude.

For Akçura, the idea of *İslamalık* also originated from Western Europe, and began to be used during the reign of Abdülaziz when the idea of *Osmanlılık* began to weaken. Initially used by diplomats, it was taken up by the Young Ottomans after they began to abandon the idea of a fatherland (*vatan*) comprised of all the inhabitants of the empire. Akçura, like the Arab nationalists, saw *İslamalık* as a magnificent but unattainable ideal. For him, the negative points of this policy included the problems of different laws and the likelihood of an increase in enmity between Ottoman citizens, especially after the equality measures of the *Tanzimat* period. Additionally, the Great Powers would be against it due to the potential problems with their own Muslim inhabitants. It would also disrupt relations with other Islamic Asian states. On

---

[67] *Ibid.*, p. 20.
[68] *Ibid.*

the positive side, such a policy, if carried out, would found a powerful Muslim community with a strong basis of religious unity.[69]

Akçura states that after they abandoned the idea of *Osmanlılık*, the Young Ottomans realised that even if there was complete freedom and legal equality for non-Muslims, the Christian communities would still refuse to join the proposed nation; hence, they began to view Christian Europe with great hostility. He also states that Midhat Paşa accused Abdülhamid of applying such a policy even though it had by then been abandoned by most of its adherents. Thus, for Akçura, Abdülhamid's policy was very similar to that of the Young Ottomans:[70] he was using the railways to promote pan-Islamism and had turned back to the theocratic state abandoned by the *Tanzimat* reformers.[71]

Akçura's third and final idea was *Türkçülük* (which can roughly be translated as 'Turkish nationalism'). This he saw as the quality of being a Turk ('*Türklük*'), Turkish national politics, or unification of the Turks. He pointed to the huge number of Turks in Asia outside the Ottoman Empire. He argued that the Turks of the Ottoman Empire were not the totality of Turks, and that if all the Turks could unite then they would be very powerful. However, he saw that the idea of Turkish unity was very new, and without precedent in history. He emphasised that while Turks could at that moment look back to their military and political contribution to the Ottoman Empire, as yet they could not look back to ancient 'Turkish' heroes such as Oğuz, Cengiz, Timur, Uluğ Bey or others outside the Ottoman Islamic framework.[72]

As regards non-Turks in the area of the proposed unified Turkish state, Akçura was not opposed to assimilation and Turkification. Among the advantages of Turkic unification, he stated that

.... those united by religion [Islam] who were essentially not Turks but who to a certain extent had become Turks would become more assimilated with Turks, and even those who had never identified themselves as such could themselves be made into Turks.[73]

---

[69] To make this easier, Akçura saw the need for the consent of the Caliph and the use of Arabic as language of religion and science, etc; Karal, *op. cit.*, p. 7.

[70] Akçura, *op. cit.*, p. 22.

[71] *Ibid.*, p. 23.

[72] *Ibid.*, p. 35.

[73] *Ibid.*, p. 33.

He ends by asking which of the policies of Islamism or *Türklük* is more harmful to the Ottoman Empire and which is more possible.[74] It is clear that he preferred *Türklük*.

Thus, Akçura firmly comes out in favour of an ethnic nationalism in which all the Turks should unite into one large nation state. Given their background in Russia, where the Turks and Turkic peoples were under threat from the assimilatory Great Russian authorities, it is not surprising that he and other exiles should expound such an ideology. As noted in Chapter 1, nationalists often come from mixed areas, especially from communities under threat from other aggressive nationalisms – in this case Great Russian nationalism masquerading as pan-Slavism. Hence, when the pamphlet was first published in 1904, his ideas were seen by many Ottoman intellectuals as extreme.[75]

---

[74] *Ibid.*, p. 36.

[75] An immediate riposte came from Ali Kemal (1867-1922), one of the main anti-Turkists, who in his pamphlet *Cevabımız* of 26 May 1904 – reprinted in Akçura, *op. cit.* – poured scorn on Akçura's ideas. He noted that from the time of Mahmud II to Midhat Paşa, when the *Tanzimat* was in full swing, there was no trace of Bulgarians, Rumanians, Serbs or Armenians adopting the supposed Ottoman nationality. (Actually Midhat Paşa was himself from an Islamicised Slav (Pomak) family, showing that Muslim Slavs could be brought into the 'Ottoman' nation. Again, the shared religion of Islam was the key.) As regards the idea of Islamic unity, Ali Kemal considered this to be a ridiculous illusion, and one that France, Britain and Russia would not allow. Finally, as regards the idea of Turkish unity, Ali Kemal pointed out acidly that the Ottoman Turks had been unable to defend the Crimea, so how could they be strong enough to unite the Turks of Central Asia? He also pointed out that in the Ottoman Empire the concept of *Türkçülük* was non-existent. His solution to the empire's problems depended more on individual improvement, rising standards of living and the creation of a strong society through increased wealth and knowledge, with the state reaping the benefits of this progress rather than chasing what he saw as illusionary ideas of Islamic or Turkish unity. Even Akçura's close friend Ahmet Ferid (Tek) (1877-1971) in his reply to Ali Kemal's criticism (*Bir Mektup*, June 1904, reprinted in Akçura), *op. cit.*, could not wholly accept Akçura's rejection of Ottomanism. He defended the *Tanzimat* and Midhat Paşa's policies to some extent. He wrote: 'The Ottoman nationalist policy is the most easily followed at present, although it does not promise very excellent results for the future ... We devote our thoughts to pursuing the Ottoman policy, that is, to protect and assimilate all the subjects that remain under our rule. Those whom we succeed in protecting and assimilating remain among us; those who do not remain leave.'

Ziya Gökalp and the CUP

Although many in the Ottoman élite viewed Akçura's new Turkish nationalism as inappropriate in 1904 when he wrote *Üç Tarz-i Siyaset*, the continuing break-up of the empire brought about a change. The Young Turks, while paying lip service to the concepts of Ottomanism and equality of all, in reality progressively pursued a policy of Turkism. The loss of most of the Balkan provinces in the Balkan Wars and the ensuing First World War allowed these ideas to be fully aired. The main ideologue of the CUP became Ziya Gökalp who, like so many ardent nationalists, came from a mixed area – in this case the Kurdish area of Diyabakir; Gökalp himself was almost certainly of partial Kurdish extraction.[76]

Much of Gökalp's work is contradictory, but this can partly be explained by the fact that he lived through the periods of the Ottoman Empire, the Young Turks and early Kemalism, and thus was party to great changes.[77] Given the premise that reconciling Islam with modern nationalism is at times problematic, as well as the importance of culture in nationalism, detailed in Chapter 1, it is worth taking a close look at Gökalp's thinking on these issues. Gökalp attempted to draw a distinction between 'civilisation', to which he attributed Western technological achievements and cultural implements which could be shared by many societies, and 'culture', to which he assigned the latent pattern of values and beliefs which define a people.[78] He viewed the commands

---

[76] Uriel Heyd, *Foundations of Turkish Nationalism – the Life and Teachings of Ziya Gökalp* (London: Harvill Press, 1950), p. 21. Gökalp himself claimed to be racially a Turk but went on to state: 'However, I would not hesitate to believe I am a Turk even if I had discovered that my grandfather came from Kurdish or Arabic areas, because ... nationality is based solely on upbringing.' Ziya Gökalp, *Turkish Nationalism and Western Civilisation*, selected essays translated by Niyazi Berkes (London: George Allen and Unwin, 1959), p. 44.

[77] As nationalism later became the leading ideology of the Kemalist republic, the contemporary influence of Gökalp (and other nationalists like Akçura) can be overstated. However, their ideas play a crucial role in this study, precisely because of what came later. Heyd, *op. cit.*, remains the clearest treatment of Gökalp's ideas. See Niyazi Berkes, 'Ziya Gökalp; His contribution to Turkish Nationalism', *Middle East Journal*, vol. 8, no. 4, 1954, for the view that Gökalp would have, if he had lived longer, come round completely to Kemal's ideas. See also Taha Parla, *The Social and Political Thought of Ziya Gökalp, 1876-1924* (Leiden: E.J. Brill, 1985) and Z. Gökalp, *The Principles of Turkism* (Leiden: E.J. Brill, 1968).

associated with the 'proper' Islamic organisation of society as aspects of Arab culture with nothing to do with 'pristine' Islam.[79] As the Arabs in Mohammed's time had locked organised government, the institution of the religious community and the young Muslim state had necessarily to be interdependent.[80] Now was the time to separate the two; legislative powers should not be subject to the *Şeriat*. Armed with a questionable interpretation of Islamic precepts,[81] he called for Islam to be a purely ethical religion free from all legal and social rules. Thus religion and state should be separated and the domination of Islam over political (even if only nominal) and social life be ended.[82]

This interpretation also allowed him to separate religion from his definition of civilisation, and thus claim no contradiction in the adoption of European civilisation alongside Islamic values, all based upon a latent Turkish culture. As he stated:

> [we can] accept the three ideals [Turkism, Islam and modernisation] at the same time by determining the respective fields of operation of each. ... In short, the Turkish nation today belongs to the Ural-Altai group of peoples, to the Islamic community, and the West internationally.[83]

[78] Şerif Mardin, 'Religion and Secularism in Turkey' in Kazangıgil and Özbudun, *Atatürk Founder of a Modern State* (London: Hurst, 1981), pp. 206-7. See also Ziya Gökalp, *Turkish Nationalism*, and M. Arai, *op. cit.* The idea apparently came from F. Tönnies; see Heyd, *op. cit.*, pp. 66-7.

[79] Mardin, 'Religion and Secularism in Turkey', pp. 206-7.

[80] Heyd, *op. cit.*, p. 88.

[81] He came up with a novel theory regarding the sources of Islamic law, which he saw as deriving from *nas* – the divine revelation shown in the Koran and the deeds and utterances of Mohammed – and *örf*, which he saw as representing the collective consciousness of society – that is the Muslim community. Using a debatable interpretation of a saying in the Hadith ('What the faithful regard as good is good with God') he saw almost all the obligations which refer to matters of this world as deriving from *örf* rather than *nas*. As all religious obligations, except for the personal relationship between man and God, depend on 'social consciousness' for sanction, *örf* held sway over *nas*. He regarded *örf* as a form of divine revelation – i.e. God revealed through social law, in the same way that some Muslim jurists hold that God is revealed in the laws of nature; *ibid.*, pp. 85-7.

[82] *Ibid.*, p. 88.

[83] Gökalp, *Turkish Nationalism*, p. 76.

In his 1916 memorandum drawn up for the CUP government, he called for the removal of the Şeyhülislam from the cabinet, his rights to be limited to questions of belief and religious ceremonies, and for the office to be made independent of the political authorities. He also suggested the abolition of the *evkaf* (pious foundations) as they prevented the establishment of communal administration in towns due to their ownership of schools, hospitals, water reservoirs, etc.[84] He also held that because they secured unearned income for the descendants of the founder they sapped the initiative of the Turks by breeding indolence and encouraging an exaggerated reliance on God and fate – all faults which he also attributed to the *tarikats*. These were the main reasons for his opposition to the orders, despite their important role in the development of Turkish culture, which he held so dear.[85] He also called for all religious courts to be transferred to the Ministry of Justice, an end to the dualism of secular and religious schools, equality for women and 'proper' family names for all.[86]

Gökalp rejected the view that there was a fundamental contradiction between Islam and nationalism,[87] and sought dubious justification for this in the Koran.[88] In his early years, when the Ottoman Empire was struggling against hostile Christian powers, he stressed the importance of Islam for strengthening Turkish patriotism, stating that as all Turks (unlike Albanians or Egyptians) were Muslims (not strictly true as the Gagauz of Bessarabia and the Dobrudzha were Christian Turks), Turkey was the last fortress of Islam.[89] However, the Albanian revolts, the failure of the *jihad*

[84] Heyd, *op. cit.*, p. 90.

[85] *Ibid.*, p. 91. Although of course the abolition of the 'low' culture *tarikats* is fully in line with Gellner's paradigm of creating a unified 'high' culture.

[86] *Ibid.*, see also Mardin, *op. cit.* These calls bear great similarity to Kemal's sweeping reforms (see Chapter 4). Gökalp approved of Kemal's separation of the Caliphate from the Sultanate, seeing it as an opportunity for reorganising the religious institutions more along the lines of the Roman Catholic Church – that is an 'Islamic Church' with a hierarchy running from *imam* (at the local level) through *müftü* (district head) and *Şeyhülislam* (country head) to Caliph (an international head akin to the Pope); Heyd, *op. cit.*, pp. 92-3.

[87] He stated: 'In fact Turkism is the real support of Islam and of the Ottoman state'. Nor did he see any contradiction between Turkism, Islam and modernisation. Gökalp, *op. cit.*, pp. 74 and 76.

[88] Heyd, *op. cit.*, p. 101.

[89] *Ibid.*, p. 28.

declaration by the CUP in the First World War, and the participation by Muslims (Indian and others) against the empire produced a change in his views. He never entirely abandoned his Islamic patriotism, especially in the struggle with the Greeks, although he never espoused pan-Islamism except as a basis for co-operation between Muslim nations.[90] The interests of the Turkish nation were always dearer to him than those of Islam. He looked to future assimilation of non-Turkish Muslims of the empire.[91] He occasionally hinted at giving Islam a national Turkish character. In his Turanist period before and during the First World War he regretfully pointed out that Islam originated from non-Turks. He wanted Islamic elements absorbed from Arabs and Persians to be discarded, keeping only the 'genuine' beliefs and traditions of Islam.[92]

Thus, Gökalp attempted to synthesise Islam and the modern state by artificially compartmentalising his three basic components of Turkish national culture (which he saw preserved in the peasant culture of Anatolia), Islam as a matter of individual conscience, and 'European civilisation'. He did this by accepting from the West only its material achievements and scientific methods, and from Islam its religious beliefs without its political, legal or social traditions. All other elements of culture, especially emotional and moral values (apart from personal religious ones), were to come from a claimed Turkish heritage. As Heyd points out,[93] these rigid and artificial distinctions were not workable; in Gökalp's synthesis of Turkish culture and Western civilisation there was no real place for Islam. Although he was at a loss to find the roots of Islam in Turkish national traditions, he did not suggest developing a specifically Turkish Islam. His 'religious Turkism' remained one of the weakest points of his programme for cultural revival, as it only called for the use of the Turkish language in religious services. His concept of Islam as a purely ethical religion was from the start vague and unconvincing. It was never expanded,

---

[90] *Ibid.*, p. 101.

[91] Gökalp, *op. cit.*, p. 78, where he writes, '...the Pomaks now speaking Bulgarian and the Cretan Muslims now speaking Greek may learn Turkish in the future and cease to be Bulgarian – or Greek-speaking peoples. This means nationality is not determined by language alone but also by religion.'

[92] Heyd, *op. cit.*, pp. 101- 2.

[93] *Ibid.*, p. 150.

and after the collapse of the Ottoman Empire, it increasingly became the junior partner of his three pillars.[94]

As noted above, the Young Turks after the 1908 Revolution had an agenda of Turkification despite their lip-service to Ottomanism. The education system was to be used for achieving this aim:[95] while primary schooling could be in the mother tongue, there would be compulsory Turkish classes, and in middle and high schools Turkish was to be the language of instruction (although middle schools could also use local languages). From now on it would hard to become a government official without being a Turk.[96] The CUP programme of 1908 made Turkish the official language.[97] The CUP saw itself as the defender of Turkism (*Türkçülük*) in the multi-national Ottoman state.[98] Turkishness replaced Islam as the basis of governing legitimacy,[99] but this had to remain hidden as the empire was still, despite the continual losses of territory, a multi-national one with large non-Turkish provinces. Thus, the CUP attempted to square the circle by pursuing an open 'civic' nationalism of Ottomanism while simultaneously pursuing a hidden 'ethnic' variant.

The wars – firstly the Balkan Wars and then the First World War – allowed this hidden agenda to come more to the fore. One notable aspect was the economic nationalism of the war period. In the first months of the Balkan War, a National Consumption Society was founded to encourage people to buy goods produced in the '*vatan*' even if they were more expensive than

[94] *Ibid.*, p. 151.
[95] Akşin, *op. cit.*, p. 103.
[96] *Ibid.*
[97] *Ibid.*, p. 104.
[98] *Ibid.*, p. 158.
[99] In November 1908 Hüseyin Cahit (Yalçın) wrote: 'Non-Muslims and Muslims regarding the law can say 'will this state be a Greek one? an Armenian one? or a Bulgarian one?' No this state will be a Turkish state. We will all be united under the Osmanlı name. But the shape of the state will never undergo a change that will exclude the special advantage of the Turkish nation.' Quoted in *ibid.* p. 169. For a vivid personal account of the rise in assertive Turkish nationalism see Irfan Orga, *Portrait of a Turkish Family* (London: Gollancz, 1950). In this account he relates his experience when sent to military school during the First World War; the Captain in charge stated clearly to his mother: 'Our intention, *hanim efendi*, is to bring up a new generation of purely Turkish officers.' (p. 204).

imports.[100] On 9 September 1914, the Capitulations were abolished with effect from 1 October. Other measures were introduced which aimed specifically at the creation of a Turkish capitalist class.[101] On 23 March 1916 a law was introduced making the use of Turkish compulsory at work. All registers and bills as well as all street signs had to be in Turkish.[102]

While such measures can be seen as steps in Gellner's state-building model, in which a uniform language is imposed on a linguistically diverse population, making it amenable to the needs of modernisation, there were more sinister sides, the Armenian deportations and massacres being the prime example. By now the Ottoman Empire had lost virtually all its European provinces due to the gaining of independence by Christian nationalist movements; the Armenians were attempting to follow the same path and threatening the breakaway of parts of eastern Anatolia. By two temporary laws of 27 May 1915 and 26 September 1915,[103] the Young Turk government ordered their deportation from this sensitive region on the Russian border. The result was colossal loss of life. This whole sorry episode is still controversial, with competing claims as to the numbers of those who died ranging from 200,000 to one million. Also controversial is the question of whether this was a deliberate policy of genocide, as the Armenians claim, or whether the government reacted reasonably to a treasonable revolt of the Armenians in Van. The Turkish government still denies that the then government deliberately pursued a genocidal policy – and this view is usually supported by eminent Turkish historians.[104] Many others disagree.[105]

---

[100] Akçura again was one of the founders; Akşin, *op. cit.*, p. 277.

[101] *Ibid.*, p. 276. As noted above, previously the *Tanzimat* reforms had seen the rise of non-Muslim entrepreneurs at the expense of Muslim ones.

[102] *Ibid.*, p. 281.

[103] *Ibid.*, p. 296.

[104] E.g. Akşin, who covers the massacres in 3 paragraphs and puts the blame squarely on the Armenians – Akşin, *op. cit.*, p. 296.

[105] See D.M. Lang and C.J. Walker, *The Armenians*, (London, MRG Publications, 1987). Erik J. Zürcher, *Turkey: A Modern History* (London: I.B. Tauris, 1993), pp. 119-21, clearly blames the Young Turk government for deliberate genocide of the Armenians and accuses Talat of giving the order and the *Teşkilat-i Mahsusa* of carrying it out. Numerous other sources back this up, for example Ronald Grigor, *Looking towards Ararat* (Bloomington: Indiana University Press,

Turanism

The idea of Turanism – a unification of all Turkic peoples from the Balkans to China in one country called 'Turan' – can be seen initially in Akçura's ideas. The Turanian movement, which can be regarded as the purest manifestation of ethnic nationalism,[106] began in earnest after the Young Turk revolution, and was led by *émigrés* from Russia. Akçura set up the *Türk Derneği* (Turkish Association) publication in November 1908 in Istanbul to help spread his ideas.[107] In August 1911 the influential magazine *Türk Yürdü* (Turkish homeland) was founded, again on Akçura's initiative.[108] This followed the *émigré* line more closely, and three of the six founders were from Russia.[109] It was avowedly pan-Turkist and non-Ottoman.[110] At about the same time the *Türk Ocağı* (Turkish Hearth) was founded, initially by students at the Military Medical School who asked for help from the intellectuals. The Hearth was officially launched in June 1911, with Akçura

---

1993) pp. 109-15. The *Teşkilat-i Mahsusa* (Special Organization) was set up in the Balkans in 1913 to organise guerilla warfare after the Ottoman defeats. It was later expanded to cover Anatolia and the Arab provinces.

[106] See Jacob M. Landau, *Pan-Turkism in Turkey* (London: Hurst, 1981), for the classic account of the ethnic variant. See also Chapter 5.

[107] See M. Arai, *op. cit.*, pp. 6-14 which shows that this publication concentrated on the language issue.

[108] Y. Akçura, *Türk Yili: 1928* (Istanbul 1928), p. 437, referred to in Arai, *op. cit.*, p. 49. *Türk Yürdü* had especial influence on the 'economic nationalism' which came to the fore in the First World War.

[109] As well as Akçura, there were the *émigrés* Ahmet Ağaoğlu and Ali Hüseyinzade; *ibid.*, p. 435, in Arai, *op. cit.*, p. 49.

[110] Its editorial programme, written by Akçura, stated: '1. The periodical shall be written in the style read and understood by as many people of the Turkish race as possible. ... 2. The periodical shall try and promote ideals acceptable to all Turks ... 4. To make Turks aware of their common destiny, the periodical will record events which arouse brotherly feelings, those occurring in all parts of the Turkic world, and currents of thought produced in various places of the world of Turks. It is hoped that literary works composed by various ethnic groups of the Turkic nation will be circulated to every member of that nation ... 6. The periodical shall strive as much as possible to develop the Turkish national spirit among Ottoman Turks ... 7. The periodical's principle regarding international politics is to defend the interests of the Turkic world.' *ibid.*, pp. 437- 9, in Arai, *op. cit.*, pp. 49-50. See also Hüseyin Tunce, *Türk Yurdu üzerine bir inceleme* (Ankara: Kültür Bakanlığı, 1990), which gives details of the topics covered in the publication.

again prominent as vice-president and one of the founders. This was another essentially pan-Turkist organisation which saw education as the key.[111] The Hearths in particular were extremely influential in spreading the ideas of Turkish nationalism and Turanism amongst students and the intellectual élite.[112] However, such ideas were still confined to a small section of the population; it needed the cathartic Independence struggle for the ideas of modern nationalism to spread to the mass of the people.

The idea of 'Turan' as the homeland of all Turks gained ground at this time. Already in 1911 Gökalp had published in Salonika his poem called 'Turan', which ended: 'The country of the Turks is not Turkey, nor yet Turkestan. Their country is a broad everlasting land – Turan.'[113] The First World War saw a rise in pan-Turkic hopes,[114] but these were dashed by the Ottoman defeats. The Russian Revolution provided a fleeting glimpse of pan-Turkic dreams, of which the adventurer Enver attempted to take full advantage,[115] but military defeat and the regaining of control by

[111] Its regulations, published for the first time in 1913 stated: 'Article 2: The object of the association is to strive for the totality of the Turkish race and language by promoting national education and improving intellectual, social and economic standards of the Turks, who are the most important of the Islamic nations. Article 3: The association shall open clubs named Turkish hearths to accomplish its objectives; it shall arrange lectures and entertainment; it will publish books and brochures, and it is hoped that it will also open schools ...' Akçura, *op. cit.*, pp. 439-40, in Arai, *op. cit.*, footnote to p. 75.

[112] See Halidé Edib, *Memoirs of Halide Edib* (London: John Murray, 1926), for a vivid personal account of the impact of the *Türk Ocağı* on intellectual life during the Young Turk era.

[113] Heyd, *op. cit.*, p. 126.

[114] A full description of the pan-Turkist wartime ideology is given by Tekin Alp – a Jew originally named Moise Cohen who became firstly a staunch pan-Turkist CUP supporter and later a staunch Kemalist – in *The Turkish and the Pan-Turkish Ideal* (London: War Staff Intelligence Division, Admiralty, 1917). This was probably written just after the outbreak of war and first published in German in 1915. This document gives a brief history of Turkish nationalism in the Ottoman Empire and looks forward to the creation, with German military help, of a Turkish state including Azerbaijan (which he sees as essentially Turkish) and the 'Caucasian Turks' of Kazan and the Caucasus. For more on Tekin Alp, see J.M. Landau, *Tekinalp, Turkish Patriot, 1883-1961* (Amsterdam: Netherlands Historical-Archaeological Institut at Istanbul, 1984).

[115] There was briefly an independent Republic of Azerbaijan, declared on 28 May 1918, which looked to Turkey for help. See Mehmet Saray, *Azerbaycan Türkleri Tarihi* (Istanbul: Yeni Türk Cumhuriyetleri Tarihihi Serisi – 1, 1993),

the centre of the new Soviet state ended these illusions.[116] In place of the dream of Turan, there was the real possibility of the almost complete dismemberment of even the Anatolian heartlands.

To summarise this and the preceding chapter, it can be said that until the need for change became intense, the Ottoman Empire followed a policy of classifying its citizens according to religion – the *millet* system. Despite welcoming converts to Islam, the Ottoman Empire was essentially non-assimilative and allowed the separate Balkan peoples to retain their individual cultures and identities – this was aided by the geography of the region. In this respect, the Ottoman Empire seems to fit Ernest Gellner's paradigm of a pre-modern society where the mass of the general population lived according to the precepts of their own local 'low' cultures. Conversely, the 'high' culture of the state was a minority achievement of privileged specialists, differentiated from the fragmented, uncodified majority folk cultures. These specialists tended and aimed to be trans-ethnic and trans-political, employing an elite idiom with no interest whatever in ensuring continuity between their mode of communication and that of the masses. The majority

---

pp. 30-42. Halidé Edib, *op. cit.*, p. 320, asserts that, parallel to Gökalp's pan-Turanianism was Enver's 'pan-Islamic ideal'. This was only seen as pan-Turkic during the war, as the Muslims he tried to unite were Turanians. However, a *Report on the Pan-Turanian Movement* by A.J.T. (Arnold Toynbee – London: Intelligence Bureau Department of Information, Admiralty, L/MIL/17/16/23, 1917) notes in appendix ii, p. 23, 'Anti-Islamic Tendencies in the Pan-Turanian Movement' and points to Enver as one of the main instigators. Specifically, the report says that he was the patron of the 'Boy Scout' movement using Turanian names, carrying the *Bozkurt* (Grey Wolf) emblem and cheering for the 'Khahan of the Turks' instead of the 'Padishah'. The report also details a Turkish army order which directed troops to include the 'Grey Wolf' in their prayers and a captured circular from the *Türk Ocağı* on a Turkish officer. This stated amongst other things: 'That monstrous figment of the imagination which is known as the Community of Islam, and which has for long past stood in the way of present progress generally, and of the realisation of the principles of Turanian Unity in particular, has now entered on a phase of decline and ruin. We need not apprehend from it any further danger to the execution of our hopes and principles. This is abundantly shown by the state of affairs among the Moslems in India ...'

[116] In his classic account of the Young Turk era, Akşin dismisses the whole Turan movement in under ten lines as an insane idea; Akşin, *op. cit.*, p. 304.

were excluded from power and from the 'high' culture, and were tied to a faith and a church rather than to the state and a single pervasive culture. In Benedict Anderson's terminology, the 'real' community was the family, the village or city quarter or tribe, while the 'imagined' community was the religious group rather than one making up the state or even a geographic part of it.

The nineteenth century and the rise of nationalism in Western Europe saw a profound transformation. On the one hand, the Ottoman state attempted to change its fundamental basis and treat all its citizens as equal, regardless of religion. It thus moved towards attempting to create an Ottoman citizen. In this category would be included non-Muslims – an attempt which was resisted by many sections of the Muslim population both within and without the governing élites. On the other hand, the impact of Western nationalism had a profound effect on how the Christian groups identified themselves. The *millets* became progressively identified with national groupings. At the same time, the new radical nationalists were competing with the old traditional leaders within the *millets*. Added to this was the interference by the Great Powers in the internal affairs of the ailing empire, sometimes encouraging and sometimes discouraging particular emerging national groups according to the way they perceived their own interests.

The *Tanzimat* reforms did not lead to the creation of an 'Ottoman nation'; nationalism continued to affect the Christian populations and helped to tear the empire apart in the Balkans. Indeed, it can be argued that the *Tanzimat* reforms actually aided this process by undermining the conservative *millet* leaders and thus allowing nationalists greater influence. The reaction among the Turkish-speaking Muslim population began with the Young Ottomans with their emphasis on a return to Islamic precepts and was amplified during the reign of Abdülhamid. In this period, despite the Sultan's emphasis on Islam as the cementing force in the empire, there was a noticeable growth of a sense of Turkishness among Ottoman intellectuals. This process was aided by the Western usage of terms like 'Turk' and 'Turkey' in place of Ottoman forms, as well as the penetration of the new ideas of nation and race.

Especially influential in this process were the Turkic *émigrés* from the Russian Empire who had been galvanised into nationalist action as a defensive measure against increased Russification in the second half of the century. These *émigrés* began to spread ideas of Turkish unity among sections of the elite. In addition, the concept of Anatolia as a Turkish heartland began to take hold, aided by the retreat in the Balkans. The Turkish peasant of Anatolia, previously the object of contempt by the elite, began to be romanticised as the embodiment of national values. However, these processes remained incomplete. The majority of Ottoman intellectuals, even those who were in the vanguard of the new movement, remained ambivalent as to exactly how they defined themselves in group terms and particularly unsure of how much weight to give to the three apparently competing ideas of Ottomanism, Islamism and Turkism.

The 1908 Revolution and the ensuing Young Turk era saw these trends deepening, with Turkism gradually coming to the fore – albeit secretly in the initial Young Turk phase. The continuing loss of territory in the Balkans and the rise of nationalism among hitherto loyal Muslim Albanians and Arabs helped Turkism rise over both Ottomanism and Islamism. The outbreak of war allowed the Young Turk regime to espouse Turkish nationalism more openly, both socially and economically. The ideas of Turkic unity espoused in the Turanist movement – again started by Russian *émigrés* – spread among sections of the elite, aided by the influential *Türk Ocağı* and the *Türk Yurdu* periodical. During the First World War, these ideas came to the fore; the Russian Revolution afforded a brief illusionary vista of this utopian ideal which was dashed by military defeat.

4

THE TOP HAT: SECULAR KEMALIST NATIONALISM

This chapter concentrates on the official nationalism of Kemalism, how this ideology was formed and propagated, and how it relates to the general framework of nationalism as detailed in Chapter 1. It begins with a brief look at the growth of Turkish nationalism in the 'war of national resistance' (or Independence War) as well as the founding of the republic and the abolition of the Caliphate. It then concentrates on the nationalist ideology of the initial Kemalist state, beginning with the views of Kemal himself, especially regarding Islam and the non-Turkish Muslims of Anatolia. The consolidation and homogeneity of the élite's ideology will be considered, as will the 'Turkish History Thesis' proclaimed at the First History Congress in 1932 and incorporated in school textbooks for successive decades. A consideration of Turkish nationalism as defined in the statutes of the ruling Republican People's Party (CHF – CHP after 1935) and propagated by the party-state follows, together with an account of the purification of the language, and the 'Sun Language Theory'. How the new ideology viewed minorities, both Muslim and non-Muslim, within the new Turkey and how these minorities were treated in practice is finally examined.

The Independence War, the founding of the republic and the abolition of the Caliphate

Kemalist historiography, beginning with Kemal's classic account of the Independence War as detailed in his famous speech of October 1927 – Nutuk[1] – likes to portray the founding of the

---

[1] Mustafa Kemal Atatürk, *Nutuk* (Kültür Bakanlığı Yayınları: Ankara, 2 vols,

republic and the abolition of the Caliphate as revolutionary measures which owed their inspiration and execution to the 'genius' of one man – Mustafa Kemal. In this version of history, Kemal left Istanbul for Samsun in 1919 when the Ottoman Empire was on its knees, and then almost single-handedly organised the national resistance and revived 'the Turkish nation' against external enemies, despite the treacherous activities of the Sultan, the previous authorities, and some of his erstwhile colleagues. The establishment of a republic with its legitimacy based upon the Turkish nation in place of the traditional Ottoman Empire with its Islamic roots and strong absolutist tradition was a major change. However, as the previous chapter indicates, this transformation can be seen as having occurred over a longer period than the Kemalists claim, and there were fairly solid antecedents to many of Kemal's sweeping reforms.[2] Additionally, despite Kemal's version, there were strong links between him and the previous Young Turk regime since he had been a trusted CUP member – albeit one at odds with Enver's faction.[3] This continuity is further illustrated by the fact that 85 per cent of the Ottoman Empire's civil servants and 93 per cent of its staff officers retained their positions in the new republic.[4] However, the changes in the 1920s were huge. It would

---

1980) – all further references to the *Nutuk* refer to this edition.

[2] As Rustow states, few of the sweeping reforms of the 1920s were original to Kemal since all had been advocated in the period 1908 to 1919 and some had solid antecedents in the 19th-century Ottoman reforms. Almost the whole programme actually appeared in 'A Very Wakeful Sleep' by the Young Turk writer Abdullah Cevdet which was published in 1912. An exception was republicanism, but even here the Young Turks, by curbing the Sultan's power and effectively removing him from the power centre, as well as by their new emphasis on the Turkish nation, can arguably be seen as having laid the essential preconditions for the acceptance of a republic and the concept of popular sovereignty. Dankwart A. Rustow, 'Atatürk as Founder of a State' in Nermin Abadan (ed.), *Yavuz Abadan'a Armağan* (Ankara: Sevinç Matbaası, 1969), p. 550.

[3] See Erik Jan Zürcher, *The Unionist Factor – The role of the CUP in the Turkish National Movement, 1905-1926* (Leiden, E.J. Brill, 1984), which convincingly shatters the myth of Kemal's self-professed distance from the Young Turk regime. In his latest book, *Turkey: A Modern History* (London, I.B. Tauris, 1993), Zürcher goes so far as to extend the Young Turk period right up to the advent of real multi-party politics in 1950.

[4] D.A. Rustow, 'Atatürk as an Institution Builder' in A. Kazancıgil and E. Özbudun (eds), *Atatürk: Founder of a Modern State* (London: Hurst, 1981), p. 73.

be wrong to see them merely as part of a logical and inevitable progression from 1908 without taking into account the changes in society brought about by the continual wars from 1912-22 or the character of Kemal himself. As McCarthy points out,[5] reform needs a constituency, and the bureaucracy is not enough on its own. The *Tanzimat* and the Young Turk reforms were gradual precisely because they had limited constituencies. Religious schools were left to coexist with new Westernised academies; new alphabets were experimented with but not adopted; parliaments were called but the Sultan-Caliph remained. Only in the military were radical changes completely accepted due to the repeated military defeats which forged a constituency for them. McCarthy sees Kemal's reform constituency as being the Turkish people who, due to the battering they had received during the wars of 1912-22, had become aware of the possibility of change. This draws attention to the role of war as the engine of social transformation which, as we have seen in Chapter 1, can greatly accelerate the growth of nationalism. Furthermore, the economic conditions of the post-war period caused the population to see the changes as beneficial, and thus to support them.[6]

McCarthy lists a number of factors as being responsible for this change, but emphasises mortality and migration as the most important. Anatolia suffered huge mortality in this period. Its population fell by 30 per cent, of which some 10 per cent was due to emigration. The population in the east suffered the highest mortality; in the Ottoman province of Van, over 60 per cent of the Muslim population died, in Bitlis over 40 per cent, and in Erzurum over 30 per cent.[7] Such a huge loss of life often leads to desire for and acceptance of radical change – as in the cases of the Black Death and the Thirty Years War in Europe. At the same time there were almost half a million immigrants to the new Turkey, as well as massive internal migration as Turkish Muslims refilled the places left in cities by departing

[5] J. McCarthy, 'Foundation of the Turkish Republic: Social and Economic Change', in *Middle Eastern Studies*, vol. 19, 1983, p. 139.

[6] *Ibid.*

[7] *Ibid.*, p. 140. McCarthy however repeats the common error of attributing to Turkey the highest mortality rate among all the First World War combatants. This ignores the case of Serbia, which lost some 25 per cent of its total population. Zürcher makes the same mistake (Zürcher, *Turkey*, p. 171).

Christians.[8] By definition, migrants are uprooted, and are thus more open to political and social change. These, McCarthy asserts, were the constituents for Kemal's reforms.

The period also saw an extension of nationalist ideas which had affected intellectual circles and had become government policy under the CUP, but which had probably not yet penetrated to the mass of the population. The Independence War changed all this; it is noticeable that the resistance movements sprang up initially in the east, due to the fighting with the Armenians and the Russians, and only spread to the west with the Greek invasion. The direct foreign threat sharpened the 'us against them' mentality, aided the spread of Turkish nationalism, and laid the foundations for the ideas of popular sovereignty and a republic. Here, the role of Kemal himself does need emphasising. He strongly embodied many traditional characteristics held in high esteem by Turks – for example military prowess, organisation, and respect for law[9] – and had also succeeded against outside forces after a century and a half of failed attempts. He was the *Ghazi*. Reforms introduced by him were not seen as forced under duress by the outside; they could thus be accepted with pride rather than shame.

The Sultantate had been partly discredited and bypassed after the failed 1909 counter-revolution following the restoration of the Constitution in 1908. Now, the Sultan's collaboration with the occupying forces and his opposition to the nationalist movement in Anatolia sealed the fate of the dynasty. In the debates on the 1924 Constitution, anti-Sultanate and pro-republican sentiment permeated the Control Commission report, and was clearly observable in the debates. The Independence War and the experiences under the Sultanate had had a profound impact on the deputies; loyalty to the new 'nation-state' of Turkey, to the Republic of Turkey and to republicanism was very evident in the debates.[10] As Weiker states, 'even had Atatürk wanted to retain the monarchy, he could not have done so without compromising his entire

---

[8] The departure of the Christian minorities greatly facilitated the promotion of a Turkish national state. The rationale for this huge forced transfer of population will be looked at in more detail below.

[9] Rustow, 'Atatürk as Founder of a State', p. 568.

[10] See Suna Kili, *Turkish Constitutional Developments and Assembly Debates on the Constitutions of 1924 and 1961* (Istanbul: Robert College Research Centre, 1971), *passim*.

revolution.'[11] It is highly significant that ever since the abolition of the monarchy in 1922 there has never been any real movement for restoration.

Thus, the establishment of a republic can be seen as the logical result of political developments since 1908; the Independence War and the ensuing spread of Turkish nationalism forced the pace of change but did not alter its path. The abolition of the Caliphate was different. Unlike the Sultanate, Islam was not discredited during the Independence War – on the contrary, Kemal used it as a rallying cry against the foreign invaders.[12] As noted in Chapter 3, CUP ideologues like Ziya Gökalp tried to reconcile Turkish nationalism with Islam. However, their attempts were not very intellectually satisfying and the essential contradiction between Islam and nationalism remained. Gökalp proposed keeping the Caliphate as a non-political spiritual body for all Muslims akin to the papacy. However, Islam is very different to Christianity in its outlook and origins, and not so easy to separate from politics or neatly compartmentalise.[13]

How important the Caliphate was to Turkish Muslims is a moot point. As noted in Chapter 2, it was Abdülhamid who really stressed the Caliphate's role, which had not been so strongly emphasised earlier. The Young Turks had used the Caliphate to agitate among the Muslim populations of the Entente powers, especially Russia and Britain. Kemal set up a committee at the time of abolition in 1924 which, to back up his view, pointed out that the Ottoman claim to the Caliphate was illegitimate and had ceased to exist in 1258 when the Mongols conquered Baghdad. However, there appears to be more evidence for the view that the abolition was engineered primarily by Kemal himself (the

---

[11] W.F. Weiker, *Political Tutelage and Democracy in Turkey – The Free Party and its Aftermath* (Leiden: E.J. Brill, 1973), p. 11.

[12] Although the failure of the CUP *Jihad* call and the Arab Revolt had to an extent discredited Islam for some intellectuals, in a proclamation of 16 March 1920 Kemal stated: 'God's help and protection are with us in the sacred struggle which we have entered upon our fatherland and independence.' (*Nutuk*, vol. 1, p. 513). See also Binnaz Toprak, *Islam and Political Development in Turkey* (Leiden: E.J. Brill, 1981), p. 63.

[13] This relationship between Islam and Turkish nationalism is a perennial feature of this study; the attempted Turkish-Islamic synthesis of the 1980s (see Chapter 6) runs into similar intellectual problems.

ulema on the committee were hand-picked by him) and that he adroitly used the intervention on behalf of the Caliphate by the Agha Khan and another prominent Indian Muslim to discredit it.[14]

In her account of the constitutional debates,[15] Suna Kili notes that the trail-blazing 1921 Constitution makes no mention of the Sultan-Caliph and that the 1924 Constitution states in Article 2 that Islam is the religion of Turkey (this was withdrawn in 1928). In the debates on the 1924 Constitution there appears to have been no debate on the issue of the Caliphate. However, unlike the abolition of the Sultanate, there was opposition to the abolition of the Caliphate from within the nationalist camp. Senior figures in the independence struggle like Ali Fuat, Kâzim Karabekir and Rauf opposed the abolition. One reason for Kemal's insistence on its abolition was perhaps the possibility that it might provide a focus for opposition to him and his sweeping plans. Although the religious hierarchy had become progressively incorporated into, and thus controlled by, the central government apparatus, the religious establishment remained a nucleus of potential opposition to Kemal, both in the official hierarchy and in the *tarikats*.[16] Indeed, just before the abolition of the Caliphate, *hocas* and dervishes were preaching against Kemal in mosques and market places, and caricatures of him were circulated.[17]

Kemal's ideology of nationalism

Kemal was primarily a pragmatic soldier-turned-politician who

---

[14] The Agha Khan had in fact consistently supported the nationalist cause but this was not well known in Turkey. He was also not an orthodox Muslim but head of a branch of the Ismailis – regarded by the orthodox as heretical. As Geoffrey Lewis points out in *Turkey* (London: Benn, 3rd edn, 1966), p. 83, his intervention was counter-productive, and the Kemalists spread the story that he had been set up in India by the British as a rival Islamic leader.

[15] Kili, *op. cit.*, p. 18.

[16] Weiker, *op. cit.*, p. 12. See also Mete Tunçay, *Türkiye Cumhuriyet'inde Tek-Parti Yönetiminin Kurulması, 1923-1931* (Ankara: Yurt, 1981), pp. 208-25, and Niyazi Berkes, *The Development of Secularism in Turkey* (Montreal: McGill University Press, 1964), pp 446-60.

[17] H.C. Armstrong, *Grey Wolf: Mustafa Kemal – An Intimate Study of a Dictator* (London: Arthur Barker, 1932), p. 244, and *Nutuk*, vol. 2, p. 314.

did not indulge in the writing of long theoretical tomes. His attitude to the new state and its borders appears wholly pragmatic. Regarding President Wilson's famous fourteen points – which represent the ethnic variant of defining national boundaries – Kemal stated:

> I confess that I too tried to define the national boundaries somewhat according to the humanitarian purposes of Wilson's principles. ... On the basis of those humanitarian principles, I defended boundaries which Turkish bayonets had already defended and laid down. Poor Wilson, he did not understand that lines that cannot be defended by the bayonet, by force, by honour and dignity, cannot be defended on any other principle.[18]

This can be seen as representing Kemal's pragmatism (after all, the national boundaries laid down by 'Turkish bayonets' did not include his birthplace of Macedonia) and emphasises the 'territorial' aspects of his vision of the new Turkey. For him the 'natural' boundaries were those militarily defensible. In relation to the old question of Islamic or pan-Turkic solidarity, he maintained that 'we all wish to see our Muslim brothers live free. Beyond our wishes we can give them no help.' However, in the Assembly he stated:

> I am neither a believer in a league of all the nations of Islam, nor even in a league of the Turkish peoples. Each of us here has the right to hold his ideals, but the government must be stable with a fixed policy, grounded in facts, and with one view and one alone – to safeguard the life and independence of the nation within its natural frontiers. Neither sentiment nor illusion must influence our policy. Away with dreams and shadows! They have cost us dear in the past.[19]

But what were the 'natural frontiers'? At the Sivas Congress in September 1919, the nationalist movement spoke of itself as

---

[18] *Büyük Gazinin Hatıratından Sahifeler* – a series of reissues published by *Hakimiyeti Milliye* (Ankara) and *Milliyet* (Istanbul), 13 March to 12 April 1926, instalment 26 – and F.R. Atay (ed.), *Atatürk'ün Hatıraları 1914-1919* (Ankara 1965) p. 71, quoted in D.A. Rustow, 'The Founding of a Nation State: Atatürk's historical achievement' in *Papers and Discussion: Türkiye İşBankası International Symposium on Atatürk (17-22 May 1981)* (Ankara: TISA, 1984), p. 349.

[19] H.C. Armstrong, *op. cit.*, pp. 218-9, and similarly in *Nutuk*, vol. 2, pp. 6-7.

the 'Union for the Defence of the Rights of Anatolia and Rumelia'[20] – that is, including an undefined part of the Balkans. Right from the start there had sprung up societies to save Eastern Thrace and, if possible, form 'a Turco-Muslim community that would include Western Thrace.[21] However, Kemal was always the practical soldier, and by 3 February 1920 he was stressing that while Eastern Thrace was 'an integral part of our country', Western Thrace was not.[22]

However, it was apparent that in contrast to Smith's 'territorial' nationalist model, Kemal did not view the Turkish nation as equivalent to all the citizens living within the 'natural frontiers', however defined. The Christian populations in particular were seen (with historical justification) as hostile, and as not belonging to the 'nation'. The result was the mass population transfers with Greece, using religion as the criterion for differentiating populations rather than race, ethnicity or language. However, it seems that initially at least, Kemal leaned more towards Smith's 'territorial' concept. In a telegram of 16 March 1920 he wrote:

> The humane attitude which we shall adopt towards the Christian population dwelling in our country will be all the more appreciated at the present time. ... [and] will be conclusive evidence of the civilising factors existing in the character of our race.[23]

The change in policy must surely have come about due to the life-or-death struggle with the Greeks in the west and with the Armenians in the east.[24]

Thus, the 'natural boundaries' of the 'Turkish nation' were to equate roughly to the militarily defensible Anatolian heartland. Kemal stated:

> I expressed clearly [at the Erzurum Congress on 23 July 1919]

---

[20] *Nutuk*, vol. 1, p. 296.

[21] *Ibid.*, vol. 1, pp. 5–6.

[22] *Ibid.*, vol. 1, p. 495.

[23] *Ibid.*, vol. 1, p. 504. It is interesting that in the massive speech Kemal never once refers to the population exchanges with Greece.

[24] As Kemal stated, 'Christian elements were also at work all over the country, either openly or in secret trying to realise their own particular ambitions and thereby hasten the breakdown of the Empire.' *Ibid.*, vol. 1, p. 4.

that the will of the Turkish nation to be master of her own destiny could only spring from Anatolia.[25]

Within this area the Christians would not be included, even if their mother tongue was Turkish, with the exception of the Christian population of Istanbul and two islands, who were protected by the Treaty of Lausanne.

But what of non-Turkish-speaking Muslim populations in this area? The clauses for protection of minorities in the Lausanne treaty were, in Kemal's words, 'only applicable to non-Muslims.'[26] Thus, all the Muslims of the new state were seen as members of the majority – that is the 'Turkish nation'. However, despite Islam's supranational attraction, nationalism had already deeply affected the Muslim Albanian population as well as the majority Muslim Arab populations of the old Ottoman Empire (even if in the latter case the initial impetus had come from the Arab Christian communities). As Kemal himself admitted:

> In today's Turkish national, political and social community we have patriots and citizens who have been subjected to propaganda about Kurdish, Caucasian and even Laz and Bosnian nations. But these are misnomers, which are a result of the despotic ages of long ago, had no influence on the individuals of this nation, except for a new enemy agents and brainless reactionaries, and have left our people in grief and sorrow. Because the individuals of this nation, as members of the integrated unified Turkish Community have a common past, history, morality and law.[27]

In fact, as Kemal repeatedly details in the *Nutuk*, the 'few enemy agents and brainless reactionaries' were especially active during the independence struggle and the majority of these were Kurds. From the start there was a 'League for the Resuscitation of the Kurds' based in Diyarbakır, Bitlis and El Aziz (now Elazığ) provinces, with its head office in Istanbul, aiming to set up a Kurdish state under foreign protection.[28] On 18 June 1919 Kemal claimed that:

[25] *Ibid.*, vol. 1, p. 78.
[26] *Ibid.*, vol. 1, p. 375.
[27] A.A. İnan, *Medeni Bilgiler ve M. Kemal Atatürk'ün El Yazıları* (Ankara: Türk Tarih Kurumu, 1969), p. 23.

.... from one end to the other of Anatolia the population is united. ... The propaganda aiming at the erection of an independent Kurdistan under English protection has been successfully countered ... The Kurds have joined the Turks.[29]

Thus, at this time Kemal saw the national movement as embracing Turks and Kurds (separately identified). This was emphasised in a telegram from Kemal to Kurdish notables in September which appealed to common Islamic bonds, and spoke of Turks and Kurds as two inseparable brothers ('öz kardeş').[30] Nevertheless, Kurdish insurrections continued. Thus, it appears that Kemal shifted his stance on the issue of the Kurds. Initially, he appealed to them as fellow Muslims but as a separate people (ethnie). However, faced with continuing Kurdish insurrections, he began to emphasising the unity of the 'nation'. Henceforth, all manifestations of Kurdish nationalism were proscribed.

How nationalist these insurrections were in character, and how much merely part of the traditional tribal conflicts and general anarchy in the east, remains a moot point. Kemal reports united action among the Kurdish tribes around Malatya in September 1919 in terms which clearly indicate Kurdish national objectives.[31]

[28] *Nutuk*, vol. 1, pp. 8-9.

[29] *Ibid.*, vol. 1, p. 25.

[30] *Atatürk'ün Tamim, Telgraf ve Beyannameleri, 1917-1938*, vol. 4, (Ankara: Türk Inkılap Tarihi Enstitütü, 1964), p. 63. Moreover, at a meeting in İzmit in 1923, Kemal reportedly promised the Kurds autonomy in areas where they made up substantial populations. However, the Sheikh Said revolt in 1925 (see below) resulted in all references to this promise subsequently being censored from official accounts of the meeting. See *2000'e Doğru*, 1987, no. 35, and 1988 no. 46, and Baskın Oran, *Atatürk Milliyetçiliği: Resmi İdeoloji Dışı Bir İnceleme*, (Ankara: Bilgi Yayınevi, 3rd edn, 1993), p. 211.

[31] 'He [Faruk Bey, 'a trustworthy man'] states that the Kurds belonging to the tribes in these districts as far as Siverek are ready to join the others, and the tribes of Dersim itself had been summoned to come there in the name of the Kurdish cause. ... It is rumoured that the Kurds regard the expulsion of the Mutessarif from Malatya as a serious offence against their Kurdish reputation ... after Malatya has been occupied ... they will hoist the Kurdish flag.' *Ibid.*, vol. 1, p. 162. Other non-Turkish Muslim opponents are mentioned by Kemal, like Circassians, but there is no indication of any national basis in their opposition to his forces. For more details on the Kurdish insurrections and Kurds in general see M.M. van Bruinessen's classic *Agha, Shaikh and State* (Utrecht: Rijswick, 1978), which concludes that the great Sheikh Said revolt of 1925 was not really a Kurdish national rebellion but more a mixture of religious and tribal matters

The treaty of Sèvres foresaw a commission of the Allied Powers for the area east of the Euphrates, which was openly referred to as 'Kurdistan'. It suggested that if a majority of the Kurds wished to be independent of Turkey then this would be achieved. It is clear that, whatever Kemal's claims, the Muslim population of Anatolia – including many Turks loyal to the Sultan as well as Kurds – was definitely not totally united behind his forces.[32]

Kemal's nationalism was a mixture of Smith's two variants – the 'ethnic' and the 'territorial'. The territory was to be essentially Anatolia. Despite the existence of potential members of the nation – whether measured by language, race or religion – living outside the area, they were not to be claimed as such. Conversely, Christians inside the territory were to be rejected. Kemal's attitude to religion is worthy of close inspection – especially given Islam's importance in group identity in the region. As noted above, Kemal saw Christians as unsuitable material for becoming 'Turkish', and the greater part of them were expelled. Thus, Islam was initially seen as a basic component of being a member of the new Turkish state. The Kurdish insurrections in the Independence struggle as well as later were seen as examples of 'fratricidal war' inspired by the treacherous Sultan's authorities.[33] Kemal had also countered the *fetva* of the Istanbul authorities with one by the *müftü* of Ankara and had called the Independence struggle a 'Holy War'.

However, he saw the religious hierarchy both in the *ulema* and in the *tarikats* as potential centres of power and opposition, and he rightly regarded them – especially the *tarikats* with their system of countrywide lodges – as a danger to his sweeping reforms. He was always the modernist and Westerniser; to make Turkey catch up with the West and assume its 'rightful place' as a modern

---

(see below). Also, see the less impressive Robert T. Olson, *The Emergence of Kurdish Nationalism and the Sheikh Said Rebellion, 1880-1925* (Austin: University of Texas Press, 1989) which rather unconvincingly backdates Kurdish nationalism to this period, and even before.

[32] In the *Nutuk* both the number of occasions on which Kemal speaks of the 'united Turkish nation' as standing solidly behind his organisation and the repeated lists of internal upheavals which belie these claims are noteworthy. This is most notable in vol. 2, pp. 13-14, where he states that in 1920 'The clouds of treachery, of ignorance, of hatred and fanaticism darkened the sky and threw the whole country into deep shadow. The waves of insurrection surged even up to the walls of our headquarters in Ankara.'

[33] *Ibid.*, vol. 1, p. 168.

civilised state and society was always his aim. If traditional aspects
of Islam impeded this process, then Islam itself would have to
be tamed. Hence, as soon as the independence struggle was won,
the role of Islam as a crucial component of Turkish nationalism
was downplayed. The Caliphate was abolished, but the new constitution emphasised the central place of Islam in Articles 2 and
26. Article 2 stated that 'That State religion of Turkey is the
Muslim religion', while Article 26 mentioned the *Şeriat* as the
holy law. Kemal himself was obviously not happy with this. In
the *Nutuk* he stated:

> The superfluous expressions which were incompatible with
> the modern character of the new Turkish State and our
> republican regime, contained in Articles 2 and 26 of the Act,
> constitute compromises to which the revolution and Republic
> ought to have agreed so as to satisfy the exigencies of the
> time. When the first favourable opportunity arises the nation
> must eliminate these superfluities from our Constitution Act.[34]

Mardin asserts that, with the loss of the Arab provinces, the
link between Turks, Arabs and Islam could be more easily jettisoned,
and that it was remarkable that Kemal did not immediately do
this.[35] It is not easy to accept this assertion. Jettisoning Islam was
surely no easy matter. Despite the loss of the Arabs it was still
a crucial, perhaps the main, component of identity in the 'imagined'
community of Benedict Anderson's terminology; after all, in the
same article Mardin goes on to say that at the time no Turkish
nation existed. The Turks/Arabs/Islam linkage also ignores the
other Muslim populations of Anatolia, especially the Kurds. The
Sheikh Said revolt of 1925, which was more a religious and tribal
revolt than a national uprising, suggests that Islam was definitely
the main component of group identity for large numbers of Kemal's
new subjects. Indeed, the Alevi Kurds opposed Said, who was a
Sunni dervish Sheikh.[36] Thus, in the east, nationalism had not

---

[34] *Ibid.*, vol. 2, p. 328.

[35] Ş. Mardin, 'Religion and Secularism in Turkey' in Kazancıgil and Özbudun,
op. cit., pp. 208-9. For more on the secularism/Islam debate see N. Berkes,
The Development of Secularism in Turkey; U. Heyd, 'Islam in Modern Turkey',
Royal Central Asian Journal, vol. 34, 1947; and H.A. Reed, 'Secularism and
Islam in Turkish Politics', *Current History*, vol. 32, no. 190, 1957.

[36] Van Bruinessen points out that non-tribal Kurds were not considered by

yet replaced the traditional differentiators of tribal or non-tribal and religious cleavages.[37] In view of Gellner's observations explored in Chapter 1 regarding the folk cultures of the *tarikats*, the 1925 Law No. 677 banning all the *tarikats* and closing down their lodges and the *türbes* – shrines of holy sheikhs – makes perfect sense: it can be seen as a move to smash the localised folk cultures and replace them by a unified national culture, as well as removing a perceived reactionary countrywide alternative power network.[38] The official urban *ulema* were not eliminated. On the contrary, they were further incorporated into the central state authority,

---

Said and his followers as fit to fight. In any case, they preferred Kemal's secular republic where for the first time they were officially regarded as equals with rights and laws to protect them. Similarly, the Yormek and Lolan Alevi Kurdish tribes opposed the revolt as they did not want to be in an independent Kurdistan controlled by Sunni sheikhs (*op. cit.*, p. 399). This role of the Alevis, both Turkish and Kurdish, their support for Kemalism, and their current situation in the countryside with the rebirth of more active Sunnism, will be returned to later.

[37] Some at the time, like TGNA member (and later speaker) Abdülhalık Renda, who was of Albanian origin, believed that the Said rebellion 'was a national movement under the cover of religion and reaction.' – from his report reprinted in Mehmet Bayrak, *Kürtler ve Ulusal-Demokratik Mücadeleleri*, (Ankara: Öz-Ge, 1993), p. 454. He called for assimilation of the Kurds by: population transfers which would move Kurds westwards and transplant Turkish migrants to the main lines of communication; disarming the local population; and breaking up the Kurds' tribal structures; *Ibid.*, pp. 452-67. The Minister of the Interior, Cemil Bey (Ubaydın) also called for such a 'colonial' style solution to the Kurdish problem. However, after visiting the area he stated that while the local intellectuals were all Kurdish nationalists and the local population 'strongly attached to its language and ethnicity', Kurdish nationalism was not 'deep, all-embracing or dangerous'; *Ibid.*, p. 468. The 'colonial' style solution of population transfers was later effectively implemented in areas where the rebellion had been based (see below).

[38] Mardin, *op. cit.*, hypothesises that Kemal's secularising reforms were linked to the common denominator of liberating the individual from the collective constraints of Muslim community and sees the attack on the *tarikats* in 1925 as an attempt 'to set free the individual from the stifling gemeinschaft.' Of course this can also be seen as replacing one group loyalty – the *tarikat* – with another – the nation. As noted above, whether one is more stifling than the other is open to question. For an opposing view that Sufism was not low but actually mainstream culture, and that the current revival is a return to this, see Cemal Kafader, 'The New Visibility of Sufism in Turkish Studies and Cultural Life' in Raymond Litchez (ed.), *The Dervish Lodge: Architecture, Art and Sufism in Ottoman Turkey* (Berkeley: University of California Press, 1992).

and attempts were made to confine Islam to the sphere of private life.

So if Islam was not a crucial component of being 'a Turk' in Kemal's ideology, what was? In view of the conclusions of Chapter 1, it is not surprising that language and history were given great prominence, along with the territorial unit. Regarding language, Kemal wrote:

> The Turkish national tongue is Turkish. The Turkish language is one of the easiest, richest and most beautiful in the world. ... [it] is also a sacred treasure for the Turkish nation.[39]

However, large numbers, especially in the southeast of the country, did not speak Turkish as their mother tongue. The relationship between the Turkish state and minority languages within it, particularly Kurdish, is a topic which we shall return to later.

Kemal stated that while the Turks as an ethnic group had lived in Asia, Europe and Africa, they were now quite content to live in their new state without pretensions of expansion.[40] There is an obvious ethnic mix in much of the Muslim population of Anatolia, which many see as due to repeated intermarrying and assimilation throughout the ages. Kemal claimed this was actually the result of changes in Turkish stock brought about by life in different climatic regions, suggesting that:

> Never, anywhere do people from even a small family totally resemble each other. It is not true to see the Turks as setting out from a narrow area which had no climatic changes.[41]

As a summary of what makes the Turkish nation, he argued that:

> These are the historical and natural facts regarding the basis of the Turkish nation: a) Political unity; b) linguistic unity; c) territorial unity; d) unity of lineage and roots; e) shared history; f) shared morality.[42]

---

[39] Nurhan Tezcan (ed.), *Atatürk'ün Yazdığı Yurttaşlık Bilgileri* (Istanbul: Çağdaş 1989), p. 14. See also A. Afet Inan, *Medeni Bilgiler*.

[40] *Ibid.*, p. 14. This became the basis of the Kemalist slogan of 'peace at home peace abroad'.

[41] *Ibid.*, p. 15.

[42] *Ibid.*, p. 20.

Kemal's notion of what constituted a nation was also bound up with the idea of national independence; he went as far as to negate the idea that the Chinese, Afghans or Indians were even nations, as they were not free.[43] The absence of religion is noteworthy. In his writings, while admitting the role of religion in the forming of some nations, he stressed that: 'The Turks were a great nation before adopting Islam.'[44] After it had played its role in uniting the population in the struggle against internal and external enemies, religion was to be discarded as a component of Turkish nationalism. Secularism, and great emphasis on the Turks as historical figures outside the Islamic framework – the 'Turkish History Thesis' – were to be put in its place.[45]

The Turkish History Thesis

As noted in Chapter 1, the interpretation of history is a crucial tool for nationalists in propagating their ideologies. Towards the end of the 1920s, the writing of history was high on the agenda due to the perceived need for new high-school history textbooks which would inculcate Turkish nationalism. The result was the 'Turkish History Thesis', which was effectively launched at the First History Congress in Ankara in 1932 after elements had been incorporated in *lycée* and intermediary school textbooks in the preceding three years. The thesis was a combination of a reaction against perceived European perceptions of the Turks as an inferior race, and the need for nation-building along the lines of Gellner's paradigm. The Ottoman period was seen as discredited, due to

[43] *Ibid.*, p. 25. The ideas of joining the 'advanced' nations and independence were entwined by Kemal in his writings: 'Turkish nationalism, in addition to being the process of advancing with, and parallel to, the contemporary nations in mutual harmony along the path of progress and development, and in international intercourse and relationships, also serves the social and special characteristics of Turkish society and rights of identity which, in themselves, depend on freedom.' (Afet İnan, *Medeni Bilgiler*, p. 25.) This notion of nationalism as a way of advancing and modernising fits in with Gellner's paradigm. Thus, Kemalism can be seen as combining parts from all the different nationalist theories outlined earlier.

[44] *Ibid.*, p. 18.

[45] Interestingly, despite attracting strong support from religious conservatives, the Free Party, set up in 1930, did not appear to openly challenge this thesis. See Walter F. Weiker, *Political Tutelage and Democracy in Turkey, passim.*

military defeat. As we have seen, Kemal rejected Islam, which was also tainted with the Ottoman defeat, as the basis of social cohesion, and tried to relegate it to private life. Instead, pre-Ottoman Turkish identity was stressed. It was even claimed that the Turks were the descendants of the founders of civilisations in Iraq, Anatolia, Egypt and the Aegean.

The thesis quickly became the official line. After the First Congress there was little further discussion, as the Kemalist state pushed forward 'Kemalism' as a single idea for the nation and the only legitimate ethic for the new state.[46] In this ideology 'Turkish nationalism' as defined by the Kemalists was seen as a monolithic solution to all social, political, economic and cultural problems. Competing variants of 'nationalism' – whether pan-Turkist or Islamic in inspiration – were proscribed. The party-state took over the cultural organisations like the Turkish Hearths.[47] The thesis became the basis for all school history textbooks for almost two decades, with only minor changes.[48]

---

[46] For further reading on Kemalism as a whole see Suna Kili, *Kemalism*, (Istanbul: Robert College Research Centre, 1969) and D. Mehmet Doğan, *Kemalizm*, (Istanbul: Alternatif Üniversite, 1992).

[47] *Cumhuriyet*, 18 March 1931 stated: 'The Turkish Hearths joined the Republican Peoples Party (CHF). The General Assembly will convene before the Party Congress. The Hearths will be the cultural branch of the party. The name will be changed and the property turned over to the Party.' Yunus Nadi, then editor-in-chief of *Cumhuriyet*, wrote on 28 March 1931, 'It is only natural that instead of developing national culture in different organisations, all national forces unite.' Quoted in B. Ersanlı-Behar, 'The Turkish History Thesis: A Cultural Dimension of the Kemalist Revolution' (unpubl. Ph.D. thesis, Boğaziçi University, Istanbul 1989), p. 120.

[48] See Türker Alkan, *The Political Integration of Europe: A Content Analysis of the Turkish, French, German and Italian History Textbooks* (Ankara, METU Publications, 1982), *passim*. The legacy of this thesis lives on. The section entitled 'A New Conception of History' of a secondary school history textbook states: 'We know that the Turks, starting from Central Asia, went all over the world, founded states and civilisations and often changed the course of history. We know all this thanks to historical research done under the guidance of Atatürk' –M.K. Su and A. Mumcu, *Türkiye Cumhuriyeti İnkilap Tarihi ve Atatürkçülük* (Istanbul, 1986), p. 208, quoted in Ersanlı-Behar, *op. cit.*, p. 281. For other examples, see also Hercules Milas, 'History Textbooks in Greece and Turkey', *History Workshop* (spring 1991), pp. 25-31. Milas also details public criticism of this blinkered official line by leading historians like Mete Tunçay in the late 1970s, although the latter had little apparent effect. For these criticisms see also *Felsefe Kurumu Seminleri* (Ankara: Türk Tarih Kurumu Basımevi, 1977), pp. 278-311.

It is noticeable in this period that many of the republic's leading historians were really politicians or political figures. This continued the pattern of the Young Turk period, when most historians were political figures working for nationalism in the form of Turkism – for example Yusuf Akçura, Ziya Gökalp, Fuad Köprülü, and Ahmet Ağaoğlu. Some, like Akçura, lived through to the new thesis. The Turkish History Research Society (which later become the Turkish History Society)[49] was really a branch of the CHF.[50]

Afet İnan, who was to became the veritable commissar of the new ideological purity, relates how she became a historian in 1928 when she showed Kemal a French book which stated that Turks were yellow skinned and considered by Europeans as a 'secondary human type'. She asked him if this was true and he replied 'No, that is impossible, we should investigate this. Start working!'[51] Mete Tunçay argues that the history thesis was first formulated by Yusuf Ziya (Özer), Law Professor at Istanbul University, against opposition from Fuad Köprülü, who did not hold to the theory that the Turks were the origin of all Anatolia's inhabitants.[52] Tunçay points to a gradual sophistication in interpreting

---

[49] The Turkish History Research Society was founded in 1929 as an evolution of the Turkish Hearths, despite the worries of the Hearths' first president, Hamdullah Suphi who wanted them to remain an intellectual club. See Mete Tunçay, *Türkiye Cumhuriyetinde Tek-Parti Yönetiminin Kurulması 1923-1931* (Ankara: Yurt, 1981), pp. 296-8. The second president of the Hearth was Reşit Galip, who was closer to Kemal, was more in favour of them becoming politicised and an appendage of the CHF. He had been president of one of the Independence Tribunals – the executive tool for purging Kemal's opponents – and later became Minister of Education. See F. Georgeon, 'Les Foyeurs Turcs à L'Epoque Kemaliste', *Turcica*, vol. 14, 1982, p. 176. Other sociopolitical organisations were similarly liquidated or became CHP branches in 1930-1 during this veritable *Gleichanschaltung* of political life. See Tunçay, *op. cit.*, p. 297.

[50] Ağaoğlu for example believed that the Turkish Hearths needed close links with the government. After the end of Ottoman rule he advocated government support and even direct control of them; see Frank Tachau, 'The Search for National Identity Among the Turks', *Die Welt des Islams*, vol. 8, no. 3, 1963, p. 174. Akçura, although never a CUP member, was always in harmony with the CUP, especially when collaborating with Gökalp. After the revolution he became CHF member and deputy for Istanbul; see F. Georgeon, *Aux origines du nationalisme Turc: Yusuf Akçura (1876-1835)* (Paris: Institut d'Études Anatoliennes, 1980), p. 82.

[51] Afet İnan, 'Atatürk ve Tarih Tezi', *Belleten*, vol. 3, 1939, pp. 234-6.

[52] Tunçay, *op. cit.*, pp. 300-3.

'nation' and 'nationalism' in the first three CHF party statutes of 1923, 1927 and 1931.[53] In the 1923 statutes, the adoption of Turkish 'culture' was regarded as indispensable for CHF membership. In 1927 other key words appear for defining 'national solidarity' as dependent on unity of language, sentiment, 'idea' and 'progress of Turkish culture and language'. In the 1931 programme the 'nation' is defined as 'a political and social whole which is made up of a unity of language, culture and idea and solidarity of patriots.' The 'unity of idea' meant a single monolithic ideology to unite all nationalists. A strict homogeneity in the élite was seen as essential to promote the new ideas among the masses.[54]

The new history textbooks

The new republic needed new history textbooks. The first was *Türkiye Tarihi* by Hamid Muhsin, which was published three times and used between 1924 and 1929 mostly in intermediary schools (*ortamektepler*). Unlike those which followed, it concentrated mostly on the Ottoman Empire, with only the last chapter (Chapter 7, 'Ottoman-Turkish civilisation'), devoted to the new interpretation of Turkish nationalism. In this history the Turks were presented as a tribal people before adopting Islam (later this would be something of an insult). Due to outside influences – mainly Islam – they had allegedly lost the factor of racial unity.[55] The last chapter stressed the nineteenth-century reform movement and Westernisation and the need 'to build a homogeneous society and a modern national state.'[56]

[53] *Ibid.* See the Appendices pp. 362, 382 and 447.

[54] Mardin, *op. cit.*, p. 212, points out that 'solidarism' (which was also the official ideology of the French Third Republic) was in retrospect one of the main planks of Kemalist ideology and came from Durkheim through Gökalp. It postulated that class conflict in modern society was not necessary, and that social equilibrium could be maintained through peaceful co-operation between different economic groups. Such views are essentially nationalist, as defined in Chapter 1, in that they see the unity of the group – the nation – as paramount, and overriding possible divisive forces.

[55] '.... in tribal life, the crucial element of solidarity was the solidarity based on common blood ... Therefore with the impact of Islam and the influence of Christianity, racial features had lost their determining character as a factor of solidarity during the middle ages ...' *Türkiye Tarihi* (Ankara, 1924), p. 470.

[56] *Ibid.*, p. 475.

The next textbook, and the first to try to rewrite history along the lines of the Kemalist history thesis, was *Türk Tarihinin Anahatlan*, written in 1929-30 by selected members of the Turkish History Research Society including Yusuf Akçura. However, Kemal did not approve of it, due apparently to the many inaccuracies in the hastily prepared text, and only 100 copies were printed for others to comment on.[57] It concentrated on the spread of the Turks through history and continents. The Introduction explained that it was written to answer the need to upgrade the historical role of the Turks and to negate false information regarding the creation of civilisations stemming from the Jews and the Bible.[58] It stated that:

> The Turks, who brought civilisation to the whole world, had already founded great civilisations in their fatherland, Central Asia, in various periods. ... [but there had been discontinuity] due to climatic reasons, namely drought.[59]

There was great emphasis on the Turks as creators of state structures as opposed to the 'importance of Arabs and Persians.'[60] The new emphasis on the pre-history and racial characteristics of the Turks was illustrated by the fact that the situation in the republic since 1923 was only covered on the last page (page 605).[61] Despite the errors and Kemal's disapproval, there was support for its general theoretical framework. In 1931 30,000 copies of a condensed seventy-four page version were published as *Türk Tarihinin Anahatlanna Medhal* by the Ministry of Education. This version left out the Ottoman Empire entirely, illustrating the new priorities.[62]

In 1931 the process continued with the publication of the four-volume *Tarih*. It was used in *lycées* and immediately simplified for intermediary schools in three volumes as *Ortamektep İçin Tarih*. These last two publications were used for decades virtually unchanged.[63] Once more, the racial aspects were stressed, as was

57 B. Ersanlı-Behar, *op. cit.*, p. 127.

58 *Ibid.*, pp. 128-29.

59 *Türk Tarihinin Anahatlan*, p. 403, quoted in *ibid.*, p. 130.

60 *Ibid.*

61 *Ibid.*, p. 131.

62 *Türk Tarihinin Anahatlanna Medhal* (Istanbul, 1931).

the claim that Turks were the founders of great civilisations. In the introduction to the intermediary version, Gobineau's classification of people by colour and Eugene Pittard's classification by skeletal type were used.[64] The Turkish language was seen as the most important in the world, and the Turkish race as the motor of history.[65] The Ottoman Empire is presented as a retrograde phase, and the Ottoman experience as alien and non-Turkish. The close identification with the party-state is shown by volume 4 of *Tarih*, which deals with the history of the Turkish republic and is in two sections: the first up to the Lausanne Treaty and the second on the period afterwards. The identification of the CHF with the 'nation' is illustrated in the second section, which even had three pages on 'currents of opposition' (i.e. the Progressive Republican Party) which were portrayed as hostile to the nation.[66]

The racism portrayed in these books can be seen as a part of the prevailing pattern of the times, with the rise of fascism in Europe. However, they were not fundamentally changed in subsequent decades; only in the late 1940s did more balanced views on the Ottoman Empire and the period immediately preceding

[63] See T. Alkan, *op. cit.*

[64] *Ortamektep İçin Tarih*, vol. 1, 3rd reprint (Istanbul, 1936), p. 7.

[65] The first peoples in Asia Minor in historical times were seen as the Hittites (claimed in the book to be Hata Turks – *ibid.*, p. 112) and the Phoenicians, later known as Sassanites, who were also 'Turks' as 'shown' by skeletal research on their graves (*ibid.*, p. 134). The book claims the Turks brought civilisation to the Chinese (*ibid.*, p. 40). This can be seen as a kind of 'positive discrimination' used by the Kemalist state to try to counter on inferiority complex *vis-à-vis* the West. It also reflects the common nationalist trait, as shown in Chapter 1, of moving from claiming an equal place with other nations to that of claiming a preeminent place for one's own national group.

[66] *Tarih* vol. 4 (Istanbul 1931). For more information on the Progressive Republican Party see Weiker *op. cit.*, and E. Zürcher, *Political Opposition in the Early Turkish Republic: the Progressive Republican Party 1924- 1925* (Leiden, E.J. Brill, 1991). This characteristic of viewing opposition as illegitimate can be seen as a continuation of the problems of legitimate opposition in Islam (see Chapter 2). It continued in the nationalist republican era and is demonstrated in Kamil Su and Kazim N. Duru, *Ortaokular İçin Tarih III* (Istanbul, 1943-9) pp. 212. Here, the 3rd National Assembly was portrayed as being constituted by the CHF without any opposition at all, while the Free Party was characterised as a tool of conservatives and religious reactionaries; see Ersanlı-Behar, *op. cit.*, p. 142.

it appear. In school textbooks the revolutionary pragmatic mentality continued unabated – indeed, if any change occurred it was for the worse.[67]

The First History Congress

The First History Congress took place in Ankara and was hosted by the Minister of Education and Kemal himself. It took place to introduce the new thesis formally. Education was seen as the key – along the lines of the Gellner modernisation paradigm mentioned in Chapter 1 – and secondary-school teachers made up the bulk of the participants. There were 198 *lycée* and intermediate school teachers, eighteen university professors or assistant professors and twenty-five History Society members (mostly parliamentarians).[68] Only thirty-three people actively took part and there were fifteen papers presented around four topics: the use of prehistoric sources; debates concerning the Turkish languages; debates on geographical change in central Asia resulting in migration (a central point in the new thesis); and debates on 1932 history books. The main figures in the debates were Fuad Köprülü, Afet İnan (representing the two views on the thesis – Fuad critical and Afet strongly partisan), Yusuf Akçura, Ahmet Ağaoğlu, Samih Rıfat (another thesis loyalist), Zeki Velidi (Togan), Sadri Maksudi (Arsal),[69] Ahmed Refik (Altınay) – a prolific history-book writer, and Reşit Galip. In the debates, İnan ensured there was no outright opposition, which was seen as anti-national. The need was for an unassailable myth to build the new nation. İnan spelt it out in the conclusion to her appear:

> Many European scholars think their [that is European] ancestors came from the tribes of Central Asia, which they call Aryans, Indo-Europeans or Indo-Germans, who originated from the Altai-Pamir plateau and brought their high culture to Europe and all of humanity both in prehistoric and historic times ... The Turkish race had attained a high level of culture in its

[67] See Alkan, *op. cit.*

[68] *Birinci Türk Tarih Kongresi: Konferanslar Müzakere zabıtlaln*, (Istanbul: T.C. Maarif Vekâleti, 1932), p. vii-xiii.

[69] These latter two were both educated in Russia – Maksudi only coming to Turkey after 1923.

homeland while the peoples of Europe were still ignorant savages. ... Turkish children will learn that they are part of an Aryan, civilised and creative people descended from a high race who have existed for tens of thousands of years, not from 'a tribe of 400 tents' [a reference to the previous Ottoman mythology of the original Ottoman Turks].

The last remark was greeted by prolonged applause.[70]

When Fuad mildly criticised the methodology of İnan's paper he was himself criticised, and backed down. Rıfat's paper tried to show that many languages like Chinese and Persian actually originated from ancient Turkish.[71] The only real confrontation occurred over the theory of a great drought in Central Asia which started the supposed migrations and brought 'civilisation' to other lands; Galip was a main protagonist of this view.[72] Zeki Velidi opposed this thesis,[73] but was himself attacked by Galip, Maksudi and Şemseddin (Günaltay). It appears that much of this debate, which resurfaced again and again in the conference, was due to old quarrels among the Russian *émigrés*, specifically about Velidi's actions after the Russian Revolution while he was still in Russia.[74] Despite the personal animosity between them, Maksudi and Velidi, who were both impassioned Turkists, were better informed than others in the congress. Both later joined the dis-organised opposition to rigid one-party rule and the excessive simplification by the Kemalist state in pushing its nationalist agenda

---

[70] *Birinci Türk Tarih Kongresi*, pp. 40-1.

[71] *Ibid.*, p. 59.

[72] *Ibid.*, pp. 99-161 for his paper detailing this.

[73] *Ibid.*, p. 169.

[74] Şemseddin said at the conference: 'Zeki Velidi and Sadri Maksudi Bey had been strong opponents on the question of Turkism. Two congresses aiming at unification were convened by the Turks after the end of the Tsarist system in Russia, one in Moscow and one in Ufa. However, Zeki Bey at the Ufa Congress strongly opposed the unification of the Turks and wanted to separate the Bashkirts from the Turkish associations [cries of shame from the participants]. Zeki Velidi Bey contributed to the promotion of linguistic and cultural division among the Turks of Russia. ... Does Zeki Velidi Bey also want to play the same role in this congress? However he can be assured that all the participants at this congress are burning with the fire of nationalism. All forces against this fire are doomed to failure [prolonged and intense applause].' *Ibid.*, p. 400.

forward.[75] In accordance with the new emphasis on archaeology and pre-Islamic Turkish history, and the corresponding downgrading of the whole Ottoman experience, there was no paper at the congress directly about Ottoman history or its bearing on Turkish history in general. The prolific history writer Ahmed Refik (Altınay) contented himself with criticising his own previous work in a manner reminiscent of Stalinist self-denunciation.[76]

Language Reform and the First Turkish Language Congress

The First History Congress showed that the political leadership had clearly decided to explain national identity in terms of race and language, with language also seen as a racial characteristic similarly to German in Kedourie's model of nationalism. However, it was also apparent that the delegates were unsure exactly how to go about this; Samih Rıfat's paper was particularly ineffective in its arguments and produced some criticism.[77] Soon after the First History Congress the First Turkish Language Congress was convened.

As noted in Chapter 2, language reform had been consistently to the fore in the latter period of the Ottoman Empire. Ottoman Turkish corresponded to Gellner's model of the official state language of a pre-modern society, which was largely unintelligible to the mass of the population. The first stage in the Kemalist language reform was the 1928 decree on replacing the Arabic script with a more easily learnt Latin alphabet based on strict phonetic principles. This crucial measure was undertaken – like so many of Kemal's sweeping reforms – with military precision. The preparatory committee was allowed just three months to

[75] Ersanlı-Behar, *op. cit.*, pp. 175 and 187-8.

[76] Refik had been tried in 1925 for 'anti-republican activities' by the Independence Tribunal in Ankara, which included Reşit Galip among the judges, *ibid.*, p. 193. At the end of the congress he stated: 'I think that my honourable friend Yusuf Akçura's criticism of our history textbooks are positive and justified. I also know that my own books are, as has been pointed out, far from being error free. From now on I will try and correct my past errors and try to compensate by enlightening our youth and people in future work. My new books will be mainly devoted to correcting my previously published errors.' *Birinci Türk Tarih Kongresi*, p. 609.

[77] *Ibid.*, p. 84.

draft the proposals, with 1 January 1929 the deadline by which the use of Arabic characters became illegal. All officials were obliged to learn and use the new script; the penalties for not doing so were loss of appointment, and even loss of nationality and expulsion from the country. Even prisoners were not released on expiry of their sentences if they could not use the new script.[78] By 1929, Arabic and Persian were no longer taught in the schools, and in 1930 Kemal proclaimed the defence and enrichment of the Turkish language as the guiding principle of the language reforms. This meant, on one hand, the purging of Arabic and Persian loanwords, and on the other, the coining of new words based on Turkish elements.[79] The objectives of all these moves were the sponsoring of a literate population, combined with a break with the Ottoman Islamic heritage and a reinforcing of the new Turkish national identity. The advent of mass literacy was also an essential precondition for the propagating of a unified high culture to create a national consciousness.

The First Turkish Language Congress was another stage in this military-style campaign. It was held in late September and early October 1932 in the continual presence of Kemal himself, and in Istanbul – the country's intellectual and press centre – rather than Ankara, where the new Kemalist bureaucracy was less in need of indoctrination. It also generated wide press coverage.[80] Immediately after the History Congress, a Society for Research on the Turkish Language had been set up to simplify the language. Its chairman was Samih Rıfat, who was Vice-president of the First Language Congress.[81] As in the case of the History Congress, teachers were the largest group, making up 312 of the 711 registrants. The agenda covered four main topics starting with

---

[78] H.C. Armstrong, *op. cit.*, pp. 306-7. For more on the language reform see U. Heyd, *Language Reform in Modern Turkey* (Jerusalem: Israel Oriental Society, 1954) and G.L. Lewis, 'Atatürk's Language Reform as an Aspect of Modernisation in the Republic of Turkey', in J.M. Landau (ed.), *Atatürk and the Modernisation of Turkey* (Boulder, CO: Westview Press, 1984).

[79] A.S. Leverend, *Türk dilinde ve sadeleşme evreleri* (Ankara: Türk Dil Kurumu, 1972).

[80] Jacob M. Landau, 'The First Turkish Language Congress' in Joshua A. Fishman (ed.) *The Earliest Stage of Language Planning: The 'First Congress' Phenomenon* (Berlin: Mouton: De Gruyter, 1993), p. 274.

[81] *Ibid.*, p. 277.

the origin of language (Turkish and other languages) and the expansion of Turkish in its own environment (this section covered dialects, grammar and vocabulary, and the contemporary situation of Turkish). Other sections covered morphology, syntax, vocabulary (again) and terms, and the prospects for development in line with the march of civilisation.[82]

Rıfat opened the proceedings and showed the way. According to him, Kemal had single-handedly saved Turkey from the Ottoman defeat. The proposed language reforms, he claimed, were a step confirming the original Turkish personality, which had been submerged in the anti-Turkish Ottoman society. The Ottomans had mocked the simple Anatolian Turk, even though his civilisation was more advanced than that of the other communities in the empire.[83] In this, Rıfat echoed the classic nationalist line that the peasant was the repository of true national values. Reşit Galip, as Minister of Education, was next. He emphasised that Ottoman Turkish was a cosmopolitan language of the élite, and that no more than 10 per cent of the Turks of Anatolia could understand it. He went on to stress that Turkification of the language was an absolute necessity for the future of national culture, and suggested that there may have been about 80,000 words in the Turkish spoken in Anatolia, and that these could be supplemented by words borrowed from other dialects and ancient documents. A powerful language, he argued, was a fact of life and highlighted the objective of making Turkey one of the world's most advanced nations.[84] The congress then went on to reinforce the History Thesis by purporting to show that Turkish was the most aristocratic, powerful, lively and ancient of languages, and that it had a very special role. This thesis was extended (some may say even vulgarised) into what became known as the 'Sun Language Theory', in which it was argued that science and archaeology had 'shown' the predominance of the Turkish race in world history. Hence, it was only natural that a race which was the source of civilisation should provide a mother language to all the others.[85]

[82] *Ibid.*, p. 276.

[83] *Ibid.*, p. 278.

[84] *Ibid.*, p. 279.

[85] *Ibid.*, pp. 280-1. Another 'rationale' for the 'Sun Language Theory' (SLT) was that Atatürk aimed to purge all foreign words from Turkish, but this was

Landau points out that with the exception of the eminent journalist Hüseyin Cahit (Yalçın), who argued in the press against artificial language manipulation and was castigated as a reactionary because of this, there appears to have been virtually monolithic unanimity within the congress regarding the approved Kemalist approach.[86] Turkey in the 1930s was an authoritarian statist polity with strong corporatist aspects akin to national socialism. The CHP party-state actively pursued this along with state nationalism, as the programme accepted by its Fourth Grand Congress on 9 May 1935 clearly spelt out, stating (in the official translation):

Article 1. *The Fatherland* is the sacred country within our present boundaries where the Turkish Nation lives with its ancient and illustrious history and with its past glories still living in the depths of its soil ...

Article 5. ... (b) The Party considers it essential to preserve the special character and the entirely independent identity of the Turkish social community. ... (c) ... It is one of the main principles to consider the people of the Turkish Republic not as composed of different classes, but as a community divided into various professions according to the requirements of the division of labour for the individual and social life of the Turkish people. The aims of the Party are to secure social order and solidarity instead of class conflict, and to establish harmony of interests ...

Article 41. Our main principles for national education and instruction are as follows: ... (b) The training of strongly republican, nationalist, populist, etatist and secular citizens must be fostered in every degree of education. To respect and make others respect, the Turkish nation, the Grand National Assembly of Turkey, and the Turkish State must be taught as a foremost

---

not always possible. However, by adopting the theory he could overcome this problem as it claimed that all languages derived from Turkish in the first place; see Yakup Kadri Karaosmanoğlu, 'Atatürk ve Türk Dili' in *Atatürk ve Türk Dili* (Ankara: 1963, pp. 109-10). However, G. Lewis discounts this because Atatürk normally acted decisively rather than in such a subtle manner; see G.L. Lewis, 'Atatürk's Language Reform', pp. 207-8.

[86] *Cumhuriyet*, 10 October 1932, depicted those who did not understand the language reform as having a reactionary mentality encouraged by enemies but who would not be believed by anyone 'in whose breast a Turkish heart beats'; quoted in Landau, 'The First Turkish Language Congress', p. 285.

duty. ... (e) Education must be high, national, patriotic, and far from all sorts of superstitions and foreign ideas. (g) Our Party lays an extraordinary importance upon citizens knowing our great history. This learning is the sacred essence that nourishes the indestructible resistance of the Turk against all currents that may prejudice the national existence, his capacity and power, and his sentiments of self-confidence. (h) We shall continue our serious work in rendering the Turkish language a perfect and ordered national language. ...

Article 50. The Turkish youth shall be brought up with the conviction that the *defence* of the *Revolution* and the Fatherland is the highest duty. They shall be taught to be ready to sacrifice everything in order to fulfil this duty ...[87]

This is all fully in line with the nationalist view, as expounded by Kedourie, of society as an organic whole, as well as Gellner's view of the central state pushing a unified high culture primarily through the education process. The army and compulsory national service for all young men was another tool to train youth in national values; as well as a means of teaching illiterate peasants how to read and write. In recruitment posters of the 1930s shifty looking youths were transformed into fit strapping young men wearing modern Western clothes in contrast to the old days of bearded turbaned men.[88]

By the time of the Second History Congress of 20 September

---

[87] Reprinted in Lilo Linke, *Allah Dethroned: A Journey through Modern Turkey* (London: Constable, 1937) pp. 327-32. The programme further stated: 'Article 5. The Party considers the *radio* to be one of the most valuable instruments for the political and cultural education of the nation. We shall erect powerful broadcasting stations, and shall provide for the easy purchase of cheap receiving sets ... Article 52. The national *opera* and the national *theatre* are among our important tasks.' Radio sets were introduced in large numbers in the 1930s: by 1935 there were 8,082 sets of which 2,838 were in rural areas; see Martin Stokes, *The Arabesk Debate: Music and Musicians in Modern Turkey*, (Oxford: Clarendon Press, 1992), p. 36. This use of radio, as shown in Chapter 5, became something of a two edged sword as foreign radio stations could also beam in perceived alien cultural influences like 'Arabesk' to rival the TRT cultural norms. The opera and theatre as components of the new high culture seem to have owed much to Kemal's personal preferences or his desire to appear Western and modern at all time; see Lord Kinross, *Atatürk: The Rebirth of a Nation* (London: Weidenfeld and Nicolson, 1964), pp. 469-70.

[88] Linke, *op. cit.*, p. 330.

1937 the 'Sun Language Theory' – which also to an extent 'freed the Turkish language from the Islamic yoke'[89] – was official dogma. This congress, which was characterised by complete lack of debate or argument, emphasised archaeology, which was used for the territorial realisation of the nation. Anatolian civilisations were 'shown', using the results of the excavations of the mid-1930s, to have been the work of Turks. Again, the Ottoman period was ignored as 'the dark age'.[90]

The Kemalist state and minorities

Many scholars have claimed that Kemalist nationalism was not racist, but rather a state-building nationalism along territorial models proposed by Gellner and Smith, which did not persecute minority groups.[91] The above discussion, however, would tend to conclude that there were strong racial aspects in Kemalist nationalism as it came to be defined and propagated in the 1930s. We should therefore briefly look at how minorities within the new Turkey were treated. As earlier, Orthodox Christian minorities were seen as suspect almost from the start, and with the exception of communities in Istanbul and the islands of Gökçeada and Bozcaada, they were expelled. Contrary to Bernard Lewis's assertion,[92] the Kemalist state never admitted that the Young Turk regime pursued a deliberate genocidal policy against Armenians, and

---

[89] Ersanlı-Behar, *op. cit.*, p. 230. For the congress itself see *İkinci Türk Tarihi Kongresi, 20-25 Eylul, 1937: Kongrenin Çalışmaları ve Kongreye Sunulan Tebligler* (Istanbul, 1943).

[90] Afet İnan, quoted in *ibid.*, p. 242.

[91] Suna Kili in 'Kemalism in Contemporary Turkey', *International Political Science Review* vol. 1, no. 3, 1980, states 'Kemalist nationalism is not racist and it is not a persecuting nationalism. According to Kemalist ideology one's Turkishness is not determined by one's race or religion but by the degree a person associates himself with the ideals and goals of the Turkish republic and through commitment to Turkey's independence and modernization.' Bernard Lewis states that Kemal's 'nationalism was healthy and reasonable: there was no arrogant trampling on the rights or aspirations of other nations, no neurotic rejection of responsibility for the past', *The Emergence of Modern Turkey* (Oxford University Press, 1961) p. 286. For more details on Turkey's minorities see P.A. Andrews, *Ethnic Groups in the Republic of Turkey* (Weisbaden: Dr Ludwig Reichert Verlag, 1989).

[92] See footnote 91. One could add that the denial of any worth in the whole Ottoman period was indeed a 'neurotic rejection' of the past.

continues to this day to refuse to acknowledge it. The defining and official propagation of the new nationalist thesis in the 1930s saw a rise in the official attitude of 'Turkey exclusively for the Turks'.[93] To a large degree, this can be seen as 'healthy and reasonable', as a Turkish national identity was needed to weld the nation together. The Koran and New Testament were to be translated into Turkish and the call to prayer in all mosques had to be in Turkish, not Arabic.[94] Foreign schools were discouraged, especially missionary ones. All primary education was in Turkish schools, and the foreign schools which remained had to omit all reference to religion, to teach Turkish, and to employ a given percentage of Turkish teachers.[95] In the economy, each firm had to have a high percentage of Turkish capital as well as Turkish directors and staff. Heavy import duties and quotas tried to keep out foreign goods, and there were campaigns to buy Turkish products. Again, these measures can be seen as predictable – and to some extent, economically rational – given the recent history of foreign or non-Turkish domination of the economy. Economic nationalism does not always equate with racism. Moreover, the quotas only came into effect in the 1930s, partly as a reaction to the 1929 world economic crisis and the fact that other countries were doing likewise.[96]

More chauvinistic perhaps was the fact that many professions, including medicine, law and even wheelwrighting, were closed

[93] H.C. Armstrong, *op. cit.*, p. 292.

[94] Kemal did look at the possibility of constructing a Turkish Islam, with a Turkish translation of the Koran, and wanted the 'religious poet' and author of the national anthem Mehmet Akif to do this. Funds were voted by the National Assembly in 1926 and Akif, who was then in Egypt in protest at Kemal's reforms, was formally invited. He initially accepted but then refused as he would not override the consensus of the Muslim *ulema*, who opposed translation of the Koran, even though Kemal renewed the invitation as late as 1936. See Edward Mortimer, *Faith and Power: The Politics of Islam* (London: Faber and Faber, 1982) pp. 144-5. However, ultimately Kemal and his collaborators were convinced that Islam and Turkish nationalism were incompatible. As noted above, Islam was rejected as a main base of social cohesion.

[95] H.C. Armstrong, *op. cit.*, p. 292.

[96] For economic policy see William Hale, 'Ideology and Economic Development in Turkey, 1930-1945', *British Society for Middle Eastern Studies Bulletin*, vol. 7, 1980, and Hale, *The Political and Economic Development of Modern Turkey*, (London: Croom Helm, 1981), pp. 33-85.

to all but Turks.[97] Worse were the several official expressions of anti-semitic and anti-minority policies. In 1934, for example, Law 2510, regulating the distribution and settlement of Turkey's population, saw Eastern Thrace restricted to inhabitants of purely Turkish upbringing and education and the forced removal of the historic Jewish communities of Edirne and the Straits zone.[98] This anti-Jewish campaign, orchestrated by the Turkish press,[99] led to the flight of 8-10,000 Thracian Jews to Istanbul in the space of a couple of weeks. The 1935 law which required all Turkish citizens to adopt surnames produced pressure on Istanbul's Jewish, Greek and Armenian populations to give up their traditional surnames and adopt new ones,[100] while the language campaign – the *Vatandaş Türkçe Konuş* (Citizen Speak Turkish) movement – also put pressure on the minorities. A bill was even put forward to compel Jews to speak only Turkish; in 1938 the British Ambassador Sir George Clark reported that 'local Greeks and Jews were fired or blamed for speaking a non-Turkish language.'[101]

İsmet İnönü and Fevzi Çakmak were apparently more fanatically pro-Turkish than Kemal himself.[102] After Kemal's death, with İsmet İnönü at the helm, the situation deteriorated.[103] Soon after

[97] H.C. Armstrong, *op. cit.*, p. 292.

[98] *The Times*, London, 4, 5, 6, 7 and 16 July 1934. While such campaigns to remove potentially suspect populations from sensitive border areas was by no means a purely Turkish innovation this does not justify such actions. See H. Poulton, *The Balkans: Minorities and States in Conflict* (London: MRG Publications, 1983), p. 178, for Greece's similar actions.

[99] *Zaman*, of 9 July 1934 told the Jews to stop complaining and instead adopt Turkish culture. For a contrary view see S. Shaw, *The Jews of the Ottoman Empire and the Turkish Republic* (London: Macmillan, 1991), who points to the continuing of Sephardic Jewish culture in the 1920s and 1930s and the support for Kemal's reforms by the Jewish community. However, even in his somewhat rosy picture, he mentions (p. 251) that Tekin Alp (a Jewish extreme Kemalist –see below) formed the *Türk Kültür Birliği* (Turkish Cultural Union) and the *Türkçe Konuşturma Birliği (Union for Speaking Turkish)* and claimed that assimilation was very successful.

[100] See David Brown in Foreword to Faik Ökte, *The Tragedy of the Turkish Capital Tax* (London: Croom Helm, 1964), p. x.

[101] *Annual Report on Turkey (1983)*, Foreign Office 371/23301/E1214, in *ibid.*

[102] İsmet was reportedly at times unintelligible in his speeches to the Assembly due to his use of the new Turkish; see H.C. Armstrong, *op. cit.*, p. 292.

[103] İnönü is characterised by Armstrong as 'an extreme nationalist and hater of foreigners', *ibid.*, p. 312. However, this characterisation must be treated with care.

the outbreak of the Second World War, the government mobilised all Jewish, Greek and Armenian males between 18 and 45 years old. At the time of the signing of the agreement between Turkey and Hitler's Germany in June 1941, they were sent to special camps in the Anatolian interior where there were reports of harsh treatment and high mortality rates.[104]

The most notorious incidents of this trend relate to the Capital Tax of 11 November 1942, which best illustrates the official mistrust of minorities. The severe economic crisis of 1939-42 was blamed on Jewish and Christian businessmen, and the Turkish press launched a vicious campaign against them.[105] Religion and ethnicity were the criteria used to define how much tax a person should pay. Initially, there were two lists: one for Muslims and one for non-Muslims. Later, separate lists were made for foreigners and for *Dönmes* (Jews who had converted to Islam). The latter paid twice the Muslim rate, while non-Muslims paid up to ten times as much as Muslims. Foreigners were supposed to be charged the same as Muslims. In practice many were charged like non-Muslims, eliciting protests from embassies.[106] Defaulters were deported to camps like Aşkale labour camp, an inaccessible spot in the mountains west of Erzurum.[107] The boards made arbitrary demands with no recourse of appeal. However, under the constitution there was a right of petition. By January 1943 there were over 10,000 petitions, almost all of which were rejected. The published list of defaulters revealed that they were almost all Greeks, Jews and Armenians. In December 1943 the last deportees were allowed home and a law of 15 March 1944 cancelled all unpaid dues.[108] Cynics would point out that the change of

---

İnönü's policy after the Second World War hardly supports Armstrong's view.

[104] The camps held about 5,000 men each and the inmates were instructed in non-combative skills like road building. See *Ankara Chancery to Southern Department* 4 June 1941 FO/371/30031/R5813 quoted in D. Brown, in Ökte, *op. cit.*, p. x. Despite pro-German sentiment after Hitler's attack on the USSR, Turkey continued its *de facto* neutrality.

[105] For example the semi-official *Ulus* of 24 November 1942 accused the 'Yorgis, Salamons, Kyriakos, Artins' – i.e. Greeks, Jews and Armenians – for the economic ills; quoted in D. Brown, in Ökte, *op. cit.*, p. x.

[106] B. Lewis, *Emergence*, p. 290.

[107] D. Brown, in Ökte, *op. cit.*, p. xi.

[108] B. Lewis, *op. cit.*, p. 292.

heart was due to the course of the war, given that the deportees were allowed home a week before İnönü met Churchill and Roosevelt in Cairo. The period 1941-3 had seen a rise in anti-Semitism and anti-minority feeling in Turkey, with investigations into past family records of officials to see who was of Jewish origin. A bitter campaign was launched against the Jews and the *Dönmes*, in which the latter were seen as 'being worse than the Jews' as they 'wanted to have the best of both worlds.'[109] Ahmet Emin Yalman, a *Dönme*, had his newspaper *Vatan* suspended for criticising the tax, and he was deported to Aşkale.[110]

Another aim of the tax – not formally voiced but understood by all – was that it would purposely destroy many of Istanbul's non-Turkish businesses which had survived the economic nationalism of the 1920s and 1930s.[111] Istanbul's non-Turkish residents were especially numerous among those interned; out of a total of 2,057 interned for deportation 1,869 were from Istanbul. Of these 2,057, 657 either died or paid up; the remaining 1,400 were deported to camps where twenty-one died – all from Istanbul.[112] There was no respite for the old, sick and infirm.[113] The

[109] D. Brown, in Ökte, *op. cit.*, p. xiii.

[110] *Ibid.* Interestingly, in his memoirs, *Turkey in My Time*, (Norman: University of Oklahoma Press, 1956), Yalman does not relate his personal experience, but merely refers to the Tax as a huge public relations blunder (p. 204). He had suffered from the repressive side of the Kemalist state previously in 1925, when he and six other journalists seen as hostile to the government were sent to Elazığ for trial by the dreaded Independence Tribunals in the wake of the Sheikh Said revolt. On the journey he 'became aware that Turkey as a whole did not present a uniform pattern with normal deviations, but displayed discrepant stages of development in different sectors. We saw an over-all picture of heterogeneity and retardation which called for maximum unity, harmony, and co-operation by us all.' (p. 153) As a result, all seven backed down and supported the government.

[111] Nadir Nadi, then the owner of *Cumhuriyet*, later wrote: '... a second objective of the tax was to free the market from the control of the minorities and open it to the Turks ... Thus our Jewish, Greek Orthodox, Catholic and Georgian subjects who were proud of being Turkish citizens had to sell out their property and wealth for nothing.' Nadir Nad, *Perde Arkalarından* (Istanbul: n.p., 1964), pp. 178-9.

[112] Ökte, *op. cit.*, pp. 73-4.

[113] As shown by the deportation of a 70-year-old half-paralysed Jew named Shaban and a 65-year-old handicapped Jew named Behar – *Memorandum on conditions in the assembly camp of Demirkapı*, Col. Binns to the British Consul-General in Istanbul FO/371/37402/R2416, 24 January 1943, quoted by D. Brown in

Director of Finance, who personally supervised every taxpayer over TL 50,000, was Faik Ökte. Ökte pinpoints Prime Minister Saraçoğlu (who took office in June 1942 and was seen as being close to İnönü) as the man who conceived the bill.[114] To get the bill through parliament, Saraçoğlu strongly indicated that only the minorities would be taxed, and many deputies were later angry that (Muslim) Turks would have to pay anything at all. Some governors even refused to collect taxes from Muslim Turks, forcing the Finance Minister Fuat Ağralı to personally intervene and explain that Muslim Turks had to pay at least a token levy.[115] Ökte and others refused to dispatch Muslim Turks to Aşkale, and managed to avoid deporting them if they defaulted.[116] While Ökte's obvious personal discomfort at being party to this disgraceful measure is apparent in his account of it,[117] the reader is struck by the fact that the deputies only really objected to Muslim Turks' being taxed even a token rate, and not to its blatant anti-minority aspect.

The situation regarding non-Turkish Muslims was also problematic. As noted above, Kemal conceived the new Turkish nation as being constituted by the Muslim population of Anatolia. However, the new state introduced sweeping reforms aimed at relegating Islam to the personal domain, and secularism became an essential component of the new nationalism. As we have seen, this resulted in a serious revolt of Zaza-speaking Sunni Kurds led by Sheikh Said which was ruthlessly put down. The *tarikat* brotherhoods were also banned. Said and hundreds of his supporters were hanged. Anything between 40,000 and 250,000 died in the 'pacification', and Ankara decided to forcibly remove large numbers of Kurds from the area.[118] Immediately afterwards, another revolt broke

---

Ökte, *op. cit.*, p. xi.

[114] Ökte, *op. cit.*, p. 21.

[115] *Ibid.*, p. 23.

[116] *Ibid.*, p. 72.

[117] He states 'Turkey needed an extraordinary tax on capital. What it did not need was this misbegotten offspring of German racialism and Ottoman fanaticism.' *Ibid.*, p. 14. As Bernard Lewis points out, the tax resulted in the closing of many small businesses, and actually helped the black market. It shook and dislocated the business world, and badly besmirched Turkey's international reputation. B. Lewis, *op. cit.*, p. 295.

[118] D. McDowall, *The Kurds: A Nation Denied*, (London: MRG, 1992), p. 37.

out around Ağrıdağ (Mt. Ararat). This time a more overtly nationalist – as opposed to a religious *tarikat* – movement was involved along with the traditional sheikhs and *ağas*, with assistance from Reza Shah in Iran.[119] However, the Shah cut off his support and the revolt was crushed. Law 1850 of 1930 eloquently illustrates the official line by stating that there would be no prosecutions for crimes, including murder, committed against Kurdish insurgents.[120] In August, Prime Minister İnönü announced:

> The revolution [the Kurdish uprisings], fanned by foreign intrigue in our Eastern provinces, has lasted for five years, but today it loses half its strength. Only the Turkish nation is entitled to claim ethnic and national rights in this country. No other element has any such right.[121]

Minister of Justice Mahmut Esas Bozkurt reinforced this view by stating:

> I believe that the Turk must be the only lord, the only master of this country. Those who are not of pure Turkish stock can have only one right in this country, the right to be servants and slaves.[122]

Mass deportations were used again and Turks were encouraged to settle in Kurdish areas by a law of 5 May 1932.[123] This law

---

[119] Kendal [sic], 'Kurdistan in Turkey', in G. Chaliand (ed.), *People Without a Country: The Kurds and Kurdistan* (London: Zed, 1980), p. 64-5.

[120] Law 1850, Article 1, stated: 'Murders and other actions committed individually or collectively, from 20 June 1930 to 10 December 1930, by the representatives of the state or the province, by the military or civil authorities, by the local guards or militiamen, or by any civilian having helped the above or acted on their behalf, during the pursuit and extermination of the revolts which broke out in Ercis, Zilan, Aúgrıdağ and the surrounding areas, including Pulumur in Erzincan province and the area of the First Inspectorate, will not be considered as crimes.' Quoted in *ibid.*, p. 65. The First Inspectorate covered a far larger area than the actual revolt. See also Hikmet Özdemir, *Rejim ve Asker*, (Istanbul: Afa Yayınları, 1989).

[121] *Milliyet*, 31 August 1930, quoted in *ibid.*, p. 65.

[122] *Milliyet*, 16 September 1930, quoted in *ibid.*, pp. 65-6.

[123] Tekin Alp justified such actions as ensuring a homogeneous Turkish culture in areas where the populations had 'not assimilated enough to Turkish culture.' See Tekin Alp, *Le Kemalisme* (Paris: Alcan, 1937), p. 255. Alp (a *Dönme* previously called Moise Cohen) had been an ideologue for the Young Turk regime. He

legalised the evacuation of certain areas including one, Dersim (now Tunceli), which was not then totally government controlled, and where three Turkish army corps were engaged in fighting a guerrilla war until the end of 1938. Kurdish villages were closely policed, the use of Kurdish language, dress, folklore and names prohibited, and the area remained under martial law until 1946.[124]

As we have seen, the Kemalist state actively pursued an aggressive Turkish nationalism. The Kemalist catchphrase 'What happiness to call oneself a Turk' was displayed in all schools and army barracks throughout the country, as well as being prominently displayed in public places. In this view, there was no place for a separate Kurdish identity. In the 'Turkish History Thesis,' the Kurds were of Turanian origin, had come from Central Asia five thousands years ago and now spoke a 'dialect' which was a 'mixture of old Turkish, Persian, Arabic and Armenian' as 'lost in their inaccessible mountains, the Kurds ended up by forgetting their mother tongue and fell under the influence of their Persian neighbours.'[125] They were henceforth to be designated as 'mountain Turks' by the Kemalist state.

However, the Kemalist 'revolution' was not as thorough going as, for example, that of Stalin in the USSR in the same period. Kemalism was essentially the creed of the new rulers in the urban centres; while the education process and the army were seen as modes of transmission for the new ideology, much of the countryside continued to live according to traditional, usually folk-Islamic, values. Here one must take issue with Metin Heper's assertion that '[A]mong anthropologists there is a consensus that the secularizing reforms had a strong impact in Turkey not only at the level of the elite but also at the mass level.'[126] On the contrary, numerous anthropological works stress the reverse: that

---

later whole-heartedly embraced Kemalism and became something of an official ideologue for the new regime (see below). Along with Karabet Devletliyan, another pro-Kemalist from the minorities, he was even exempted the Capital Tax because of this – see Ökte, *op. cit.*, p. 74.

[124] D. McDowall, *op. cit.*, p. 38.

[125] Quoted in Kendal, in Chaliand, *op. cit.*, p. 69.

[126] M. Heper, 'Political Culture as a Dimension of Compatibility' in M. Heper, Ayşe Öncü and H. Kramer (eds), *Turkey and the West: Changing Political and Cultural Identities* (London: I.B. Tauris, 1993), p. 9. Heper is a political scientist, and in many ways a product of Kemalism.

at the mass level, society was not greatly influenced by Kemal's sweeping reforms. Traditional modes of thought continued, at least until the integration of the countryside into the economy in the 1950s, thanks to mass migration to the urban centres. This was especially so in the underdeveloped southeast.[127] The relevance of this lack of Kemalist penetration has been seen in the last twenty or so years with the rise of a rival Kurdish nationalism. This was a more 'modern' nationalism than the tribal-cum-religious revolts of Sheikh Said and others. It was helped by Barzani's success in Iraq, competed with the Turkish state for the loyalties of Kurds, and to an extent succeeded due to the obvious strength of its claim based on language. This is covered in greater detail in Chapter 7.

Aggressive Kemalist Turkish nationalism also affected other non-Turkish Muslim groups. Whether of Laz, Circassian, Slav, Albanian or Georgian descent they, like the Kurds, were actively discouraged from using their mother tongue in public or in written form, especially during the *Vatandaş Türkçe Konuş* movement.[128]

---

[127] See particularly, P. Stirling, *Turkish Village* (Weidenfeld and Nicolson, 1965); C. Delaney, *The Seed and the Soil: Gender and Cosmology in Turkish Village Society* (Berkeley: California University Press, 1991); and P. Stirling (ed.), *Culture and Economy: Changes in Turkish Villages* (Huntingdon: Eothen Press, 1993). For a firsthand account of village life and the failure of Kemalist penetration in this period see M. Makal, *Bizim Köy*, translated as *A Village in Anatolia* (London: Vallentine Mitchell, 1954). These standard anthropological works deal with Turkish villages in Anatolia. For Kurdish village society in the southeast, which remained even more 'traditional' with continuation of patron-client relations etc. see L. Yalçin, 'Kurdish tribal organization and local political processes' in A. Finkel and N. Sirman (eds) *Turkish State, Turkish Society* (London: Routledge, 1990), and Bruinessen, *op. cit.*, *passim*.

[128] Migrant families from Georgia related to me how such usage of their mother tongue was forbidden. A Cherkez respondent recalled how she spoke Cherkez at home but it was frowned upon outside. While there were no actual penalties, she and her relatives strongly felt that it would count against them in terms of job prospects, etc., if it were known that they spoke another mother tongue. Of course this could have been merely mild paranoia, but it does illustrate the pressures of the times. The Kurds did face actual punishment. Kurdish nationalist Musa Anter in his memoirs (*Hatıralarım*, Istanbul: Yönayncılık, 1991) p. 29, relates how Kurdish-speakers were fined according to a tariff for every Kurdish word spoken. This prohibition on Kurdish remained until the multi-party system took over in 1950. It was reintroduced following the 1980 coup, to be once more rescinded in 1991 (see Chapter 7).

Leading CHF member Recep Peker spelt this out in October 1931 when he said:

From our conception, nationalism has no connection with the masses whose political destinies are separated from ours. We preserve a warm affectionate interest for Turks outside our frontiers, as an independent state, as belonging to other states ... In this context we consider as ours those of our fellow citizens who live among us, who politically and socially belong to the Turkish Nation and who have been inculcated with ideas of sentiments like 'Kurdism', 'Circassianism' and even 'Lazism' and 'Pomakism'. We consider it as our duty to end, by sincere efforts, these false conceptions inherited from the absolutist regime [i.e. the Ottoman Empire] and which are the product of long historical oppression. Today's scientific truths do not admit the possibility of an independent existence for a Nation of several thousand nor even a million.[129]

Leaving aside the notion that there is a minimum number, of over one million, below which a nation cannot exist, this speech underlines certain key elements in Kemalist thinking on the nation. While there are Turks outside the new Turkey, they are not claimed as part of the nation. In spite of the romantic ethnic components of Kemalist nationalism, irredentism is not on the agenda. In line with the territorial model of nationalism, all citizens within the territory of the Turkish state are, or are to become, Turks. As Tekin Alp stated:

Regarding the question of national minorities, the Turkish Kemalist has never admitted this principle. The New Turkey does not recognise in its citizens any but Turks. If today the New Turkey, due to past survival, includes several hundred thousand citizens who have not yet adopted Turkish culture, it is certain that in several dozen years they will have done so. The Kemalist regime is based on national unity.[130]

However, for Tekin Alp, this does not mean 'renouncing Kurdish, Laz, Armenian or Jewish particularism.' The principle is, he asserts, demonstrated in countries like France, Italy and Britain where

[129] Quoted in Tekin Alp, *Le Kemalisme*, pp. 253-4.
[130] *Ibid.*, p. 267.

the Scots, Welsh, Bretons and Corsicans 'jealously preserve their national peculiarities but are not regarded as minorities.'[131] As regards the Christian minorities' guaranteed protection under the Lausanne Treaty, Tekin Alp denies the validity of such treaty guarantees:

> Treaties with special chapters for minority protection do not solve problems but aggravate them ... the provisions signed by İnönü are now a dead letter due to the Kemalist Revolution ... the government has ended the Muslim/non-Muslim divide by laicism ... The fundamental Law has recognised as Turks all the citizens of the country without distinction of race or religion, and has prepared the way for a complete integration of minority elements into Turkism.

But he adds that in practice this has still not happened with non-Muslim minorities like Greeks, Armenians and Jews because 'the watertight compartments that separated them before Kemalism are still not completely destroyed.'[132] However, he believes that in time the process of assimilation will be complete.[133]

On the other hand, the 'Outside Turks' (those who remained outside the new territory) were welcome to come to Turkey – indeed they were seen as a resource for aiding the Turkicisation of the territory and the building of the nation, especially in potentially problematic border areas. The Minister of the Interior at the Fourth CHP Congress made this clear when he said:

> One of our resources to arrive at this end is the flow of immigrants. Large numbers continually arrive from Romania, Bulgaria and Yugoslavia. They make up a contingent of 1,200,000. Being unprepared we have tried to dam this flow. We will have the possibility of installing 600,000 of them in Thrace in the Dardanelles region in the space of five to six years.[134]

Tekin Alp goes on to comment that 'Kemalist Turkey throws

[131] *Ibid.*, p. 268. This is somewhat problematic, since the Welsh and Scots are regarded as national minorities. It also remains unexplained how, in the Turkish case, such people can 'preserve their peculiarities' when they have to speak the dominant language and adopt the unified culture, as Tekin Alp suggests.

[132] *Ibid.*, p. 269.

[133] *Ibid.*, p. 270-1.

[134] *Ibid.*, p. 256.

open its doors not only to Muslim Turks from Romania but also Christian Turks called "Kara Oğuz" [Gagauz] who live in Bessarabia in compact masses.'[135]

The large Turkish (as opposed to Kurdish) Alevi community appeared to have been supportive of Kemalism. Here, the secular nature of the new regime appears crucial. For Alevis, this was preferable to a Sunni regime in which they would face possible persecution. Alevis often claim that they were instrumental in

---

[135] *Ibid.* As regards the question of who is eligible for Turkish nationality, there have been three successive laws defining nationality in modern times in the Ottoman Empire and the Turkish republic. The first was in 1869, with the Ottoman nationality legislation which followed in the footsteps of similar European legislation. This was replaced in 1929 and again in 1964. According to Law 403 of 11 February 1964, Turkish nationality is given from birth to those born within or outside the country of a Turkish father; or those with a Turkish mother but unable to assume the father's nationality; or illegitimate children of Turkish mothers (Article 1). Citizenship is also given from birth to illegitimate children with foreign mothers who are either claimed by Turkish citizens or who can by law be attributed to Turkish citizens (Article 2). Adoption in childhood by Turkish citizens is another option (Article 3). Citizenship is available to those born in Turkey who are unable to assume their mother's or father's nationality. Such legislation is common to many countries, and displays a common mix of ethnicity and territorial criteria. A standard law textbook at Ankara University, Erdogan Göger, *Türk Tabiiyet Hukuku* (Ankara: 3rd edn, 1975, p. 18), notes that the Prussian nationality law of 18 December 1842 which, in line with German romantic ethnic nationalism, for the first time stressed the superior claims of blood (i.e. race and ethnicity) over residence, opened the way for similar nationality laws. The Ottoman law, however, was based more on the 1851 French citizenship law – which was more in line with the territorial aspect than the ethnic one. This law, which Göger sees as being in tune with contemporary ideas on nationality (presumably by not stressing the ethnic component), lasted until Law 1312 of 1 January 1929. However, as Göger asserts, this suffered from important defects in that it aimed at increasing the population after the colossal loss of life in the long wars during and preceding independence, and sacrificed the rights of the individual to those of the state (in line with the étatist/nationalist thinking of the time). This law lasted until Law 403 of 22 May 1964, which is still operational. The evolution of the complexities of the modern concept of nationality is shown by the increase in the number of Articles these successive laws consisted of; 9 in 1869; 17 in 1929 and 48 in 1964. A simpler if less legalistic way of defining who is a Turk is given in school textbooks like *İlkokullar için Sosyal Bilgiler 5* (4th edn, Ministry of Education, 1993), p. 207, which says that anybody despite their language or religion who feels themselves to be a Turk, lives like a Turk and respects himself as one, is a Turk. This is similar to Renan's 'daily plebiscite' (see Chapter 1).

the success of Kemal's journey across Anatolia by drumming up support in the initial phase of the Independence struggle.[136] There are also many parallels between Kemalist republican ideology and the Alevi way of life – such as emphasis on correct conduct, responsibility to the community, and collective music, poetry, dance and song. As a result many *dedes* (Alevi spiritual leaders) venerate Kemal today.[137] Alevi villagers have no sense of attachment to Iran and tend to see Hacı Bektaş (one of the founders of Anatolian Alevism) as a great Turkish leader, with few Arabic (that is Sunni Islamic) influences. More extreme Alevis see him as a representative of pre-Islamic shamanism (supposedly the 'true' Turkish religion).[138] Alevis also use Turkish prayers rather than Arabic ones, and prefer the word *Tann* to *Allah*. This is again reminiscent of early Kemalist attempts to make a Turkish Islamic religion.

In 1926, *Türk Yurdu*, the publication of the Turkist *Türk Ocaği* organisation, even went as far as to claim that the Turkish national ideal was kept alive by the Alevis, who consistently held to the Turkish language instead of Arabic, thus intentionally preserving the Turkish tongue, race and blood.[139] The Alevis were sympathetic to the script reform and the language reforms of the Turkish Language Foundation (*Türk Dil Kurumu*), and regretted its closure after the 1980 coup.[140] It is interesting that while Kemal closed

---

[136] See Cemal Sener, *Atatürk ve Aleviler* (Istanbul: Alev Yayınevi, 1991), p. 12, for the claim that he was smuggled secretly from Alevi village to Alevi village.

[137] D. Shankland, 'Alevi and Sunni in Rural Turkey: Diverse Paths of Change' (unpublished Ph.D. thesis, Darwin College, Cambridge, 1993), p. 172, and footnote 20. Shankland points out that according to republican ideology, folk dances are a way to celebrate the Turkish roots of the nation, and that there is now even a government department to collect folk tales. Every child is taught folk dances while at school and folk dances and folk tales are still the subject of government conferences and publications such as *Türk Halk Kültürü Araştırmaları* (Ankara, 1991). In villages, school teachers are encouraged to make pupils perform folkdances as a way of celebrating national holidays, and thus reinforce republican history and national solidarity. While the song and dance aspect of this clashes with strict Sunni religious believers, it poses no problems for Alevis, who traditionally use dance as a way of celebrating their culture.

[138] *Ibid.*, p. 174.

[139] Baha Sait, 'Türkiyede Alevi, Zumreleri', *Türk Yurdu* no. 21, September 1926, quoted in J.K. Birge, *The Bektashi Order of Dervishes* (London: Hartford, 1937), p. 16.

[140] Shankland, *op. cit.*, p. 175.

down the *tarikats*, which included the Bektaşis, the Alevis were often held up as original Turkish patriots. In 1930 the government's education department printed 3,000 copies of a book of 180 Bektaşi poets, with biographical data and selections from their religious verses, which were seen as examples of the original Turkish language and original Turkish literary forms.[141] A forty-instalment series in the daily *Yeni Gün* in early 1931 on the Bektaşis by Ziya Bey (himself a Bektaşi) claimed that the Bektaşi rituals, in which men and women are present and women are treated as social equals, were continuations of old Turkish national rites. The articles ended by agreeing with the view that since government action had accomplished what the Bektaşis had long stood for – e.g. abolition of the Sunni Caliphate and freedom and equality for women – there was no longer need for the order.[142]

While the proscribing of the Bektaşi order must have been opposed by many Alevis, in practice this would not have much significance as they had long experience of operating semi-clandestinely during the Ottoman period, when Sunni orthodoxy was more pronounced. In addition, the Kemalist cadres did not really push their revolution right down to the village level. On the other hand, it is certain that many Alevis, probably a majority, saw the Kemalist regime as an improvement over the previous ones, by whom they were always regarded as suspect. The presence of large numbers of Alevis in a crucial central area (they tend to live in an arc to the east of the capital) and the fact that they saw the Kemalist reforms as beneficial to them, must surely have been a factor in the success of the reforms.[143]

---

[141] Sadettin Nüzhet, *Bektaşi, Şairleri* (Istanbul, 1930), referred to in Brige, *op. cit.*, p. 17.

[142] *Yeni Gün*, 26 January–8 March 1931 referred to in Birge, *op. cit.*, pp. 20 and 85.

[143] Given this, it is perhaps ironic that Shankland (*op. cit.*) and others like Ragner Ness, conclude that Alevism as a way of life is seriously on the decline in Turkey mainly because the Alevis cannot integrate into modern Turkey without huge difficulties. This is primarily due to contradictions between their way of life, with their traditional hierarchies and *dede* authority figures, and life in a modern state, especially in the cities (see Chapter 8). R. Ness, 'Being an Alevi Muslim in S.W. Anatolia and Norway: the impact of migration on a heterodox Turkish community' in T. Gerholm and Y.G. Lithman (eds), *The New Islamic Presence in Western Europe* (London: Mansell, 1988). See also Chapter 8.

The above discussion has concentrated on the official nationalist ideology of the Kemalist state. From this it can be seen that Kemalist nationalism displays strong elements of Smith's 'ethnic' and 'territorial' models as well as much of Gellner's state-building/high-culture-forming paradigm. The ideology of Kemalist nationalism was not fixed from the start. In particular, its relationship with Islam underwent a fundamental change in the initial republican period. Whereas at first Islam was exploited as a rallying cry in the independence struggle, and was used to define who were to be the new Turks (that is the Muslim population of Anatolia), this was quickly abandoned. Instead, attempts were made to relegate Islam to the private sphere. In its place, language and history were stressed as the elements which both defined and cemented the fledgling Turkish nation.

To counteract the long and strong influence of Islam as one of the main factors of national identity in Ottoman times, the pre-Islamic history of the Turks was given great emphasis, as was the purification of the language to make it more 'Turkish'. This pre-history was also used to underwrite the Turkish claim over Anatolia as the Turkish homeland. Part of this process entailed the intrusion of strong ethnic components in the official nationalist ideology, which saw the Turks held up as the founders of many civilisations and eventually found expression in the bizarre 'Sun Language Theory'. This phase saw the Turks held up as culturally superior to other nations.

While this can be seen as equating to Kedourie's model of German ethnic nationalism, with its innate chauvinism and stress on the purification and superiority of the given language, Kemalist nationalism continued simultaneously to display strong elements of Smith's territorial model, both by adamantly negating any form of irredentism (with the possible exception of Hatay/Alexandretta) and by refusing to recognise minorities within the state. In practice, this entailed assimilation and pressure culminating in the infamous Capital Tax of 1942. The large Kurdish minority of the southeast posed a special problem for the new state, and necessitated repeated large-scale military action to subdue revolts. These, while not nationalist in the modern sense, certainly entailed a direct challenge to the secularist nationalist ideology.

In line with the model detailed in Chapter 1, Kemalist nationalism was essentially totalitarian in its attitude, and all competing forms of nationalism, whether pan-Turkic (that is a purer form of the Kedourie/Smith ethnic model), proto-Kurdish, or based on Islamic values, were suppressed. The 1930s saw a *Gleichschaltung* of political and cultural life, in which the CHP party-state took over all forms of cultural activity and the official ideology was propagated through the educational system. The army was used in a similar role as a 'builder of the nation'. However, unlike examples such as the Stalinist regime with its brutal upheavals in the 1930s, the Kemalist revolution was not totalitarian in practice.[144] While the masses of the population outwardly accepted the new rules (or were seen by outside observers to outwardly accept them), in reality they tended to carry on as before. While the great reforms were carried out in the centres of power in the cities, for millions of citizens they remained relatively marginal, at least initially.

Thus, the Kemalist revolution, while certainly spreading its ideas to large sections of the urban population, did not penetrate all of society. This allowed large sections of the population to carry on using other criteria for self-identification. Often, this remained the traditional village unit. In this way many people were largely unaffected by the strident new Turkish nationalism, or by any other membership of a greater 'imagined community' other than the religious one. This continued until the greater mass mobility of the 1950s and 1960s. They were thus not thoroughly inculcated with Kemalist nationalism, and were prone to competing variants – notably, that of Islam. For Kurdish mother-tongue speakers, a modern Kurdish nationalism only began to emerge later, aided by events in Iraq. These two competing currents will be dealt with more fully in chapters 6 and 7. The next chapter concentrates on the more extreme 'ethnic' variant which, although controlled and subdued by the Kemalist state, was not completely destroyed, and came to the fore as a competitor to the idea of the territorial 'nation' at certain times.

---

[144] Paul Stirling notes that the Kemalist elites charged with enforcing the new rules were themselves not keen on their ruthless application, while 95% of the population were still engaged in traditional occupations, and 75% still lived in villages in 1950; see his 'Social change and Social Control in Republican Turkey' in *Papers and Discussion, Türkiye İş-Bankası International Symposium on Atatürk* (17-22 May 1981) (Ankara: TISA, 1981), pp. 583-8.

5

THE GREY WOLF: THE PAN-TURKIST FRINGE

This chapter will look at the ideology of pan-Turkism and the radical right, the study of which has remained a somewhat neglected area. It has been a consistent competitor to the official secularist Kemalism, as detailed in Chapter 4. As we have seen, the official Kemalist nationalism resolutely turned its back on pan-Turkism and all forms of 'Turanism', and under the slogan 'Peace at home, peace abroad' pursued a nationalist policy of attempting to create a Turkish secular national consciousness which would include all, or virtually all, the citizens within the boundaries of the Turkish Republic. As we shall see, this ideology, despite claiming to speak on behalf of all those it defined as Turks and simultaneously negating all other competitors,[1] has had and continues to have a number of rivals who likewise claim to speak on behalf of the Turkish nation. As shown in the previous chapter, Kemalist secularist nationalism, despite exhibiting some tendencies towards Smith's 'ethnic' model, can be seen as predominantly 'civic' in its underlying principles of nation-building within the given boundaries along the lines of the Gellner modernisation paradigm. However, pan-Turkism and its associated nationalist ideological variants of the radical right fall more squarely within the 'ethnic' model.

Pan-Turkism and radical right politics in Turkey up to 1960

The year 1960 is seen as something of a watershed in Turkish

---

[1] As noted in Chapter 1, this is a common feature of nationalisms, which all display similar totalitarian pretensions in claiming to uniquely speak for the 'nation' however defined.

politics. Before the 1960 coup, Turkey can effectively be seen as a one-party tutelary polity. It can be argued that the multi-party system which allowed the change in government in 1950 was in reality an ersatz one – one-party rule by the Republican People's Party (CHP) was replaced by one-party rule by the Democrat Party (DP). For most of the 1950s, the CHP programme was not radically different to that of the DP. Only after 1960 did it become possible to differentiate the DP from the CHP in conventional political terms like 'left' or 'right'.[2] Also, while the 1924 Constitution had few safeguards to protect fundamental rights and left power firmly in the hands of the National Assembly, allowing Adnan Menderes and the DP to effectively establish an 'elected dictatorship', the 1961 Constitution allowed the formation and legal operation of radical parties from both ends of the political spectrum. Furthermore, the introduction of proportional representation made it possible for such parties to take an active part in the nation's political life.

This came at a time of dramatic social change. Industrialisation was transforming the country and large numbers of people were flocking to the cities and establishing themselves in squatter settlements (*gecekondular*). In 1950 the industrial working class and their families accounted for about 5 per cent of the population; by 1965 it was over 20 per cent, while wage earners had risen in the same period from under 400,000 to almost 2 million – of whom 600,000 were in the agricultural sector.[3] At the same time improved communications had resulted in greater social mobility and greater social awareness.

Before 1960, radical-right politics was almost exclusively confined to advocates of pan-Turkism (*Türkçülük*) or Turanism (*Turanalık*) – the uniting of all Turkic peoples in one state[4] – and

---

[2] W. Hale, 'The Turkish Army in Politics 1960-73' in A. Finkel and N. Sirman (eds), *Turkish State, Turkish Society* (London: Routledge, 1990), pp. 53-77.

[3] K.H. Karpat, 'The Turkish Left', *Journal of Contemporary History* vol. 1, no. 2, 1966, pp. 169-71.

[4] Although Turanism originally had a wider meaning than pan-Turkism and referred to all peoples considered to be Turanic, thus including Hungarians, Finns and Estonians, by the 1920s the two terms came to be seen as interchangeable and referred only to the unity of all Turkic peoples. It is in this sense that the two terms will be used in this study. See Jacob M. Landau, *Pan-Turkism in Turkey* (London: Hurst, 1981), p. 1.

was not politically organised along party lines. This Pan-Turkism – as detailed in Chapter 3 – originated in the late nineteenth century in intellectual circles, in no small part as a reaction to pan-Slavism in the Russian Empire. Many of the leading figures in the early days of pan-Turkism were *émigrés* from the Russian Empire. The Young Turk period, especially during the First World War, saw Pan-Turkism as the ruling ideology for a short time. Members of the nationalist organisation *Türk Ocağı* (Turkish Hearth) first founded in 1911 and officially established on 12 March 1912, quickly grew in numbers from 3,000 in 1914 to 30,000 by 1920. Writers like Ziya Gökalp, the main Young Turk ideologue, espoused the cause, and there was 'hardly an intellectual during this period not captivated by the spell of Turanism.'[5] However, the demise of the adventurer Enver Paşa in the Caucasus and Central Asia, chasing the Turanist dream, and the success of Mustafa Kemal (Atatürk) in founding the new Turkish Republic changed all this.

As shown in Chapter 4, Kemal, aided perhaps by Lenin's repudiation of pan-Slavism, firmly rejected all Turanist notions. Many pan-Turkists joined Kemal in the War of Liberation and were co-opted into the new regime. However, some who joined Kemal, like Yusuf Akçura, Mehmet Emin (Yurdakul) and Ahmet Ağaoğlu, did not entirely abandon Turanist goals. The *Türk Ocağı*, closed by the British in 1920, resumed activity in 1924, and by 1930 had 257 branches and 32,000 members. It displayed Turanist tendencies, especially in its publication *Türk Yurdu*, and potential members were even screened for racial purity. Atatürk tried in 1927 to curb such activity by putting them under CHP control, but this was not wholly successful and they were closed down in 1931. However, pan-Turkist symbols like the Grey Wolf (*Bozkurt*) were used by the state on stamps and currency and the government even approved a resolution by the National Turkish Student Union to have the emblem affixed on university caps. The policies pursued by Atatürk in building a Turkish national consciousness, as detailed in Chapter 4, to some extent coincided with such currents. As Islam was rejected as a basis of social cohesion and relegated to private life, the new state exalted Turkish-

---

[5] Mehmet A. Ağaoğulları, 'The Ultranationalist Right' in I.C. Schick and E.A. Tonsk (eds), *Turkey in Transition – New Perspectives* (Oxford University Press, 1987), p. 182.

ness, and Atatürk 'even provided material for racists.'[6] However, the racist currents can be seen as a unifying element rather than a divisive one. Whereas for example in Nazi Germany minorities were seen as foreign bodies to be uncovered and removed, in Turkey after the mass population exchanges based on religious not ethnic criteria, non-Turkish Muslims like the Kurds were officially seen as Turks and subjected to assimilation. This exaltation of Turkishness in the drive for promoting national unity reached its apogee in the 'Turkish History Thesis' and the 'Sun Language Theory' (see Chapter 4).

Thus, the new regime assimilated some Turanist and pan-Turkist elements and co-opted their ideologues. All saw the survival of the new republic as essential, even if Kemalists saw this as the end, while Turanists saw it as the beginning, with the new state providing the nucleus for a future 'Greater Turkey'. Despite the *Türk Ocağı* membership, Turanism had remained limited to a relatively small circle and did not serve as a serious threat to the new regime, unlike religion, which in 1925 did serve as vehicle for serious protest.[7] The authorities, however, continued to see pan-Turkism as a rival to its own version of Turkish nationalism, and in the 1920s along with the closing of the *Türk Ocakları* several *émigré* periodicals were closed down and the import of others banned.[8]

However, the new regime's education policies can paradoxically be seen as having aided and nurtured a new generation of pan-Turkists who manifested more open racist attitudes than the 'first generation' like Gökalp (who died in 1924) and Akçura and Ağoğlu (both of whom died in the 1930s). In 1931 the *Atsız* Review by Hüseyin Nihal Atsız appeared; students organised demonstrations in support of the 'Outside Turks' (*Dış Türkler*) and against the annexation of Hatay. Landau[9] identifies five Pan-Turkist groups

---

[6] *Ibid.*, pp. 185-7.
[7] As in the initial period of Turkish nationalism in the late 19th and early 20th century (see Chapter 3), many leading pan-Turkists originated from outside Turkey, especially from the USSR. For example, the militant pan-Turk ideologue, Zeki Velidi Toğan (Ahmet Zeki Validov), before his move to Turkey in 1925 was briefly president of the Bashkirian Soviet Republic (1919-20). In Turkey he was a professor but was purged in 1933; *ibid.*, footnote 44 on p. 209.
[8] *Ibid.*
[9] Landau, *Pan-Turkism*, pp. 93-4.

in the inter-war period: the first led by the distinguished Professor Ahmed Zeki Velidi Toğan (1879-1970), who was born in Turkistan; the second led by the openly racist Atsız (1905-75) and his brother Necdet Sançar (1910-75); the third led by Riza Nur (1879-1942), a one-time ally of Atatürk who later pronounced a form of 'Islamic nationalism' akin to that of Necmettin Erbaken in the 1970s;[10] the fourth led by the racist Reha Oğuz Türkkan (b. 1920); and finally those who looked back to the ideas of Gökalp and others and were based around the periodical *Cınaraltı* (1941-5). All these groups were united in being heavily anticommunist, and in aiming to 'make Turkey great again'.[11] In the 1930s the *Kadro* movement – 'a superficial combination of Marxism, nationalism and corporatism with a strong dose of élitism'[12] – and other authoritarian tendencies also surfaced, but the government remained in control. *Kadro* was shut down in 1934. The trend towards a mono-party state along Italian fascist lines favoured by the Recep Peker faction in the CHP ended with Atatürk's intervention and Peker's resignation in 1936.[13]

Pan-Turkist sentiments revived on the eve of the Second World War and grew stronger after the Nazi attack on the USSR in 1941, with the Germans apparently pursuing similar policies towards Turkey as in the First World War.[14] Pan-Turkist sympathies were also evident in the armed forces in this period – a direct parallel with the First World War, when the weakness of Tsarist Russia

[10] J.M. Landau, *Radical Politics in Modern Turkey* (Leiden: E.J. Brill, 19074), p. 192.

[11] *Ibid.*, p. 199.

[12] Ergun Özbudun, 'The Nature of the Kemalist Political Regime' in A. Kazancıgil and E. Özbudun (eds), *Ataturk: Founder of a Modern State* (London: Hurst, 1981), p. 92.

[13] Feroz Ahmad, 'The Political Economy of Kemalism' in Kazancıgil and Özbudun, *op. cit.*, p. 160.

[14] German aims were not clear in this respect, with the Foreign Ministry apparently against such actions but the military in favour. The Germans set up units from captured Soviet prisoners such as the SS East Muslim Division, the Timur Battalion and the Turkestan Legion, which fought for pan-Turkic aims. See R. Tuzmuhamedov, *How the National Question Was Solved in Soviet Central Asia (A Reply to Falsifiers)* (Moscow: Progress, 1973), p. 42-5, and Baymirza Hayit, *Sovyetler Birligi'ndeki Türklüğün ve İslamın Bazı Meseleleri* (Istanbul: Türk Dünyası Araştırmarları Vakfi Yayını, 1987), pp. 174-207, and *passim* for a picture of pan-Turkist claims over Soviet territory as far as Siberia.

also gave rise to pan-Turkist dreams. However, as the war developed it became apparent that Nazi Germany would be defeated. The authorities clamped down on pan-Turkism, with the celebrated trial in 1944 following the anti-communist demonstration on 3 May 1944. Those tried included Toğan, Türkkan, Atsız and his brother Sançar as well young army officers like Alparslan Türkeş and Fethi Tevetoğlu.[15] However, renewed tension with the USSR immediately after the war over Soviet claims on territory and the Bosphorous allowed greater freedom to all forms of anti- communism, including pan-Turkism. In 1946 the *Türk Kültür Ocağı* – essentially a nationalist grouping with pan-Turkist tendencies –was set up to spread and defend Turkish culture from internal and external attacks by foreign ideologies.[16]

What were the essential components of pan-Turkism in this period? Atsız in 1950 defined a pan-Turkist as:

A Turk who believes in the superiority of the Turkish race, respecting its national past and ready to sacrifice himself for the ideals of Turkdom, especially in the fight against Moscow, the implacable enemy.[17]

Ağaoğulları[18] identifies five basic tenets of pan-Turkist ideology. These include: Turanism; racism – including the rejection of Turkish-speaking 'alien blood' (for example the Jews of Turkey) and supporting a state based on racial unity; militarism (Atsız claimed that nations could only survive through war, and his brother Sançar wrote that 'Turk, army and war are inseparable'); anti-communism (Atsız defined communists as 'Enemies of race and family, opponents of religion and war, ... excessive fondness for the minorities in our country ... attacking nationalism as racism ...'[19]); and what he calls 'other components', which include the perceived need for a disciplined hierarchical society, obedience, glorification of the leader and self-sacrifice for the state. These lead him to favour a single-party authoritarian state headed by a single leader along fascist or national socialist lines. However, this

---

[15] Ağaoğulları, *op. cit.*, p. 188.

[16] Landau, *Pan-Turkism*, p. 130.

[17] Quoted in *ibid.*, p. 127.

[18] Ağaoğulları, *op. cit.*, pp. 190-1.

[19] *Ibid.*, footnote 64 to p. 191.

ultranationalist right remained in the wilderness in the 1950s, due in no small part to the success of the DP. In 1959 Karpat could state:

> The developments of the past ten years – the relative democratisation, the increase in economic activity, and the new general atmosphere in favour of tolerance – have deprived the racialists of suitable grounds for success and have isolated them as a small group lacking relationship with reality.[20]

The coup of 27 May 1960 and the young radical officers

The prime movers of the coup of 27 May 1960 were middle-ranking army officers who had become increasingly impatient with the 'elected dictatorship' of Menderes and the DP. They stressed economic development and social justice and some were highly ambivalent about multi-party democracy – or at least viewed its introduction in Turkey by İnönü as premature – and openly preferred authoritarian methods. In view of the later prominence in radical-right circles of some of these radical young officers, especially their leader, Colonel Alparslan Türkeş, it is worth studying what they wanted in 1960 in greater detail, and why the fourteen leaders of this group were expelled on 13 November 1960 from the ruling National Unity Committee (NUC) set up after the coup.

The Turkish officer corps had inherited a long Ottoman tradition of the virtual identity of state authority with military power, amplified by the nineteenth-century reform programme, which aimed primarily at modernising the armed forces. As a result, it saw (and continues to see) itself as a modernising political force and in effect a separate class in Turkish society rather than a mere instrument of one or another class.[21] Atatürk had to a large extent withdrawn the army from politics in the sense of day-to-day government but the officer corps saw itself in the continuing vanguard role as the defender of the republic and 'Atatürkism' as it perceived it.[22]

---

[20] Kemal H. Karpat, 'Turkey's Politics', quoted in *ibid.*, p. 191.

[21] Hale, *op. cit.*, p. 53.

[22] *Ibid.*, *passim.*

One of the leading radical officers, Muzaffer Özdağ, the youngest member of the NUC and then close associate of Türkeş, explained their viewpoint:

The coup was performed to prevent civil war. The Turkish army is a national army not an imperial army ... The army belongs to the nation and is not for or against any one party but serves the people and the Constitution and is subject to the national will ...

The conflict with the fourteen was, according to Özdağ, over how long the NUC should remain in power before reverting to civilian government. Özdağ states that the majority of the NUC shared his view and that of the other radicals that they should remain in power for some years 'as a non-political government of national unity to make the new Constitution and usher in reforms.' However, the senior Generals in the NUC disagreed. What were the reforms the radicals envisaged? Özdağ answers that they were:

Certain social reforms especially in education and the social services as well as financial reforms and rapid industrialisation to be undertaken by the state rather than private enterprise. The aim was to establish the legal basis for national unity.

It seems that the officers saw themselves in classic nationalist manner as representing 'the national will'. Anti-communism was a strong factor in their outlook. The analogy used by Özdağ was with the British in the Second World War:

The Russia of 1960 was our neighbour then, and was just as much a threat to us as Hitler's Germany was to Britain in the 1930s.[23]

Thus, the fourteen wanted dynamic authoritarian rule, akin to that of Atatürk, to secure the social justice, mass education and economic development which the politicians, due to their sectarian and petty interests, were apparently unable to do. Although the authoritarian strains and proposed reforms of the fourteen bear resemblances to the radical rightist programmes which came later (see below), the lack of any real organisation or of any apparent

---

[23] Quotes from an Interview with M. Özdağ, Ankara, 15 July 1992.

ideology other than that of 'doing what was needed for the country' (as seen by the military as 'objective' representatives of the state) indicate that they should not at this time be seen as a radical nationalist force. Things were very different when they returned from their various exiles in the mid-1960s.

Despite the above, it is apparent that Türkeş at least was, even at this time, attempting to organise and move into politics properly with a clear nationalist platform. The NUC, despite sharing the suspicion of the bureaucratic intelligentsia towards the apparent Islamic resurgence, did not repudiate the DP policy of greater leeway for Islam. Accepting that Islam was a vital ingredient in the Turkish character, they accepted the newly set up *Imam-Hatip* schools and the advanced Islamic Institute opened in 19 November 1959 and tried to encourage the Turkification of Islam.[24] Türkeş, however, wanted to substitute nationalist ideology for Islam through education and propaganda and tried to set up the Union of Ideal and Culture in June 1960 for this purpose.[25] This would indicate that at this time Türkeş saw Islam as a rival ideology to his view of Turkish nationalism. He was also in the process of forming a political party with two post-coup cabinet ministers, Ekrem Alican – a former dissident DP member who joined the Freedom Party and was then Finance Minister in the post-coup government, and who formed the New Turkey Party – and Abdullah Gözübüyük.[26] Both these developments were curtailed by his ousting from the NUC in November 1960 and subsequent exile to New Delhi.

Radical rightist organisations and their ideology

Outside the army, nationalist currents were aided by the persecution of Cypriot Turks by Greek Cypriot communists (see Chapter 9). In March 1961 there were marches in support of the Turks in Kirkuk, who were facing pressure from the Iraqi authorities.[27] The new political situation of the 1960s allowed the formation

---

[24] F. Ahmad, *The Turkish Experiment in Democracy, 1950-75*, (London: Hurst, 1977), p. 375. See also Chapter 6.

[25] *Ibid.*, p. 374. The idea was vetoed by Gürsel and was one of the reasons for the expulsion of the 14 from the junta.

[26] *Ibid.*, footnote to p. 233.

[27] Landau, *Radical*, p. 201.

and operation of left-wing parties and a corresponding rise on the right in reaction – anti-communism being a basic tenet of all right-wing groups. As early as November 1962, meetings in Istanbul of the newly formed Worker's Party of Turkey (TIP) were attacked by organised mobs.[28] The Association for Fighting Communists in Turkey, originally operating in 1950-3 under Necdet Sançar's leadership and based in Zonguldak, then in Istanbul from 1956-60 under Burhanettin Şener, involving students and professors, was revived in 1963 in Izmir. Pan-Turkist in its inspiration and strongly supported by conservative Islamic circles, it reportedly had 110 branches throughout Turkey in 1965, and President Cemal Gürsel even briefly stood as honorary president. In August 1964 the Union of Turkish Nationalists was founded in Ankara from the Association of Turkists, with Necdet Sançar as chairman and branches and 'ocaklar' (hearths) throughout the main urban centres. A rival congress, unequivocally pro-Islamic, was convened in 1967, with a second congress in May 1969 in Istanbul led by rival personalities like Professor Ibrahim Kafesoğlu.[29] However, the first real organisation of the radical right into a political force began in 1963 with the return of Türkeş and others from exile.

The fourteen had kept in touch from their various places of exile, and in May 1963 Türkeş and his then closest associates Rıfat Baykal and Muzaffer Özdağ published a seventy-two-page booklet, *Some Truths (Defences)*.[30] They considered forming their own party but instead decided to take over the Republican Peasants Nation Party (RPNP), a small conservative party that had won 14 per cent of the vote in the 1961 National Assembly elections.[31] A group of supporters joined, followed by Türkeş and four of 'the fourteen' on 31 March 1965. By June that year ten of the fourteen had joined.[32] With ruthless efficiency, Türkeş and his associates rapidly took over the party. At a special congress held on 1 August 1965 the old leaders were defeated and abandoned the party; Türkeş became Chairman with Özdağ Assistant Secretary-General.[33]

---

[28] Ahmad, *Experiment*, p. 219.
[29] Landau, *Radical*, pp. 201-4.
[30] *Ibid.*, p. 207.
[31] *Ibid.*, p. 208.
[32] *Ibid.*, p. 209 and Ağaoğulları, *op. cit.*, p. 193.
[33] *Ibid.*

The party was renamed the Nationalist Action Party (MHP) in 1969. Türkeş personally dominated the radical right until the military coup of 1980. Despite disagreements and resignations like those of Nihal Atsız and other leading pan-Turkists, who themselves tried to dominate the party but were outmanoeuvred by Türkeş,[34] there was no real rival to the MHP in the field of radical-right politics or pan-Turkism in this period. As Landau, writing just before the 1980 coup, stated:

> By its virtual monopolising of Pan-Turkism together with those groups of Idealists close to the party ... the NAP [MHP] has to some extent preempted the Pan-Turkist activities of other groups in Turkey, which must now reckon with the former in all moves they undertake.[35]

Such dominance was no doubt aided by the death in 1970 of the leading pan-Turkist Professor Toğan and the deaths in 1975 of Atsız and his brother Necdet Sançar. (Atsız had been imprisoned in 1973 for writing an article about the Kurds and for criticising presidential speeches on Turkishness, but was pardoned in 1974.)[36]

The situation after the military coup of 1980 was somewhat different, with greater fragmentation evident, as the previous politicians were again allowed to enter the political arena by the military. As the reasons for the various splits and ensuing micro-parties detailed below were ostensibly ideological – although in reality personal rivalry was surely a major factor – a brief survey is in order. Many previous MHP activists joined Özal's Motherland Party (ANAP), where they formed an Islamic nationalist faction with Islamic conservatives led by Mehmet Keçeciler and Mustafa Taşar.[37] Türkeş, who spent four years in detention from September

---

[34] Landau, *Pan-Turkism*, p. 153.

[35] *Ibid.*, p. 166.

[36] Ayşe N. Çağlar, 'The Greywolves as Metaphor' in Finkel and Sirmen, *op. cit.*, p. 86.

[37] This was the so-called 'Holy Alliance' of ex-members of ultra-nationalist and Islamic groups banned by the 1980 coup leaders who resurfaced in ANAP. Keçeciler was mayor of the religious stronghold of Konya before the coup and was vetoed from standing in the 1983 election by Evren. In 1980, a year after the Iranian Revolution, he was a main figure in a rally in Konya calling for the abolition of the secular state and a return to Islamic rule (J. Owen-Davies, Reuter, 20 June 1988 – see also Chapter 6).

1980, was the driving force behind the Nationalist Work Party (MÇP), which was founded on 7 July 1983 as a successor to the MHP, with a similar party programme and ideology. When circumstances allowed, he formally assumed its leadership.[38] An electoral alliance with Erbakan's Welfare Party (RP) and another smaller party to overcome the 10 per cent electoral barrier resulted in the MÇP's gaining nineteen seats in the National Assembly in the October 1991 elections. However, it initially appeared that Türkeş did not have the same control over the radical right as before the coup. On 8 July 1992, six MÇP deputies led by Muhsin Yazıcıoğlu, deputy for Sivas, left the party, taking with them a host of provincial and district level activists, and set up a new party known as the Great Unity Party, with its founding congress to be held in August in Ankara.[39] On 11 July Riza Müftüoğlu, one of the MÇP's vice-presidents, also resigned, saying that the party had become 'too radical'.[40] Some reports[41] indicated that Yazıcıoğlu and his five associates left as they saw MÇP departing too far from Islam. Other reports[42] indicated that Yazıcıoğlu, in view of the global changes with the break-up of the USSR, wanted a more radical policy towards Central Asia – Türkeş was advising against any form of Islamic Union with fellow Turkic nationals in Central Asia despite his activity in places like Baku (see below). Whether the split was ideological or merely one of competing personalities is debatable. Officials in the MÇP HQ stated that there had been disagreements with Yazıcıoğlu for some years before the split. They blamed the lack of discipline among some party supporters, evident in the split, on the fact that until 1987 the party was not well organised, since many young militants remained imprisoned after the coup, and thus outside party control.[43]

[38] He was elected unopposed as leader in December 1991 (TRT TV Ankara, in BBC SWB, 31 December 1991).

[39] *Sabah*, 11 July 1992.

[40] *Cumhuriyet*, 11 July 1992.

[41] *Milliyet*, 8 July 1992.

[42] TRT TV, 20 July 1992. Yazıcıoğlu and his associates, who included Kahraman Maraş MP Ökes Sendiller, were seen as the most radical wing of the MÇP (*Briefing*, no. 896, Ankara, 13 July, 1992).

[43] These militants were said not to read newspapers much, but rather relied on what they were told for information. Interview with MÇP Press attaché, Ahmet Anzerlioğlu and other unnamed MÇP officials, 21 July 1992.

At the same time, Sadi Somuncuoğlu, a former MHP vice-president and cabinet minister (along with Türkeş) in Demirel's first National Front government from 21 July 1977 to 5 January 1978, who had not joined the MÇP, was also organising a rival party. Despite Türkeş's insistence on the 'unique place' of the MÇP in nationalist politics,[44] Somuncuoğlu was not deterred. The lifting of the ban on the use of pre-1980 coup political party names brought the splits to a head, with Türkeş and other leading MÇP members announcing the reopening of the MHP in Ankara on 23 July while Somuncuoğlu simultaneously opened a second, rival MHP at Kocatepe,[45] with Yazıcıoğlu's new party also in the offing.[46] This fragmentation and confusion on the extreme right was aided by the disappearance of the MHP archives after the last pre-coup MHP congress,[47] and Türkeş's advanced age, as his rivals obviously attempted to keep him out of a revived MHP.

However, Türkeş was eventually able to reinstate his authority as 'the leader'. Despite a poor showing in local elections held on 1 November 1992, when the MÇP won only 1.47 per cent of the vote in the twenty or so municipalities contested,[48] Türkeş retained control of his followers in parliament. In March 1993 the breakdown of MPs on the far right was thirteen for the MHP (formerly the MÇP and now once more under Türkeş's control); seven for Yazıcıoğlu's Great Unity Party, which now proposed a Turkish identity which was clearly Islamic, and two for the Nation Party of former Democracy Party leader Aykut Edibalı.[49] The new tensions in the country over the Kurdish issue (see

---

[44] *Cumhuriyet*, 20 July 1992.

[45] *Cumhuriyet*, 23 July 1992.

[46] A factor in the split appears to have been over control of former MHP property. At the time of the military coup, the MHP deliberately transferred its property to Türkeş to avoid possible sequestration. A court later ruled that it did belong to the party and seized it. However, the law under which the old parties were allowed to reopen was amended at the last minute to allow Türkeş to regain control of the property. This amendment was supported by Demirel's True Path Party (DYP). Some critics saw this as a sign that Demirel was again looking to Türkeş and his fellow MÇP MPs as coalition partners in reserve if the coalition with SHP failed; see *Briefing*, nos 893, 22 June, and 896, 13 July 1992.

[47] *Cumhuriyet*, 20 July 1992.

[48] *Briefing*, no. 912, 2 November 1992.

[49] *Briefing*, 929, 1 March 1993, and 1003, 22 August 1994.

below and Chapter 7) saw a revival in the MHP's fortunes, Prime Minister Çiller courting its support by bringing prominent rightist Ayvaz Gökdemir into the cabinet. She also appeared with Türkeş in Yozgat where she spoke of 'unity and togetherness' and kissed the Koran three times in front of an MHP crowd.[50] A further temporary split in MHP ranks occurred on 3 October 1994 when Istanbul MP Tunce Toskay set up Call for Unity Party with other MHP dissidents. However, within a matter of days they had rejoined the fold.[51]

The Türk Ocağı organisation revived

Somuncuoğlu's supporters appear to be strong in the *Türk Ocağı* organisation, which was revived again in 1986, Somuncuoğlu being a member of the nine-person central committee.[52] The *Türk Ocağı* organisation had reopened in 1949 after its closure by Atatürk in 1931 but had been closed again in 1971 after the army 'coup-by-memorandum', and its HQ confiscated and taken over by the Ministry of Culture. In the 1970s its activities were subsumed by the MHP in other organisations, most notably the Association of Hearths of Ideals and later its successor, the Association of Idealist Youth. This was one of the largest groups in Turkey in the 1970s, with about 100,000 members, mostly youths organised in some 1,500 hearths.[53] Although never officially acknowledged, MHP control was often alluded to buy its leaders and generally accepted as such.[54] The new *Türk Ocakları* stress their independence

---

[50] *Briefing*, no. 1003, 22 August 1994. Gökdemir is a DYP member but in the 1970s had close links with the MHP when he was in the Education Ministry. He is the author of *Türk Kimliği* (Ecdad: Ankara, 1990), which is a collection of speeches he made in many conferences, some of which had previously been published in the *Türk Ocağı* publication *Türk Yurdu*. The book is a right-wing nationalist tract which bears many similarities to Türkeş's own writings on the subject of Turkish nationalism, rejecting any notion of other nations within Turkish territory and at the same time pan-Turkist. He also tries to reconcile Turkism with Islam and, without naming him, criticises Atatürk strongly for attempting to remove Islam as a crucial component of Turkish identity.

[51] TRT TV, Ankara, 5 October 1994, in BBC SWB EE/2121, B/7, 8 Oct. 1994.

[52] *Türk Yurdu*, vol. 12, July 1992.

[53] *Çağlar, op. cit.*

[54] Interview with *Türk Ocağı* President Orhan Düzgüneş and Central Committee

from political parties and ostensibly espouse purely cultural aims 'to defend Turkish values.' They view Turkey purely as a unitary state and, while acknowledging some minor cultural differences, deny the existence of any minorities in Turkey. Unsurprisingly, they are especially hostile to all forms of Kurdish nationalism.[55] As such they appear to follow the traditional *Türk Ocaği* line of Turkism/pan-Turkism and see no apparent contradiction in supporting the classic Atatürk line that all those within Turkey's borders belong to the Turkish nation while still claiming affinity with their 'brothers' outside the country, most notably now in Central Asia. In other words, Turkey has no minorities but her neighbours have Turkish minorities.[56]

The chairman, Professor Orhan Düzgüneş, still adhered to aspects of the 'Turkish Historical Thesis' which attempted to show the crucial importance of the pre-Islamic Turkish contribution to civilization. For example, he stated that 'Human Rights are now discussed all over the world, but it is historically proven that Turks established and applied human rights wherever they ruled.' At the same time he claimed that democracy, due to early Islamic practices like the consultative councils, has always been a facet of Turkish history.[57]

Despite the somewhat confused ideology, the *Türk Ocaği* movement, with its forty-one branches and 6,000-7,000 members, has participated in joint ventures with the Ministries of Culture and Education. With the Ministry of Culture, it has since 1991 organised courses for Turkish citizens to learn 'different dialects e.g. Azerbaijani etc.' It claims that it is working 'closely' with the Ministry of Education to explain general questions of nationalism and questions regarding the 'Turkish populations' outside Turkey, as well as explaining to young people such essential components of Turkish culture as music, religion and literature.[58] In this context, *Türk*

---

members Yücel Hacalaoğlu and Kerim Ünal, 22 July 1992, and Landau, *Pan-Turkism*, p. 166.

[55] *Türk Ocağı* interview, and *Güney-Doğu Anadolu'nun Tarihi Kültürel Ekonomik Jeo-Politik ve Sosyal Durumu* (Ankara: Türk Ocakları Merkez İdare Heyeti, 1992), *passim*.

[56] *Türk Ocağı* interview.

[57] *Ibid.*

[58] The attitude to music is especially interesting as it relates directly to notions of what is 'true Turkish culture' and what is not, and thus to the whole

Ocağı is especially hostile to Arabesk music which is seen as foreign and insidious.[59] Overtly, Western cultural penetrations such as US films and pop music were not seen as so problematic since they were obviously perceived as non-Turkish.[60] However, Arabesk – dismissively referred to as '*Dolmuş* music' (the music of the distinctive shared taxis of Turkey) – was seen as different, as its roots were similar to Turkish roots, and thus may fool people into thinking that it was 'really Turkish'. 'Authentic' Turkish music was collected and vetted by 'experts' at TRT who decided what to broadcast. Interestingly, *Türk Ocağı* seems to be in agreement with the classic Turkish state bureaucracy, who viewed Arabesk music as a negative reaction by 'malcontents' in the cities opposed to Atatürk's reforms, and who excluded it from the main TRT airwaves. In this respect *Türk Ocağı* is at odds with other elements of the extreme right who view Arabesk as 'real culture' and a positive cultural element.[61] Despite their agreement with TRT over the negative aspects of Arabesk music, *Türk Ocağı* has so far been unsuccessful in its applications in 1991 and again in June 1992 to have a joint programme with TRT to explain its concepts of Turkish culture and values.[62]

MHP/MÇP ideology

Despite this fragmentation after 1980, due to the prolongation

---

nationalist debate.

[59] *Türk Ocağı* interview.

[60] It is interesting to note that Atatürk strongly supported 'Western' culture like opera, and the Kemalist state subsidised opera houses and schools like the Atatürk Kültür Merkezi in Istanbul. In this Atatürk followed the precedents of the nineteenth and twentieth-century Sultans who brought over touring opera troops from Italy. In 1936 the Turkish government invited Karl Ebert to found an opera company. He brought over musicians from Nazi Germany, and within three years there was a Turkish opera company. Opera remains supported by only a small élite group in Turkey but it is, as one acolyte noted, 'an indication of where we want to fit into the Western world.' – 'A Night at the Opera', *Rear Window* (Channel 4 TV, London), 31 August 1993.

[61] Martin Stokes talk on Turkish Arabesk music, SOAS, London University, 13 December 1991. For a full discussion of 'The Arabesk Question', see his *The Arabesk Debate: Music and Musicians in Modern Turkey* (Oxford: Clarendon Press, 1992).

[62] *Türk Ocağı* interview.

of Türkeş's leadership, as well as that of its basic ideology and aims, this study views the MÇP as the continuation of the MHP, and will treat the parties' political programmes as interconnected. The common basis of RPNP (post-1965)/MHP/MÇP policy was and remains 'the nine lights', which first appeared in 1963[63] and were first published in 1965. Özdağ claims to have prepared the party programme while in exile in Japan but states that it was felt to be too complicated and needed to be reduced to nine simple principles.[64] The number nine was chosen as Atatürk had talked about nine principles when founding the CHP, and thus had an accepted tradition behind it.[65] Türkeş also stated on numerous occasions that he had paid special attention to formulating the principles in nine categories because that number had been considered auspicious by Turks,[66] and some of the 'lights' are similar to the 'Six Arrows' of the CHP in the 1930s. The exploitation of symbolism like this, and the use of the *Bozkurt* (Grey Wolf), which figures prominently in the mythic origins of the Turks, and the *Başbuğ* (Leader), which is also borrowed from Central Asian lore, was obviously important to Türkeş and his associates as a tool for mass mobilisation;[67] both were also used by Enver Paşa for the same purpose.

Unsurprisingly, 'Nationalism' (*Milliyetçilik*) was the first and most important 'light' and essentially defined as serving the Turkish nation, with all the other 'lights' interpreted and evaluated in terms of service to the Fatherland.[68] Türkeş stated:

[63] F-W. Fernau, 'Le Retour des 'Quartoze'' en Turquie', *Orient*, vol. 7, no. 25, 1963, p. 14.

[64] Özdağ interview.

[65] *Ibid.*

[66] Ağaoğulları, *op. cit.*, footnote 82 on p. 194.

[67] Çağlar, *op. cit.*, p. 80, and Ağaoğulları, *op. cit.*, footnote 100 on p. 196.

[68] Landau, *Radical*, p. 227. The other 'lights' are idealism (*ülkücülük*), morality (*ahlakçılık*), social-mindedness (*toplumculuk*), scientism (*ilimcilik*), the guaranteeing of freedoms (*hürriyetçilik*), peasantism (*köycülük*), development and populism (*gelişmecilik ve halkçılık*), industrialisation and technology (*endüstricilik ve teknikçilik*). Together with the first light 'nationalism', the principles, with some minor changes in order and emphasis, have remained the core of Türkeş's doctrine since his return from exile in 1963. As noted above, they bear resemblance in part to the six arrows of Kemalism. The programme was originally called the 'Nine principles of the renaissance of Kemalism' before being named 'the Nine lights'; Fernau, *op. cit.*, p. 22.

In addition our nationalism means Turkism [*Türkcülük*]. Ideologically, this means conforming in all spheres to the Turkish spirit and traditions and to assistance to all Turks and the Turkish nation in everything.[69]

The pan-Turkist aspect of this was made clearer in Türkeş's explanation of the 'Nine Lights' in 1972:[70] 'Our nationalism also includes this demand: wherever in the world there is a Turk, then that becomes part of our sphere of interest'; and in the 27 December 1988 MÇP programme: 'Nationalism which we believe is formed ... in the entering along the road of the Great Turkish Ideal (*Büyük Türkiye Ülküsü yolunda*).'[71] He often ended his speeches with the slogan 'Victory to the Great Turkish Nation!'[72] Thus Pan-Turkist overtones can be seen to have been constantly present in Türkeş's views. This aspect is not so surprisingly given that Türkeş himself was born and raised in Cyprus. His participation in the Turanist anti-communist demonstrations of 3 May 1944 has obviously been of great importance in influencing him, and these events are given great prominence in the MÇP General Education Programme.[73]

However, while the MHP became the dominant factor in radical-right politics by the end of the 1960s and subsumed other pan-Turkist groups, pan-Turkism was by no means the sole component of MHP ideology. The pan-Turkist theme was often played down when political considerations seemed to warrant this.[74] Ağaoğulları goes further and states that there was little emphasis on pan-Turkist views, noting that the MHP programme only referred to 'outer Turks' twice, and then only with the neutral term 'the Turkish world'. This was exemplified by Article 6, which states that the MHP's aim is 'To bring about the total unification of language in the Turkish world', and Article 41: 'To develop relations ... with the Turkish world.'[75] Özdağ confirms

[69] Landau, *op. cit.*, p. 224.
[70] Alparslan Türkeş, *Yeni Ufaklara Doğru* (Istanbul: Kutluğ, 1973), p. 19.
[71] *Milliyetçi Çalışma Partisi Programı* – MÇP programme (Ankara, 27 December 1988) p. 17.
[72] Türkeş, *op. cit.*, p. 119.
[73] *MÇP Genel Merkezi Eğitim Programı* (Ankara, n.d. but probably 1988), p. 22.
[74] Landau, *Pan-Turkism*, p. 166.
[75] Ağaoğulları, *op. cit.*, p. 194 and footnote 85.

that overt political Turanism was never part of the party programme but its cultural aspects always were. In his words:

> Part of the Turkish community was being oppressed by other imperialist countries who had absolutely no respect for human rights and due to a great inferiority complex were destroying our cultural riches. It is only natural that we should love them ['outer Turks'] but countries with common sense have to have realistic policies and the aim in the 1960s was to protect Turkey rather than expand.[76]

'Realism' in the context of the late 1960s excluded overt aggressive intentions against the USSR. It is noteworthy that up to the sudden collapse of the USSR, when discussing the *Dış Türkler* Türkeş, emphasises the plight of Turks in Greece and Bulgaria (and occasionally Iran and Iraq) and appears to ignore the Turkic peoples of Central Asia. For example his article 'Foreign Policy and the Outer Turks' of 1972[77] concentrates on the Turks of Western Thrace and then moves into a general discussion on 'Turkism', 'Ottomanism' [Islamic] Community' (*Ümmetçilik*) and so on. Again the MÇP programme of December 1988 mentions Turks from Bulgaria, Iran and Iraq and even Afghanistan, but not the USSR.[78]

This reticence was almost certainly due in part to the fear of giving too much ammunition to the frequent accusations of Turanism. In the MÇP Education programme it is noted bitterly that the 'love and interest' shown by the Turkish nationalist for Turks outside Turkey 'has for years been accused with the name of being Turanism' and 'Turanism was seen as bad.'[79] At least the Turks in Greece, Bulgaria and Iraq were generally accepted by world opinion (if not by internal rulers at various times) as being Turks. This is not so for the Turkic peoples of Central Asia where, it can be argued, Stalin and the Soviet State had pursued a deliberate policy of ethnogenesis to both divide a potentially large and problematic Turkic area into smaller more manageable units (Azerbaijan, Turkmenistan, Uzbekistan, Kyrgyzstan,

---

[76] Özdağ interview.
[77] Türkeş, *op. cit.*, pp. 72-80.
[78] *MÇP Programı*, p. 79.
[79] *MÇP Eğitim Programı*, p. 35.

Kazakhstan, etc.) and keep them away from possible Turkish influence. For instance, Stalin originally chose the Latin alphabet for the new Central Asian languages but switched to Cyrillic after Atatürk also adopted the Latin script. Expressing public concern for the Turks who remained outside Turkey as remnants of the Ottoman period was safer than overt statements about Central Asia.[80] Despite this reticence in party programmes or communiqués, Türkeş did on occasions define Turkism as the idea of achieving a powerful all-Turkish union, claiming than this was not utopian. He called for cultural and diplomatic assistance to 'captive Turks', help for emigrants, and preparations for the day when each Turkic land would achieve independence.[81]

Furthermore, many believe that Türkeş clandestinely made and kept contacts with Central Asia, and that this is one reason why Demirel took him there in April 1992. The right nationalist penetration of the ANAP in the early 1980s noted above surfaces again here, as the 1983 ANAP government put, on an official basis, organisations set up by pan-Turkists to propagate their views in Soviet Central Asia and the Caucasus. These organisations were set up specifically to promote the Turk/Islamic model of pan-Turkism in these areas.[82] Certainly, Türkeş was close to the Azeri nationalist leader Abulfaz Elchibey, and some claim he heavily financed him.[83] The collapse of the USSR allowed him to come out more into the open. On 12 December 1991 he introduced a proposed motion to the Turkish parliament chastising the govern-

---

[80] For more on attitudes to Central Asia and the Balkans, see Chapter 9.

[81] Ağaoğulları, *op. cit.*, p. 194.

[82] See F. Bilici, 'Acteurs de développement des relations entre la Turquie et le monde turc. Les *vakı(s)*' given on 28 October 1991 at the conference *La Turquie et L'Aire Turque dans la Nouvelle Configuration Régionale et Internationale: Montée en Puissance ou Marginalisation?*, and report of the same in *CEMOTI (Cahiers D'Études sur la Méditerranée Orientale et le Monde Turco-Iranian)*, no. 13, 1992, pp. 216-17. See also F. Üstel, 'Les 'Foyers Turcs'' et les 'Turcs de l'Éxterieur''', *CEMOTI*, no. 16, 1993, pp. 55-9. She makes the point again that Cyprus was neglected in favour of Central Asia by pan-Turkists and that since the beginning of the 1990s, the Kurdish problem came to be seen by the far right as the main danger and thus there were more articles about the Kurdish problem in *Türk Yurdu* – the main Pan-Turkist publication – than about the 'Outer Turks'.

[83] S.T. Hunter, 'Will Azerbaijan's new rulers safeguard Western interests?' in *Middle East International*, 24 July 1992.

ment for not seizing the opportunities offered by the emergence of the 'Turkish Republics' (*Türk Cumhuriyetleri*) of Azerbaijan, Uzbekistan, Kazakhstan, Kyrgyzstan and Turkmenistan. In the MÇP presentation attached to the motion and Türkeş's speeches, his life-long dedication to the outside Turks was noted, as were the frequent accusations of his being a 'chauvinist' and a 'dreamer'. It was stated (with some satisfaction) that now, with 'nearly 200 million Turks in the world', Turanism was not a fantasy but a reality.[84]

The plight of Turkish *Gastarbeiter* in Western Europe was also a MÇP policy issue in the 1980s.[85] The main nationalist concern here was that Turkish children born, for instance, in Germany might be subjected to alien denationalising influences. The lack of preschool crèches was noted and it was seen as undesirable to send Turkish children to normal crèches where they were subjected to 'Christian propaganda' (the confusion over 'national' and 'Islamic' identity is again noteworthy). At the same time, older children needed protection from being pushed into crime and from bad Western habits like gambling machines and nihilism (*başıboşluk*). What was needed was a system of Turkish Houses (*Türk Evleri*) or carefully chosen personnel sent by the state to safeguard Turkish children living in such a perceived hostile environment. The solution was seen as being the use of a combination of teachers, Imams, citizens and foreign affairs functionaries all co-ordinated by the state. The MÇP programme laments the authorities' neglect of this issue and proposes the setting up of a special ministry to deal with the problems of the millions of *Gastarbeiter* and their hundreds of thousands of children.[86]

[84] A. Türkeş, 'SSCB'ndeki Türk Cumhuriyetleri ve Muhtar Bölgeleri ile İlişkiler, konusunda meclis konuşmaları', *Birleşim TBMM Tutanakları*, 12 and 17 December 1991.

[85] *MÇP Programı* pp. 57-9. In March 1992, the MÇP held a demonstration in Germany (as well as in Istanbul) where the slogan 'A Turkish Islamic World Empire is coming' was displayed (*The Month in Turkey*, no. 15, London, March 1992). Furthermore, 'Grey Wolves' were blamed by the Belgian Interior Minister for organised attacks on PKK sympathisers in Brussels in January 1994 (*Briefing*, no. 972, 10 January 1994).

[86] *Ibid.* The rise of neo-Nazis and subsequent attacks on Turks in Germany must also have had an effect on this concern for the *Gastarbeiter*. There is also the factor of looking to build up a support base among Turks in Germany which would be outside Turkish government control.

The basis of society was seen as the family. As in the case of nationalist movements in other countries, traditional family values were extolled and an expanding population was regarded as beneficial. There was open opposition to any form of birth-control, which was seen as a scheme by Turkey's enemies to limit its population.[87] This outright opposition to birth-control has become somewhat tempered. The MÇP 1988 programme – while rejecting the view that Turkey's population increase is a factor in its economic predicament and calling for a larger population – is ambiguous on birth-control measures other than abortion, which is roundly condemned. Feminism too is 'resolutely rejected' and modern developments like artificial insemination and test-tube babies are also rejected.[88]

The MHP, while pledging to abide by accords with international organisations like NATO, was hostile to the West and also openly opposed 'Common Market slavery' for both economic and political reasons,[89] preferring to build contacts with neighbouring Islamic countries (similarly to the Islamic RP – see Chapter 6). This opposition has become somewhat reduced of late, as the MÇP 1988 programme sees further application for membership of the European Community as unavoidable. However, while economic links were regarded as inevitable, aims of political and social integration were firmly rejected and stress was put on the protection of Turkish beliefs and values from foreign elements.[90] With the events in Eastern Europe since 1988 making Turkey's full membership of the European Community perhaps more unlikely, this line may revert back to more open hostility. The distrust of the West is also well illustrated by the MÇP view of the Gulf crisis of 1990. Saddam Hussein was severely criticised, and the generally poor relations with Turkey's Muslim neighbours were lamented and blamed on the persecution in those countries of minority Turks. However, the prospect of a Kurdish autonomous state in northern Iraq was seen as the real threat; the West, and the United States in particular, was accused of deliberately trying to set up such a client state – 'a boil like Israel' – which would destabilise

[87] Landau, *Radical*, p. 230.
[88] *MÇP Programı*, pp. 7–8.
[89] Ağaoğulları, *op. cit.*, p. 195.
[90] *MÇP Programı*, pp. 40–1.

Turkey.[91] The new situation after the collapse of the USSR has allowed a more active foreign policy and there have been reports in the Turkish media of several thousand radical-right volunteers fighting with the Azeri forces in and around Nagorno-Karabakh.[92] The debate in June 1994 about US aid, and the strings attached concerning the use of military aid against internal PKK insurgents, saw Türkeş urging the government to categorically refuse the conditional aid, asserting that the same amount could be collected from Turkish workers in Western Europe.[93]

The attitude of Türkeş and the MHP/MÇP towards Turkey's internal minorities also deserves attention. As noted above, racism was an evident feature of pan-Turkists like Atsız and Türkkan. Özdağ, however, denies any charge of racism, claiming that Turks have historically never been racist.[94] This historical refutation of charges of racism was also used by Türkeş, who denied any evidence of genocidal practices in Turkish history (no mention of the Armenian tragedy here) and pointed to the refuge given by the Ottoman state to the Jews of Spain, exiles from Poland and persecuted sects from Russia. He states, in refuting charges of Nazism, that:

> Because of this historical achievement it is not possible to apply in Turkish society any idea like extermination of people belonging to different race or religion.[95]

The MÇP programme of December 1988, without further explanation, baldly states that 'Turkish nationalism because it is a cultural movement ... rejects racism.'[96]

However, as Ağaoğulları points out, Türkeş and the MHP used two separate modes of discourse. Hence, unofficial publications of the MHP, as well as journals linked to it, need to be looked

[91] *Körfez Krizi ve MÇP* (Ankara, September 1990), *passim.*

[92] The fighting in Nagorno-Karabakh has aided the rise of Turkish nationalism and the fortunes of politicians like Türkeş, Erbakan, and Ecevit who play the nationalist card – albeit from different perspectives. Even a 'liberal' like Mesut Yılmaz could state in a press conference that Turkey had some kind of right to protect Azerbaijan under international law (*Briefing*, no. 879, 9 March 1992).

[93] Turkish TV, Ankara, 19 June 1994, in SWB EE/2027, B/9, 21 June 1994. The USA decided to end grant aid in 1996 anyway.

[94] Özdağ interview.

[95] Türkeş, *Yeni Ufaklara*, p. 110.

[96] *MÇP Programı*, pp. 4-5.

at to uncover the real ideology. While overt racist-Turanist ideology was dropped from official doctrine to address a wider electorate, it remained a constant thread. 'Commerce will be purged of non-national elements' and '[t]he term national state implies that the state is founded upon a single homogeneous nation' are clear statements of this.[97] More extreme attitudes appeared in militant publications. Muhsin Yazıcıoğlu wrote:

> We firmly believe in the theory of superior race ... Turkishness is an essence (*cevher*) comprised of religion and race ... The Turkish race is more precious than all others.[98]

A pamphlet distributed to Turkish workers in Germany by the MHP prior to the 1977 elections went further:

> Those who have destroyed [the Ottoman Empire] were Greek-Armenian-Jewish converts, Kurds, Circassians, Bosnians, and Albanians. As a Turk, how much longer will you tolerate these dirty minorities? Throw out the Circassian, that he may go to Caucasia, throw out the Armenian, throw out and kill the Kurd, purge from your midst the enemy of all Turkdom.[99]

In areas where there were ethnic and religious (primarily Alevi) minorities, the minorities were presented as the main enemies after the communists, while badly-off sectors of the Turkish and Sunni majority were stirred up against them.[100] Indeed, this policy appears to have born some fruit, as MHP and MÇP electoral successes appear to have come almost entirely from these mixed areas. Regarding the Kurds, Türkeş would combine the two traditional hostilities of the radical right and urge his *Bozkurtlar* to fight against the 'communist-Kurd' danger.[101] In this, of course, he was aided by the growth of the violent Marxist PKK. Unsurprisingly, hostility to all forms of Kurdish aspirations in Turkey has remained constant. At the MÇP convention of 29 December 1991, there were anti-Kurdish speeches and Yazıcıoğlu stated

---

[97] *MHP 1973 Seçim Bildirisi*, quoted in Ağaoğulları, *op. cit.*, footnote 106 on p. 197.

[98] Quoted in Ağaoğulları, *op. cit.*, footnote 107 on p. 197.

[99] *MHP İddianamesi*, quoted in *ibid*.

[100] Ağaoğulları, *op. cit.*, p. 197.

[101] Türkeş, *Yeni Ufaklara*, p. 58.

'Turkey belongs to the Turks.'[102] Türkeş himself reacted with predictable fury to President Özal's suggestion of a Kurdish TV channel stating that this would lead to a division of the country; he warned Özal to 'remember the right' – an allusion to the threat of possible action.[103]

However, in July 1992, he appeared to change his views following a meeting with Kurdish politicians in HEP (Peoples's Labour Party) and ÖZDEP (Freedom and Equality Party). Türkeş than stated that his party now saw Kurds as brothers even if they belonged to the PKK and claimed he was for a solution without bloodshed. He went on to say: 'My sister is married to a Kurd. How can I become an enemy of my nephew? Everyone in this region is our children.' He even opposed the closing of HEP (see Chapter 7), saying that all political views should be allowed. He and other right wing leaders including his rival Muhsin Yazıcıoğlu also made appeals to their followers not to get involved in conflict with the PKK.[104] This extraordinary about face must surely have been merely tactical and part of a possible overture to Prime Minister Tansu Çiller. Nonethless, the 'Kurdish Question' has aided the revival of right-wing nationalist forces within the country with a groundswell of anti-Kurdish feeling (see Chapter 7). Türkeş soon reverted to his usual line, and at a rally in the southeast in March 1994 he accused the PKK of collaboration with the violent anti-Turkish Armenian organisation the Armenian Secret Army for the Liberation of Armenia (ASALA). Türkeş then stated:

> All of us are brothers, we come from the same ancestors. The terrorists are trying to force our citizens in the east and southeast to flee to other regions so as to realise their dreams of greater Armenia.[105]

---

[102] *Turkey Confidential*, no. 25, January 1992.

[103] *Tercüman*, 24 April 1992. At a Turkish Cypriot Association meeting in London on 13 February 1992, Türkeş stated that most Kurds were in fact Turks and that Kurdish nationalism was a Greek plot to break up Anatolia with Armenian and Western support. He went on to blame Özal for separatist tendencies within Turkey (*The Month in Turkey*, no. 14, February 1992).

[104] *Briefing*, no. 897, 20 July 1992.

[105] *Anatolia*, Ankara, 15 March 1993. However, this can also be seen as more of an attack on the PKK than on the Kurdish community as a whole.

Despite denials of complicity by Türkeş, there were reports of MHP/MÇP violence against HEP and socialist members in Iğdır and Istanbul during the 1 November 1992 local elections.[106] On 20 September 1992 Musa Anter, a founding member of HEP, was gunned down in Diyabakır by an obscure Turkish nationalist group, 'Boz-Ok' (Grey Arrow).[107] This last outrage raises the whole question of extreme-rightist involvement in the large number of unsolved assassinations of left-wing and politically active Kurds in the southeast, ostensibly by members of the shadowy 'Hizbollah' movement, which is covered in greater detail in Chapter 7. At this stage, we shall merely note that the raised nationalist tensions over the Kurdish issue had, by late 1992, seen a number of cases of near lynchings and destruction of Kurdish property in several parts of the country – and not just the troubled southeast – where no perpetrators were brought to justice. This raised severe doubts as to the impartiality of the security forces in cases of racist attacks on Kurds within Turkey.[108]

Thus, the nationalist ideology of the MHP/MÇP is very similar to that of the *Türk Ocaği* in its denial of minorities within Turkey and insistence on a unitary state, while at the same time championing the cause of Turkish and Turkic peoples outside the country. Despite official denials, there is also an undeniable racist component which goes much further than the Atatürkist integrationist denial of minorities like the Kurds.

Pan-Turkism and Islam

It is in its attitude to religion that perhaps the only real change has taken place in the radical-right ideology. The 1965 RPNP programme spoke of a secular state. At this time Türkeş often ended his speeches 'God protect the Turks' (the slogan of the pan-Turkist Association of Turkish Youth immediately after the Second World War, and even ended the 1965 Nine Lights

---

[106] *Briefing*, no. 912 and 913, 2 and 9 November 1992.

[107] *Mideast Mirror*, 21 September 1992.

[108] *Briefing*, no. 916, 30 November 1992, comments on the wave of Turkish nationalism and contrasts the mass reportage in Turkey of the deaths of three Turks killed by German nationalist arsonists in Germany with the lack of coverage of similar incidents against Turkey's own citizens within the country.

programme with an appeal to 'Almighty God' for strength to carry out the party's tasks. In both cases, however, he uses the non-Islamic Turkish term '*Tann*' rather than 'Allah' for God.[109] As noted above, in 1960 Türkeş had wanted to substitute nationalist ideology for Islam in the education process. Özdağ confirms that at that time religion was not seen by his party as having a political connotation: 'God's ['*Tann*] wish is that human beings govern world affairs.'[110] However, by the late 1960s the relationship with Islam became the most hotly debated issue in radical-right circles. Some saw it as a rival ideology while others, including it seems Türkeş, wanted to harness its continuing emotional appeal (despite almost fifty years of Atatürkist secularism) to large sectors of the population.[111]

The issue came to a head in 1969. A seminar of Turkish nationalist leaders in Istanbul in May clearly stated that Islamism (*Müsülmanlık*) was and should remain an integral part of Turkish nationalism, and the 1969 MHP electoral campaign openly appealed to Islamic sentiments.[112] This apparent tactical move to try to win votes caused a rift, leading to the departure of some senior members like Ismail Hakkı Yılanlıoğlu. The third MHP Congress in Adana adopted the more Islamic symbol of three crescents as the party emblem in place of the *Bozkurt* (which was however retained for the youth organisation). Nihal Atsız and his followers, as well as a group known as the 'Shamanists', left the party in protest at the new developments.[113] Özdağ, who also left the party at this time, states that the new emphasis on Islam was one reason for his departure. He goes further and states that this new direction was symptomatic of a general abandoning of basic principles in favour of an opportunistic approach which eventually led, so he claims, to the MHP becoming a tool of Demirel's Justice Party.[114]

How sincere Türkeş was in espousing Islam – he even went on a pilgrimage to Mecca and established close links with some

---

[109] Landau, *Radical*, pp. 218 and 227.
[110] Özdağ interview.
[111] Landau, *Pan-Turkism*, p. 148.
[112] *Ibid.*, p. 153.
[113] *Ibid.*, p. 153 and Ağaoğulları, *op. cit.*, p. 198.
[114] Özdağ interview.

tarikats[115] – is debatable. At the time some, like the Nurcu leader
Bekir Berk, were highly sceptical, pointing out that he had up
till then consistently shown a secularist approach.[116] This drew
the predictable response from Türkes – while admitting that there
had been 'a decision to raise the profile of our religion in our
doctrine', he rejected the charges of insincerity and opportunism.[117]
What is incontestable is that henceforth Islam came to the fore
in party programmes and publications. Whereas in 1965 the
'Morality' section of the 'Nine Lights' does not mention Islam
and refers only to 'Turkish traditions, spirit and to beliefs of the
Turkish nation',[118] by 1972 'Islamic principles' had been added,
and the preamble to the 'Lights' stresses the Islamic contribution
to world civilisation. Furthermore, Türkes stated:

> Nations [*milletler*] cannot live without religion. Every nation
> has a religion. ... The basis and sources of the Nine Lights
> are these: Turkish consciousness, Islamic belief, Islamic morality
> and virtue.[119]

More definitely, in a speech addressed to 'Young Grey Wolves'
Türkes says, with almost Jihad overtones, 'Allah is with us, because
he supports the truth. We are invincible because our belief is
complete.'[120] It seems that the religious aspect was more than
mere window-dressing for the electorate. A former MHP party
leader said that for imprisoned MHP militants in 1979,

> Koran courses were compulsory. Islamic subjects, prayer, etc
> were also taught. Prison was referred to as the stone *medrese*
> [religious school].[121]

This new basis of Turkishness and Islam has remained a key
component of Türkes's espoused ideology and has, if anything,
become more pronounced, possibly in line with the rise of Islamic
sentiment in Turkey in the 1980s. The 1988 MÇP party programme

---

[115] Ağaoğulları, *op cit.*, p. 198.
[116] Landau, *Radical*, p. 231.
[117] Türkes, *Yeni Ufaklara*, p. 64.
[118] Landau, *Radical*, p. 224.
[119] Türkes, *Yeni Ufaklara*, pp. 16, 17 and 20.
[120] *Ibid.*, p. 84.
[121] Ağaoğulları, *op. cit.*, p. 198.

stated: 'Every human being is accepted as a sacred/holy receptacle created by His Excellency Allah [*Cenab-ı Allah*]' and notes that of 3,000 years of Turkish history, 1,400 have been Islamic.[122] Throughout the MÇP party and education programmes there is frequent reference to 'Allah (C.C.)' – the '(C.C.)' appendage signifying great religious respect. The Islamic as well as the Turkish nationalist roots of the MÇP are stressed at every opportunity.[123]

The radical right in practice

As shown in Chapter 1, nationalist movements are essentially totalitarian in their claims to represent the whole nation, however defined. In view of this, a brief look at the practice of the radical right is in order. Was the MHP/MÇP essentially totalitarian and even fascist? In their regulations and programme, the political parties of the radical right espouse democracy both internally for party organisation and externally as a system of government. Seizure of power by means other than election was officially opposed.[124] Özdağ states that in the 1965-9 period, when he was one of the leaders of the party, the twenty-nine member General Administrative Council was elected according to democratic norms laid down in the regulations, and all party decisions were taken democratically. Thus, he refutes for this period the charge that Türkeş was a dictator within the party.[125] However, as Landau notes,[126] the 1969 MHP regulations laid great powers on the centre and were reminiscent of those used by military organisations – hardly surprising given the military background of Türkeş and other leading MHP members. The indictment against the MHP brought after the 1980 coup charges that 'genuinely democratic elections were not held' and that absolute power was held by Türkeş, who prepared candidate lists for election at all levels which were then ratified without debate. It also states:

The MHP headquarters, the youth branches, all the idealist

[122] *MÇP Programı*, pp. 2 and 6.
[123] *MÇP Programi* and *MÇP Eğitim Programı, passim*.
[124] Landau, *Radical*, p. 200, and *MÇP Programı*.
[125] Özdağ interview.
[126] Landau, *Radical*, p. 213.

associations and their 'oba' [a term borrowed from Central Asian lore originally referring to nomad encampments] organisations in schools, neighbourhoods, and government offices, and the units of the 'oba', constituted a centralised, totalitarian pyramid stratified from the top down, where military discipline reigned.[127]

These charges are hard to evaluate. In all Turkish political parties the role of the leader is very powerful and parties often become personal fiefdoms of individuals. However, it seems incontestable that, due in no small part to Türkeş's military background, the radical right was run internally on lines more akin to the military than were other political parties.

In electoral terms, the RPNP/MHP was always a small party. Even in the 1977 elections when it won sixteen parliamentary seats with almost one million votes, its share of the votes cast was only 6.4 per cent. In 1965 it won eleven seats with 2.2 per cent of the vote; in 1969, due to the abolition of the 'national remainder' system, it won only one seat (Türkeş's) with 3 per cent; and in 1973, three seats from 3.4 per cent of the poll. This electoral weakness continued in the case of the MÇP, which won 2.8 per cent of the vote and no seats in 1987, and about 5 per cent in 1991 (or nineteen seats in alliance with the RP, to overcome the electoral hurdle). Thus, the radical right has never achieved electoral breakthrough. As noted above, what electoral success the MHP/MÇP has been able to garner has come from areas like Yozgat, Kahraman Maraş, Sivas and Çorum, where different ethnic and religious groups coexist, or from provinces in Central Anatolia where a stagnant rural population has been more receptive to its ideology.

However, in the confused political situation of the 1970s, it was able, through coalitions with Demirel's Justice Party (AP), to achieve influence greater than its parliamentary representation warranted. In the first National Front government of 1 April 1975 it held two ministries despite only having three deputies, and in the second National Front government on 22 July 1977 it secured five ministries. During its tenure in government, the MHP took over many public organisations and exploited state resources as much as possible, packing its supporters and members

---

[127] *MHP Iddianamesi*, quoted in Ağaoğullan, *op. cit.*, pp. 194 and 198.

into key positions. This practice was, however, pursued by all the parties in the 1970s, leading to the polarisation and politicisation of the bureaucracy. As noted above, by the 1980 coup the MHP also controlled several large organisations as well as some trade unions.

Why did Demirel give the MHP such representation? At this time, the CHP under Ecevit was pressing for early elections so as to reap the benefit of his popularity over the Cyprus crisis of July 1974, and Demirel's AP was faced with a fragmentation on its right. Ecevit had managed to transform the CHP into a left-of-centre party which, after the outlawing of the TİP in 1971, had no real legal party to its left. Left-wing violence, which had begun in the late 1960s, continued, especially as left-wing militants, after the TİP electoral disappointments in the 1960s, now saw no chance of power through the ballot box. In this situation Demirel played for time by delaying the election. He was apparently waiting or hoping for the offshoots from the AP to wither and their membership be brought back into the AP fold, while he continued his policy of attacking the left as communist and revolutionary. The MHP role in street violence (see below) can be seen as part of this strategy, as the continuing violence kept the issue of communism and revolution in the limelight. Certainly, Demirel was guilty of having as his Deputy Prime Minister someone like Türkeş, who was openly heading paramilitary organisations fighting on the streets. This analysis tends to see the MHP and Türkeş in the 1970s as being merely tools of Demirel – an accusation which Özdağ repeats and which is also shared by some commentators from the left who see fascist or radical-right movements as the last defence of the 'capitalist class'.[128] Some form of alliance was certainly there – mirrored in the slogan of the right wing press: 'Demirel in Parliament, Türkeş in the Street'[129] – and the two appear to have kept their relationship to the present day. However, the classic Stalinist interpretation of the radical right is surely too simplistic. Türkeş was not Demirel's poodle by any means. The violence can just as easily be seen as a develop-

---

[128] A. Gil, 'La Turquie. Crise Economique et Péril Fasciste', *Le Monde Diplomatique*, February 1979.

[129] Ahmad, *op. cit.*, p. 347.

ment in which the two wings of the anti-systemic political periphery were fighting for control of the streets.

This raises the question of whether the MHP, despite its official espousal of democracy and renunciation of armed revolution, hoped to gain power through extra-parliamentary means. Alternatively, were the *Bozkurt*/commando units merely set up to fight 'the communist threat'? The 'Commandos' (*Komandolar*) began to appear on the scene at the end of 1968, with their first open violent action on 31 December against left-wing students at Ankara University. They were probably set up in the summer of 1968, with three main training camps near Istanbul, Izmir and Ankara and others reportedly near Samsun and in Anatolia. The Ankara and Izmir camps were directed respectively by two of Türkeş's closest collaborators and members of 'the fourteen', Dündar Taşer and Rıfat Baykal.[130] In 1970 estimates of the numbers of commandos, later called '*Bozkurtlar*' or 'Idealists', put the figure at up to a few thousand.[131] Until 1974 their activities were staged in universities and other higher institutions, and targeted left-wing revolutionary groups.[132] As noted above, the extreme left had begun to use violence in the late 1960s, and the 1961 Constitution had allowed the universities so much autonomy from the state that extreme groups could operate from their premises with some impunity. Radical-right violence can thus be seen in this period as essentially anti-communist rather than as being aimed at seizing the state or instigating wide-spread terror. However, a report by the internal ministry and directorate of security presented to Demirel in 1970 stated that the commando camps were 'akin to Hitler's Nazi organization' and that the MHP was

.... aiming at the destruction of the existing democratic order, the expulsion of minorities, ... unification of Turks living within the boundaries belonging to other states ... weakening the government and taking over power ...[133]

The report was evidently seen as exaggerated and alarmist by Demirel and ignored.

---

[130] Landau, *Radical*, pp. 215-16.

[131] *Ibid.*, p. 215.

[132] Ağaoğulları, *op. cit.*, p. 204.

[133] Quoted in *Ibid.*, footnote 25 on p. 201.

The scope of their activities escalated after the CHP-led coalition came to power, with attacks on CHP members and leftist professional organisations like the Confederation of Revolutionary Workers. The beginning of 1975 saw radical-right violence escalate dramatically.[134] Indeed, the scale of political violence from both right and left escalated as the decade wore on, with nine deaths in 1969; 27 in 1974; 319 in 1977; 1,362 in 1979; and 2,206 in 1980.[135] Journalists seen as hostile to the radical right cause also became targets and the terrorism finally acquired mass proportions with widespread violence against Alevis and leftists, including CHP members, in Malatya, Sivas, and notoriously Kahraman Maraş in 1978, and in Çorum and other locations in 1980.[136] This phase of the violence, which eventually also turned against some of its own members in line with Türkeş's declaration 'Shoot anyone who joins the cause and then turns back',[137] can be seen as having much wider aims than the first essentially anti-communist or terrorist period. As early as 1975, some believed that Türkeş was trying to create chaos in the country, leading to martial law and a state of emergency. In this, the CHP would be banned and Türkeş would establish an essentially fascist regime.[138] Ahmad suggests that the MHP tactics used when Türkeş visited Diyabakır on 23 June 1975 resulted in riots and nearly led to martial law, which he sees as being Türkeş's aim. MHP commandos had arrived before Türkeş and stirred up trouble in this predominantly Kurdish area with slogans of 'Flee, the Turks are coming.' At the same time, MHP gangs attacked Ecevit, but he refused to be intimidated.[139] In places which fell under MHP control in the so-called Devil's Triangle of Erzurum, Yozgat and Adana, similar tactics appear to have been used in which militants arrived and caused disturbances and terror as a preliminary to the MHP takeover of local authorities.

It appears that the MHP had supporters in the army, and that

[134] Ahmad, *op. cit.*, p. 347.
[135] Ruşen Kele, sand Artun Ünsal, *Kent ve Siyasal Siddet*, (Ankara: Ankara Üniversitesi Siyasal Bilgiler Fakültesi Yayınları, 1982), p. 35.
[136] Ağaoğulları, *op. cit.*, p. 204.
[137] *Ibid.*
[138] Ahmad, *op. cit.*, p. 351.
[139] *Ibid.*, pp. 352-3.

the MHP was careful not to oppose the armed forces in any way.[140] Türkeş, of course, was a retired officer, as were many other MHP leaders. The 1971 coup by memorandum had been greeted with enthusiasm by the MHP and the party line was that the commandos and 'Idealists' were assisting the security forces against revolutionary communists.[141] When martial law was proclaimed on 26 December 1978, the MHP leadership ordered its rank and file to minimise actions so as not to antagonise the army, and to allow the army to concentrate on armed left-wing groups.[142] Whether the MHP was actively aiming at a military coup is debatable. Some on the left claim this, and state that although the 'authoritarian, repressive, and nationalistic concepts' of the Evren military regime converge at some points with those of the MHP, Türkeş and his associates were unable to take advantage of the coup.[143] To support this, they point to the petition by Türkeş's lawyers after the coup, which calls for his acquittal as

> .... the requests outlined in the MHP electoral manifesto have been realised ... The attitudes and actions of Alparslan Türkeş and his party are today actually under implementation.[144]

Since this view sees Türkeş and the MHP as openly fascist in 1970s, such an interpretation implies that the post-coup military regime was also fascist. This view is hard to justify, since fascism entails more than an authoritarian regime which represses the left.

Turkish fascism? Comparison with other European movements

Was or is the RPNP/MHP/MÇP movement a fascist movement, and how does it compare with other similar movements in Europe? A distinction has to be made between fascist movements in power and those either in opposition or on the way to power. The Turkish radical right, despite being a coalition partner, has never

[140] Ağaoğulları, *op. cit.*, p. 205.
[141] *Ibid.*, p. 205 and footnote 142.
[142] *Ibid.*, p. 205.
[143] *Ibid.*, p. 206 quoting Vaner, 'Violence Politique en Turquie' [no further details].
[144] *Cumhuriyet*, 5 October 1982.

achieved absolute power. Thus, what sort of state it would usher in is by no means definite. Despite this, there is enough evidence manifest in its ideology and practice to make judgment possible. In Europe during this century there have been a number of different radical-right movements which can be termed fascist.[145] Juan Linz defines fascism as:

> A hypernationalist, often pan-nationalist, anti-parliamentary, anti-liberal, anti-communist, populist and therefore anti-proletarian, partly anti-capitalist and anti- bourgeois, anti-clerical, or at least, non-clerical movement, with the aim of national social integration through a single party and corporative representation not always equally emphasised; with a distinctive style and rhetoric, it relied on activist cadres ready for violent action combined with electoral participation to gain power ...[146]

The 'distinctive style' Linz refers to is the rituals of marches, uniforms, symbols, etc. often used by these movements. To this definition can perhaps be added the cult of a leader and élitism (not seen as essential by Linz),[147] and a national state-centred socialism. This entails a strong authoritarian centralised state and often an autarchic economic policy. Linz also emphasises fascism's essential dynamic and mobilisatory concepts, which differentiate it from traditional conservative parties.[148]

On almost all counts, the MHP of the 1970s, with its paramilitary organisations and other manifestations, would appear to fit this definition. The only exception is perhaps 'the anti-clerical, or at least, non-clerical aspect (although this also applies to some fascist movements like the Romanian Iron Guard and perhaps Spain). As shown above, even here there is some doubt as to Türkeş's sincerity in espousing Islam, which has striking similarities to Le Pen's apparent espousal of religion for political ends in France.[149]

---

[145] See J.J. Linz, 'Some Notes Towards a Comparative Study of Fascism in Sociological Historical Perspectives' in W. Laquer (ed.), *Fascism – A Reader's Guide* (London: Pelican, 1982) *passim.*

[146] Linz, *op. cit.*, p. 25.

[147] *Ibid.*, p. 37.

[148] *Ibid.*, p. 25.

[149] In 1951 Le Pen reportedly went to mass in a resort in Aix-les-Bains drunk and abusive. He refused the host and the police had to be called to eject him.

Another interesting point of comparison with modern European radical-right movements like Le Pen's lies in the expressed attitude to minorities and race. In Western Europe today, racism and the immigration issue is the main, often the only, real factor in radical-right politics. This is combined with playing down the Nazi Holocaust, and an obsession with Hitler.[150] In Turkey these factors are not so marked, and the main emphasis is on ultra-nationalism, anti-communism and social solidarism. Nazism and Hitler are not held up as models, and the MHP/MÇP attitude to minorities, although perhaps similar in its real hostility to that of West European parties, is not unduly publicised, except in an unofficial manner in areas of mixed populations, where its racism can be used to electoral advantage. The difference in attitude to immigrants, of course, is certainly due to the fact that Turkey's immigrants are often Turks fleeing neighbouring countries as opposed to 'foreigners' arriving for scarce jobs. Turks in Western Europe are also one of the targets of rightist parties there. Since the 1980s coup, the radical right's activities have been severely curtailed and perhaps can no longer be seen as truly fascist. Fascism, as is often observed, flourishes in times of economic hardship. The 1970s, not just in Turkey, were also a decade of fervent ideological ferment, with groups like the Red Brigades operating in a number of European countries. Rising living standards and a decline in ideological fervour have affected the radical right as well as the radical left – as has the apparent collapse of Soviet communism, the traditional enemy. This, combined with the above- mentioned fragmentation, and the advanced age of Türkeş, would indicate that the radical right is destined to remain a peripheral force in Turkish politics for the near future at least – despite the openings in Central Asia which has seen 'cultural Turanism' become official policy.[151] In this context, the emergence of the Islamic RP as a

---

Later, when he married in 1960, he expressed relief that his wife's divorced status saved him 'from being inflicted with a marriage in church.' In recent times Le Pen, since then divorced and remarried himself, has claimed to be an ardent Catholic and peppers his speeches with references to the Virgin Mary; see J. Nundy 'Le Pen: A Fear in Provence', *The Independent*, 20 March 1992.

[150] *Committee Inquiry into the rise of fascism in Europe* (European Parliament Working Document, A Series A 2-160/85, December 1985), *passim*.

[151] Examples of Turkey's official attitude of cultural solidarity to the Turkic states of the former Soviet Union are many. Here are just two: the first by

more effective radical force is relevant. However, the continuing 'Kurdish Question' and the escalation of the war with the PKK, which is detailed in Chapter 7, have allowed extreme nationalist groups to continue to attract support among sections of society. Additionally, the Turkish economy has so far failed to live up to expectations raised in the 1980s, and while these problems remain the extreme right will continue to be a factor.

As we have seen, despite the seemingly absolute monopoly of official Kemalist secular nationalism in the early decades of the republic, pan-Turkism remained as a competitor. Whilst this 'ethnic' challenge was often a marginal one confined to peripheral elements, it has remained a constant. It has shown signs of rejuvenation at certain critical times, due to events in Central Asia or internally with the campaigns against the PKK. Whenever the control of the USSR over the Turkic states of Central Asia appeared weak, pan-Turkism in Turkey would revive – most notably during the Second World War and especially following the collapse of the Soviet Union and the emergence of the independent states of Azerbaijan, Uzbekistan, Turkmenistan, Kyrgyzstan, and Kazakhstan. However, the reality of serious political or territorial union with perceived 'kin' in Central Asia has remained a chimera.

Since the 1960s, the pan-Turkist wing has been closely associated with the personality of Alparslan Türkeş. He has dominated the radical right, and has managed to control to some extent the fissiparous tendencies inherent in the extreme right. Whether his

---

then Prime Minister Demirel, who on a visit to UK in 1992 while rejecting political pan-Turkism spoke of a 'Turkish world to the Great Wall' and said that Central Asia was 'our fathers' land ... [who] came to Anatolia 900 years ago ... Now is the time for the Turkish world ... [we] share the same language, the same culture and the same history.' – *Turkey Briefing*, vol. 6, no. 6, 1992, p. 33; the second by Prime Minister Çiller opening the 2nd Turkic States and Commonwealth Friendship, Brotherhood and Cooperation Congress in Izmir on 20 October 1994: 'I welcome to our country my brethren, who are united in their lullabies, legends, pasts, ancestors, language, religion and enthusiasm ...' TRT TV, Ankara, 20 October 1994). Turkey saw and portrayed itself as a model for the new emerging Turkic states to follow but the attraction has somewhat dimmed of late due to the internal economic and political problems facing Turkey.

party can continue to play a leading role in the radical-right periphery after his death remains an open question.

A major development in pan-Turkism has been the adoption of Islam in an apparent attempt to appeal to the Islamic sensibilities of the mass of the population. However, the pan-Turkist parties have been faced with a more effective rival here in the shape of the Islamic RP of Necmettin Erbakan. This is the central topic of the next chapter.

6

THE CRESCENT: THE
ISLAMIC VARIANTS

This chapter will examine the relationship between Islam and Turkish nationalism in the post-Kemalist era. It will look at the re-emergence of Islam in the 1950s with the advent of multi-party democracy, and the growth of the National Salvation Party and its participation in coalition governments in the 1970s. It will then study the post-1980 military governments' attempts to co-opt Islam as a force to bind society together in the service of essentially nationalistic ideals – the so called 'Turkish-Islamic Synthesis'. The success of this policy will be looked at both with reference to élite attitudes and to those of the general population. The penetration of Islamists and Islamic ideology into crucial state bodies like the Education Ministry during the Özal era will also be discussed, as will the rise of the Welfare Party (RP) in the late 1980s and the 1990s. This discussion will encompass the opportunities afforded Islamists by the Özal privatisation programmes and the general modernisation of Turkish society, and how they have taken advantage of this. The chapter will also look at radical Islamist groups who have used violence to further their aims of establishing an Islamic state in Turkey.

Islam, the early Turkists and Atatürk

As we have seen in Chapter 3, some early Turkists like Yusuf Akçura called for a modern Turkish nationalism to take preference over ties of Islam as the primary focus of loyalty of the 'imagined community'. Ziya Gökalp, the official ideologue of the first essentially Turkish nationalist regime, attempted to synthesise Islam and the modern state by artificially compartmentalising his three basic components of Turkish national culture (which he saw as

168

being expressed in the peasant culture of Anatolia), Islam as a matter of individual conscience and 'European civilisation'. As has been shown, these rigid and artificial distinctions were not really workable, and in his synthesis of Turkish culture and Western civilisation there was no real place for Islam.

In Chapter 4 we saw how Kemal and his collaborators did initially use Islam in the struggle against the Greeks and did apparently look at the possibility of constructing a Turkish Islam. However, they were ultimately convinced that Islam and Turkish nationalism were incompatible. Hence, Islam was rejected as a main basis of social cohesion. They also saw the impossibility in Islam of separating religion from state and made no real attempt to create an autonomous structure for Islam such as Christian Churches have in some Western states,[1] and which Gökalp saw as a possibility. They opted instead for making it subservient and state controlled, and keeping it out of the political arena by imposing state control over all political activity regarding the promotion of religious interests. However, many of Gökalp's suggestions were implemented. An attempt was made to transform Islam into an individualistic religion relegated to private life. The office of the Şeyhülislam, who was already virtually a civil servant by the late Ottoman period, was abolished, and what remained of his functions transferred to a government department. The *tarikats* were closed down and the *ezan* (the call to prayer) was to be in Turkish only.[2] The dual school system was abolished and control over the *evkaf* (the charitable religious foundations) were transferred to the state. In place of Islam, Kemal and his associates looked to Turkish nationalism in the form of the 'Turkish History Thesis' and the 'Sun language Theory' as pillars of the new ideology to promote national identity.

Thus, Kemal essentially built on Gökalp's ideas by continuing

---

[1] Binnaz Toprak, 'The Religious Right', in I.C. Schik and A.E. Tonak (eds), *Turkey in Transition* (Oxford University Press, 1984), p. 220. See also Niyazi Berkes, *The Development of Secularism in Turkey* (Montreal: McGill University Press, 1964), and Binnaz Toprak, *Islam and Political Development in Turkey* (Leiden: E.J. Brill), 1981.

[2] In 1933 it was recommended the *ezan* be in Turkish, but there were no legal sanctions to enforce this till 1941. See Andrew Mango, 'Turkey: The Emergence of a Modern Problem' in W. Hale (ed.), *Aspects of Modern Turkey* (London: Bowker, 1976), pp. 10 and 14.

the emphasis on adopting 'Western civilisation', stressing Turkish national culture and making Islam a matter of personal conviction. However, he went further by removing Islam from the position of junior partner in Gökalp's trinity, and making it a state captive, under close supervision, so as to prohibit its use as a legitimisation of political or social goals. We have seen, however, that Kemal's reforms effectively took place in the centres of power – in the cities and larger towns. Until the 1950s, they remained marginal to the majority of the population living in villages, who continued to live as they had always done according to traditional Islamic precepts. Indeed, religion also remained important to many of the urban intelligentsia.[3] The new élites in the urban centres espoused the 'secular' creed of Kemalism almost as a substitute religion, and the gulf between them and the Islamic masses widened considerably. Despite this, when faced in the late 1940s with a serious rival in the shape of the Democrat Party (DP), the ruling Republican People's Party (CHP) was not averse to appealing to the religious sensibilities of the masses in an attempt to win votes. In January 1947 the CHP Supreme Council permitted religious instruction in schools and in 1949 Prime Minister Şemsettin Günaltay opened the Theological Faculty at Ankara University as part of a liberal government policy towards Islam. Even CHP leader İsmet İnönü admitted that before the elections of 1950 the CHP exploited Islam for political ends.[4] The advent of multi-party politics and the victory of the DP in 1950 allowed the Islamic feelings of the countryside to come out more into the

[3] A survey in the 1960s of religious attitudes among male students at the School of Social Welfare in Ankara and the Academy of Economics and Business Sciences in Eskişehir found that 40.3% of respondents said religion was very important to them, 27.6% moderately so, and only 32.1% said it was of little importance. H.G.R. Field, 'Religious commitment and work orientations of Turkish students', *Human Organisation*, vol. 27, no. 2, 1969, pp. 147-51.

[4] Feroz Ahmad, *The Turkish Experiment in Democracy, 1950-1975* (London: Hurst, 1977), pp. 21, 38 and 364. The first such university theological faculty had been opened in 1900. It was closed in 1919 to become the Department of Religious Sciences. This was reestablished in the new republic in 1924 but the period 1924-33 saw a decrease in the number of students. In 1933 Istanbul University established a Theology Faculty, but this was closed in 1936 at the height of the state-propagated Kemalist nationalist alternative ideology. Susannah Pickering, 'Islamic Education and the State in Turkey since 1980' (talk at SOAS, London University, 31 January 1992).

open, and some contemporary observers mistakenly saw this as
a religious revival.[5]

The 1950s and the 1960s

The DP, which was seen by many in the country as pro-Islamic
compared to the CHP, continued with the latter's new-found
liberal policies. The obligation for the *ezan* to be delivered in
Turkish was removed, and on 5 July 1950 the ban on religious
radio programmes was lifted. In October religious lessons in school
became the norm and those who did not want this had to opt
out by parental letter.[6] The government made available substantial
funds for religious education in *Imam-Hatip* schools.[7] However,
it would be a mistake to view the DP as an Islamic party. A
demand at the DP Konya Congress after its election victory to
lift the ban on wearing the fez or the veil and the use of Arabic
script was not accepted. In practice, the DP appealed to the
religious sentiments of the people, but clamped down on overt
politicisation of Islam. In 1950 and 1951, after the DP victory,
there was a religious reaction against the years of CHP control,
with the radical Ticani *tarikat* responsible for vandalising busts
and status of Atatürk. The DP government responded in June
1951 with a round-up of Ticani members and on 27 June the
sect's leader Kemal Pilâvoğlu was arrested and sentenced to ten
years' imprisonment. On 25 July an act of parliament was passed
protecting Atatürk's statues. The DP government also moved
against overtly Islamic publications. In February 1952 the all-party
Clubs of the Turkish Revolution were set up to protect Kemalist

---

[5] For example Lewis V. Thomas, 'Recent Developments in Turkish Islam',
Middle East Journal, vol. 6, 1952, pp. 22-40.

[6] Ahmad, *op. cit.*, p. 365. However, *Temel Eğitim ve Ortaöğretim Din ve Ahlak
Dersi Programı* (Ankara: no date but prepared in 1982), states that this was
introduced in 1948. This appears to be a confusion with the 1948 move which
saw religious education restored in primary schools as an elective subject. Either
way, this period saw a change in the emphasis on religious education which
was to last until 1961 when those who wanted to attend such classes had to
actively request it. As we shall see, the policy was reversed again after 1980.

[7] These were schools for prayer-leaders and preachers which offered the regular
Turkish high-school education but where almost half the curriculum was study
of Arabic, the Koran, and religious instruction.

traditions and reforms, and the radical Islam Democrat Party was closed. After an attack on Ahmed Emin Yalman, a Kemalist writer and newspaper proprietor, Prime Minister Menderes promised to crush the religious right, and the Nurcu leader, Said Nursi, was arrested and tried in January 1953. On 23 July 1953 the 'Law to Protect Freedom of Conscience' was passed to prevent the politicisation of religion. The right-wing Islamic party, the Nation Party, was accused of exploiting Islam for political ends and calling for a return of *Şeriat*. It was temporarily banned on 8 July and dissolved by court order on 27 January 1954.[8]

Despite this, both the DP and the CHP continued to use religion to gain votes. CHP leader İnönü co-operated with the Nation Party's successor, the Republican Nation Party, and CHP support in central Anatolia was dependent on the Bektaşi vote (see Chapter 8). Similarly, as the DP began to lose its outright majority, it began to appeal more and more to Islam for support. This was no doubt aided by the formation of the Freedom Party on 20 December 1955, which saw the DP lose its more secular members to the new party. In February 1957 Menderes survived an aeroplane crash at Gatwick airport, and he subsequently openly

---

[8] Ahmad, *op. cit.*, pp. 41, 47, 367-70. Said Nursi (1873-1960), an ethnic Kurd, had a long history of religious political activity dating from 1908/9. He espoused an Islamic revivalist movement and founded the Nurcus, a movement which some see as a traditional *tarikat*, others as a *tarikat* in formation, and others as one in degeneration (from the Nakşibendis). Others see his movement as one to bring all Muslims together against secularisation and to restore an Islamic state (thus not a *tarikat* at all). After 1950 he emerged again and began to publish *Risale-i Nur* (Journal of Light). He reportedly demanded in a letter to Menderes that: his collection of speeches be in the curriculum of all Turkish schools; as Islam contains everything it should be the basis of the state; the head of State and National Assembly members should be religious Turks; there was no need for a constitution other than the Koran; and Şeriat should be the law. Saudi Arabia was cited as a successful example for Turkey to follow. In fact, despite the ostensive repression against Nursi, the DP flirted with the Nurcus for electoral reasons. The movement grew in the 1950s and 1960s throughout Turkey and abroad thanks to propaganda from its centre in Berlin. In Turkey the bulk of support came from small towns in Anatolia. See Şerif Mardin, *Religion and Social Change in Turkey: The Case of Bediüzzaman Said Nursi* (Albany: State University of New York Press, 1989), *passim*; Jacob M. Landau, *Radical Politics in Modern Turkey* (Leiden: E.J. Brill, 1974), pp. 184-5; and Paul Dumont, 'Disciples of the Light: The Nurcu Movement in Turkey', *Central Asian Survey* vol. 5, no. 2, 1986, pp. 33-60. The Nurcus became increasingly important in the 1980s, see below.

identified with Islam, using this 'miracle' for political ends. Moreover, in the October 1957 election he claimed that some 15,000 mosques had been built in Turkey in the previous seven years.[9]

The Kemalist elites, long used to their paternal role towards the general population, viewed this perceived Islamic resurgence from below with great unease. However, the military National Unity Committee (NUC), which took over in the 1960 coup, effectively kept the same policy and tolerated the religious *Imam-Hatip* schools as well as the Advanced Islamic Institute, which had been opened on 19 November 1959. The NUC was sophisticated enough to realise that Islam was a vital ingredient in the Turkish national psyche, and tried to encourage the Turkification of Islam, but was not in power long enough to achieve this.[10] The 1961 Constitution reaffirmed the separation of religion and state but banned politicised religion. In practice, there was little change from the 1950s. Between 1960 and 1964, some 6,000 new mosques were built and the number of *Imam-Hatip* schools rose throughout the decade, especially in the late 1960s.[11] The 1960s were a turbulent decade for Turkey, with the growth of left-wing forces (which under the 1961 Constitution were allowed to operate openly for the first time), as well as accelerated industrialisation. In this period, Islam became increasingly identified with anti-liberal and anti-socialist forces, and in opposition to the 1961 Constitution. In 1964 there was a resurgence in attacks on statues of Atatürk as well as a Nurcu revival. Leftwingers were castigated as communist lackeys of Moscow (and attacked by *Imam-Hatip* students), while the emerging capitalists were attacked as Masons or Zionists.[12] This period also saw the growth of 'petty-

---

[9] Ahmad, *op. cit.*, pp. 57, 370-1. There is some controversy over the actual number of mosques built in this period. G.L. Lewis writing in *The Muslim World*, vol. 56, no. 4, 1960, p. 235, states that 15,000 mosques were built in Turkey between 1950 and 1960, while Bülent Dâver in 'Secularism in Turkey', *SBFD*, vol. 22, no. 1, 1967, p. 59, says that only 5,000 were built in this decade.

[10] Ahmad, *op. cit.*, p. 375. As shown in Chapter 5, at this time NUC member Alparslan Türkeş wanted to substitute nationalist ideology for Islam but he was ousted from the NUC before this could take effect.

[11] In 1960-1 there were 337 teachers and 4,548 pupils in these schools; a decade later there were 1,547 teachers and 49,308 pupils. Landau, *Radical Politics*, p. 176.

[12] Ahmad, *op. cit.*, pp. 376-8. Even Süleyman Demirel was accused of being a Mason by Islamists, and in 1965 the Justice Party (AP), which was the successor

bourgeois' trade and artisan associations with a religious bias as self-defence units against the new capitalism, as well as Koran schools, which especially proliferated in the villages.[13] Despite the poor showing of left-wing parties like the Turkish Labour Party in successive elections in the 1960s, the Demirel governments appeared to view them as a grave threat and tolerated attacks by radical Islamists on leftwingers. The 1961 Constitution had allowed the universities great autonomy and left-wing radicalism among students was a feature of this period (as was right-wing radicalism in some). In 1966 the government promised that *Imam-Hatip* students would be able to go to university.[14] The decade also saw a proliferation of cheap religious literature (some of which even tried to show that Atatürk was a good Muslim), in which Landau[15] notes six reoccurring themes: Islam is a morally desirable way of life; the decline in the Muslim faith led to he fall of the Ottoman Empire and thus a return to faith would see a return to a 'Great Turkey'; there is no basic contradiction between secularism and Islam, and Turkish secularism is not anti-religious, indeed enlightened secularism *supports* Islam; there is no contradiction between Turkish nationalism and Islam, rather they complement each other as both are sacred foundations of Turkey, and Islam is an important element in Turkish culture; Islam is compatible with Western culture; and, lastly, Islam is *not* a reactionary force. Politicised Islam was forbidden in Turkey, and the 1965 Party Law specifically forbade political parties to campaign against secularism. Thus, the attempts to reconcile both secularism and Turkish nationalism with Islam were to some extent a matter of

---

to the banned DP, changed its emblem of an open book with the letters 'A' and 'P' on either side (which could be seen as symbolising the Koran with 'A' standing from 'Allah' and 'P' for *Peygamber*, the Prophet) to a less religiously-imbued grey horse symbol. However, Demirel continued to use Islam to further his political aims.

[13] In the late 1960s there were about 10,000 extra-curricular Koran courses under government supervision and another 40,000 privately arranged ones each year; Landau, *op. cit.* p. 176.

[14] In April 1968 a boycott at the Ankara University Theological Faculty took place over a female student who insisted on wearing the traditional head-scarf in class – an issue which has remained problematic to this day; Ahmad *op. cit.*, p. 381.

[15] Landau, *op. cit.*, p. 178.

self-defence. Nonetheless, the strong emphasis on Islam as an essential component of 'Turkishness' is notable.[16]

The 1950s and the 1960s saw the moderately Islamic centre-right forces of the DP and its successor the AP as the dominant popular political party. In line with this there was a re-emphasis on and support for moderate Islam as a component of Turkish national identity. However, the political climate did not allow overtly Islamic parties to operate, and those that did were closed. There were radical Islamic groups operating, of whom the Ticanis were to the fore in the early 1950s but came to be superseded in importance by the Nurcus and other small groups of radicals like the Süleymancıs. The latter were based in the east of the country and took their name from their founder Süleyman Seyfullah (1863-1946), whose goal was a theocratic state.[17] In early 1968 a national convention of *mukaddesatçılar* ('those revering sacred things') was held in Bursa, and claimed sovereignty belonged to Islam not to the nation. This convention also called for the return of the *Şeriat*, and a sustained effort by Islamists to infiltrate the education system (especially the universities), the press and judicial system, and even the military.[18] Thus, there were radical groups who called for Islam to be the main, if not the sole, component of national identity, but these remained peripheral. For the most part, this period saw the growth of a 'moderate Islam' in which Islam was once again seen by large sections of the mainstream political forces as a component of national identity, but one subordinated to the goals of Turkish nationalism.

The 1970s and the emergence of Necmettin Erbakan

The late 1960s saw a fragmentation of the right, with a number of new parties forming. Of particular significance in this respect was the National Order Party (MNP) of Necmettin Erbakan

[16] As noted in Chapter 5, the late 1960s also saw the pan-Turkist radicals move towards accommodating Islam.

[17] How influenced these groups were by outside ideologies is an open question. From 1967 Ahmed Selah el-Ali, a Palestinian radical based in the Lebanon, was reportedly increasingly active in Turkey among radical Islamic groups like the *Hizb-üt Tahrir*. This was broken up by the police, with many arrested in August and September 1967; Landau, *op. cit.*, p. 187.

[18] *Ibid.*, p. 187.

founded on 26 January 1970. Erbakan had been a contemporary of Demirel at the Istanbul Technical University, where he was a professor of engineering, and on 24 May 1969 had become president of Union of Chambers of Commerce and Industry.[19] He was also a follower of the Nakşibendi leader Halidi Shaikh Mehmed Zahid Kotku in Istanbul.[20] He thus presented the new 'technocratic' face of political Islam, one which was at home in the modern industrial world of big business but with an Islamic agenda in internal policies and an anti-European one abroad. In place of the perennial orientation towards Europe and the 'Christian' European Economic Community, he proposed that Turkey should look instead towards her Muslim neighbours. At a press conference of 26 January 1970 Erbakan stated that the MNP was against Freemasons, Communists and Zionists, and stood for democracy, social justice, freedom of conscience and other liberties. It was opposed to population planning and birth control. Among other things it wanted the strengthening of national morals in universities, radio and television, and the overhauling of education. Erbakan castigated the EEC (at that time, six Christian states) as being essentially Jewish and Zionist, and instead looked towards the '1,000 million world Muslims'.[21]

The return of the military to the political stage in 1971 saw the dissolution of the MNP on 20 May 1971, by order of the Constitutional Court, for violating Articles 2, 19, and 57 of the 1961 Constitution relating to the secular character of the state. In fact, only one paragraph out of the 100 in the MNP's 'Basic Aims' programme related directly to Islam, but its programme did contain as much Islamic content as it thought it could get away with. Despite the ban, the MNP leaders like Erbakan were not penalised, and in October 1972 they regrouped in the shape

[19] He had been prominent in the AP on the conservative Islamic wing, where he had been a fervent advocate of private initiative, but had fallen out with Demirel just prior to the 1969 elections. His candidacy had been vetoed in these elections by the AP but he had been elected as an independent for the religious stronghold of Konya.

[20] Binnaz Toprak, 'The Religious Right', p. 226. See also Şerif Mardin, 'The Nakşibendi Order in Turkish History' in R. Tapper (ed.), *Islam in Modern Turkey* (London: I.B. Tauris, 1991), p. 15.

[21] Landau, *op. cit.*, pp. 191-2. For more on Erbakan's views see his *Millî Görüş* (Istanbul: Dergâh Yayınları, 1975).

of the National Salvation Party (MSP). Despite (or perhaps because of) his background in big business, Erbakan argued that capitalism was undermining the traditional socioeconomic base of Anatolian society. He was successful in mobilising large-scale support from this sector, making the MSP the third largest party in the 1973 election[22] – albeit a long way behind the AP and CHP in popularity. Thus, the MSP's official doctrine had three main thrusts: a religious view of the world; a call for swifter industrialisation; and a redistributive populist economic and social ethic.[23] The MSP was to remain a significant force in politics in the 1970s, serving as a coalition partner in successive governments from January 1974 to December 1977 – initially in partnership with Ecevit's CHP, and then from 1975 in Demirel's 'National Front' government against the left.

Some saw the coalitions embracing the MSP, especially that with the CHP in 1974, as proof that it was 'part of the system' and was not trying to impose its own Islamic vision in an hegemonic fashion.[24] On the other hand, participation in government gave Erbakan badly needed legitimacy after his previous party, the MNP, had been banned as unconstitutional.[25] Participation in governments by the MSP can also be seen as a strategy by which it could take over key ministries to further its own ends. In this it was not alone, and parties like it and Türkeş's Nationalist Action Party (MHP) could thus exert greater influence than their electoral strength warranted. For example, in the first Demirel 'National Front' coalition of 1975-7, the MSP gained the Ministries of Justice, the Interior and Labour (but not Education, which was the one they particularly wanted). The 1970s were a decade of increasing turbulence in Turkish politics, leading to increasing

---

[22] Ahmad, *op. cit.*, pp. 318-19.

[23] Ş. Mardin, 'Religion in Modern Turkey' in *International Social Science Journal*, 1977, p. 292.

[24] Ahmad, for example, states that the MSP along with the CHP stood for 'fundamental freedoms' and this was one similarity between the two which helped explain their surprise coalition in 1974; Ahmad, *ibid.*, p. 332. The main similarly was probably shared opposition to Demirel.

[25] In the 1974 MSP/CHP coalition there were points of confluence like shared antipathy to the 'capitalist' EEC, and commitment to protection of tradesmen and 'the small man' against exploitation by 'big capital'. There were, however, obvious major differences, and the subsequent coalitions by Erbakan with Demirel were perhaps more rational.

anarchy and violence in the streets, and ultimately to the military coup of 1980. While there were many reasons for this collapse of democracy, one aspect relevant to the present discussion is the attempts by parties to take over key areas of the bureaucracy, especially the Education Ministry, thus propagating their ideologies and their notions of what constitutes the 'Turkish nation', and conversely negating other competing versions.[26] As noted in Chapter 1, this is essentially a classic nationalist policy.

As Landau points out, organisations like the MNP/MSP and the Nurcus differed in ideology from the *tarikats* and other strictly religious organisations as regards their attitude towards Turkish nationalism. They propagated an 'Islamic nationalism' (*İslam milliyetçiliği*). This attempted to identify Turkish nationalism with Islam by emphasising that Islam was a strong factor in the founding of the Turkish nation and that Turks were the foremost soldiers of Islam.[27] This contrasted strongly with the original Kemalist formulation which, as we have seen in Chapter 4, emphasised the pre-Islamic roots of the Turks and largely ignored the Islamic Ottoman period. It was, however, much closer to that propagated by Demirel and the centre-right, and similar to that later used by the post-1980 military regime (see below). The difference between the attitude of Erbakan and his followers on the one hand and that of the centre-right on the other related to the politicisation of Islam. Both groups appear to see Islam as a basic component of national identity, but for those like Menderes and Demirel it appears to have been seen as more of a personal matter. The state could and should aid Islam by government funding but should always be in control, and any form of overt Islamist politicisation was taboo. This was essentially a Kemalist approach, but one modified to take into account the overwhelming Islamic sympathies of the nation. For the Islamists this approach did not measure up to the basic precepts of Islam. They wanted Islam to be a basic component not just of individual identity but of the politics of the state. The stance of Erbakan and others was also superficially

[26] As Şerif Mardin notes, in connection with the MSP's natural power base, the combination of the lower-middle-class businessmen (the *ensaf*) and the *tarikats*, 'strengthened by the national scope of this operation [the MSP] will eventually try to capture the machinery of the state.' Ş. Mardin, 'Religion in Modern Turkey', p. 292.

[27] Landau, *op. cit.*, p. 192.

much closer to that adopted by Alparslan Türkeş and his followers from the pan-Turkist wing by the end of the 1960s (see Chapter 5). The difference between them was that Türkeş appears to have turned to Islam in an attempt to make his essentially pan-Turkist message more palatable to the populace. Erbakan on the other hand saw Islam as the main component. This may help to explain why Erbakan has succeeded to a larger extent than Türkeş in continuing to appeal to the disaffected. What this period does clearly illustrate is that the original Kemalist nationalism, in which Islam was largely ignored, had become untenable. Turkey was now a truly multi-party system in which the voting populace was overwhelmingly Muslim. As such, Islam was bound to be a factor.[28]

The Hearth of the Enlightened

The Hearth of the Enlightened (*Aydınlar Ocağı* – AO) was an influential organisation founded on 14 May 1970 by a group of university professors, *hocas*, and businessmen who viewed with alarm the penetration of left-wing ideologies in Turkey, especially in the universities. This was in many ways an extension of the Club of the Enlightened (*Aydınlar Kulübü*) set up in May 1962 by rightist intellectuals taking advantage of the new liberal climate following the 1960 coup. In both cases the basic aim was to strengthen the right-wing ...tionalist forces in the face of a growth in left-wing ideology. For the AO, humanism was seen as the enemy of national culture, as humanists defend laicism. This contributes to cosmopolitanism within the essentially Muslim Turkish culture. For the AO there were five main groups of enemies: atheists (which included materialists and communists); enemies of society (which included 'dividers' (*bölücüler* – that is Kurdish separatists), humanists and communists); other religious groups

---

[28] As we have seen, the main secularist Kemalist party, the CHP, even resorted to playing the Islamic card for electoral purposes. Despite such attempts to co-opt Islam, and its appeal to Atatürk's charismatic legacy, as well as its mass support from the Alevis who make up some 20% of the population (see Chapter 8), it is noteworthy that the CHP *never* gained an outright majority in elections after 1950 when multi-party politics became the norm. In contrast, recent elections have shown that the moderately Islamic centre-right combined with the Islamic right have a clear majority.

(like Christians); those responsible for the collapse of the Ottoman Empire; and 'forward and governing intellectuals'. The AO viewed the post-1960-coup democracy as a 'false democracy', in which the state-controlled religious authorities had not given rights to Muslims, and was thus inimical to the national ideal. Japan was cited as an example of how a country could adopt some Western modes of modernisation but still retain its 'national' values. As Turkey was overwhelmingly Muslim, there was a need to reassert a place for Islam in the secular Turkish Republic.[29] A leading ideologue of the AO was İbrahim Kafesoğlu, its first chair, who formulated what became later known as the Turkish Islamic Synthesis (see below). This was the attempted synthesis between Islam and Turkish nationalism which was adopted by the nationalist right (see Chapter 5). Other AO members included Turgut and Korkut Özal and others who were later to be leading members of the Motherland Party (ANAP) and the True Path Party (DYP) of the 1980s. The AO opposed Ecevit and the CHP, who were seen as leftist, and AO influence rose in Demirel's National Front governments of the late 1970s. Many AO publications appeared at this time. As noted above, the AO was a natural supporter of Türkeş's MHP, and in the increasingly polarised political climate of the late 1970s it was not hard for it to co-operate with Demirel. However, Erbakan and the MSP were less inclined to support the AO despite the confluence of Islamic ideas.[30] This was probably because, as noted above, for the AO and for Türkeş and his followers, Islam was seen as a way of strengthening Turkish nationalism, whereas Erbakan and others had an essentially Islamic view of the world.

By the end of the 1970s Islamists everywhere were emboldened by the Islamic revival in Iran.[31] Despite a decline in their electoral support in 1977 compared with that of 1973, the MSP and other Islamists were beginning to openly attack the foundations of the

---

[29] This was all spelt out in *Aydınlar Ocağı'nın Görüşü: Türkiye'nin Bugünkü Meseleri* (Istanbul: 1973), quoted in Bozkurt Güvenç, Gencay Saylan, İlhan Tekeli and Şerafettin Turan, *Türk-Islam Sentezi Dosyası* (Istanbul: Sarmal, 1991), pp. 41-3, 65, 67.

[30] *Ibid.*, pp. 187-91.

[31] While the revival in Iran was Shiite as opposed to Sunni, there were similarities between Reza Shah's attempted modernisation of Iran, and Atatürk's policies in Turkey, both of which engendered radical opposition from Islamists.

regime's ideology. In May 1980 worshippers at Istanbul's Fatih mosque jeered and booed at the mention of Atatürk in a service which was broadcast. Erbakan said he was sorry for such 'un-Muslim' behaviour but made no attempt to defend Atatürk's memory. On 6 September at a mass rally in Konya, MSP supporters from all over the country refused to sing the national anthem and called for the return of the *Şeriat*.[32]

The 1980 military authorities and the 'Turkish-Islamic Synthesis'

The military regime of 1980–83 closed down all political parties and banned their leaders from political life. Unlike previous army interventions in 1960 and 1971, when the military control was of deliberately limited duration, this time the military seemed determined to remain in power long enough to cement changes in attitudes and avert a repetition of the anarchy of the late 1970s. Despite the army's seeing itself as a bastion of Kemalism, it appears that the military rulers believed a lack of religious instruction in Turkey's youth had led to a proliferation of anti-systemic ideologies like Marxist-Leninism and fascism. Correspondingly, Article 24 of the 1980 Constitution stated that: 'Instruction in religious culture and moral education shall be compulsory in the curricula of primary and secondary schools.'[33] However, this state-propagated religion was not a recipe for rampant Islamism, and the same article mentioned that religious practices could not violate Article 14 of the Constitution, which expressly forbade a theocratic government (as well as a class-dictatorship). The strategy of this compulsory religious and moral education was spelt out in a report to the military rulers in September 1981.[34] This stated that religious education had passed into the hands of 'irresponsible people' outside state control, and as a result 'the current negative and political currents (*Ticanilik, Nurculuk, Süleymanalık*, etc.) were born.' It concluded that there should be compulsory classes, in primary

[32] Clement H. Dodd, *The Crisis of Turkish Democracy* (Huntingdon: Eothen Press, 2nd edn, 1990), p. 24, and Erik J. Zürcher, *Turkey: A Modern History* (London: I.B. Tauris, 1993), p. 282.

[33] *The 1982 Turkish Constitution*, Article 24, reprinted in Dodd, *op. cit.*

[34] *Milli Eğtim Bakanlığı Din Bilgisi Öğretimi* (Ankara, September 1981).

schools on subjects such as 'I am a Muslim Turkish child' (class one), and in secondary schools 'Turks and Muslims' (class eight), 'love of the Prophet' (class nine), and 'Turkish-Islamic culture and civilisation' (class 11).[35] The basic thrust of this policy was amplified in 1982.[36] The 'General Aims of Religious and Moral Education' were given as:

> To learn in basic and middle education enough basic knowledge of Islamic religion and morals in accordance with Atatürk's laicist and other principles, along the lines of the general aims of the Turkish national educational policies; thus the populace will obtain good morals and virtues to ensure in them a love of people, religion, morals, Atatürkism (*Atatürkçuluk*), national unity and togetherness.

Among the 'Principles' it was stated that:

> The aims of religious education will 1. Always take into consideration our state's secular basis and always defend this principle. ... 4. Take care to inculcate by the instruction of religious knowledge into the pupils the exalted concept of the national value as a *gazi*, or martyr, and of the value of the standard, flag, nation, and fatherland, and to strengthen brotherly and friendly relations, respect, love, togetherness and national unity. 5. To always keep in mind the national worth of our traditions, customs and practices ... 6. Lesson subjects should always be integrated with Atatürk's principles.

Specifically, the programme called for two hours a week of basic education in religion and morals for classes one to eight, which would include in classes four to five the aim: 'to consolidate the love of Atatürk, the fatherland, and nation.'

In classes six, seven and eight the aim was

> .... to bring about heroic feelings concerning the history of the Turks ... and in defence of the fatherland, and to bring

---

[35] *Ibid.*, p. 4.

[36] The following excerpts are taken from *Temel Eğitim ve Ortaöğretim Din ve Ahlak Bilgisi Dersi Programı* (Ankara, n.d. but proposed in 1982 after religious and moral education had become compulsory). This is still in force although a new draft Religious Education Programme is being prepared.

about knowledge of the Turks' service to Islam throughout history.[37]

When we look at the actual subjects the aims of the state become clearer:

> Class seven, unit ix, *Secularism and Islamism*, 1. What is Secularism? 2. Atatürk and secularism. 3. Atatürk's views regarding Islam. 4. A choice of Atatürk's quotations concerning Islam.
> Class eight, unit iii, *Secularism and Islamism*, 1. The place of religion in the understanding of secularism. 2. What is secularism according to Islamic understanding?
> Unit vi, *Love of Nation and Fatherland*, 1. Why must we love our nation and our fatherland? 2. Defence and protection of the fatherland ... 4. The giving to M.K. Atatürk the title of *Gazi*. 5. Views in connection with the merits of Atatürk's morals. 6. Respect for the sacred merits concerning war: a) respect for the flag and the National Anthem; b) respect for the army and standard; c) respect to national heroes and great men of state; d) the sacredness of military service.
> Unit viii, *The Turks and Islam*, 1. How and why did the Turks become Muslims. 2. The Turks' contribution to Islam. 3. The spread of Islam ... 4. The Turks' attitudes to those of other religions.[38]

In junior high school (*ortaokul*) education, which was to have one hour per week of such classes, the stated basic aims were virtually identical to those in primary education. Here the topics covered included:

> Unit iv, *Turkish-Islamic Culture and Civilisation*.
> Unit v, *Atatürk and our Religion*, 1. Atatürk's views concerning secularism and our religion. 2. What is secularism? 3. Atatürk's understanding of secularism. 4. Atatürk's views concerning our religion.[39]

This curriculum closely corresponded to the so-called 'Turkish-Islamic Synthesis' (TİS) which had been worked out by Ibrahim Kafesoğlu, a leading ideologue of the 'Hearth of the Enlightened'

---

[37] *Ibid.*, pp. 4 and 10.

[38] *Ibid.*, pp. 17-20.

[39] *Ibid.*, pp. 21, 26 and 27.

of the 1970s (see above). This TİS held that Islam had a special attraction to Turks due to supposed similarities between pre-Islamic Turkish society and Islamic civilisation including a sense of justice, monotheism, belief in the immortal soul, and a strong emphasis on family life and morality. Given this, the Turks were to be 'the soldiers of Islam'.[40] As noted, this ideology had been taken up by the MHP and the extreme right in the 1970s as it emphasised both Islam and the pre-Islamic history of the Turks. It was an attempt to bring supposedly shared values to the surface, peel away the 'false Western veneer' which was seen as responsible for such ills of modern society as drug addiction and crime, and recognise a national synthesis of fundamental values under the labels of 'Turk' and 'Islam'. As Richard Tapper points out, this synthesis aimed at an authoritarian but not an Islamic state where religion was seen as the essence of culture and social control, and should thus be fostered in the education system but not politicised.[41] This policy had similarities with Abdülhamid's use of Islam as a form of 'social cement' in the late nineteenth century (see Chapter 3).

The TİS became widely propagated. It was the basis of the State Planning Department's National Cultural Report of 1983,[42] which despite being ostensibly a democratic project was 'really a totalitarian, authoritarian cultural plan.'[43] Additionally, after the 12 September 1980 coup, personnel of the new bodies overseeing education and culture – TRT (radio and television broadcasting), YÖK (Board of Higher Education, the supreme body overseeing educational matters, with ministerial functions and staffed by government appointees), university rectors and the Education Ministry – were all leading AO members.[44] The 1980-3 period saw a veritable legislative blitz by YÖK to purge the universities of politically undesirable teachers and bring them into line with the new policies.[45] After 1983 the TİS was carried on by the Özal

---

[40] E.J. Zürcher, *Turkey: A Modern History* (London: I.B. Tauris, 1993), pp. 302-3.

[41] R. Tapper, 'Introduction' in R. Tapper (ed.), *Islam in Modern Turkey* (London: I.B. Tauris, 1991), p. 16.

[42] *Milli Kültür Raporu*, (Ankara: Devlet Planlama Teşkilatı Yayını, 1983).

[43] Güvenç, Saylon, Tekeli and Turan, *Türk-Islam Sentezi Dosyası*, p. 61.

[44] *Ibid.*, p. 192.

[45] Ayşe Öncü, 'Academics: The West in the Discourse of University Reform'

regime. It was clearly evident in school textbooks. For example, the *İmam-Hatip* high schools educational programme published in 1985 reiterates the basic aims of national education. Along with the usual Kemalist aims of duty and responsibility to the indivisible Turkish state, and the adoption of Turkist (*Türklük*) principles, the programme stresses that the Turks were 'the leaders in the rise and spread of Islam in the world.' It also stresses the importance of 'the union of Turkish moral values with Islamic belief', and that 'amongst the fundamentals of the Turkish way of life is the need for the Islamic religion.'[46]

While politicised Islam still remained relatively taboo, the penetration of religious ideology into mainstream politics was a marked feature of the 1980s. The education ministry was again a prime post and in 1984, the Minister of Education Vehbi Dinçerler, reportedly a Nakşibendi member, banned the teaching of Darwin in primary and secondary schools.[47] The growing influence of the TİS in the late 1980s saw a reaction from staunch Kemalists, especially those from the *Cumhuriyet* newspaper, and a series of articles attacking its penetration into the government appeared.[48]

The scope of government support by both the 1980-83 military authorities and the Özal governments for the spread of Islamicisation in Turkey is clearly shown in a pamphlet of early 1990 by the head of the Directorate of Religious Affairs, Professor Yazıcıoğlu, which describes and details the activities of his department in the previous ten years. In 1989 the department had a budget of TL 232 billion and over 84,712 employees – up from 50,765 in 1979. Of these 84,712 employees, 77,722 were in religious service,

---

in Metin Heper, Ayşe Öncü and Heinz Kramer (eds), *Turkey and the West: Changing Political and Cultural Identities* (London: I.B. Tauris, 1993), pp. 166-7.

[46] *İmam-Hatip Liseleri Öğretim Programları*, T.C. Millî Eğitim Gençlik ve Spor Bakanlığı, Dinöğretimi Genel Müdürlüğü (Ankara: Millî Eúgitim Basımevi, 1985) pp. 15-17.

[47] Güvenç, Saylan, Tekeli and Turan, *Türk-İslam Dosyası*, p. 204.

[48] The term TİS is almost never used by right-wing nationalists or Islamists, who view its use as hostile as it implies that the ideology is somewhat artificial. The term is most commonly used by opponents of the ideology in the Kemalist secular camp. It is rarely referred to in the popular press and 'the man in the street has no knowledge of the TİS'; *ibid.*, p. 18. For a detailed list of such articles attacking the TİS, see *ibid.*, pp. 17-24.

4,994 in general management and 1,976 in supplementary services. While Turkey had 20 religious personnel working in offices abroad in 1980, by 1989 there were 628 such staff (see Chapter 9 for the activities of the department outside Turkey). The number of *İmam-Hatip* graduates in the department rose from 2,688 in 1973 to 39,907 in 1988. The report stated that an average of 1,500 mosques were being built each year and that the ratio of mosques to the general population was 1:857. In 1984 there were 54,667 mosques in Turkey and a further 8,280 new ones were constructed in the next four years. There were 62,947 by the end of 1988. Of these, 49,040 are in sub-districts, towns and villages, and 13,907 in provincial centres. Regarding Koran schools, 234 new ones are being opened each year. In 1979-80 there were 2,610 such schools in the country. This figure rose to 3,047 by the end of the military regime in 1983, and increased to 4,715 in 1988-9. While 68,486 pupils attended such schools in 1979, the figure had risen to 155,403 in 1989 of whom 97,053 were male and 58,350 female. The number of Korans inspected and approved annually by the ministry rose sharply after the 1980 coup from 31,075 in 1979 to 259,731 in 1981. A further sharp increase was noted in 1985 when 599,629 were approved, and this rose to 964,973 for 1987 alone. All in all in the 1980s, 4,057,942 new Korans were passed by the ministry.[49]

As well as the huge budget for the Directorate of Religious Affairs (in 1995 TL 12.3 trillion, which is equal to that of five ministries: Tourism, Environment, Industry, Transport, and Energy and Natural Resources), TL 4.8 trillion from the Education Ministry's 1995 budget is earmarked for religious educational needs. Some of this goes to the 476,000 pupils in the 454 İmam-Hatip schools. When these are added to the number of previous graduates from these schools which are set up to train religious functionaries, it appears that over one million have been trained, and there are plans to open more such schools.[50] On the other hand, at the end of November 1989 some 14,000 Islamists were reported to have been tried for Islamic political activity since the 1980

---

[49] These figures are taken from the 32-page pamphlet details of which were published in *Briefing*, no. 784/5, 23-30 April 1990, p. 19. In 1993 the numbers of Korans passed numbered a staggering 820,000. *Hürriyet*, 30 August 1994.

[50] This adds up to about one trained religious functionary for every 50 people in Turkey, a huge figure. *İnfo-Türk*, E. 217, November/December 1994, p. 11.

coup.[51] While Islamists appeared successful in penetrating many state and government bodies, the armed forces, the bastion of secularist Kemalism, regularly purged would – be infiltrators.[52]

The Welfare Party and Erbakan's return

Thus, the penetration of Islamic notions of what constituted Turkish identity continued apace in the 1980s, initially propagated by the military but then taken up by the Özal governments. When the referendum of 6 September 1987 lifted the ban on the pre-1980 leading politicians, Erbakan returned as official leader of the reconstituted MSP, now known as the Welfare Party (RP). the RP continued with the MNP/MSP emphasis on Islam as the primary focus of loyalty. This is clearly shown in the answers given by the Executive Committee of RP District organisation in Trabzon on 29 August 1994:[53]

> Q. Turkey is an overwhelmingly Muslim country. Is Islam an essential component of Turkish identity? Can one be a Turk without being a Muslim?
> A. Islam is sent to the whole of the human race. It is a supranational religion. When one says 'Turk', one thinks of Islam. This is because the Turks accepted Islam and served it.
> Q. How does RP view the Alevis – are they true Turks? Is there assimilation of them by the Sunni majority as they allege?
> A. RP sees no difference between Alevis and Sunnis. Nobody is oppressed because of his/her belief. For the Alevis it is not important being a Turk, being human is enough. There is no assimilation of the Alevis by the Sunnis.
> Q. How does RP view non-Muslim Kemalists – are they true Turks?

[51] *Mideast Mirror*, 23 November 1989, quoting *Cumhuriyet*.

[52] In early 1990 there was a spate of stories in the Turkish press about attempted Islamic penetration of the armed forces. On 19 May Defence Minister Safa Giray said that 114 Air Force personnel had been dismissed for 'Islamic fundamentalism', adding to the 364 dismissed from the combined armed services in the previous seven years for such reasons. See *Mideast Mirror* and *Turkish Daily News*, 21 May 1990.

[53] I submitted the questions to them in writing the previous day and the answers were also in writing.

A. RP's view is that everybody should have freedom to live according to what they believe in. Being a Kemalist or not does not matter.

Q. How does RP view minorities like the Kurds?

A. RP sees no division between Turks and Kurds and accepts them all as brother Muslims.

Q. How does RP view Turks and Turkic people outside the country?

A. RP accepts that there is a Turkish identity but does not put it in first place. Islamic brotherhood and human rights are the essentials.

Q. How does RP reconcile notions that ethnicity is divisive and that all Turks and Kurds are brother Muslims with modern nationalism and Turkey's borders?

A. RP wants to establish and maintain human rights and justice throughout the world. To accomplish this, it calls for the establishment as soon as possible of an Islamic United Nations, and Islamic Common Market, and Islamic Cultural Union (akin to UNESCO). All Muslims are brothers and equal: superiority comes in serving humanity. RP works for salvation and prosperity of all humanity whether Muslims or non-Muslims.

Q. Atatürk created the secular Turkish state. In the light of this, how does RP view him, and especially the all-pervasive pictures and statues of him?

A. RP believes that Atatürk and his legacy is exploited by certain circles in Turkey. This exploitation must be overcome.

Q. Is there such a thing as the TİS and if so does RP adhere to it?

A. There is no deficiency in Islam as a religion. Thus there is no need for any synthesis or analysis for Islam. The TİS is an idea only put forward in recent times.

These answers, besides illustrating the RP's emphasis on Islam as the main focus, also display its caution at accusations of being anti-Atatürk, and totalitarian in the sense that it would not tolerate other groups with radically differing ideologies if it gained power – both of which are against the law and could lead to its closure and prosecution. Again, we are faced with the question as to whether the RP, like the MSP before it, is anti-systemic in the sense that it ultimately aims at total hegemony. Of course, all political parties aim for 100 per cent support, but the question here is how tolerant would it be of opposing ideologies if it took power on its own. Some like Nilülfer Göle believe that while Islam has penetrated the Turkish state, 'modernism' has also penetrated Turkish Islam, which is now, she believes, essentially democratic and tolerant.[54] Conversely, one could point to the increasing number of violent incidents like the attacks on Alevis in Sivas and Istanbul (see Chapter 8) and against those not observing Ramadan.[55] Erbakan himself commented on the difficulties of restraining his supporters from using violence to achieve political success.[56] Moreover, he himself has made ambiguous statements along these very lines.[57] Perhaps the true face of the RP is more clearly shown by the more outspoken Istanbul deputy Hasan Mezarcı, who on 27 April 1992 criticised Demirel for saying it was possible to be both secular, democratic and Muslim. Mezarcı stated:

> I am not secular or democratic. I am a Muslim. Did Allah make some mistake which Demirel has to put right? You cannot be a Muslim in the way that Demirel is. Muslims with Demirel's identity cannot go to heaven. Democracy and secularism do not promise us heaven.

Mezarcı also attacked Demirel for saying that there should be no distinction between believers and non-believers, and he further asserted that the parliamentary oath and the constitution were not binding on Muslims.[58] Mezarcı led a group of twelve deputies who attempted to rehabilitate those accused of plotting to kill

---

[54] See her quotes in Nicole Pope and Yves Heller, 'Turkey divided over emerging Islamism', *Le Monde*, 31 May 1995.

[55] For example, on 22 February 1995, thirty people armed with knives, meat cleavers and clubs raided a restaurant and cafeteria in the Göztepe campus of Istanbul's Marmara University and attacked those not observing the fast. *Turkey Briefing*, vol. 9, no. 1, 1995. There have been many such incidents in recent years.

[56] *Briefing*, no. 929, 1 March 1993.

[57] For example, in mid-April 1994 after the dramatic gains for the RP in nationwide local elections of 27 March that year, Erbakan stated that the RP would inevitably take over 'whether in peaceful or bloody fashion, depending on the will of the people.' *Turkey Briefing*, vol. 8, no. 2, 1994.

[58] *The Month in Turkey*, no. 16, April 1992, which noted that Mezarcı was spokesman for the GNA's Human Rights Commission, and described him as a 'fairly typical RP representative'.

Atatürk seventy years earlier.[59] However, such outspokenness proved too much for Erbakan, and Mezarcı was expelled from the RP.[60]

Quite what the RP would actually do if it gained power remains unclear – probably deliberately so given Turkey's current penal code. The two crucial questions concern the situation as regards the Kurds and the legal system. Regarding the Kurds, Erbakan has often pointed out that this problem can, in his view, be overcome by emphasising the bonds of Islam instead of the divisive ones of ethnicity.[61] Would a majority RP government attempt to reintroduce the *Şeriat*? Erbakan has said that in the next elections:

> Our aim is to obtain an absolute majority at the National Assembly, necessary to modify the constitution.[62] It is no longer possible to stop the 'Just order' storm which began at the 27 March [local] elections.[63]

[59] Of these twelve, eight were from RP, two from the Democracy Party, and one from DYP and 1 from the Great Unity Party. *Anatolia News Agency*, 24 February 1994, in BBC EE/1933, B/8, 28/2/94. Mezarcı's outspokenness in parliament against Atatürk led to trouble with the state security authorities and his parliamentary immunity being lifted. He had alleged that Atatürk's mother was a prostitute and that Atatürk was born out of wedlock during the extraordinary 'respect for Atatürk week' in early 1994 – see *Briefing*, no. 980, 7 March 1994. However, the case against him was dismissed on 17 February 1995. See *Turkey Briefing*, vol. 9, no. 1, 1995.

[60] He tried to form a new political movement with two other former RP deputies in August 1994. *Anatolia News Agency*, 5 August 1994, in SWB EE/2068, B/5, 7/3/95.

[61] For example, in an interview with Mehmet Ali Birand and Can Dundar, he stressed that his mission was to give the 60 million people of Turkey 'a sense of love and brotherhood.' He stated: 'There is nothing more absurd than ethnic differentiation among Muslim brothers.' *Show TV*, Ankara, 31 January 1994, in SWB EE/1914, B/8, 5/2/94. See also Chapter 7.

[62] The aim was to change Article 24, which banned religiously based parties. In the debates of 1994 and 1995 on liberalising the constitution, ANAP was also in favour of changing this article but the SHP/CHP were strongly opposed. The RP made its support for lifting the repressive measures contingent on removing Article 24. When this was not included in the reform package, the RP became isolated and was the only party to vote against the changes on 23 July 1995; even then some RP members must have abstained or voted for the changes as only 30 voted against; *Cumhuriyet*, 24 July 1995. See also *Probe*, 24 June 1994, for the previous discussions.

[63] To the RP's National Vision Organisations in Europe (AMGT) annual congress in Antwerp in 11 June 1994. *İnfo-Türk*, E. 212, June 1994, p. 4.

While this 'just order' was not explicitly stated to be Islamic (as it is still against the law to say this), it certainly has this connotation. The return of the *Şeriat* is a frequent call at RP mass rallies. The RP mayor of Bingöl, Selahattin Aydar, was dismissed from his post for calling for the return of the *Şeriat* on the TV programme Kanal-6 prior to the March 1994 local by-elections.[64] The RP mayor for Rize, Sevki Yılmaz, was also under investigation for inciting religious discrimination in his speeches.[65]

The RP successes in the local elections of March 1994, when it won the mayoralties in Istanbul and Ankara and other municipalities, especially in the southeast, were followed by reports of attacks on women in Western dress in a number of places including Istanbul's social centre, Beyoğlu. One report told of Islamists stopping a computer train and ordering all the women to sit in a separate compartment.[66] The Istanbul governor, Hayri Kozakçıoğlu called on security forces to prevent such measures and Erbakan said that there would be no 'bans' on private behaviour.[67] Since then, the new RP municipal authorities have kept a relatively low profile and not attempted to radically Islamicise city life in Ankara and Istanbul, the two metropolitan centres. Conversely, large numbers of secularists in the main centres have taken to wearing badges of Atatürk, and his 'personality cult' in the shape of numerous huge banners of his likeness reached new heights on Republic Day 1994. This struggle, which is essentially a nationalist one between competing visions of the basic elements of the Turkish nation continues and is reflected in the controversy over what symbol should be used to represent the capital, Ankara. The old Kemalist symbol was a Hittite one (linking in with the 1930s History Thesis – see Chapter 4). The RP proposed a new, more Islamic one of two minarets on top of a crescent, provoking much dissent. While this symbol still needed to be officially passed, in July 1995 it was already being used on the city's buses by order of the RP mayor.[68]

[64] He reportedly said: 'If I had 10 heads, I would sacrifice all 10 of them for *Şeriat*.' Kanal-6 TV, London, 9 July 1995, in SWB EE/2350, B/3, 11/7/95.

[65] TRT TV, Ankara, 5 January 1995, in SWB EE/2194, B/3, 7/1/95. Videotapes of his rousing speeches were being shown at Trabzon RP headquarters to the party faithful to help inspire them to greater successes in the future.

[66] *Turkey Briefing*, vol. 8, no. 1, 1994.

[67] TRT TV, Ankara, 1 and 3 April 1994, in SWB EE/1963, B/5, 5/4/94.

[68] Claire Poynton, *Newsdesk*, BBC World Service, 4 July 1995. Ankara, unlike

What is clear is that in the 1990s the RP has managed to break out of its previous minority role and become a mass party attracting almost 20 per cent of the national vote. One reason for this success has been its policy of providing services to the dispossessed in the *gecekondular* as well as its reputation of being far less corrupt that other main political parties.[69] In addition, the RP has shown itself adept at using modern technology with, for example, lists of all Istanbul's 4.4 million voters on computer disc. This allowed it to know exactly how to target the electorate.[70] By 1994 the RP had succeeded in entrenching itself in the Interior Ministry, with some 700 of the 1,500 key administrators in the country, such as provincial and county governors or inspectors, believed to be RP supporters.[71]

The new Islamic intellectuals

Many in the Kemalist élite see Islamic forces as a conservative phenomenon which modernisation will sweep away. In line with this classic Kemalist view, they view the recent growth of Islamic political forces with a mixture of incomprehension and distrust, and often attempt either to belittle it or label it as a passing

---

Istanbul, does not have a skyline dominated by huge mosques, with the exception of the Kocatepe Mosque, completed in 1987, which competes with Atatürk's mausoleum, the *Anıtkabır*, in the centre of town. The old citadel to the north, and the commercial buildings to the south in the new elite areas like Gaziosmanpaşa make up the other 'dominant' buildings. For a full discussion of the competing symbolic values represented by the Anıtkabır and the Kocatepe Mosque, see Michael E. Meeker's paper, 'Once there was, once there wasn't: National Monuments and Interpersonal Exchange', presented at the MIT conference 'Rethinking the Project of Modernity in Turkey', Massachusetts Institute of Technology, March 1994.

[69] Especially in comparison to the centre-left SHP, whose control of cities like Istanbul became notorious for corruption. The RP was accused of misappropriating a large amount of funds destined for Bosnia in 1995; see *Turkey Briefing*, vol. 8, no. 4, 1994. However, the party managed to ride this out and still retain its image of relative probity.

[70] *Briefing*, 10 January 1994.

[71] Of the country's seventy-six provincial governors, twenty-four had performed the pilgrimage to Mecca in the last few years at the invitation of the Saudi Arabian authorities. *Cumhuriyet*, 2 May 1994.

symptomatic reaction to modernisation.[72] On the other hand, it can be argued that the rise of Islam which began in the 1970s in Turkey (and elsewhere[73]) was due in no small part to the process of its *political* revival and re-emergence as an ideology legitimising political action. This new radical Islamism is unlike that of the Young Turks or the modernisers of the Ottoman Empire who attempted to justify modernisation and Westernisation in terms of Islamic principles (see Chapter 2). Rather, it is a political cultural movement radically opposed to Western civilisation and the Western model of modernisation, which is seen as being in contradiction to Islam.[74] The new radical Islamists pose what they see as the contradictions between the Western model adopted by the secularist Kemalist élite and what they consider to be the basis of an Islamic society, and they find the Western model wanting.[75]

Thus, the new Islamic intellectuals attack the basis of the Western ideals of development to which the secularist Kemalists hold fast. Their critique is basically that the emphasis on consumption and materialism is obliterating the 'true' values of Islamic civilisation. The Western ideal promises 'paradise on earth' but fails to deliver.[76] Included in this critique is an attack on the drive for incessant

[72] For example Binnaz Toprak, 'The Religious Right', and Türker Altan, 'The National Salvation Party in Turkey' in Metin Heper and Raphael Israeli (eds), *Islam and Politics in the Modern Middle East* (New York: Croom Helm, 1984). In this matter, the writings of Şerif Mardin stand out in contrast.

[73] Interestingly, Turkish Islamists rarely refer to similar movements in other countries, instead keeping their gaze focused on Turkey.

[74] Haldun Gülalp, 'Modernisation Policies and Islamist Politics', delivered at the conference 'Rethinking the Project of Modernity in Turkey' (see footnote 68).

[75] This links in with wider discussions of 'modernism' versus 'post-modernism', and 'individualism' (associated with the former) versus 'community' (associated with the latter, with the added connotations of discipline, etc.). This can even be seen to link with feminism, which may support a 'holistic' view of society as opposed to the rampant 'male' individualism of Western modernity. The latter viewpoint is discussed below in relation to the new Islamic women radicals.

[76] See: Ali Bulaç, *Din ve Modernizm* (Istanbul: np, 1991), p. 27; Ismet Özel, *Üç Mesele: Teknik, Medeniyet ve Yabancılaşma (Istanbul: np, 1992), p 151;* and İsmet Özel, 'Kalkinma? Ilerleme? Varolma?' and Ahmet Tabakoğlu, 'İslam Iktisadı Açısından "Kalkınma"' both in Ahmet Tabakoğlu and İsmail Kurt (eds), *Iktisadi Kalkınma ve İslam* (Istanbul: np, 1987), pp. 232 and 241-3 respectively. See also Binnaz Toprak, 'Islamist Intellectuals: Revolt against Industry and Technology' in Heper, Öncü and Kramer (eds), *Turkey and the West*, pp. 245-9.

economic growth, which is seen as leading to an increase in the individual's narrow self-interest at the expense of the values of a wider community.[77] As Haldun Gülap points out,[78] this critique bears some striking similarities to the Western environmentalist critique of constant economic growth. In both cases, the ideal is one in which humans live in harmony with 'the natural order' as opposed to striving for endless consumption of material objects. In this essentially 'post-modernist' critique of modernism, Islam is held up as a superior value system. As such, the Islamists condemn official Kemalist nationalism, which is seen as an imitation of the West, and in its place espouse one based essentially on Islam.

An important point concerning these new Islamic intellectuals is that they are themselves products of the Kemalist modernising education system. They are all university graduates (indeed some, like civil servant Rasim Özdenörem and *Zaman* correspondent Fehmi Koru, were educated at US universities). They are well versed in essentially secular modes of discourse which, thanks to universal mass education, are readily understandable by all. This places them in an advantageous position over, for example, the traditional *tarikat* leaders, who use a language and terminology which is much less accessible to a mass audience. For example, the books of İsmet Özel, a former Marxist poet and now leading Islamist intellectual,[79] sell in huge quantities, with many in their

[77] Other examples include Ersin Gündoğan, *Teknolojinin Ötesi* (Istanbul: np, 1991), pp. 20 and 125, and Besir Hamitoğullan, 'İktisadi Vahşi Büyümenin Bunalımları ve İslam Kalkınma Modelinin Vaadettikleri' in Tabakoğlu and Kurt, *İktisadi Kalkınma ve İslam*, pp. 10-12 and 16- 17.

[78] Haldun Gülalp, 'Modernization Policies and Islamic Politics', paper at MIT conference (see footnote 68).

[79] This switch from active Marxist in the 1970s to radical Islamist in the 1980s and 1990s appears not to have been as unique as might be expected given the mutual antagonism between Marxists and Islamists. See Michael Meeker, 'The New Muslim Intellectuals in the Republic of Turkey' in R. Tapper (ed.), *Islam in Modern Turkey*, pp. 189-219. One explanation could be that both Marxism and Islam offer the acolyte an all-inclusive system of beliefs and life which appeals to certain individuals. The military take-over and the general world crisis of socialism has seen many former Marxists 'lose their faith', and some have moved straight over to Islamism. Similar switches across the political spectrum were observable in Weimar Germany in the late 1920s and early 1930s when Marxists moved in large numbers straight to Hitler's party, when it was seen as being on the rise. These examples perhaps indicate that there is an essential political conflict between an 'individualistic' viewpoint – the classic Western

fourth or fifth editions. Indeed, many of the new young radicals are not from the 'backward, ignorant' elements of society, rather they are likely now to be university graduates from economics faculties – the very people whom classic Kemalists originally saw as the harbingers of secularism. The wearing of the head-scarf for women in public buildings, especially in the universities, became a battle-ground between the two viewpoints in the late 1980s. Under the Kemalist regimes, this had been banned as one of Kemal's secularist policies. However, in the late 1980s Islamist female students began to flout the law and the issue came to a head. Özal's ANAP party, influenced by its strong Islamic/ nationalist faction – the so-called 'Holy Alliance'[80] – passed a law allowing the wearing of the head-scarf in public buildings like universities, but President Evren referred it back to the Constitutional Court. Eventually in December 1989 the ban on head-scarves was lifted, and the question left to university rectors to decide individually in each case.[81]

This struggle over the veil raises interesting points about the position of women. On the one hand it is seen by many secularists as one of the classic elements of Islam which counters modernisation – that is that veiling subjugates women and thus works against their equality. On the other hand, some point out this most visible of Islamic symbols can be seen as a way in which women themselves can make radical political statements, and that the

liberal one – and an essentially 'communal one' – whether this be Marxist, fascist or religious (in this case Islamist). This line of argument may help explain such switches, as many with a penchant for 'communal' values would tend to support whichever 'communal' force was in the ascendant at a particular time.

[80] This was an alliance of those ANAP members who had a specifically Islamic viewpoint (some of whom were members of the MSP in the 1970s) and those whose more right-wing nationalist viewpoint had a distinctly Islamic tinge along the lines of the TİS (some of the latter were former members of the MHP). See Üstün Ergüder, 'The Motherland Party, 1983-1989' in M. Heper and J.M. Landau (eds), *Political parties and democracy in Turkey* (London: I.B. Tauris, 1991), p. 160. See also Jermey Salt, 'Nationalism and the Rise of Muslim Sentiment in Turkey', *Middle Eastern Studies*, vol. 31, no. 1, 1995, pp. 13- 27.

[81] Erik Zürcher, *Turkey: A Modern History*, p. 304. This also illustrates the attitude to Islam of Evren and the military authorities in 1980-3 – namely that it was to be used to help promote solidarity in Turkish society, but not when it attacked the foundations of Kemalism. It can be argued that their policy ran the serious risk of getting out of control, with the Islamic tail wagging the Kemalist dog.

veiling by young female radicals is not docile or passive but a powerful sign of Islamism.[82] This may be true for the university-educated urban élites, many of whom are graduates of the *Imam-Hatip* schools but also include some children of Kemalist secularists (here, inter-generational differences and tensions play a part); conversely, it also seems true that for many women veiling is a docile measure imposed either by their dominant Islamist men or by the prevailing norms by which they live.[83]

Either way, it seems that there is a powerful coalition between the traditional religious support of the *esnaf* and others, who see their way of life threatened by the rapid changes in Turkey in the 1980s, and a new breed of university-trained intellectuals. As noted below, Özal's privatisation wave (in the sense of wider opportunities in the social and cultural spheres) has allowed Islamists to propagate their message widely, along with their critique of modern Turkish society, which includes a critique of Turkish nationalism. The crux of the matter relates to concepts of Turkish identity. The new Islamists promote a view which is based on Islamic precepts, and which negates what is seen as false Western ones, to a ready audience. The gulf between the old secularist Kemalist élite and the new rival Islamic ones with their mass audiences in the *gecekondular* has become especially acute.[84] The rise of the RP and its success in capturing the mayoralties of

[82] For example Nilüfer Göle, 'The Quest for the Islamic Self within the context of Modernity', paper at the MIT conference 'Rethinking the Project of Modernity in Turkey' (see footnote 68).

[83] This is readily observable in religious strongholds like Erzurum where the veiling of women is clearly not such a radical personal gesture. For a discussion of the varying content and different target groups of three Islamic women's journals, two Nakşibendi ones, *Kadın ve Aile* and *Mektup*, and one Nurcu one, *Bizim Aile*, see Feride Acar, 'Women in the Ideology of Islamic Revivalism in Turkey: Three Islamic Women's Journals' in R. Tapper (ed.), *Islam in Turkey*, pp. 280-303.

[84] This is especially evident in the 'Arabesk' debate. Here the Kemalist elites controlling TRT looked down on Arabesk (a popular fusion of Turkish and Egyptian music with a strong pessimistic lyrical content often reflecting the problems of recently arrived migrants to the cities). They did not see it as truly 'Turkish' (neither did the pan-Turkish right – see Chapter 5); see Martin Stokes, *The Arabesk Debate: Music and Musicians in Modern Turkey* (Oxford: Clarendon Press, 1992), *passim*. Another aspect of the gap is reflected in the '*maganda*' and '*zonta*' stereotypes of the Arabesk-loving *gecekondu* Turk which first appeared in cartoon strips in newspapers in the mid-1980s.

Istanbul and Ankara has put the old élite into something of a panic. The current debate revolves around the issue of Turkish identity as reflected in 'lifestyles'. On one side stand the Islamists and the RP propagating a 'pure and just order' based on Islamic principles. On the other side is a group of the radical bourgeoisie, state bureaucrats, high army personnel, Kemalist intellectuals, and 'Second Republicans'[85] with perhaps only the ideal of secularism as a common value between them.[86] Between them both is the 'soft' Islamic right which tries to continue the Kemalist line of Islam as essential for Turkish identity, but argues that it should be private and not challenge the basic precepts of Kemalist nationalism. The secularist élite are now in the unaccustomed position of being in retreat. Whether this retreat is temporary or permanent remains to be seen. What is incontestable is the real clash of two radically differing outlooks on what constitutes the essence of the Turkish nation.

The Islamist radical fringe

In January 1993 the leading secularist journalist Uğur Mumcu, of *Cumhuriyet*, was assassinated. The perpetrators were believed to radical Islamists. Thousands of people attended his funeral in an open display of solidarity for secularism. While his death was perhaps the most notable, it was one of many such outrages, and radical Islamist groups using violence have made a great impact on Turkey's recent political life. They have assassinated many perceived enemies, predominantly leading secularists and left-wing Kurds in the southeast. As such, they represent the radical wing of Islamists who want a united Islamic state and are willing to openly use violence to achieve this. Their violent tactics make clear that they seek a hegemonic position in society for their vision of the nation, and that they will not tolerate competing claims. The violence began in earnest in 1990 with some 20 killings. For example, on 6 October 1990, Bahriye Üçok, a retired

---

[85] Those who call for Turkey to become truly 'Western' and base itself more on pluralism, market values, and human rights, and thus negate classic Kemalism with its insistence on national unity and past connotations with étatism.

[86] Meral Özbek, 'Arabesk Culture: A Case of Modernisation and Popular Identity', paper at the MIT conference (see footnote 68).

professor of religion, was killed by a parcel bomb. Her death was claimed by an extremist Islamic group because of her 'opinion on the veil'. The group reportedly stated that they were 'at war with all those who try to limit the expansion of Islam.'[87] An organisation often linked to the killings was the Great Eastern Islamic Raiders - Front (İBDA-C). This organisation was reportedly responsible for a number of bomb attacks on secularists like that of 30 December 1994, when journalist-writers Onat Kutlar and Yasemin Cebenoyan were killed. By the beginning of 1995 it had claimed responsibility for some ninety violent incidents, including five bombings in various cities.[88] Like Hizbullah (see below) many of İBDA-C's members are ethnic Kurds who espouse Islamic brotherhood with Turks in place of a separate Kurdish nationalism.[89]

While such killings of prominent secularists in Ankara and Istanbul continued, 1991 saw political killings of left-wing Kurds by radical Islamic organisations, especially the shadowy Hizbullah group (which has no connections with the Lebanese organisation with a similar name), become systematic in the southeast of the country. There have been a number of allegations of official complicity in these killings. While such allegations are hard to confirm or deny it is noticeable that Hizbullah, which was set up in Batman in 1987 and is committed to establishing a Sunni Islamic Turkish state, appeared as a prominent actor in the southeast after a purge of pro-Islamic police officers from Ankara in July 1991 and their transfer to the region. This purge did not apparently affect the reputed ultra-nationalist domination of the country's political police.[90] This move was combined with a spate of killings of left-wing Kurds in cities like Diyabakır and Batman.[91] It appears that Hizbullah is a radical Islamic group in the southeast primarily composed of Kurds who oppose separatist Kurdish activity by

[87] See *Turkey Briefing*, vol. 5, no. 5, 1990, and *Le Monde*, 9 October 1990.

[88] *İnfo-Türk*, E.218, January/February 1995, p. 10.

[89] See *Cumhuriyet*, 11 September 1994, for a detailed breakdown of İBDA-C's leadership and aims.

[90] İsmet G. İmset, 'Police reshuffle ousts fundamentalist', *Turkish Daily News*, Ankara, 25 July 1991. This noted that the new security chief Ünal Erkan initiated the purges after military intelligence chief General Teoman Korman warned the previous year of Islamic infiltration of the police force.

[91] Hugh Pope, 'Kurds fall victims to new wave of killings', *The Independent* London, 10 July, 1991.

the PKK (see Chapter 7) and others.[92] As such, its policy of assassination of perceived enemies appears to have been initially tolerated by the authorities, as the victims were seen as working against the unity of the Turkish state. Indeed, the authorities refused to even use the name Hizbullah until 1994; the large numbers of murders remained unsolved and were officially ascribed to 'unknown assailants'.[93] It was not until mid-1994 that Hizbullah members began to be arrested and charged with murder.[94]

Popular attitudes to Islam and Turkish nationalism

While the 'Turkish Islamic Synthesis' is rejected both by hard-core Kemalists and Islamists as an artificial concept, it appears to strike a chord among sections of the populace. Indeed, as shown in Chapter 7, it is even possible to speak of a form of 'Kurdish Islamic Synthesis'. Anthropologists have observed over a long period the importance of religion in everyday life in Turkey, and some have chronicled a strong symbiosis between Kemalist nationalism and Islam. This seems to have occurred especially in the small town setting, where ideas about Turkey as a nation-state and

[92] This was stated in the indictment of four Hizbullah members tried in Mersin in September 1994; *Anatolia News Agency*, Ankara, 24 September 1994, in SWB EE/2111, B/11, 27/9/94. On 26 October 1994, *Hürriyet* claimed that Hizbullah had links with Iran to destabilise Turkey – a charge denied by Teheran; *IRNA* news agency, Teheran, 22 October 1994, in SWB EE/2136, B/5, 26/10/94. At the major trial of 21 alleged Hizbullah members charged with 66 incidents involving death and injury during 1992-4, the prosecutor stated that the organisation had split into factions: the 'pro-knowledge' (*ilimciler*) and the 'couriers' (*menzilciler*) named after book-shops which formed the meeting place for each group; TRT TV, Ankara, 23 January 1995, and Amnesty International, *Turkey: A Policy of Denial* (London, Al EUR 44/01/95, February 1995), p. 14.

[93] There were 20 such killings in 1991, 362 in 1992, over 400 in 1993, and 380 in 1994 by November. Some of the victims appear to have been killed as a result of internecine feuding in Hizbullah. Most, however, occurred due to their political background as Kurdish activists; see *ibid.*, p. 14.

[94] It could be argued that the tardiness in arresting suspects was due to normal delays in police investigation. However, the number of the assassinations over a period of some years in an area under emergency legislation akin to martial law inevitably gives rise to suspicions of government complicity. Amnesty International stated that there was compelling evidence that the security forces were involved in at least some of the hundreds of political killings committed in the southeast; see *ibid.*, pp. 14-18.

ideas about Islam are mutually reinforcing, leading to an almost 'fundamentalist' homogeneity.[95] In this symbiosis the contradictions between the two sets of ideas are disregarded whenever possible in favour of points of confluence: for example that both Atatürk and Mohammed were founders of states who won power through military campaigns. Even army training in the 1950s culminated in the storming of a hill with cries of 'Allah, Allah'.[96] Atatürk can also be seen as a kind of Sufi leader pointing the way forward.[97] Similarly, Atatürk's great speech, the *Nutuk*, has a position akin to a holy book.[98] Richard and Nancy Tapper point out that even his pronouncements, which are taken by the secular Kemalist élite almost as texts of faith, are couched in language which is redolent of religious meaning due to the fact that he was often by necessity using vocabulary from the pre-language reform era of the 1930s.[99] When there are outright contradictions between the two sets of ideas, the majority of townspeople opt for republicanism over Islam. However, there are areas where a measure of accommodation occurs to bridge the gaps.[100]

---

[95] Richard and Nancy Tapper, 'Religion, Education and Continuity in a Provincial Town' in R. Tapper (ed.), *Islam in Modern Turkey*, p. 60. See also their "Thank God we're secular!" Aspects of fundamentalism in a Turkish town' in Lionel Caplan (ed.), *Aspects of Religious Fundamentalism* (London: Macmillan, 1987).

[96] Şerif Mardin, 'Ideology and Religion in the Turkish Revolution', *International Journal of Middle Eastern Studies*, vol. 2, 1971, p. 208.

[97] The symbiosis of Kemal with the Bektaşi sufi sect is studied in greater detail in Chapter 8.

[98] İlter Turan, 'Religion and Political Culture in Turkey' in R. Tapper (ed.), *Islam in Modern Turkey*, p. 50.

[99] For example in the Kemalist slogan '*Hayatta en hakiki mürşit ilimdir*' ('the surest guide in life is scientific knowledge'), *mürşit, iliim*, and *hakiki* are all primarily religious terms; R. and N. Tapper, 'Religion, Education and Continuity', p. 67. This point about the use of language has many ironies. In contemporary Turkish one can often ascertain a person's viewpoint on Islam by the everyday language he uses: ardent secularists use the modern state-propagated *öztürkçe* while Islamists use older Ottoman forms (which ironically are often the same as those used by the arch-secularist Kemal himself). An example is the use of *ulusal* as opposed to *milli* (national).

[100] The Tappers (*ibid.*) identify three such frequent accommodations. First, over the use of alcohol. This is justified as it is argued that the Islamic ban on its use was introduced by Mohammed because all Arabs are drunkards. In fact, the argument goes, Islam favours moderation in all things so moderate consumption

Despite the above 'small-town' symbiosis, which appears to place Turkish nationalism in a superior role over Islam, and although Islam remains a crucial component of this nationalism, surveys since the 1960s have continued to show that for a significant section of the population, the relationship between the two is reversed. For example, studies in 1969 of workers in the Sümmerbank Factory in Izmir found that 38 per cent of respondents saw themselves as Muslims rather than Turks (only 50 per cent saw themselves as Turks foremost). Even more revealingly, when asked how they perceived others in society, 52 per cent replied 'religious brothers' as opposed to 36 per cent who said 'fellow nationals'. The latter group was almost entirely comprised of *lycée* students.[101] It must be borne in mind that the findings of all such polls are open to question.[102] Also, while this survey took place in Izmir and thus relatively in 'the centre', the date (1968) would indicate that many of the factory workers would have been recent migrants from 'the periphery' of the villages. Here, the fact that *lycée* students with their greater exposure to state education were the ones who identified themselves primarily as part of the Turkish nation rather than of the Islamic community is relevant. Despite this, the survey indicates that Islam remains a key component of identity to many Turks.

The result of another detailed poll of Istanbul residents was published in early 1993. Covering 15,683 respondents over 18 years of age, it found that 69% defined themselves as 'Turks', 21% defined themselves as 'Muslim Turks', and only 4% defined

---

is acceptable. The second accommodation argues that republican institutions function in the same way as Islamic ones did, for example modern taxes are akin to the old alms and tithes. The third rationalises religious values and customs by appealing to modern secular values; for example, prayer and fasting are good for one's health by purging the body, thus Islamic wisdom anticipated modern science.

[101] Binnaz Toprak, 'The Religious Right', p. 221.

[102] For example, Metin Heper uses the same findings as backing for his claim that Kemalist values inculcated in the 1930s penetrated deeply into society, and that the mass media, Peoples' Houses of 1932-54, flag saluting, national anthem, singing, state parades, etc. helped 'a continuing and consistent socialisation aimed at producing a Turkish rather than a Muslim identity.' See his 'Political Culture as a Dimension of Compatibility' in Heper, Öncü and Kramer (eds), *Turkey and the West*, pp. 9-10. While there appears some truth in this, it is surely an overstatement – see Chapter 4, p. 122 for other views.

themselves solely as 'Muslims'. (The remainder identified themselves as members of other groups like Kurds or Caucasians.)[103]
While Istanbul is Turkey's largest and most cosmopolitan city, it
has a huge population of migrants from other areas. Thus, bearing
in mind the caveat about the accuracy of the poll sample, the
low number of those identifying purely by religion is notable.

When comparing the two polls, one in Izmir in 1968, and
one in Istanbul in 1983, one may tentatively conclude that in
the last twenty-five years the process of inculcating a primary
loyalty to the Turkish nation has enjoyed some success. Conversely,
the growth in the popularity of the RP, and the readily observable
rise in the number of women who are *kapalı* ('covered' by the
head-scarf) would indicate that there are many, and perhaps a
growing number of people who do not accept this symbiosis
between Islam and Kemalism, especially regarding the role of
women in Turkey. Here, observers point to the pressures that
modernisation and capitalism have brought to bear on small artisans
and traders, the *esnaf*, and their subsequent espousal of Islam as
a form of protest.[104] Studies in the late 1970s and early 1980s
found that migrants exposed to the upheavals associated with
transition often visibly turned to religion but that this was a passing
phenomenon for each wave.[105] However, these studies were carried
out before the rise in mass popularity of the RP, and at a time
when seasoned observers like Binnaz Toprak argued that Islamic
forces were and would remain marginal and were just one of
several ideological movements represented by various political parties which had appeared due to the institution of political
pluralism.[106]

Throughout the 1980s, Islam appeared to be on the rise in
Turkey. One reason for this was that the modernisation which
staunch Kemalists called for had sometimes had results which
they did not anticipate. This is especially evident in the Özal era,

---

[103] *Milliyet*, 27 February 1993.

[104] For example, B. Toprak, 'The Religious Right', p. 222.

[105] For example, Kemal Kartal, *Kentleşme ve İnsan* (Ankara: np, 1978), p. 111,
and Ned Levine, 'Value Orientations among Migrants in Ankara, Turkey: Case
studies', *Journal of Asian and African Studies*, vol. 8, 1983, p. 58.

[106] Toprak, 'The Religious Right' p. 226. Even at that time such complacency
was questionable due to the penetration of religious values into mainstream
political parties like the ANAP.

which both expanded the boundaries of private experience and opened new opportunities for religious organisations to market and propagate their wares and thus their ideology.[107] One aspect of this has been the huge number of Islamic publications which have appeared on the market. The main Islamic daily, *Zaman*, for example, appeared in 1986 with a circulation of some 10,000, but by 1990 it had 50,000.[108] By May 1994 it had a circulation of 259,000 while its fellow Islamist mass daily, *Türkiye*, had a circulation of 341,000.[109] The *Zaman* organisation has also expanded, with television programmes as well as outlets in central Asia including schools in places like Samarkand.[110] Additionally, the *tarikats*, formally banned in 1925, have revived in new forms more adapted to the modern state. Despite Atatürk's ban, they continued to play the role as arbitrators of disputes in eastern Turkey among tribal Kurds and also among the Alevis and Bektaşis (see chapters 7 and 8). In western Turkey they have revived, due in no small part to the opportunities of privatisation and mass literature. Universal mass education and mass communications have opened up new possibilities for them. In their new form, the charisma of the religious leader, the traditional focus of authority in the *tarikats*, 'is rivalled by an increasing need to understand the message and to focus on the charisma of the text.'[111]

[107] As Şerif Mardin notes: 'As the boundaries of the private have become enlarged [by modernisation] in Turkey an unforeseen development has occurred. As private every-day life has increasingly been given a new richness and variety, religion has become a central focus of life and acquired a new power. Religion has received a new uplift from the privatisation wave: private religious instruction, Islamic fashion in clothes, manufacturing and music, Islamic learned journals, all of them aspects of *private* life, have made Islam pervasive in a modern sense in Turkish society, and have worked *against* religion becoming a private belief'; Mardin, *Religion and Social Change in Modern Turkey*, p. 229.

[108] Figures from *Zaman*'s chief political columnist Fehmi Koru in *The Guardian*, London, 6 January, 1990.

[109] *Türkiye* was the third largest mass-circulation daily behind *Sabah* (482,000) and *Hürriyet* (438,000), with *Milliyet* (283,000) fourth and then *Zaman*. The flag-bearer of Kemalist secularism, *Cumhuriyet*, was in 11th place with a circulation of 56,000. However, these circulations constantly fluctuate.

[110] John Simpson, 'The New Great Game', (BBC TV, Channel 2, London, 13 December 1992).

[111] Mardin, *Religion and Social Change in Modern Turkey*, p. 230.

From the above it is clear that the nature of Turkish nationalism has undergone a significant change since the ending of one-party rule in 1950 (and even before). While the classic Kemalist secularist model attempted to relegate Islam to the private sphere, the fact that Turkey is overwhelmingly a Muslim country has seen Islam reassert itself as an important factor. The breakdown in society of the 1970s, with radical anti-systemic groups fighting on the streets, made the military authorities, the bastions of secularist Kemalism, attempt to instil 'Islamic' values into the population through the education system. This, they hoped, would end the attraction of Marxist and fascist ideologies by reinforcing respect for society and Turkey's traditions. At the same time, they hoped that this education would always be subordinated to the goals of Kemalist nationalism. The result had striking similarities with Abdülhamid's use of Islam as a solidifying element in society. The combination of Turkish nationalism and Islam became known as the 'Turkish-Islamic Synthesis' (TİS), a symbiosis which had already been adopted by such groups as the extreme nationalists led by Alparslan Türkeş. The basic tenets of the TİS were carried on by the Özal governments in the late 1980s. As the decade wore on, Islamic sympathisers continued to penetrate the central apparatus, especially the Education Ministry, and the relationship which the military rulers envisaged between Kemalism (which they always saw as paramount) and Islam (which they saw as a means of social control) became somewhat confused as the Directorate of Religious Affairs grew in size and power. Despite this, and despite the religious backgrounds of many leading figures in ANAP (including Özal himself), it would be a mistake to exaggerate these developments. The ANAP governments, and their successors led by DYP were essentially Kemalist with a strong religious tinge. The tenets of Turkish nationalism remained intact but were bolstered by Islam. As Turkey was an overwhelmingly Muslim country, majority electoral success depended in some degree on appealing, or at least seeming to appeal, to religious sentiments,[112]

---

[112] For example, even Ecevit on the left played the religious card in the 1991 elections by frequently referring to religion in connection with 'Turkishness'; John Norton, 'Islam in Turkey', talk at SOAS, London University, 1 November 1991. The use of religion by centre-right politicians is well illustrated by Prime Minister Tansu Çiller's meeting in December 1994 with Feyzettin Erol, nephew of the late Nakşibendi leader Muhammed Raşit Erol, as well as her meetings

and anthropological studies appear to confirm that this hybrid of Kemalist Turkish nationalism and Sunni Islam is popular among large sections of the population. This development has occurred in spite of intellectuals' dissatisfaction at its contradictions which has led to the TİS becoming somewhat discredited.

This rise of Sunni Islam as a seemingly crucial component of Turkish nationalism has been paralleled by the rise of a rival ideology that puts Islam above Turkish nationalism. Such overt politicisation of Islam remains taboo in Turkey, and a number of people have been prosecuted and political parties closed down because of this. However, since 1970, Necmettin Erbakan has managed to form and keep a mass Islamic party just within the accepted boundaries. This party, which has undergone several name changes but whose political programme has remained essentially unchanged, has a primarily religious outlook. It has found mass appeal in the squatter settlements of major cities among migrants from the countryside whose lives have been disrupted by modernisation. For similar reasons, it has also had a strong appeal to small businessmen. Perhaps because of this natural power base of those disenchanted by modernisation, many élite (secularist Kemalist) commentators saw it merely as a transient phenomenon which would fade away. However, instead of 'fading away' it has continued to grow and to a large extent confound its critics. It has also bred a new generation of Islamic intellectuals who have come through the modern education system and are willing and able to take on the previous secular élites over the whole process of modernisation. Despite protestations by both sides, it seems that both aim for the hegemony of their particular viewpoint. This is essentially a nationalist argument over what is the essence of the Turkish nation. The new Islamists have been aided by the very process of modernisation, which the old élites initially thought would sweep them away. This is especially noticeable in the results of the privatisation drives of the 1980s and 1990s (in the sense of greater freedom in the cultural and social spheres) which have allowed them to take full advantage of the new possibilities in publishing and broadcasting their ideology. Some observers see these new intellectuals as essentially working within the system

---

with the Fethullacı *tarikat* leader Fethullah Hoca, and with a Nurcu leader, Mehmet Kutlular; see *Milliyet* and *Hürriyet*, 13 December 1994.

and not aiming to overthrow it and set up a theocratic state. On the other hand, it can be argued that there are certainly many within the Islamic movement who are merely using the present system as a means towards this end, while partly hiding their real aims (the present legal system makes overtly calling for a return of the *Şeriat* illegal). Either way, there is a readily observably struggle in process for 'the soul' of Turkey between the previous Kemalist elites, who for decades have been used to paternally defining the essence of 'Turkishness', even down to what constitutes 'real Turkish music', and the new Islamic challengers.

For some of the latter, the struggle is actually physical. While the legal mass party, the RP, has to remain somewhat ambivalent, fringe Islamic groups operating outside the law and using violence and assassination to achieve their ends, are not. They are fighting (literally) for an Islamic state and are willing to kill competitors. Interestingly, the two main organisations have a large ethnic Kurdish membership. The two main targets for these Islamic death squads are a handful of leading secularists in the 'centre', and large numbers of left-wing Kurdish activists in the 'periphery'. The latter essentially espouse a Kurdish national consciousness, separate from the Turkish one, and are thus seen as traitors who are artificially dividing the Islamic nation. The whole 'Kurdish Question' is the subject of the next chapter.

7

THE KURDS: REPRESSION
AND REBELLION

The following two chapters will look at the situation of population groups in modern Turkey who are outside the Turkish-speaking Sunni majority, and how they have reacted to recent developments in the evolution of official Turkish nationalism. This will cover in detail the large Alevi minority and their reactions to the penetration of Sunni Islam into the state nationalist ideology, as detailed in the previous chapter. It will also look at the growth of a militant Kurdish ethnic nationalism, the corresponding rise of the Kurdistan Workers Party (PKK) of Abdullah Öcalan, and how the state has reacted to this direct challenge to the official variants of Turkish state nationalism and their attempted hegemony. By way of contrast and comparison, it will consider the situation of other smaller minorities, both Muslim and non-Muslim, who do not speak Turkish as their mother tongue. This category will, for Muslim communities, include the Laz, Muslim Georgians, Arabs and Gypsies (Roma), as well as immigrant Muslim communities from the Balkans (Bosnians and Albanians) and the Caucasus (Circassians, Chechens, etc.), and for non-Muslims the Orthodox Greek and Armenian populations, the Jews and the diminishing number of Assyro-Chaldeans.

The Kurds

The Kurds predominate in the southeast of the country. There are a number of traditional social cleavages among them based on differences in dialect (Zaza and Kurmanci are the most widely spoken variants of Kurdish in Turkey), tribal structures and whether they belong to nomadic or semi-nomadic groups. There are also religious cleavages, the majority being Sunni Muslims with an

Alevi minority living mainly in Tunceli and Maraş provinces (there are also a small number of syncretic Yezidis).[1] With the mass internal migrations to the cities since the 1950s and the 1960s, huge numbers have moved out of the predominantly Kurdish southeast to cities like Istanbul, often resulting in a process of 'natural' assimilation into the Turkish mass. As noted in Chapter 4, Kemal's conception of the new Turkish nation included the Muslim Kurds of Anatolia. At the same time the sweeping secular reforms of the 1920s resulted in a series of revolts in Kurdish southeastern regions. While some see these revolts as nationalist, it is perhaps more correct to view them as essentially religious. The 'Kemalist revolution', despite some claims to the contrary,[2] was essentially an urban one, and did not penetrate to the villages. This was especially the case in the more backward and mountainous southeastern regions where the Kurds predominate. As such, they continued to live in 'pre-modern' societies where notions of national allegiance were weaker than the traditional ones of tribe and religion. This tardiness of the state in the inculcation of the new Turkish nationalist ethos was to allow the growth of a rival form of nationalism to the state-sponsored Kemalist version. This nationalism was 'ethnic' in character and appealed to the Kurds through ties of language. It was almost certainly aided by the struggles of the Kurds, led by Mulla Mustafa Barzani, in neighbouring Iraq.[3] Hence, when the concepts of modern nationalism

[1] The Alevi Kurds and the Yezidis are discussed in Chapter 8.

[2] E.g., Metin Heper: see Chapter 4, P. 122.

[3] Anthropologist Lale Yalçın-Heckmann, studying Kurds in the Hakkari region, noted that in 1974/5 many from the area went to fight with Barzani and brought back the *peshmerga* mentality (in Turkey called '*Dağdakiler*' – 'those from the mountains'); Lale Yalçın- Heckmann, 'Global Ideologies, Local Strategies: Notes on the recent history of a Kurdish village in Hakkari', talk at SOAS, London University, 8 December 1994. The Kurds in Iraq have been officially recognised by Iraqi regimes to a far greater extent than either in Turkey or Iran. Much of this recognition, however, has been wrenched from Baghdad by struggle at times when the centre was weak, only to be taken away when the centre reasserted its authority. For example, the new constitution after the overthrow of the Hashemite monarchy by General Qasim's coup of 1958 stated: 'The Kurds and Arabs are partners within the nation. The Constitution guarantees their rights within the framework of the Iraqi Republic.'; E. Ghareeb, *The Kurdish Question in Iraq* (Syracuse University Press, 1981), P. 38. Actually gaining autonomy was a different matter, however, in the volatile Iraq of those times. Similarly, Barzani's relations with the Iraqi Ba'ath party fluctuated between the

finally penetrated into the rural southeast, Kemalist nationalism and its successors/rival variants were faced with a formidable rival.

The Kurdish problem is absolutely central to the whole question of ethnicity and nationalism in Turkey today, and there is little up-to-date and reasonably reliable literature on this topic. We should therefore take a brief look at the whole problem and the Turkish state's handling of the Kurdish question.

The Kurds and the Turkish Left

The Kurdish areas in the southeast were the most underdeveloped regions in Turkey. As noted in Chapter 4, the Atatürk regime in the 1920s and the 1930s dealt harshly with successive uprisings in Kurdish areas, and between 1925 and 1938 large numbers of Kurds were deported to western regions of Turkey. The state simultaneously embarked on a programme of assimilation where the educational system and national service were used as means of spreading Turkish national identity to ethnic minorities like the Kurds. The advent of democracy in 1950 saw an easing of this situation with the victory of the Democrat Party (DP). This triumph of the 'periphery' over the Kemalist 'centre' resulted in the reinstatement of many exiled *ağas* and *sheikhs* who had supported the DP, and the return of their property. These people quickly resumed their positions as brokers in the patronage system, whereby they delivered votes for government in exchange for state favours for them and their followers. A new philosophy called *Doğuculuk* ('Eastism') which advocated economic development of the east sprang up. This appeared partly as a response to Kurdish activism in neighbouring Iraq and the exposure of the eastern region to Kurdish-language radio programmes from neighbouring countries. The proponents of this doctrine studiously avoided any reference to Kurds or Kurdistan, but the implication was there. Fifty Kurdish leaders of this movement were arrested, showing the limits of

---

high spot of the peace agreement of 1970, which effectively made Iraq a bi-national Arab and Kurdish state, and its watered down version in the Autonomy Declaration of 1974 (which while granting the Kurds autonomy gave them less than the 1970 agreement). Outright repression reached its height with Saddam Hussein's poison gas attacks in 1988; see D. McDowall, *The Kurds: A Nation Denied* (London: MRG Publications, 1992), pp. 84-111.

the DP's liberalisation.[4]

The aftermath of the 1960 military coup and the 1961 Constitution saw greater opportunities for freedom of expression, the press and association. For the first time, socialist parties were allowed to operate freely and the Marxist Turkish Workers Party (TİP) was set up. A clandestine party, the Kurdistan Democratic Party was established in 1965 by 'traditionalists' who looked to and copied Barzani's nationalist movement in Iraq, but this specifically Kurdish party which was explicitly separatist remained illegal.[5] Many leading Kurdish intellectuals looked instead to left wing parties like the TİP, which welcomed them into its ranks, took up the Kurdish cause and established branches throughout southeast Turkey.[6] These left-wing parties, while acknowledging and using the Kurdish cause to attack the 'capitalist-bourgeois state', saw the cure in Marxist-Leninism whereby the establishment of a Marxist state would, so the dogma asserted, inevitably lead to a solving of national questions.[7]

Kurdish and Marxist groups became increasingly vocal in the 1960s. However, despite the support of a large selection of the intellectual élite, the left significantly failed to attract widespread support and failed miserably in the 1965 and 1969 elections. The implication was that Kurdish nationalism (and Marxism for that matter) was very much an élite phenomenon, as the bulk of the

---

[4] McDowall, *op. cit.*, p 39.

[5] It seems that support for this party was small as its 'natural' supporters were already often well integrated into the Turkish political patronage system.

[6] McDowall, *op. cit.*, p. 40. Left-wing parties also attracted many Turkish intellectuals in this period. The attraction of left-wing parties for intellectual Kurds can perhaps also be explained by the under development of the southeast and state policy towards the area which Kurdish nationalists tend to refer to as 'colonial oppression'. See also Igor Lipovsky, *The Socialist Movement in Turkey, 1960-1980* (Leiden: E.J. Brill, 1992). Andrew Mango makes the point that the Turkish ruling class of the Kemalist era took it for granted that the wild southeast should be pacified by firm government, and that this could only be effected using the methods of the French in Algeria and the British in India – i.e. 'colonialism' was not seen as the inherent evil it tends to be seen as today; Andrew Mango, 'Turks and Kurds' [forthcoming].

[7] Such views have interesting parallells with the Islamist view. Both tend to hold that in the ideal state, whether Islamic or Marxist, national differences will 'fade away' as the universalist bonds of either religion or class (depending on the viewpoint) will predominate.

Kurds continued to follow the preferences of their traditional leaders. Despite this electoral failure, the Demirel governments viewed both Marxists and Kurdish sympathisers with hostility. In January 1967 many bilingual Kurdish-Turkish left-wing journals which had appeared in the mid-1960s were prohibited by decree and their editors arrested. From 1967 onwards, actions by special military groups against suspected left-wing Kurds became more prevalent. In reply, mass demonstrations by Kurdish students and militants, apparently instigated by the TİP, took place on 3 August 1967.[8]

The electoral failure of the TİP led to a radicalisation of the Turkish left, amplified by external events like Mao Zedong's radicalism in China during the Cultural Revolution of the late 1960s and the student revolt in Paris in 1968. Armed struggle began to be increasingly advocated on the extreme left.[9] Radical Kurds followed this trend, and in 1969 the Eastern Revolutionary Cultural Hearth (DDKO) was set up – initially in Ankara, then in Istanbul and in the urban southeast. Many of the DDKO's leaders were TİP members.[10] The proliferation of militant Marxist Kurdish groups in the southeast led to violent clashes with right-wing groups like those of Alparslan Türkeş (see Chapter 5). In

---

[8] In this first mass demonstration by Kurds since the 1930s, over 10,000 took part in Silvan and over 25,000 in Diyarbakır; McDowall, *op cit.,* p. 40.

[9] See Igor Lipovsky, 'The Legal Socialist Parties of Turkey 1960-1980', *Middle East Studies*, vol. 27, 1991.

[10] Kurdish intellectual and leftist nationalist Musa Anter (who supported the DDKO) relates in his memoirs that 'in spite of my warnings' the DDKO committed 'childish' acts of violence in university centres in Ankara and Istanbul 'which even if they had borne fruit, would not have helped the enslaved Kurdish nation' but merely gave the government an excuse for repression in the shape of the 12 March 1971 coup by memorandum; Musa Anter, *Hatıralarım* (Istanbul: Yönayıncılık, 1991), p. 223. Andrew Mango in a perceptive article notes that Anter's memoirs are very much in the tradition of Istanbul drinking parties where, in a continuation of the Ottoman multi-ethnic tradition, everyone was both teased about their ethnic origins (Turkish, Albanian, Kurdish, etc.), and jealous of the good name of their particular *millet*. As such talk could bring down the wrath of the authorities, it was wrapped in humour. Regarding the Kurds, Mango points out that there were parallells with the Irish in British society before 1916, in that they were both insiders and outsiders who knew 'the rules of the game' in the country in which they operated – Turkey not Kurdistan: these are rules that the PKK is now trying to change. Andrew Mango, 'Turks and Kurds' [forthcoming].

October 1970 the TİP became the first legal party in Turkey to openly recognise the Kurds. This led to its being closed by the Constitutional Court and its leaders' being prosecuted and imprisoned for encouraging activities to divide the country.[11] Open advocacy of the Kurdish cause remained illegal in the 1970s but Kurds remained prominent in Marxist groups. These continued to engage in street fighting with extreme right-wing groups until the military coup of 12 September 1980.

State policy since the 1980 coup

Despite the liberalisation following the advent of multi-party democracy in 1950, the modern Turkish state has remained antithetical to a Kurdish national consciousness separate from the Turkish one. As shown in Chapter 4, the Kemalist state in the 1920s and 1930s forcibly put down a number of revolts in the southeast. While these revolts were often essentially religious rather than ethnic or national in character, the state consciously propagated the new 'Turkish' values for all its Muslim citizens. This has remained an enduring policy. After the 1980 military coup, the military regime further clamped down on any form of distinct Kurdish identity. The 1982 Constitution reiterated in Article 2 that the state was 'loyal to the nationalism of Atatürk'. Article 3 stated that 'The Turkish state, with its territory and nation, is an indivisible entity.' Article 5 laid down the fundamental duty of the state to safeguard Turkey's indivisibility. While Article 10 guarantees equality before the law for all citizens regardless of language, race and the like, Article 26, dealing with 'Freedom of Expression and Dissemination of Thought' states:

> No language prohibited by law shall be used in the expression and dissemination of thought. Any written or printed documents, phonograph records, magnetic or video tapes, and other means of expression used in contravention of this provision shall be seized ...[12]

[11] Feroz Ahmad, *The Turkish experiment in Democracy, 1950-75* (London: Hurst, 1981), p. 311.

[12] The 1982 Constitution is reprinted in Clement H. Dodd, *The Crisis of Turkish Democracy* (Huntingdon: Eothen Press, 2nd edn, 1990), pp. 154–220.

The application of this provision and Law 2932 of 1983 which declared the mother tongue of Turkish citizens to be Turkish resulted in use of the Kurdish language being criminalised for over a decade. The restrictions on the private use of Kurdish were not enforced by the end of the 1980s, apparently due to Turgut Özal's initiative.[13] Law 2932 was finally abolished along with Articles 142, 142 and 163 of the Turkish Penal Code (which penalised Marxist and Islamic political activity) in April 1991. In February 1991 the government adopted a new bill regarding the use of regional languages.[14] However, the Law to Fight Terrorism of April 1991, while repealing Law 2932, once more carried stiff prison sentences of between two and five years and a large fine for any written or spoken propaganda aimed at dividing the Turkish state or nation.[15]

[13] *Briefing*, no. 825, Ankara, 11 February 1991. Özal himself was of Kurdish origin but his attitude towards the Kurdish question remained ambivalent (see below). John Owen-Davies of Reuter reported on 31 March 1988 that there was now no penalty for speaking Kurdish (which remained officially unrecognised as a language) and that Ankara had recently allowed Kurds in the military prisons of Diyarbakır to speak freely in Kurdish to their visiting families after a mass hunger-strike by prisoners demanding 'freedom of Kurdish'. Note that the constitutional clause (Article 26) does not by itself have legal effect unless it is supported by a specific statute (for example former Law 2932).

[14] *Antolia News Agency*, Ankara, 1 February 1991. Law 2932 of 1983 never explicitly referred to Kurdish but rather banned the use of 'any language aside from those used by states which have formally been recognised by the state of Turkey, to explain an opinion verbally or in print.' The new bill, which was drafted by the Minister of Justice, stated its intentions in Article 1 as being to regulate 'the use of Turkish as the official language and the principles and arrangements for other languages to be used in Turkey, with the aim of protecting the indivisible unity of state, territory and nation, national sovereignty, the Republic, national security and public order.' Despite this somewhat standard Kemalist insistence on the unity of the state and nation, the bill went on to define the languages allowed in various forms of discourse: Turkish alone for state bodies; in printed works and on radio and TV and film, Turkish or the first official language of states which Turkey recognises (i.e. not Kurdish); in education, Turkish except where appropriate legislation allowed for education in English or French, etc; in writing or orally at public demonstrations, Turkish. Penalties for breaking the law were to be fines in place of previous imprisonment. The main concession came in Article 6, which stated 'Turkish citizens ... may speak local languages and dialects. They may use these languages in music and in utilising records, sound and video tape and other means of expression.' See *Briefing*. no. 825, 11 February 1991.

[15] 'Terörizm ile Mücadele Kanunu', *T.C. Resmi Gazete*, no. 20,843, Ankara,

While there has thus been some relaxation on the private use of the Kurdish language, any discussion of the 'The Kurdish Question' has remained subject to prosecution in the State Security Courts, especially under Articles 6 and 8 of 'the Law to Fight Terrorism'.[16] These articles have been frequently used against pro-Kurdish newspapers and others.[17] In early 1986 a fact-finding

---

12 April 1991, Article 8.

[16] The Law to Fight Terrorism was introduced to replace the restrictions on political activity which had been relaxed with the repealing of Articles 141, 142 and 163 of the Turkish Penal Code. Article 1 of the law defines 'Terror' as any act which 'abuses state authority' or 'disturbs the general public order and the internal and external security of the state.' See *Turkey Briefing*, vol. 6, no. 3, 1991. For a full critique of the anti-terror law see Helsinki Watch, *Turkey: New Restrictive Anti-Terror Law* (New York: Helsinki Watch, 10 June 1991). Following Turkey's signing of a customs union with the European Union on 6 March 1995, there were moves by the government to withdraw Article 8 of the law. However DYP backbenchers wanted the measure to remain on the statute book. Eventually Article 8 was modified in October 1995 so that the maximum sentence was reduced to three years' imprisonment, the phrase 'irrespective of methods and aims and ideas' was removed, and the courts given discretion to impose fines or suspended sentences in place of custodial ones. As a result 100 prisoners were released, but some prisoners of conscience still remained.

[17] For example, statistics from the Ministry of Justice showed that in 1994, press offences made up 1,162 (65% of the total of 1,774) trials undertaken at the State Security Court (DGM) in Istanbul. At these press trials 2,098 people, of whom 336 were under arrest, were prosecuted. The trials were mostly connected with the newspapers *Özgür Gündem*, *Özgür Ülke Azadi* and *Denge Azadi*, which regularly printed articles on the struggle with the Kurdistan Workers' Party (PKK) in the southeast. The highest profile case was that of the famous writer Yaşar Kemal, who is of Kurdish origin and author of *Mehmed, My Hawk* and other internationally renowned works. He was charged on 23 January 1995 by Istanbul DGM under Article 8 of the 'Law to Fight Terrorism' for having written an article for the German periodical *Der Spiegel* strongly criticising Turkish policy towards the Kurds. He was released pending the trial and in March 1996 received a suspended 20-months sentence. Another legal action was brought against him on 8 February by Istanbul DGM under Article 321 of the Turkish Penal Code for separatist propaganda allegedly contained in a collection of essays entitled *Freedom of Thought and Turkey*. A similar action was taken against Erdal Öz, publisher of the collection, which was issued at the beginning of February 1995 but immediately confiscated. Such prosecutions are not restricted to Kurds but are also applied with equal force to Turks who criticise government policy regarding the Kurds. For example, the sentences of six years' imprisonment and a large fine imposed on İsmail Beşikçi, a writer-sociologist and many-time prisoner of conscience in 3 trials under Article 8 of the 'Law to Fight Terrorism'

mission by the SHP, which was then the main opposition party, reported that in eastern Turkey almost every citizen was treated as a suspect, and oppression, torture and insult by the military was the norm.[18] In addition to these laws which covered the whole country there have been a number of regulations affecting the southeast, which has remained under emergency legislation. This was introduced in 1987 and has been successively extended.[19] Of these regulations, Law 424 of 10 April 1990 was the most sweeping and controversial, giving the Governor of the State of Emergency Region sweeping powers including the closing of printing presses (Article 1), forcible resettlement (Article 2), and the increase of prison sentences and fines (Article 5).[20] The harsh terms of this decree were somewhat mitigated in the ensuing Law 430, promulgated on 16 December 1990, which stated that publishing houses should be given written warning before closure, which should be of a maximum of 30 days, and that people forcibly resettled should be given the right to choose where they would go.[21]

Since 1993, the displacement of large numbers of civilians in the southeast has become part of government policy in the struggle

---

in connection with his writings about the Kurdish issue. The sentences were confirmed by the Supreme Court in January 1995. Beşikçi's total prison sentences for exercising his right to non-violent freedom of expression regarding the Kurdish issue then totalled 67 years and 1 month and fines of TL5 billion and TL24 million, with current prison sentences of 22 years and 6 months and a fine of TL1 billion 850 million outstanding. On 4 February, the pro-Kurdish newspaper *Özgür Ülke* was closed by court order after the court decided that it was the successor to *Özgür Gündem* (which was similarly closed on 14 April 1994) and its publication thus violated the Press Law. Publication of the pro-Kurdish *Denge Azadi* was similarly stopped by court order in March when it was decided that it was the successor to the closed newspaper *Azadi*. All 42 issues of the *Denge Azadi*, which began publishing on 20 May 1994, were confiscated and numerous prosecutions had been launched against its staff. See *Human Rights Yesterday and Today*, daily reports by The Human Rights Foundation of Turkey, Documentation Centre, Ankara, January-March 1995.

[18] *Cumhuriyet*, 12 February 1986. See also the numerous Amnesty International reports for this period.

[19] The Emergency State legislation, which set up a regional governor, covers the 10 southeastern provinces of Bitlis, Tunceli, Sırnak, Mardin, Van, Hakkari, Diyarbakır, Batman, Bingöl and Siirt.

[20] See *Turkey Briefing*, vol. 4, no. 3, 1990, for an edited translation.

[21] *Turkey Briefing*, vol. 5, no. 1, 1991.

with the PKK (see below). The government of Tansu Çiller which took power in mid-1993 pledged to continue in the attempt to defeat the PKK by military means. In an attempt to remove the logistical base of the PKK, the security forces undertook full-scale forcible evacuations of villages and hamlets.[22]

Forcible evacuation and destruction of Kurdish villages continued, reaching a peak in late September 1994 with a three-week operation in Tunceli province when some 40,000 Turkish troops reportedly destroyed thirty villages while searching for PKK members. Deputy Prime Minister Murat Karayalçın, who had previously promised help for evacuated villagers, visited the region with Human Rights Minister Azimet Köylüoğlu, who called the destruction 'state terrorism'. On 11 October he stated that 2 million people had been displaced during the previous ten years of fighting with the PKK and that 600 villages and 790 hamlets had been evacuated – over half of these since the beginning of 1993. According to the Turkish Human Rights Association (İHD) and the opposition Welfare Party (RP), over 570 villages were evacuated or destroyed in 1994. As a result huge numbers have fled into the towns of the region, so that for example the population of Diyarbakır has more than doubled from the 400,000 of four years ago.[23] In January 1994 the İHD reported that some 1,500 villages or hamlets had been evacuated or destroyed.[24]

Of course, the Turkish government has a duty to protect its citizens, and the PKK has itself been responsible for massive human

---

[22] These evacuations were often carried out with great brutality and disregard for human rights, with houses burnt and mass detentions of villagers in appalling conditions. For example, in early July 1994, following PKK raids on an army base in nearby Mezraa, soldiers raided the villages of Evrek, Sular and Karapinar near Beytüşebap in Hakkari province because of the villagers' refusal to join the village guard system. The soldiers shot villagers' cattle, burned their beehives and some houses and barns, and forced the inhabitants of the three villages – over 1,000 people including women and children – to march to Mezraa some 10 km away. The male villagers were blindfolded. There they were held in insanitary conditions with little food. Some were tortured – see *Amnesty International*, UA286/94 (EUR 44/66/94), 22 July 1994, and further reports EUR 44/67/94, 26 July 1994, and EUR 44/79/94, 10 August 1994.

[23] For more on the evacuations see Helsinki Watch, *Forced Displacement of Ethnic Kurds from Southeastern Turkey* (New York: Helsinki Watch, October 1994)

[24] See *Human Rights, Yesterday and Today*, daily reports by The Human Rights Foundation of Turkey, Documentation Centre, Ankara, January 1995.

rights violations. Again, if the Turkish army was to withdraw, there is a strong possibility of continued fighting between rival Kurdish factions as has happened in Iraq. However, disregarding for a moment the human rights aspect of such terrible suffering, it is questionable whether the strategy of emptying villages and creating such huge shanty agglomerations in areas virtually devoid of industry will achieve its aim of diminishing support for the PKK. It can be argued that these actions will actually aid such support by creating environments conducive to PKK recruitment.[25]

Education

The educational curriculum of the Turkish Republic makes no concessions at all to the multi-national and multi-ethnic character of the republic's citizens. For example, there is no mention of the Kurds as a separate people or of the Kurdish language being spoken as the mother tongue of a sizeable percentage of the population. On the contrary, the traditional Kemalist line is continued, to the effect that the Turkish nation – apart from the small Christian populations in Istanbul covered by a convention attached to the Treaty of Lausanne – is a monolith without ethnic minorities and comprises the entire population of the republic. This is clearly stated in official texts where the general aim of state education is given as ensuring that the pupil

. . . . knows that the territory and people of the Turkish state constitutes an indivisible whole, that the Turkish Republic is a national, democratic, secular, social and legal state, and that he/she feels the individual glory of the Turkish nation, and understands his/her responsibilities.[26]

Furthermore, the aim is to teach the pupil: 'To read write and speak correct Turkish, and to know, adopt and defend the principles of Turkism [*Türklük ilkeleri*].'[27] This shows both an unstated ac-

---

[25] At the same time the continuing war is crippling the economy – according to one state minister it will take up some 20% of the national budget in 1995; see *Turkey Briefing*, vol. 8, no. 4, 1994.

[26] T.C. Milli Eğitim Gençlik ve Spor *Bakanlığı Imam-Hatip Liseleri Öğretim Programları* (Ankara: Milli Eğitim Basımevi, 1984), p. 9.

[27] *Ibid.*, p. 10.

ceptance of the presence of other mother-tongue groups as well as the clear aim of national homogenisation. In the recent past, teachers, whether they be ethnic Turks or Kurds, have faced dismissal for acknowledging the existence of the Kurdish language or Kurdish culture, and they have consequently felt obliged to pressure pupils to conform to the state's policy.[28]

The emphasis on inculcating Turkish ideals at the expense of all others is also evident in the regulations governing the religious-cum-moral classes which the military regime made a compulsory part of the primary and secondary schools' curriculum.[29] The regulations stipulate that special attention should be paid to emphasising the historic role of the Turks as leaders and propagators of Islam in the world.[30]

The Turkish élite's attitudes

Given the importance of the 'Kurdish Question' in contemporary Turkish politics, it would be instructive at this point to look in more detail at the attitude of the Turkish intellectual and political élite towards it. Following the military coup of 1980, and the ensuing political repression and ban on the use of Kurdish or discussion of the Kurdish issue, the Turkish élite, with some notable exceptions,[31] supported the traditional Kemalist nationalist line that all Muslim citizens of the state were ethnic Turks.[32]

---

[28] One former teacher recalled seeing an 8-year-old being severely beaten for saying some words in Kurdish when he could not remember the words in Turkish, and being punished for being heard to speak in Kurdish to his mother who knew no Turkish. Other teachers singled out Kurds for ridicule and discrimination. See Sarah Graham-Brown, *Education Rights and Minorities* (London: MRG Report, June 1994) reprinted in *Turkey Briefing*, vol. 8, no. 2, 1994.

[29] Religious education, had been compulsory in the early years of the republic but from 1948-61 it was possible to abstain by formal request. After 1961 a formal request had to be made to attend such classes. See *Temel Eğitim ve Ortaöğretim Din ve Ahlak Bilgisi Dersi Program* (Ankara: n.d. but prepared in 1982 and still in force).

[30] *Ibid.* This also emphasises the need for protection of and service to the 'father land' (*vatan*).

[31] For example, the sociologist İsmail Beşikçi, who, as noted above, has spent many years in prison for writing about the situation of Kurds in Turkey.

[32] This of course is the French 'civic' model of integral nationalism as detailed in Chapter 1. However, as is so often the case, Turkish officials and other

However, the rise of a militant Kurdish nationalism and the struggle with the PKK, combined with a global rise of interest in and expression of minority interests (see Chapter 1) has seen a modicum of change in this. There is now a greater readiness to accept the ethnic heterogeneity of modern Turkey.[33] This has been aided by statements form Presidents Özal and Demirel explicitly referring to 'Kurds'. Thus, there is now a greater readiness to use the term Kurd and recognise their existence as an ethnic group in Turkey's ethnic mosaic.[34] This change is very recent. The repealing of Law 2932, banning Kurdish in early 1991, saw even former President, and architect of the repression, Kenan Evren, state: 'Why should not Kurdish be spoken or sung when people can sing and

leading Turks, while espousing this model for their own country, espoused a more 'ethnic' nationalist variant in relation to perceived Turks outside the border – especially in Cyprus and the Balkans (see Chapter 8). This double attitude led to the somewhat incongruous situation whereby Turkish Embassy officials in London in 1986 and 1987 protested to international human rights organisations about the plight of ethnic Turks in Bulgaria who, they rightly pointed out, were denied the right to identify themselves as Turks or use their language or practice their customs, and whom the Bulgarian Zhivkov regime was trying to forcibly make 'Bulgarians'. At the same time, they denied the analogous situation in Turkey with the Kurds. A similar stance was taken by the leading left-wing intellectual Mümtaz Soysal at the Conference on Minority Rights in Europe at the Danish Parliament, Copenhagen, 30 March-April 1990, who made an individual protest, which essentially echoed the Turkish government line, at the summary recommendations of the Working Group on the Kurds in Turkey.

[33] This is very noticeable for frequent travellers to the country. Whereas some 10 years ago most Turkish citizens one met, apart from the Kurds, would see themselves as 'Turks' pure and simple (although as noted above intellectual Istanbul 'drinking circles' would refer to their ethnic origins), many are now proud to point out their heritage of Circassian, Bosnian, Albanian or similar ancestry. Many have only become aware of the ethnic diversity within their own identity in this recent period.

[34] In January 1995 Tansu Çiller illustrated this by rephrasing the Kemalist slogan 'How happy to be a Turk', into 'How happy to be a citizen of Turkey' (*'ne mutlu Türkiye'nin vatandşıyım diyene'*) – *Milliyet*, 1 January 1995. Even this recognition is very recent. At the conference 'Change in Modern Turkey: Politics, Society, Economy' held in Manchester, UK, 5-6 May 1993, in which 14 leading academics from Boğazi.ç University, Istanbul, took part, it was noticeable that there was no mention *at all* of the Kurds until a single question on the last day which elicited a brief response from Professor Cem Behar – who was talking about the demographic situation in Turkey – that they were numerically insignificant.

listen to songs in languages other than Turkish such as English, Arabic or Italian?'[35] However, when Özal followed this in March 1991 with meetings in Çankaya with Iraqi Kurdish leader Jalal Talabani, he and Chief of General Staff Doğan Güreş both came out against any recognition of Kurds as distinct from Turks in Turkey, and they were supported at the time by Demirel and former Prime Minister Bülent Ecevit.[36]

Much of the impetus for this change came from Turgut Özal, himself of Kurdish origin, who until his sudden death on 17 April 1993 appeared to be ahead of both public opinion and the entrenched bureaucracy on the Kurdish issue. He was behind the legalising of spoken and written Kurdish. After the bloody *Nevroz*[37] disturbances of 1991 he became bolder and criticised the army's role in the southeast, thus explicitly revealing a rift over the Kurdish issue at the top of the state apparatus. He even aired the idea that the PKK could be legalised and brought into parliament.[38] Özal also proposed that Turkish radio and television's GAP[39] channel should broadcast Kurdish programmes, but he admitted that this was a minority view in the all-important National Security Council.[40] His maverick approach was also evident in foreign policy, where he was far more willing to consider wide-ranging

[35] *Briefing*, no. 824, 4 February 1991.

[36] *Briefing*, no. 831, 25 March 1991. Demirel went as far as to describe the meetings with Talabani as a scene of 'ignorance, error and treachery. However, since 1991, the DYP government has kept up contacts with both Barzani and Talabani.

[37] *Nevroz*, the Kurdish New Year (*Newruz* in Kurdish) is celebrated on 21 March, and in recent years has often been the precedent for bloody confrontations between the PKK and the state – especially so in 1992, with major clashes in Sırnak, Cızre and Nusaybin; see *Turkey Briefing*, vol. 6, no. 2, 1992. There are currently moves to turn it into a 'national' Turkish holiday.

[38] Özal stated: 'Violence brings more violence, and bloodshed attracts more bloodshed. We must remember this, when we deal with out Kurdish citizens.' Quoted in Mehmet Ümit Necef, 'New conceptions on the Kurdish Question in the Turkish political establishment', Ms, part reprinted in 'Comment', *Turkey Briefing*, vol. 6, no. 5. 1992.

[39] The Southeast Anatolian Project (GAP) is a huge economic project involving the construction of a number of large dams on the Fırat and Dicle (Euphrates and Tigris) rivers which the Turkish government hopes will revitalise the whole area.

[40] Mehmet Ümit Necef, *op. cit.*

options, contrary to Turkey's traditional policy of extreme caution. This was especially so over the formation of a *de facto* Kurdish state in northern Iraq.[41] However, it is perhaps a mistake to view Özal as a 'closet' Kurdish nationalist. He was essentially a pragmatist: somebody who saw that the state had no option but to recognise that a Kurdish consciousness in Turkey was an unavoidable fact which military repression alone could not alter.[42]

Despite the progress spearheaded by Özal, there is still great reluctance to recognise the Kurds as a *national* minority. The élite now attempts to show that Turks and Kurds are fully equal in modern Turkey, usually pointing to leading figures like Hikmet Çetin, Kamuran Inan (who both achieved ministerial rank) and other ethnic Kurds who have risen to the political top as proof that there is no discrimination against them.[43] As such, they tend to deny that there is a 'Kurdish problem' at all. Instead, they point to the economic problems of the southeast, to the 'terrorism' of the PKK, or to the evil machinations of outsiders whom they see as using the Kurdish question as a weapon against Turkey.[44]

---

[41] Mümtaz Soysal claimed that President Özal canvassed opinion of the Turkish élite on the idea of a federal post-Gulf War Iraq in which Turkey would dominate the Turkoman and Kurdish Autonomous provinces, and Turkish journalists claimed Özal was studying government documents on Turkey's claims to oil-rich Mosul (H. Pope, 'Iraq land claim behind Özal's pledge to Kurds', *The Independent*, London, 28 January 1991). Özal's floating of such an idea provoked serious discussion in the Turkish press on whether an independent Kurdistan would join Turkey as Hatay province had in July 1939.

[42] After his death, a memorandum he had drawn up was publicised which stated that he postulated further population changes in the Kurdish areas to further dilute Kurdish nationalism. *The Guardian*, 17 November, and *Turkish Probe*, 18 November 1993, p. 13. On the other hand, it appears that he had been in (very discreet) contact with Öcalan before he died; see *Mideast Mirror*, 15 March 1993.

[43] On 12 August 1994 İrfan Acar of the Turkish Foreign Ministry stated that in fact one third of the Turkish parliament was ethnically Kurdish and thus the Kurds were actually *over-represented* in parliament. However, such figures must be seen in context. Many of these 'Kurds' kept their ethnic background hidden, while those politicians who have espoused a Kurdish political programme have been penalised heavily.

[44] These views have been frequently expressed to me by Turks from all walks of life, from government officials to 'the man in the street'. An opinion poll of 29 August 1992 showed that 39.6% of respondents blamed the rising PKK violence on 'foreign powers seeking to weaken Turkey'; *Mideast Mirror*, 7 September 1992. In May 1993 former Prime Minister Ecevit said that the then

Their solution is to increase democracy for all citizens of Turkey and not pander to group or minority rights.[45] Such views were clearly stated by former Deputy Prime Minister and SHP leader Erdal İnönü.[46] He stressed that Turkey is and must remain a unitary state, and pointed to the success of 'the terrorist movement [PKK] in using propaganda as their main agent in their efforts' – although quite what was wrong in using 'propaganda' in an ostensive democracy he did not make clear. He also stated that the Kurds had 'all cultural freedom available' and that there was 'no reason for [their] feeling oppressed'.[47] When asked whether a military solution was the only option for the Turkish state in dealing with the PKK, he stated that the only way to deal with armed groups was to use the state security forces, but that the military solution was not the only way: the only real way was to 'democratise' the country.

The attitude of Demirel, who along with Özal has been perhaps the single most important politician in Turkey in the last twenty

---

PKK cease-fire was part of 'a Western plan' to give the Kurds autonomy, then a federation and finally separation as had happened in Yugoslavia; *Turkish Daily News*, interview, 12 May 1993. The US, Britain and Germany are usually seen as the main 'outside meddlers' who, so the conspiracy theory goes, want to create a Kurdish state, divide Turkey up, and gain access to the rich oilfields of Mosul in northern Iraq. This tendency to view Kurdish nationalism as a result of outside influence fits in with the traditional Ottoman/Islamic historiography that all nationalisms are both exogenous and divisive (see Chapters 2 and 3).

[45] David Kushner, Professor of History at Haifa University, in a talk entitled 'Questions of Identity in Contemporary Turkey' at the Turkish Areas Study Group, Sixth Spring Symposium, Sawston Hall, near Cambridge, UK, 13 May 1995, pointed out the similar attitudes of the Turkish élite to religious minorities like the Alevis: i.e. stress is laid on how all groups are treated equally and thus differences are seen as insignificant.

[46] At the talk 'Democracy in Turkey since 1983' at SOAS, London University, 18 April 1994. İnönü did, however, make it clear that he personally opposed the lifting of the Kurdish DEP deputies' immunity and their subsequent prosecution and imprisonment.

[47] This line of thinking was also stressed by leading academic Metin Heper at a talk, 'The Turkish Government and the Kurdish Question', at SOAS, London University 26 September 1994. His general thrust was that neither the Ottoman nor the modern Turkish state differentiated between Turks and Kurds but treated them as equals. His presentation severely underestimated the ethnic component of Kemalist nationalism (see Chapter 3) and completely ignored the strong resentment felt by many Kurds at the policy of denial and assimilation.

years, is also instructive. His views broadly echo those mentioned earlier which view all concessions with extreme caution. After his victory in November 1991 he presented his government's programme to the Turkish parliament on 25 November. In this he stated:

> It is natural to have differences in culture, thought, belief, language and race among our citizens ... Such a plurality is not a weakness for a democratic and unitary state. In this unitary structure various ethnic cultural and linguistic identities can be freely expressed.

However, he went on to state that:

> No citizen of this country except those accepted under international agreements [i.e., the religious minorities like the Jews or the Orthodox Armenians and Greeks] are in the category of a minority. In Turkey everyone is equal and a first class citizen. Everyone is endowed with the basic human rights and freedoms to explore, develop and protect his own mother tongue, culture, history, folklore and religious beliefs ... But the official language of the state, the flag and symbols, boundaries and sovereignty of the Republic of Turkey are beyond all debate [loud applause] ... The southeast will have a special 'regional development plan'.[48]

Demirel, along with Deputy Prime Minister İnönü, Interior Minister İsmet, Sezgin, and army chief Güreş, toured the southeast on 7 and 8 December 1991 as part of his policy of recognising the 'Kurdish reality' in Turkey. This 'reality' now allowed Kurdish publications and newspapers and state backing for the SHP idea of a Kurdish Institute.[49] However, the language of education was to remain Turkish and there was to be no discussion of possible federation. In Diyarbakır Demirel stated:

> This state was set up by people who came from the Turkish race [but] the others are not second-class citizens. We set it up together ... There is no such thing as saying 'you and us' ... Turkish nationalism is a soft nationalism which [is] not

[48] Turkish TV, Ankara, 25 November 1991, in SWB ME/1241 A/8 28/11/91.
[49] The institute was opened on 19 April 1992 despite the police pulling down the sign as it was in Kurdish – *Briefing*, no. 888, 11 May 1992.

based on racism and does not isolate other ethnic groups in Turkey. You must accept contacts between those [who] say they are of Kurdish origin and people of Kurdish ethnicity in other countries.

However, he again stressed that 'We are unanimously determined to protect Turkey's unity.'[50]

Thus, Demirel's policy was one of allowing Kurdish for cultural activities,[51] but not of any recognition of group rights, or even recognition of the Kurds as an official minority within Turkey. Everyone was to be recognised as an equal citizen and the backward southeast was to be developed. Turkey was resolutely to remain a unitary state, with no possibility of even discussion on this matter. Regarding the fear that a federation would lead to partition, Demirel not unreasonably pointed to the recent events in federal structures like Yugoslavia, Czechoslovakia and the USSR – all of which had collapsed.[52]

The ambivalence of leading politicians to the Kurdish question is also evident in statements by Tansu Çiller when she became Prime Minister. On the one hand, she stated that there was 'no Kurdish problem, just a terrorist problem' in Turkey, while on the other hand she told reporters in the southeast when she toured there (like Demirel before her) that anyone who saw himself as a Kurd was a Kurd.[53] She also showed a more 'liberal' face when travelling abroad to West European countries. However, at home she, like Demirel, relied on the military to subdue Kurdish resent-

---

[50] Anatolia News Agency, 8 December 1991, in SWB 11/12/91.

[51] Demirel remained wary of setting up a Kurdish TV station and in early 1992 had a number of disagreements with Özal over this. On 22 April 1992, Altan Öyman in *Milliyet* and Hasan Cemal in *Sabah*, both wrote that Demirel's fears that a Kurdish TV station would encourage Kurdish children not to learn Turkish were unfounded, pointing to the US situation where, they said, Spanish language TV programmes did not deter US Hispanics from speaking English. As shown in Chapter 1, this claim is debatable. Later, in mid-1993, Demirel was sharply critical of Prime Minister Çiller for 'concessions' over Kurdish TV, saying that this would aid the PKK; *Sabah*, 25 July 1993.

[52] Demirel specifically mentioned these 3 examples in an interview with the pan-Arab daily *al-Hayat* on 20 November 1992; reported in *Mideast Mirror*, 20 November 1992. He did not, however, refer to other non-communist federal structures like Germany, Belgium or Switzerland which have not collapsed.

[53] *Sabah*, 25 July 1993.

ment at past repression in the southeast. On the question of Kurdish TV, over which Demirel was so critical of her (see footnote 51), she only wanted a token one hour per day.[54] She also referred to the Kurdish MPs whose immunity was lifted and who were prosecuted (see below) as 'Traitors under the roof of parliament' and she organised an anti-Kurdish, anti-Islamic rally in Istanbul's Taksim Square in honour of Atatürk on 28 February 1994.[55]

The attitude of the mainstream Turkish press towards the Kurdish problem is instructive. The problems of the press in freely reporting events or criticising government policy in the southeast have already been noted. In addition to these legal obstacles, it should be noted that Turkish national dailies are mainly geared towards readership in the big cities and few have reporters in the southeast, specialists in Kurdish affairs or Kurdish-speaking journalists. The centre of publishing remains at the opposite end of the country in Istanbul, and few editors know much or care much about the southeast.[56] The official unitary Kemalist nationalism is the staple diet of the mainstream press, and only non-Muslims, as specified in the Lausanne treaty, are recognised as minorities within Turkey. The PKK is always referred to as a 'terrorist' organisation.[57] The above-noted conspiracy theory that Western countries are involved in an attempt to divide up Turkey is also frequently reiterated in the Turkish press, as is the strong commitment to the plight of 'Turks' (however defined) outside Turkey. Conversely, there is little support for greater recognition of linguistic and cultural rights for Turkey's Kurds. Beyond some fringe pro-Kurdish papers

[54] Vice-Prime Minister Erdal İnönü was also against this 'concession', arguing that cultural rights should only be granted after military victory over the PKK – *Briefing*, no. 947, 19 July 1993.

[55] Hugh Pope, *The Independent*, London 4 March 1994. However, only some 10,000 people attended, mostly police, school pupils and state workers specially bussed in for the event.

[56] Şahin Alpay, 'The Turkish Press and the Kurdish Problem' at workshop on The Turkish Media Today SOAS, London University, 21 May 1992, on which much of this paragraph is based. It is further noticeable that few Turks who originate from outside the southeast area have ever visited it.

[57] The PKK *have*, as noted below, relied heavily on indiscriminate violence to terrorise the population. However, the use of 'terrorist' is always pejorative in the political sense. As the well worn cliché puts it, one man's terrorist is another man's freedom fighter.

which face continual legal harassment (see above) there is virtually no discussion in the press of what the PKK actually wants (however difficult to ascertain this may in fact be). Some see the Kurdish problem as a purely economic one which can be solved by development and the huge GAP project. Few Turkish journalists countenance the possibility that the rise of Kurdish nationalism may well be a result of development and change in the region (in the shape of modern nationalism finally penetrating these backward areas), or that Kurdish nationalism could be a reaction to Kemalist state nationalism. Again, few distinguish between any form of Kurdish nationalism and the PKK, which has the result of reinforcing the state branding all political activists who raise the Kurdish question as PKK supporters. Despite this sorry tale, there have been some notable exceptions[58] who have greatly contributed to the gradual change in perception.[59]

An illustration of this change is the programme of the The New Democracy Movement (YDH), which was founded on 22 December 1994 after a year and a half of preparation. Its leader is the thirty-five-year-old Cem Boyner, former President of the Turkish Industrialists and Businessmen's Association (TÜSİAD). The party is supported by reformist and liberal-minded intellectuals such as Şerif Mardin, Nilüfer Göle, and Asaf Savaş Akat, as well as journalists like Cengiz Cadar. Their programme offers a new approach to such taboo subjects as the Kurdish issue and secularism. Boyner's radical speeches have been taken up by parliamentarians and widely discussed. While most political parties still cannot admit that there is a Kurdish issue in Turkey, YDH does not hesitate to say that while Turkish people may have no problems with Kurdish people the state certainly does. Among their major aims when they come to power is to close the State Security Courts. Boyner also calls for a new role for the military which,

---

[58] For example, Memet Ali Birand who did the ground-breaking interview with PKK leader Abdullah Öcalan ('Apo') in the summer of 1988 (and who was strongly criticised for allegedly de-demonising Öcalan in it. Birand in *Sabah*, 25 April 1992, also pointed out that 'we are harvesting what we have sown' in the southeast.

[59] Example of this change are ANAP Vice General Secretary Ekrem Pakdemirli's calling for the army to pull out of the southeast (*Milliyet*, 22 December 1994) and the headline of *Milliyet*, 3 January 1995, calling for a rethink of the whole Kurdish Question.

he believes, should be used against external threats rather than for internal issues like the southeast question. Despite his approach, which is radical by Turkish standards, Boyner essentially reiterates the same policy as others in the Turkish élite. He is against any autonomy for the Kurds and is for individual rather than group rights. He claims that only about 1 per cent of Turkey's Kurds want autonomy but they do want individual liberties. His answer, again, is investment in the southeast.[60]

A precursor to Boyner's movement was the idea of a 'Second Republic' put forward by a group of liberal journalists including Çetin Altan and Alktan Öyman. They, like Boyner, called for a radical change on the Kurdish issue, as well as an end to the centralised bureaucratic étatist policies which characterised the original institution of the Turkish Republic.[61] Similar ideas were put forward by Mithat Baydur in *Nokta* in February 1993.[62]

In mid-1990 the SHP also began to move with the new times and published a thirty-six page report on the Kurdish question. The report stated that 'people should be allowed to accept their Kurdish identity and say they are of Kurdish origin and be able to freely express this identity.' It went on to declare that permission should be given for all mother tongues in Turkey to be written, spoken and read, and that the state should found an institute to study minority cultures. It also described the ban on the publishing of Kurdish literature and music as 'an implementation rarely seen

[60] This was all clearly spelt out in the talk 'Current Challenges Facing Turkey' at SOAS, London University, on 11 April 1995. It was noticeable that his definite negative answer to a question about possible autonomy for the Kurds was met with a spontaneous round of applause from the mostly Turkish audience. Quite how successful Boyner's party will be remains to be seen. While his pledges to roll back the frontiers of the all-powerful state – '*Devlet Baba*' – can be seen as commendable, quite how this will appeal to an electorate brought up in a system of state patronage as reward for political loyalty is not clear. Similarly, his pledges to completely secularise the state and remove Islam from the bureaucracy may appeal to some, but will surely not appeal to the majority of the electorate which has repeatedly shown itself in favour of state support for Sunni Islam.

[61] Perhaps unsurprisingly given the traditional political set-up of patronage and influence which the '*Devlet Baba*' affords politicians, these ideas were rejected and ridiculed by most senior politicians from the left and the right; *Briefing*, no. 901, 17 August 1992.

[62] Mithat Baydar, 'Türk'ün Yeni Kızıl Elması', *Nokta*, 7-13 February 1993.

under totalitarian rules, not even envisaged even in the 1930s when the winds of fascism swept the world.' Ankara's State Security Prosecutor reportedly wanted the Constitutional Court to decide whether this document was in violation of the Constitution,[63] but this did not happen. President Özal scoffed at the report and pointed to his own practice, which had already gone a long way towards decriminalising the speaking of Kurdish, but he stated that the teaching of Kurdish in state schools would never be allowed.[64] The merging of the SHP with the reborn CHP in 1995 under the leadership of Hikmet Çetin, an ethnic Kurd but a long-time figure of the Turkish establishment, saw further calls to amend the notorious Article 8 of the anti-terror law and more calls

> .... to solve the Kurdish problem within pluralist democracy, equality and national, unity, while respecting ethnic identity and cultural, differences, by redressing old wounds and through socioeconomic development.[65]

On 21 March 1995, following the signing of the customs union with the European Union, the DYP/CHP government coalition published a paper detailing government strategy and aims.[66] This detailed a number of proposed constitutional and legal changes for Turkey. There was no explicit reference to the Kurds. Moreover, the paper categorically stated that:

> The Turkish Republic, state, country and nation is an indivisible whole ... The unity of the Turkish state was the reflection of a traditional and historical idea of solidarity and unity ... This solidarity and unity had resulted in a common 'political culture'. This we are determined to defend.[67]

The programme did have a section aimed at restoring peace and security in the southeast. Amongst other proposals, this called for

---

[63] *Mideast Mirror*, 31 July 1990.

[64] Hugh Pope, *Middle East International*, 20 July 1990.

[65] TRT TV, Ankara, 27 February 1995, in SWB EE/2240, B/6, 1/3/95.

[66] *Doğruyol Partisi – Cumhuriyet Halk Partisi Hükümetinin Uygulama Programı*, 21 March 1995.

[67] *Ibid.*, p. 4.

the raising of the people's awareness of the difference between the security forces and 'terrorists' and efforts to end the murders by 'unknown persons'. The paper also called for the ending of the emergency legislation and for a Provincial Administration law to be implemented as soon as possible. Ethnic diversity was briefly mentioned, but only in the context of the dangers it posed for national unity.[68]

Thus, despite the other aspects of the programme, which proposed greater democratisation of Turkey, it categorically reaffirmed the basic tenets of Kemalist integral nationalism. This illustrates a dilemma for Turkey's élite. They want to be 'European' and join Europe's institutions, but being 'European' in the current context means accepting not only individual human rights, but also (less well defined) collective rights – at a minimum cultural ones.[69] This was highlighted by the European Parliament's objection to the customs union with Turkey, which again focused on the 'Kurdish problem'.

The 'hard' Kurdish opposition – the PKK

Of all the recent Kurdish groups in Turkey, the Kurdistan Workers' Party (PKK) is the most important due to the length and scale

[68] Article 6 of the section entitled 'The Project to Repair the Southeast' called for the 'planning and realising of measures for bringing into the area the understanding of national unity and the actual and legal deficiencies which occur in the development and free expression of the citizens ethnic and cultural personal characteristics.' *Ibid.*, p. 20. Of course, the question of ethnic diversity in a modern democratic state is a complicated one where there is much debate; see Arend Lijphart, *Democracies: Patterns of majoritarian and consensus government in twenty-one countries* (New Haven: Yale University Press, 1984), pp. 21-36 and *passim.*

[69] While individual human rights have been codified in a number of international conventions like the International Covenant on Civil and Political Rights (ICCPR) as well as the European Convention on Human Rights (ECHR – to which Turkey is a signatory), minority rights have until recently been somewhat neglected. The European Convention is unclear on the question, while the ICCPR only refers to them briefly in Article 27. With the collapse of the Soviet bloc, this situation has begun to change. There have been a number of movements in the international arena towards codifying minority rights. The current state of play is reflected in the *UN Declaration on the Rights of Person Belonging to National or Ethnic, Religious and Linguistic Minorities*, (adopted by UN General Assembly, Resolution 47/135, 18 December 1992).

of its continuing armed insurrection and the authorities' response to it. The PKK has a tight professional structure which comprises a political nucleus, the party, its full-time fighting force, the Kurdistan National Liberation Army (ARGK, set up in 1986), and a widespread popular front, the Kurdistan National Liberation Front (ERNK, set up in 1985).[70] Despite being characterised as 'bandits' by the authorities, and as being composed of the most marginalised elements of Kurdish society or people who felt 'excluded from the country's social and economic development',[71] the PKK has grown into a formidable force. In this it has been greatly aided by the government's repressive measures and continuing military methods, especially after March 1990 when the National Security Council decided on the full-scale evacuation of villages to create a 'security buffer zone'.[72]

The PKK was formed by Abdullah Öcalan after a meeting on 27 November 1978 in a village near Diyarbakır. Öcalan, known as 'Apo' to his supporters[73] comes from a poor peasant family in the Gaziantep region. Educated in Turkish at school, his first language is now Turkish rather than Kurdish, and in his younger days he was deeply religious.[74] His main aim as a student was

[70] There have been other associated organisations like the Kurdistan Freedom Unit (HRK), set up in 1984 and modelled on the Vietcong, but the ERNK and ARGK are the enduring sub-groups of the PKK.

[71] Martin van Bruinessen, 'Between guerrilla war and political murder: The Workers' Party of Kurdistan', *Middle East Report*, no, 152, 1988, p. 42.

[72] The fighting force of the PKK rose from about 3,000 armed militants at this time to 13,000 by November 1992 plus a reserve pool of 45-50,000 in the southeast. The relationship between state repression and PKK support is clear. In 1986, despite two years of campaigns, the PKK still lacked any mass support, the turning point coming in 1987 with the state of emergency in the southeast and the expanding of the Village Guard system set up in May 1985; İsmet G. İmset, *The PKK: A report on Separatist Violence in Turkey (1973-1992)* (Ankara: Turkish Daily News Publications 1992) pp. 215-19 and 48-50.

[73] 'Apo' in Kurdish has the same meaning as 'Dede' in Turkish, i.e. a Shiite spiritual leader. 'Öcalan' means avenger, which, given his ruthless tactics, is somewhat appropriate.

[74] Interestingly, when first a student at the Ankara Higher Educational Association he reportedly attended prayers 5 times a day and attended Turkish nationalist and religious conferences at the Maltepe Mosque as well as those staged by the Association to Fight Communism; İmset, *op. cit.*, p. 334. Regarding the language issue, he stated that 'I think and plan completely in Turkish. Kurdish comes second.' – quoted in *ibid.*, p. 333. Given the emphasis on Kurdish culture and

initially to join the Turkish army[75] but, having failed the exams, he entered the Political Science Faculty of Ankara University. There he discovered socialist literature and, like many other radical Kurdish students, became part of the fragmented Turkish left wing, being a member of the group *Devrimci Gençlik* ('Revolutionary Youth') in the 1970s. However, he came to view the Turkish left as chauvinist on the Kurdish issue. Seeing the need for a specifically 'Kurdish National Liberation Movement', he severed relations with other Turkish left-wing groups.[76] He organised seminars in which the economic exploitation of the southeast was discussed and it was stressed that the Kurds had different national characteristics from the Turks, including language, culture and economic and social structures. At these seminars, Turkish troops were portrayed as occupiers and it was stated that the Kurds should determine their own future. This was clearly a nationalist agenda, and Öcalan was accused by former left-wing colleagues of being a nationalist and resembling the racist Turkish MHP.[77]

Öcalan moved from Ankara back to the southeast in 1975 and he and his associates drew up a 'Party programme draft' in 1977. This document[78] stated amongst other things that:

> Kurdistan has been divided into four regions by the four exploiting countries: Syria, Iraq, Iran and Turkey.
> The largest part of this territory is Turkish Kurdistan (Middle-West and North of the whole).

---

language, it is ironic that the PKK uses only Turkish – one reason for this, apart from the natural preference of Öcalan and other Kurds for Turkish, is the many dialects of Kurdish and the lack, so far, of standardisation; ibid., p. 66.

[75] Entry into the highly prestigious Turkish War Academy has often been one of the main avenues of advancement in republican Turkey; see Mehmet Ali Birand, *Shirts of Steel: an anatomy of the Turkish armed forces* (London, I.B. Tauris, 1991) *passim*.

[76] Abdulkadır Aygan, *PKK'nın İçinden* (Ankara: Yeni Forum Yayınları, no. 3, 1987), pp. 99-175. A more cynical view is to say that Öcalan saw that there was a better opportunity for his personal dominance by setting up a specifically Kurdish Marxist-Leninist 'liberation movement' than by remaining within the more numerous Turkish leftist groups.

[77] İmset, *op. cit.,* p. 12-14.

[78] Information from PKK defector Şahin Dönmez to the authorities reprinted in *ibid.*, pp. 15-16.

There are semi-feudal production relations in existence in this territory. This is a classic pattern of exploitation.

In the revolution, Turkish Kurdistan will take the leadership. The structure of the revolution will be a national democratic revolution.

The minimum objective will be to establish an independent non-aligned Kurdistan State in the region.

The maximum objective will be to establish a state based on Marxist-Leninist principles.

The proletariat will be the pioneering force of the revolution ... The peasants will be the major force of the revolution ...

The allied forces in this revolution will be patriotic circles, the Turkish revolutionary movement, other patriotic revolutionary movements in Kurdistan, socialist countries, workers movements in capitalist countries and international liberation movements.

It also identified the 'obstacles in front of the Kurdish revolution' as:

1. Fascists [MHP and other radical rightist forces]
2. Social chauvinists [those on the Turkish left who held that Kurdish freedom depended on revolution in Turkey]
3. The agents and state-supporter network [those Kurds who had been co-opted and financed by the state]
4. Feudal landlords and natural collaborators.

This document clearly spelt out the later PKK programme and presaged the vicious PKK war against all perceived agents of the Turkish state, including school teachers as well as Village Guards.[79]

---

[79] The PKK campaign against teachers intensified in 1992 and peaked in 1994. A report by the Ankara-based Turkish Human Rights Association (İHD), *Training and Education in the Emergency State Region* (Ankara; November 1994), stated that 128 teachers were killed in the period between 15 August 1984, when the PKK began armed activities, and 20 November 1994. Of these, 81 had been killed by the PKK and 43 by 'unidentified assailants' (often a euphemism for Hizbullah-style death squads – see chapter 6). As a result, the Education Ministry reported that 2,000 schools were forced to close in the southeast during 1994. The PKK campaign against teachers appears to have ended at the end of 1994 with the new PKK line (see below). The brutality of the PKK attacks on perceived 'agents of the state', including families and women and

Armed activity was to be a crucial PKK weapon in both gaining support and undermining state control. In classic nationalist fashion, Öcalan also selected history to bolster his ideology. Şahin Dönmez states that:

> At about this time Öcalan created in his own mind a history of the Kurds. Because we could not obtain or find any official documents on this issue, we investigated the situation of the people in the Middle East, the history of the Ottoman–Arab Turkish relations, and brought out the concept that the people in the divided territory of Iran, Syria and Turkey had come from the Mediterranean race. We also took excerpts from Lenin's book on the right of nations to determine their own fate. As a result, all of our activities concentrated on these details.[80]

Of special interest in this programme is the 'minimum objective' to establish a Kurdish state, and whether it is foreseen by Öcalan to include the parts of 'Kurdistan' in the neighbouring countries. While the PKK is always referred to by the Turkish establishment as a separatist organisation, Öcalan, despite the 1977 programme, has been ambivalent on this crucial point.[81] A consistent theme of PKK policy has been its adeptness in changing its stance and ideology to keep up with a changing world and vital changes in regional conditions. In view of this, Öcalan has, since these early beginnings, been careful to deny that the PKK's overriding aim is an independent Kurdistan.[82] Such statements must be treated

---

children, provoked dissent among Kurdish circles inside and outside the PKK. The campaign against the Village Guards, especially in the period 1987-90, spread a terror which was compared by a leading PKK expert to that of the Shining Path guerrilla movement in Peru; İmset *op. cit.*, 101. Despite alienating many Kurds, it did to a large degree seem to achieve its aims by escalating government reprisals and state terror, which have perennially bolstered support for the PKK.

[80] Şahin Dönmez quoted in İmset, op. cit., pp. 16-17.

[81] At times he has called for an independent Kurdistan and at others for a Belgian-style federal solution within Turkey. Mehmet Ali Birand, *Apo ve PKK* (Istanbul: Milliyet Yayınları, 1992), p. 286.

[82] For example he states 'claims that the PKK is 'not prepared to consider anything less than a separate state' have no basis in fact ... We are open to all proposals and all initiatives from any country or international organisation. I would like to emphasise that we are not insistent on the division of Turkey, and that such propaganda does not reflect our approach to the question.' See

carefully. Öcalan is aware of the importance of international support
and his statements also deny that armed struggle is the PKK's
only solution. During the 1993 cease-fire with the Turkish government, the Turkish authorities refused to consider any solution
other than the military one.[83] On the other hand, Öcalan has at
times expressed a desire to expand his movement throughout
Turkey and create a Turkish left-wing organisation as well, seeing
himself as a possible future regional leader.[84] This again illustrated
his vacillation between pragmatism and ambition.

On the question of relations with Kurds in neighbouring
countries, the PKK has again shown ambivalence. The initial
1977 programme spoke of 'other patriotic revolutionary movements in Kurdistan' as allies, and from 1980 onwards, Masoud
Barzani's KDP was one of the PKK's main supporters. In 1983
Öcalan and Barzani signed a protocol on 'the solidarity principles
of the KDP and PKK', but this alliance was wearing thin by
1984 due to the PKK's vicious tactics. These were provoking
reprisals from Turkey which often hit KDP positions in Iraq.[85]
Finally, in 1987, Barzani condemned PKK massacres of fellow
Kurds.[86] The PKK responded by making overtures to Jalal Talabani
instead. ARGK leader Cemil Bayik stated in August 1991: 'Our
goal is not necessarily to unify all the Kurds. If they wish to live

his address, 'To the International Conference on North West Kurdistan' of 10
March 1994, in *Final Resolution of the international conference on North-West
Kurdistan(South-East Turkey)* (London: Kurdish Human Rights Project, 1994).

[83] *Ibid.* The cease-fire declared by Öcalan was to operate from 20 March until
15 April and then extended indefinitely from 16 April when he declared: 'We
should be given our cultural freedoms and the right to broadcast in Kurdish.
The village guard system and Emergency Legislation should be lifted. The
Turkish authorities should take necessary measures to prevent unsolved murders
and should recognise the political rights of Kurdish organisations.' It was noted
that he did not mention the right to self-determination which previously had
been a standard PKK demand. Despite this apparent concession, the authorities
continued with military operations and on 24 May the PKK resumed violent
activities; *Turkey Briefing*, vol. 7, no. 2 1993.

[84] İmset, *op. cit.*, p. 334.

[85] This continued, and in late 1985 Turkey bombed KDP positions in northern
Iraq thinking they were PKK ones.

[86] Barzani stated that the PKK 'is not struggling for the Kurdish people or
Kurdistan. The PKK is earning the hatred and disgust of all the Kurdish people
and others struggling for them.' İmset, *op. cit.*, pp. 49-51.

with the people in their countries of origin, we will respect that.'[87] Once more, pragmatism appears to be the overriding concern. The Turkish government appeared to be trying to get the KDP to police the PKK, and in 1993 the KDP carried out a full-scale campaign against the PKK.[88] This was followed by a further all-out attack by the KDP on PKK bases in northern Iraq in the autumn of 1995, in which Barzani appeared to be receiving some (undisclosed) help from the Turkish forces.

The PKK's adeptness at changing policy to suit conditions is also shown by the switch in 1989 to the exploitation of Islam.[89] PKK pamphlets signed 'Amen' and beginning '*Bismillahirrahma-nirrahim*'('In the name of Allah the merciful and forgiving') first appeared in 1989. Öcalan's *Nevroz* message in 1990 spoke of 'the positive effects of the Islamic revolution in Iran'. That year he also accused the Turkish government of 'inventing Islamic Kurdish organisations' and charged that the Van-based Islamic Party of Kurdistan (PİK) was a government-controlled organisation. The use of Islamic messages and quotes from the Koran became widespread in PKK propaganda, and the PKK even set up a unit called 'The Patriotic Men of Religion'. However, religious practices were forbidden for the inner core of the party and the ARGK, and the cadres had to accept Öcalan's interpretations of Marxist-Leninism without question[90] Öcalan has kept a rigid internal control over the PKK with frequent bloody purges.

This ability to change ideology to suit new conditions was further shown at a major meeting of activists between 8 and 27 January 1995, prior to Turkey's prolonged incursion into northern Iraq in April 1995. At this meeting,[91] the PKK not only reviewed

[87] AFF, 2 August 1991, in SWB ME/1141 A/11, 4/8/91.

[88] *Turkish Probe*, 5 October 1993, and *Anatolia News Agency*, 18 November 1993, in SWB 20/11/93.

[89] This parallels the use of Islam by both the state élites in the so-called Turkish Islamic Synthesis of the 1980s and the radical pan-Turkist right – see chapters 6 and 5 respectively – and once more illustrates the importance of Islam in the Turkish context.

[90] İmset, *op. cit.* pp. 139–42. The reference to Iran may have been due to Öcalan looking to Iran as a possible supporter. The international climate was once more changing, with Turkey steadily managing to pressure Syria to stop harbouring the PKK.

[91] Although the exact meeting place of the 317 delegates is not yet known,

twenty years of warfare, but also boasted that it had taken major decisions to transform the organisation into a contemporary, more credible, guerrilla movement. The importance of the January Congress of the PKK was that it coincided with major diplomatic moves by Turkish Kurds. Efforts to set up a Kurdish Parliament-in-Exile were finalised after the meeting.[92] Immediately before, the PKK issued a 'Declaration of Intention' to abide by humanitarian laws and rules specified by the Geneva Convention. Given the PKK's murderous past, this was clearly an attempt to upgrade its international standing.[93]

At the January 1995 meeting a decision was also taken to announce a partial amnesty for state-armed Village Guards, stating that they had until May 1995 to abandon their weapons. According to PKK sources, the meeting stressed the importance of preserving human rights during guerrilla operations and not causing any harm to innocent civilians, be they of Kurdish or Turkish origin. Military targets for future guerrilla warfare were thus carefully selected and outlined, the main aim being the creation of a fully fledged Kurdish army.[94] Turkish officials now argue that the PKK

Turkish intelligence experts believed the so-called '5th Victory Congress' was held in Haftanın, a camp area which was the focus of recent Turkish raids; İsmet G İmset, 'Comment', *Turkey Briefing*, vol. 9, no. 1, 1995, which is the source for the information on this meeting.

[92] Turkey reacted strongly to attempts to set up a 'Kurdish government-in-exile', which it saw as a plot by the PKK to dismember Turkey. On 10 January 1995 Foreign Minister Murat Karayalçın said that Turkey would not allow such a body (TRT TV), Ankara 10 January 1995, in SWB EE/2199, B/3, 12/1/95). On 18 January, Turkey protested about activity to set up such a 'parliament' in Moscow and asked Russia to stop PKK activity in the country (Anatolia News Agency), Ankara, 18 January 1995, in SWB EE/2206, B/5, 20/1/95). On 15 February, the Turkish Foreign Ministry said that 'relevant' countries had been told that a 'Kurdish parliament-in-exile' would be seen by Turkey as a move against its territorial integrity. On 17 March, Speaker Cindoruk cancelled a visit to Belgium planned for 21 to 24 March in protest at plans to set up a 'Kurdish parliament-in-exile' in Belgium. However, despite Turkey's diplomatic activity on this issue, the 'parliament' was eventually set up in The Hague, causing Turkish protests; BBC World Service, 12 April 1995.

[93] Such declarations by the PKK must be seen in the context of its past massive abuses and lack of response to calls by organisations like Amnesty International to end its human rights violations; Amnesty International, *Turkey: A policy of Denial* EUR 44/01/95 (London: Amnesty International February 1995) p. 10.

[94] Despite these decisions, the Turkish incursion into northern Iraq appeared

is aware of Western concern over human rights in Turkey and is aiming to exploit the conditions through bogus promises of respecting human rights. The PKK retaliates by pointing to Ankara's own lamentable human rights record in the southeast.

Among the most important decisions taken during the congress was the PKK's termination of the use of 'General Secretary' to describe its leader, Abdullah Öcalan. Instead, a new Chairmanship Council structure was established, in which Öcalan, as Chairman, would preside over six more members. Another highlight of the meeting was a resolution adopted to abandon the traditional cold-war symbols of the hammer and sickle, which were dropped from the PKK's party flag. The PKK later boasted of being the first post-cold war group to take such a 'pioneering step' to abandon 'the burdens of real socialism'. During the congress, the movement, which started off twenty years ago as a hard-line Marxist-Leninist Kurdish group, also rejected the concept of Soviet socialism and 'other dogmatic policies', emphasising once again that 'real socialism' and organisational structure had to keep up with changes in world history. It denounced Soviet communism as 'the most primitive and violent era of socialism.'[95]

The claim to abide by international humanitarian accords and the dropping of Marxist-Leninist symbols allowed the ERNK to compare itself with organisations like Sinn Fein in Ireland, the Palestine Liberation Organisation and even the ruling African National Congress.[96] Despite previous Turkish claims that the PKK was no more than 'a handful of terrorist bandits', the Chief of Staff office issued casualty figures in April 1995 which clearly contradicted this. According to the military, a total of 9,691 PKK

---

to strike a wrong chord in PKK ranks. Grassroots groups, mainly in Germany, ran amok, with attacks against Turkish business places and even mosques. Demonstrations spread throughout Europe, while Ankara claimed that at least 4 civilians had been killed by the PKK. In early April, the organisation further marred its diplomatic drive by kidnapping 2 Turkish reporters working for the foreign press; see *Turkey Briefing*, vol. 9, no. 1, 1995.

[95] Öcalan had already signalled his turning away from 'real socialism' in November 1991 in an interview with İsmet G. İmset in the Bekaa Valley, Lebanon; İmset *op. cit.*, p. 346.

[96] BBC World Service, 12 April 1995.

militants had been killed by troops since 1984. Along with those arrested, 16,970 PKK militants had been gaoled.[97]

Thus, under Öcalan's iron leadership, the PKK has managed to turn itself into a formidable guerrilla organisation. By a combination of its own and government terror it has grown from a few discontented members on the periphery of Kurdish society to one of the most important guerrilla groups in the area. At the same time, it has made the government react with ever-increasing repression and brutal methods which have helped gain it recognition both within the Turkish Kurdish community and in the international arena. Although for most of its history the PKK has characterised itself as a Marxist-Leninist organisation fighting for Kurdish 'national liberation', it has shown great skill in adapting itself – most notably in its use of Islamic symbols – to gain support. Thus, one can posit a 'Kurdish-Islamic synthesis' alongside the semi–official 'Turkish-Islamic' one of the 1980s. The PKK's most consistent theme, apart from Öcalan's personal dictatorship, has been its struggle for the recognition of a Kurdish identity. In this it can, with some justification, claim success.[98]

[97] *Turkey Briefing*, vol. 9, no. 1, 1995. In April 1995, several weeks into the northern Iraqi incursion, officials said that over 300 PKK militants had been killed in this region as well. But the figure was in sharp contrast to Ankara's original figure to justify the invasion, that 2,000 militants were in northern Iraq. Both Kurdish sources and Turkish soldiers accepted that the PKK had abandoned its Iraqi positions 2 weeks before the incursion, and left behind only a token resistance force to harass Turkish units.

[98] Besides this, Öcalan claims to have been instrumental in the democratisation of Turkey. In his interview with İmset in November 1991, he stated: 'We are today a movement which has enabled Demirel's democrat views to go into practice. We are aware of what we have done. The resurrection of Demirel and his coming [back] into politics with a referendum are all indirect products of our August 15 [1984] uprising. You cannot deny this. Also the end to executions, the solving of the Peace Associations and DİSK trials [two show trials by the military of leftist sympathisers after the 1980 coup] are very much linked to these developments. ... Secondly we have brought an openness to the Kurdish problem. This too is a democratic development.'; İmset, *op. cit.*, p. 346. One can answer this self-aggrandisement with the riposte that the war with the PKK has actually severely hampered the democratisation of Turkey as well as seriously undermining both its economy and international standing. Öcalan himself firmly believes that the 1980 coup was primarily due to the Kurdish question and PKK activity (*ibid.*, p. 29); far from helping democracy in Turkey, the PKK was, on this reckoning, the main reason for its overthrow.

The 'soft' Kurdish opposition – HEP, ÖZDEP, DEP and HADEP

In the last fifteen years or so there have been a number of attempts to set up legal Kurdish parties which would run for election in parliament. The People's Labour Party (HEP) was formed in 1990 by seven members of parliament expelled from the Social Democratic Populist Party (SHP) for attending a conference in Paris in November 1989 on the Kurdish situation. These seven, along with three other SHP deputies established HEP on 7 June 1990.[99] However, the SHP reabsorbed HEP just prior to the October 1991 elections in a deal which allowed the Kurdish members to stand under the SHP umbrella and which bolstered SHP showing in Kurdish areas. The tensions inherent in the deal surfaced almost immediately when several of the new deputies took the parliamentary oath, which declares allegiance to Turkey as an indivisible state in Kurdish rather than Turkish. A number of them eventually left the SHP to re-establish HEP in 1992. The Chief Public Prosecution Office of the Supreme Court launched a trial against HEP on 3 July 1993 for being anti-constitutional, as it allegedly 'functioned against the indivisible integrity of the state and of the nation, and became the focal point of illegal political activities'. It was formally closed on 14 July 1993. However, to circumvent the coming prohibition, a new party, the Freedom and Democracy Party (ÖZDEP) was founded in November 1992. This was also closed on 30 April 1993 after pressure from the Constitutional Court, which formally banned it on 23 November on charges of 'making separatist propaganda through the activities and regulations of the party.' Before ÖZDEP was banned, another new party, the Democracy Party (DEP), was formed on 7 May 1993 by eighteen Kurdish

---

[99] Just how close HEP and its successors were or are to the PKK is an open question. The state has frequently accused Kurdish MPs of being in cahoots with the PKK: indeed, this was the essence of the charges in the 1994 show trial of DEP deputies (see below). The accused denied the charges. Amnesty International believes it is likely they are non-violent political prisoners (their membership of the PKK would preclude such status). On the other hand, at the first HEP convention in Ankara on 15 December 1990 there were chants of 'long live Apo [PKK leader Abdullah Öcalan]' and 'Long live the PKK'. A standing ovation was given for the arrival of Öcalan's mother as guest of honour; Hugh Pope, *Middle East International*, 20 December 1991.

deputies.[100] DEP was similarly banned by the Turkish Constitutional Court on 16 June 1994, and this allowed thirteen former DEP MPs, whose parliamentary immunity had been lifted, to be charged with treason. Six of these fled to Belgium and the remainder were sentenced to up to fifteen years' imprisonment on 8 December 1994.[101] HEP was succeeded by the People's Democratic Party (HADEP), which was founded on 11 May 1994 and has experienced much the same hostility from the state as its predecessors.

HADEP members all came from DEP and HEP (HADEP Chair, Murat Bozlak, had been General-Secretary of HEP and Vice-Chair and General-Secretary of DEP), and the new party had the same programme and aims as its two predecessors.[102] It

---

[100] See *The Story of DEP* (Ankara: The Human Rights Foundation of Turkey, Documentation Centre, n.d.).

[101] The trial of the 7 DEP deputies and an independent deputy finished on 8 December 1994 at the State Security Court (DGM) in Ankara. All the defendants, who are Kurds, were charged under Article 125 of the penal code with betraying the state and trying to destroy Turkey's territorial integrity because of their alleged links with PKK. Mahmut Alınak, independent deputy for Sırnak, and DEP deputy Sırrı Sakık each received three and a half years' imprisonment and a fine of TL70m. The time they had already spent in detention meant they were both released. Sedat Yurtdaş was sentenced to seven and a half years' imprisonment. The other defendants – Diyarbakır deputies Leyla Zana and Hatip Dicle, Mardin deputy Ahmet Türk, and Sırnak deputies Orhan Doğan and Selim Sadak – were each sentenced to 15 years. The trial had already caused much international censure. On 29 September 1994, the European Parliament decided to suspend all contacts with the Turkish Parliament as well as to recommend that the proposed customs union with Turkey be suspended in protest. The final sentences produced further international protest but it appeared that such criticism from abroad ran the risk of inflaming nationalist passions in sections of the Turkish élite. In early October, Foreign Minister Mümtaz Soysal (who resigned in late November) stated that official visits by foreign delegates with 'hidden human rights agendas' would no longer be tolerated while President Demirel testily rejected an appeal from the European Union for the release of the Kurdish deputies, stating that the trial was an internal matter. After the trial, the imprisoned former DEP deputies revealed that they had been sent to Bekaa by the late President Turgut Özal to meet Abdullah Öcalan. In an interview with Mehmet Ali Birand, the presenter of *32nd Day* (a respected and popular television news programme), they claimed that this visit had been part of an attempt to stop the bloodshed in the southeast region; *Turkey Briefing*, vol. 8, no. 4, 1994.

[102] The following information on HADEP is based on an interview with HADEP Chair Murat Bozlak on 31 August 1994 at the party headquarters in Ankara. On the wall, along with the yellow and blue HADEP flag and *Nevroz* posters, was a picture of Atatürk and the Turkish Republic flag – presumably to show

was actually set up even before DEP was closed as those affected foresaw the coming closure. Bozlak expected that HADEP too would be closed by the authorities, and he was pessimistic about the possibilities of an open Kurdish political party in Turkey,[103] HADEP's basic programme was for the Kurds to be recognised as such, and that they should be afforded full human rights and be allowed to organise themselves freely and democratically. This, Bozlak claimed, did not mean federation or autonomy,[104] – rather it meant ending the continuing war between the government and the PKK which was devastating the southeast and causing huge refugee flows out of the region. HADEP called on both sides to end the fighting and for the government to freely allow the Kurds to identify themselves as such. The next stage would be to end the legislative system, inherited from Atatürk and expanded by the military regime of the 1980s, which codified the total hegemony of 'Turkishness' as opposed to any other identity within the state.[105] If this was achieved, Bozlak stated, then a democratic solution whereby Turks and Kurds could coexist peacefully was possible.

On the issue of those parts of 'Kurdistan' which were outside Turkey, and whether they should unite, Bozlak was reticent. However, he did point out that 'Kurdistan' had been divided into four parts by the imperial powers and the 'national colonial system', and that the Kurds had the same right as all peoples to 'national self-determination'.[106] When questioned as to how a

that the party did not aim to divide the country. Interestingly, although Bozlak was using an interpreter, he spoke in Turkish not Kurdish.

[103] Bozlak began the interview by claiming (without too much conviction or credibility) that HADEP was not an explicitly Kurdish party.

[104] This was a purely practical move; Bozlak explained that any raising of these taboo issues would lead to the instant closure of HADEP.

[105] In the interview (see footnote 102) it was very noticeable that Bozlak viewed the upheavals of recent Turkish politics purely through the prism of the Kurdish question. For example, he stated, reasonably enough, that the TİP and other socialist parties had been closed over the Kurdish issue, but went on to assert that the 1980 coup and the subsequent closing of all political parties was also undertaken purely because of the Kurdish problem.

[106] The right to 'national self-determination' as guaranteed in international covenants is an especially problematic one. Technically it refers only to 'peoples'. Commentators observe that it was introduced into the covenants on the wishes of the Soviet bloc and was primarily aimed at the colonies. As such, it referred

Kurd is defined, Bozlak asserted that despite dialectical differences between, for example, Zaza and Kurmanci-speaking Kurds, and religious differences between Sunnis and Alevis, there was a common Kurdish history, which defined the individual as a Kurd rather than a Turk. He stressed that there was no conflict with the Turkish people, but rather with the Turkish government. When asked about the cases of intermarriage between Turks and Kurds, the emigration of Kurds to western majority Turkish areas, and the ensuing 'natural' assimilation of Kurds which this often entailed, he stated that whether the people born of mixed parents or brought up in Istanbul saw themselves as Turks or Kurds was a matter of individual choice.[107]

Bozlak claimed the success of the Sunni-Muslim Welfare Party (RP) in the southeast in the 1994 elections was due to a boycott by many Kurds and an RP vote by others, which was essentially a protest vote against the system, aided by the trans-ethnic appeal of Islam. He also repeated the allegation that the military supported the RP in the southeast as a means of weakening Kurdish support for the PKK. However, he personally did not believe RP's appeals for Islamic unity. Regarding the different stances of recent major politicians, Bozlak stated that Turgut Özal may have publicly declared himself to be of Kurdish origin but 'he started the war in Kurdistan'. However, although he may have been responsible for many Kurdish deaths, Özal did look for political methods rather than solely military ones and, in this respect, had better ideas on the Kurdish issue than Tansu Çiller, Demirel, or other leading Turkish politicians, whose sole policy seemed to be war. Bozlak reserved his most damning condemnation for Hikmet Çetin, who is himself a Kurd. Çetin, Bozlak stated, was a traitor to his

---

to the whole populations of colonial states who had 'the right to self-determination' – i.e. independence from their imperial masters – rather than minorities or sections of populations within states. Conversely, the idea of the territorial integrity of states remains a generally accepted principle and is enshrined in the European Convention on Human Rights, which allows states great latitude in enforcing it. However, as noted in Chapter 1, this international consensus is beginning to change following the end of the cold war, events in the Horn of Africa and the collapse of Yugoslavia. Thus Bozlak's reference to 'imperial powers' and 'the colonial system' on one hand appeals to the spirit behind the covenants. On the other hand, its implied message of secession and redrawing of borders is contrary to the original spirit.

[107] This is essentially Ernest Renan's 'daily plebiscite' – see Chapter 1.

people and a most dangerous man as he had flaunted his own Kurdishness on the international stage, when he was Foreign Minister, as a means of justifying the Turkish government's repressive measures.

The broad thrust of Bozlak's views were echoed by a leading Kurd in exile, Kerim Yıldız of the Kurdish Human Rights Project in London.[108] He pointed out that the whole question of the position of the Kurds within Turkey had been and remains a taboo subject. In answer to the question 'What do the Kurds want?', he replied that nobody really knew, as in the modern era the Kurds had not had the opportunity to express themselves on the subject. While organisations like the PKK made statements and declarations, this was not necessarily the true voice of the Kurds. Until they were able to democratically express themselves, all answers to this question would remain conjecture. He stated that leading Kurdish organisations like his had had high level meetings with German government representatives. The German officials had suggested that a solution might be some form of autonomy for Kurds within the Turkish state, but the Kurds had pointed out that they could not decide 'for the people'. While 'all Kurds dreamt of an independent Kurdistan', in the present political context this was unrealistic. Despite stating that organisations like his were in no position to fully articulate Kurdish demands and views, he went on to elaborate some basic positions. The Kurds, he said, had no intention at this stage of separating from Turkey due to their long historical links with the Turkish state. Moreover, if the Turkish state asked them to form a separate state they would refuse. The main reason for this, he stated, was that the previous seventy years of economic development had seen many Kurds move into cities like Istanbul and Izmir, which made such a division unrealistic.[109] What organisations like his were seeking was some form of federation and autonomy which would put Turks and Kurds on an equal basis and enable them to live peacefully together. A very noticeable feature of the last fifteen years had been that the government, by repressing and outlawing any attempt to set up a legal Kurdish party, could be

---

[108] Interview with Kerim Yıldız, London, 6 June 1994.
[109] Here Yıldız stated that if they were forced to leave, then they would seek compensation.

seen as having aided the PKK. By default, this had enabled the PKK to claim to be the sole organisation championing the Kurdish cause.

This may be finally changing, thanks to a recent attempt to set up a 'middle ground' Kurdish party by Turkey's former Minister for Public Works, Serafettin Elçi. Elçi, a Kurd by origin, has, like Hikmet Çetin, been frequently held up by Turkey to prove that no discrimination exists against the Kurds. In recent interviews published in the Turkish press, Elçi emphasised the need for Turkey to open its political system to democratic demands on behalf of the Kurds, arguing that it was a mistake to regard the PKK as the sole representative of the Kurdish people in Turkey. However, he accepted that 'it does receive some popular support.' In his words, the PKK

> ....receives support from a section of the people who have been hurt and damaged by the state, and who are concerned about the possibility of losing their national identity.[110]

Elçi was careful not to antagonise the PKK, yet also wished to distance himself from violence, and claimed that his party would not be 'against' but 'different' from the PKK, which is known for its violent methods. He stated:

> Had we not been different, we would not have required to set up a separate party. The political movement we have started is named the Kurdish Democratic Platform. The masses we are directed at are masses which do not approve of violence, who are not involved in violence: Kurdish circles with liberal and democratic views.

Unlike the PKK, which started off as a secessionist group, Elçi's movement insists that many of the Turkish Kurds do not want to separate from Turkey, but want to live together with the Turks:

> This is the principle we believe in. We respect the sovereignty of the state and say the Kurdish problem should be solved within this sovereignty.

---

[110] This and the following quotes from Elçi were printed in *Hürriyet* and reprinted in *Turkey Briefing*, vol. 9, no. 1 (summer 1995).

Still, this former minister who previously hid his own Kurdish identity when entering Parliament, insisted that Ankara's problem was not one of terrorism alone. According to him:

> The Kurds want their identity to be recognized. Obviously there are also the rights which stem from such a recognition. The honour of an individual is to have an identity, to be himself. An identity can only be developed through education. Thus the most essential demand of the Kurds is to have the right for education. This is not only the demand of the Kurds but a right established by the UN for children's rights which Turkey has also signed. Every child has the right to education in his/her own language. The other demand is the right for organization in the form of political parties and cultural institutions. If this right is granted, it will be a very positive step. Because then the true representatives can be seen [meaning that the PKK will lose support].

His 'solutions' are still not welcomed in Ankara, where officials argue that giving the Kurds any 'exclusive' rights would lead to the division of the country. Yet Elçi argues that such an exceptional status would not be one that all ethnic communities in Turkey could enjoy. As he stated:

> Not everyone has the right to this exception. During the War of Liberation period, the only ethnic group mentioned aside from the Turks were the Kurds. Mustafa Kemal [Atatürk] and his colleagues, while preparing the Amasya Protocol, were promising that every kind of racial right of the Kurds would be maintained and protected. All other ethnic groups living in Turkey, the Georgians, Çerkez [Circassians], Abkhaz, Bosnians and Tatars have their own countries. They have abandoned their own countries and come to Turkey in order to benefit from the opportunities of the state. They have come having accepted the status of the state. But the Kurds are different. The Kurds have joined this state with [by virtue of] their own geography. Other ethnic groups [have not].

We shall return in the next chapter to this point about the differences between the 'indigenous' Kurds and immigrant arrivals in their attitudes to state-sponsored Turkish nationalism.

Attitudes among the Kurdish population

The brutality of the struggle between the state and the PKK, the ensuing mass displacement of large numbers of people and the state repression of virtually all forms of Kurdish political activity, whether violent or not, have made the question of what the actual Kurdish population of Turkey wants a problematic one. As noted in the statements by Kerim Yıldız above, no one can really know what the people want until they are able to be asked in appropriate conditions. Nevertheless, it is possible to make some observations from the available information.

On first sight the data seems contradictory, but this is only to be expected. Kurdish nationalism is a relatively new phenomenon and, like Turkish nationalism, has many facets and competing variants. It seems there are now two main components of Kurdish nationalism: First, the Islamist formulation of the 'Kurdish problem', which emphasises that all Muslims are brothers and attacks the current authorities and traditional Kemalists without making its own policies clear; second, the DEP/HADEP formulations which link up with those of the Kurdish socialist groups and the PKK. However, as noted above, the PKK is now trying to incorporate Islamist arguments so as to widen its appeal. Yalçın-Heckmann notes that for the Kurds of Hakkari, Islam remains the dominant force in daily life and discourse, but that Islam can and has been used by the PKK to form a Kurdish Islam. Kurdish nationalists increasingly acknowledge the power of both religion and tribal ideology in the southeast, and adapt their programmes accordingly, while the state refuses to believe that the rebels may be religiously motivated.[111]

Given this complex situation, seeming contradictions are inevitable. Thus on the one hand, it was reported in early 1992 that the results of an opinion poll commissioned by Demirel showed that 70 per cent of the population of the southeast wanted to remain part of Turkey.[112] This contrasts somewhat with the strength of support for the PKK, which is usually portrayed as a

[111] Lale Yalçın-Heckmann, 'Ethnic Islam and nationalism among Kurds in Turkey' in Richard Topper (ed.), *Islam in Modern Turkey*, (London: I.B. Tauris, 1991) pp. 102-20.

[112] Jonathan Rugman, 'Demirel plans reforms in Kurdish areas', *The Guardian*, 3 April 1992.

separatist organisation. It also contrasts with the 70 per cent vote for the HEP list featuring such personalities as leading Kurdish radical Leyla Zana, who openly stated 'we are going to parliament to be the voice of Kurdish liberation.'[113] On the other hand, the strength of religious feeling among the population of the Kurdish southeast is also often commented on.[114] The previous discussion has suggested that this may have been a major reason for the success of the RP in the southeast in the March 1994 elections. As noted in Chapter 6, there are many religious Kurds active in radical Islamist groups and implicated in the numerous killings of left-wing Kurds in the southeast by shadowy groups like Hizbullah and İBDA-C.[115] Indeed, a poll conducted in 21 August 1992 which asked Kurds which political organisation best represented Kurdish people gave figures of only 29.2 per cent for the PKK and 9.1 per cent for HEP.[116] This would indicate that the large majority of Kurds did not look to these organisations which are usually seen as primarily left-wing, nationalist and, despite the PKK's policy changes, secular in orientation.[117]

Another detailed poll of Istanbul residents was published over

[113] Hugh Pope, 'Turkey forced to face the Kurdish question', *The Independent*, 25 October 1991.

[114] For example *Briefing*, no. 984, 4 April 1994, commenting on the RP success in the March elections that year, stated that many Kurds in the southeast and the West clearly support the RP and that 'the Kurdish Islamic identity is arguably more fundamental to many than their "Kurdishness" and has been so since converting to Islam hundreds of years ago.' The article went on to note that most of the Kurdish rebellions in the last 150 years have been religious rather than national, and only in 1984 with the rise of the PKK did this change. As noted above, the PKK has recently attempted to portray itself more as a radical Islamist organisation than a Marxist-Leninist one.

[115] Another radial Islamist Kurdish organisation was the *Kürdistan İslami Partisi*, which distributed leaflets in a mosque courtyard in Erzerum on 23 February 1992 accusing the state of torture and calling the faithful to war against the authorities; *The Month in Turkey*, no. 14, February 1992.

[116] Piar-Gallup survey conducted 29 August 1992 and published in *Milliyet*, 6 September 1992.

[117] Polls are, of course, notoriously unreliable. Another poll conducted by the New York-based Kurdish Library (and thus liable to be more pro-PKK than 'Turkish' polls) gave 87% of Kurds in Turkey as viewing Öcalan as the representative leader of Turkey's Kurds. Haluk Gerger 'The Plight of the Kurds', *Balkan War Report: Bulletin of the Institute for War and Peace Reporting*, London, no. 24, March/April 1994.

five days in *Milliyet* in February/March 1993.[118] The poll found that while 13.3 per cent of Istanbul's population stated they had Kurdish roots,[119] only 3.9 per cent considered themselves to be Kurds, while another 3.7 per cent considered themselves to be Turks although their parents were Kurds.[120] On the question of Kurdish independence, 90 per cent of the respondents definitely opposed the idea, with 87 per cent also saying no to any federal state. Fewer (75 per cent) rejected autonomous units, while a majority (69 per cent) were in favour of giving more power to local government – reflecting perhaps a widespread dissatisfaction with central government. Among those who saw themselves as Kurds, 22 per cent were in favour of an independent Kurdistan, with 78 per cent saying they wanted to live together with Turks and not separate.[121] Within the same group, 23 per cent said that HEP was Abdullah Öcalan's mouthpiece in parliament while a further 28 per cent said this was possibly so. Interestingly, almost half of them (49 per cent) said the PKK was a 'terrorist organisation', while a further 17 per cent said this was possibly so, with only 26 per cent seeing the PKK as an organisation defending Kurdish national rights and a further 21 per cent saying that this was possibly so.[122]

---

[118] *Milliyet*, 27 and 28 February and 1, 2 and 3 March 1993. Despite possible sampling errors, etc., the figures given in this poll appear realistic and point to some 8% of Istanbul's population being Kurdish, which, given the Kurds are probably 15-20% of Turkey's total, appears reasonable. However, the poll was only conducted in Istanbul and is thus not necessarily representative of Kurds as a whole. Also, the whole topic is sensitive in Turkey and many respondents may have given answers which they expected the authorities to approve of. Despite this, the poll is an important source, and the fact that it was conducted at all and published in a mass-circulation newspaper well illustrates the changes in attitude by both the state and the public.

[119] A further 6.81% were from the Balkans, 5.75% from the Caucasus and 8.77% of Laz origin.

[120] Compared to 69% who defined themselves as 'Turks', 21% who defined themselves as 'Muslim Turks', and 4% who defined themselves solely as 'Muslims' – 98% of the respondents said they were Muslim by religion.

[121] Similar results were given in August 1995 in a poll of 1,200 Kurds commissioned by the Union of chambers of Commerce and Bourses executed by Doğu Ergil. This showed that only 13% wanted an independent state, but 89% supported a federation, with 63% wanting Kurdish to have equal status with Turkish; *The Independent*, 15 August 1995.

[122] Interestingly, many Kurds did not answer any of the 4 questions relating to the PKK, with 20% refusing to answer whether it was in their opinion a

The poll did show that the Kurds were low on the social scale, with Kurds most numerous among the unemployed and having the lowest educational qualifications. Those who declared themselves as Turks had the highest average wages (TL4,120,000, slightly above the average of TL4,010,000), followed by those declared as 'Muslim Turks, or 'Muslims' (TL3,820,000), then those who saw themselves as Turks but from Kurdish parents (TL3,497,000) and finally those declared as Kurds (TL2,940,000). Respondents from all groups saw the general economic situation as a more important problem for Turkey than that of the PKK.[123] This strengthened the interpretation that the Kurdish question was merely an economic one, and if the economic differences could be removed then the problem would be solved.[124]

The poll also showed that only 44 per cent of the families who considered themselves to be Kurdish spoke Kurdish as their mother tongue, but that a slightly higher figure (47 per cent) of those who considered themselves to be Kurds wanted their children also to know Kurdish. Regarding mixed marriages, 65 per cent of those who saw themselves as Kurds thought it perfectly acceptable for their daughters to marry a Turk, while conversely, only 45 per cent of the Turks saw a Kurd as an acceptable marriage partner for their own daughters. While these latter figures do not show a very high degree of segregation between the two communities, they are sizeable enough in the context of Turkey's most numerous and mixed city.

The difference in attitudes between the Kurds in the developed western part of the country and the big cities as opposed to those in the southeast, where they are subject to the harsh measures of the authorities, is very noticeable in the results of the December 1995 elections. The Kurdish party HADEP scored 20.0 per cent of the vote in the southeast, being especially successful in the provinces of Adıyaman, Ağrı, Batman, Bingöl, Bitlis, Diyarbakır, Elazığ, Hakkari, Malatya, Mardin, Muş, Siirt, Tunceli, Urfa and Van. However, in the main metropolitan areas of Adana, Istanbul,

---

'terrorist organisation'.

[123] Among all groups, 51% of the 'Kurds' and 61% of the 'Turks' cited the general economic situation as 'Turkey's most important problem', while 22% of the 'Kurds' (and 28% of the 'Muslim Turks' or 'Muslims', and 'Turks from Kurdish parents') cited 'terror, PKK..' as the most important.

[124] Yalçın Doğan, 'Kürtler Bütünlüten Yana', *Milliyet*, 27 February 1993.

Izmir and Ankara it only scored 3.7 per cent of the vote and nationally only 4.2 per cent, thus coming below the threshold for parliamentary representation. In contrast, the Islamic RP – the largest party nationally in the elections with 21.4 per cent of the total vote – scored 27.8 per cent in the southeast and 19.6 per cent in the big cities.[125] This would indicate that for the Kurds who have moved to the big cities, the appeal of outright Kurdish parties has declined along with the appeal of independence. With so many of Turkey's Kurds now outside the southeast, such attitudes are encouraging and perhaps point to the possibility of coexistence if only they are allowed full cultural freedom.

The apparent ethnic and social cleavage have sometimes given rise to violence. The escalating war in the southeast has seen a rise in inter-ethnic tensions with a number of attacks throughout the country on Kurds by local Turks. Tensions have run especially highly at funerals of Turkish soldiers killed in the southeast.[126]

It is easy to view the recent history of the Kurds as one of unrelenting oppression by the central authorities. However, whether they be viewed as brigands or freedom fighters, local Kurdish leaders – predominantly tribal ones – have arrived at accommodations with the central authorities which have, despite the prevailing under-development, brought some advantages to them and their followers. The rise of Kurdish nationalism has changed much of this. In looking at how the Kurds actually think and act in the southeast, it must be remembered that the bitter struggle between the authorities and the PKK has left the local population caught in the crossfire; in such a situation survival strategies come to the fore. Villagers joined the Village Guard

---

[125] Source: 1995 election results final.

[126] In late 1992 in Alanya, 2 Kurdish youths were rescued from a lynch mob and there were attacks on Kurdish property. In Iğdır there were anti-Kurdish riots after HEP gained a seat on the municipal council – *Briefing*, no. 913, 9 November 1992. *Briefing*, no. 916, 30 November 1992, pointed out that nobody had been brought to justice for these and other attacks on Kurds and Kurdish property. On 13 July 1993 there was an anti-Kurdish riot in Ezine in Çanakkale, with the mob of 5,000 chanting 'Death to the Kurds' after a row over a bill at a Kurdish-owned night club. The area of the town where a number of Kurdish construction workers lived had to be sealed by security forces in order to protect them; *Cumhuriyet*, 14 July 1993. I have myself been shocked by the hardening of attitudes from Turkish friends in Turkey towards the Kurds in general, due to the escalating struggle with the PKK.

system (where they were armed and paid by the government to flight PKK guerrillas) for a variety of reasons. Apart from the pay, many Kurds saw joining as a way of regaining their traditional firearms, upon which much of their male honour is based and which were taken by the authorities after the 1980 coup. Many appear to have joined hoping to avoid inter-Kurd conflict with the PKK – indeed, in the Hakkari border region many even looked to the Barzani group in Iraq for protection so as to avoid outright confrontation with the PKK. As such, many were unwilling to fight the PKK. Despite the PKK's past policy of ruthless attacks on Village Guards and their families, in some areas captured Village Guards were later released by the PKK.[127] This perhaps helps to explain the government's change of policy towards forced evacuations. However, as noted above, the huge influx to urban centres like Diyarbakır and Van from devastated villages creates ideal recruiting grounds for the PKK. Apart from the greater opportunities afforded to mass mobilisation in urban shanty towns, there is the additional factor of the breakdown of the traditional forms of authority whereby the old could more easily control the young. The evacuations have also greatly accelerated the breakdown of traditional tribal ties.

[127] Lale Yalçın-Heckmann, SOAS talk (see footnote 3).

8

THE ALEVIS AND OTHER INTERNAL
MINORITY GROUPS

The Alevis

As noted in Chapter 4, the large Alevi population, estimated to
comprise up to 20 per cent of the total population, appeared to
be supportive of Kemalism and the secular nature of the new
regime. For Alevis, this was preferable to a Sunni regime in
which they might face persecution. As such, the community as
a whole appeared even to acquiesce in the proscribing of all
Islamic Sufi sects in 1925, which included Alevi Sufi orders like
the Bektaşis, who are the most numerous of Turkey's Alevis. It
would therefore be instructive to look more closely at how Alevi
society is differentiated from Sunni society and how the differences
have been translated into political ideology.

The Alevis are Turkey's Shiite population but are distinct from
the *ashani* Shiites of Iran and the Alawis of Syria.[1] In addition

---

[1] Wandering Sufi *dervişes* who accompanied or followed in the wake of the
conquering Ottoman troops were a crucial component in aiding the conversion
to Islam of large sections of the Anatolian and Balkan Christian populations.
These Sufi organisations tended to absorb popular movements. Shiites were
particularly forced to seek asylum within Sufi groups, of whom the heterdox
Bektaşi order, which followed the teachings of Hacı Bektaş, allowed them full
expression. As a result, Bektaşis are essentially Shiite. This also held true for
Christian communities in the Balkans who adopted Islam, the process no doubt
aided by the similarity of many Bektaşi rites to Christian ones. The Bektaşi
order was especially prominent in Albania. The life of Hacı Bektaş himself
remains fairly obscure. Some sources state he was born in 1208 or 1209 and
died in 1270 or 1271, others that he was born in 1248 and died in 1337,
although the former version is the most widely accepted. Some say he was
born in Khorassan, others that he was born in Anatolia and went to Khorassan
to be educated. Either way, he came from Khorassan to Anatolia and lived in

to differences in religious belief, noted in Chapter 2, Alevism is strongly distinguished from Sunnism in the ways the sects organise their own communities and traditionally resolve disputes within them. The variety of names, *Bektaşi, Kızılbaş, Tahtacı* (literally 'board cutters') etc., for different segments of the Alevi community causes some confusion.[2] Essentially, while they have differences, they share a core of belief which separates them from Sunni groups. In Sunni Islam there is no real priestly hierarchy, as mosque officials merely lead the prayers of the faithful. In the *tarikats*, however, there is usually some form of 'master' to 'pupil' relationship.

In the Alevi community, this phenomenon is even stronger and its societies are strictly hierarchical. Among the Bektaşi community there are four grades of initiation and authority: *aşık* (lover) as the first grade; *derviş* for those formally admitted; *baba* or *dede* for those who become leaders and instructors of *dervişes* and *aşıks*; and the *Dedebaba* who is the head. The order is further divided between those *dedes* who believe that Hacı Bektaş married and had sons, who claim descent from him, and who themselves marry, with their sons inheriting their authority, and those who follow the teachings of the second leading figure in the order, Pir Balım Sultan, who established celibacy for the *dedes* in the sixteenth century. The latter are chosen for their proven worth rather than their lineage; today celibacy is not required of leaders of this branch of Bektaşism. The distinction between those who

---

Kayseri, Kırşehir and Sivas. He eventually settled in the village of Sulucakara-ahöyük, now known as Hacıbektaş, some 50 Km north of Nevşehir, where he died. His doctrines, however, are well known and have made a great impact. His teachings, as expounded in his most famous treatise, the *Makalat*, see 4 stages of development: the initial stage is *Şeriat*, the canonic Islamic law which Alevis see as the level of Sunnis; then comes *Tarikat*, the way; then *Marifet* (gnosis or knowledge of God); and finally *Hakikat*, truth or oneness with God. See J. D. Norton, 'Bektashis in Turkey' in D. MacEoin and A. al-Shahi (eds), *Islam in the Modern World* (Croom Helm: London, 1983) and R. Yürükoğlu, *Okunacak En Büyük Kitap İnsandır: Tarihite ve Günümüzde Alevilik* (Alev Yayinevi: Istanbul, 1990).

[2] Altan Gökalp divides the Babağan branch, directly attached to the Bektaşi *tarikat*, which covers the urban communities of Anatolia and the Balkans, from the Sofiyan branch, which he classifies as covering 'rural Bektaşism' and which includes the Kızılbaşis and the Tahtaas as well as the nomadic Alevis; *Têtes Rouges et Bouches Noires* (Société d'Ethnographie: Paris, 1980) p. 74.

generally call themselves Bektaşis and those who claim to be Alevi–Bektaşis is that outsiders can become Bektaşis, whereas one has to be born an Alevi or Alevi-Bektaşi.

The *dedes* traditionally had license to mediate conflicts within the community. This is done at a collective meeting, the *cem*, with participants from every household. Women are equal to men in these meetings. Before the religious rituals of the *cem*, which include music and dancing (*sema*) – again mixed – disputes are brought into the open. If participants try to hide disputes then communal pressure brings them up. The *dede* mediates and suggests solutions which the community then decides upon. If one side refuses to accept this communal decision, they face being temporarily ostracised from the community, with the added punishment of no help from others for activities like gathering in the harvest. In addition, every household has to make a confession to the *dede* once a year. The essence of this conflict resolution is an emphasis on communal decisions and pressure against intercommunal violence.[3]

In line with this communalism (as well as sympathy to Kemalism), the Alevis have traditionally supported political parties of the left. Until the 1980s they tended to vote as a solid bloc for left of centre parties.[4] However, in recent years there have been some

---

[3] Despite the rise of Alevi-Sunni tension, there is little evidence that antagonistic attitudes originate from the Alevi population; they are rather the victims, as in the case of some 40 Alevis from Sivas who were attacked and killed during a football match in Kayseri; see D. McDowall, *The Kurds: A Nation Denied* (London: MRG, 1992), p. 59. Other more recent incidents are detailed below. Indeed, in the Bektaşi centre of Hacıbektaş town there is a mosque, built in the 19th century in the heart of the monastery complex, where the town's Sunni population, some 20% of the total, come to pray. Despite their tolerance, due to their support of left-wing parties, in the troubled late 1970s the Alevis were often the target of violence by extreme right-wing nationalists. For example, there was widespread violence by MHP radicals against Alevis and leftists, including CHP members, in Malatya, Sivas, and notoriously Kahraman Maraş in 1978, and in Çorum and other locations in 1980 (see Chapter 5).

[4] This apparently included the CHP before it became a 'left of centre party' in the 1960s. Many Alevis supported communist parties, giving rise to the seemingly incongruous sight of hammers and sickles and pictures of Karl Marx alongside pictures of Hacı Bektaş and the hereditary *dedebaba* Veliyettin Ulusoy Efendi, who took over after the death of his father Feyzullah Ulusoy Efendi on 18 March 1994. The 1961 Constitution for the first time allowed socialist parties to freely operate, and even before the Constitution came into effect

changes, with sections now voting for ANAP or DYP.[5] Part of this change is a reflection of what anthropologists see as a breakdown of the Alevi way of life due to the incompatibility of traditional Alevi dispute settlement by persons claiming authority from their position in a chain leading back to Hacı Bektaş and Ali, with the normal judicial offices of the modern state. In the traditional system, banishment was the ultimate sanction, but in recent times mass migration to the cities has negated the threat of this. Modernisation seem to be rapidly undermining the basis of Alevi support for the *dede* system, with Alevi villages suffering apparent declines while Sunni villages tend to prosper.[6] Alevis have, like Sunnis, moved from the country to towns in recent years, creating compact Alevi communities in major cities like Istanbul and Ankara. In Ankara two of the city's most popular radio stations are overtly Alevi. Besides the annual festival in Hacıbektaş (see below), since 1992 there has been an annual Alevi festival in Ankara attracting

---

Istanbul trade unions had formed the Turkish Workers' Party (TİP). This gained in dynamism in 1962 under the leadership of Mehmet Ali Aybar, but despite strong support from intellectuals, performed poorly in the 1965 and 1969 elections and split into various factions; see Kemal H. Karpat, 'Socialism and the Labor Party of Turkey', *Middle Eastern Journal*, vol. 21, 1967, and Igor Lipovsky, 'The Legal Socialist Parties of Turkey, 1960-1980', *Middle Eastern Studies*, vol. 27, 1991. In the 1970s, the Unity Party, which on 28 November 1971 became the Unity Party of Turkey (TBP), was one of the main parties to the left of the CHP and was seen as primarily an Alevi party. In the 1973 election, Aybar and 7 other TİP leaders stood as independents on the TBP ticket, but the TBP had no real organisation or national leadership; Feroz Ahmad, *The Turkish Experiment in Democracy, 1950-75* (London: Hurst, 1977), p. 319.

[5] See 'Alevilik Tarihe Karışıyor', in *Nokta*, 27 August 1987.

[6] See Gökalp, *op. cit.*; David Shankland, 'Alevi and Sunni in Rural Turkey: Diverse Paths of Change' (unpubl. Ph.D. thesis, University of Cambridge; 1993) 'Alevi and Sunni in Rural Anatolia: Diverse Paths of Change' in P. Stirling (ed.), *Culture and Economy: Changes in Turkish Villages* (Huntingdon; Eothen Press, 1993); and R. Ness, 'Being an Alevi Muslim in S.W. Anatolia and Norway: the impact of migration on a heterodox Turkish community' in T. Gerholm and T.G. Lithman (eds), *The New Islamic Presence in Western Europe* (London: Mansell, 1988). Shankland concludes that while Sunnis have little or no problem in integrating into the modern 'nation state', the Alevis find this more difficult because of their different traditional structures of authority; integrating into the modern state means abandoning most of the customs and traditions which make them Alevi. As such, he concludes, Alevi villages are suffering a steep decline, helped by government policy, and Anatolia is becoming solely Sunni. As shown below, this seems somewhat exaggerated.

over 10,000 participants, with a rise in the number of books on Alevism.[7] Alevis also figured disproportionately among guestworkers in Germany[8] and there has been something of an Alevi revival among them, with a rise in interest and growth of Alevi associations in cities like Berlin.[9]

Alevi dissatisfaction with the increasingly Sunni orientation of the Turkish state under Özal began to become evident. Author and poet Seyyid Dursun Doğanay was arrested in early October 1990 in Izmir for a forthcoming book which was highly critical of President Özal's views on Alevis.[10] The DYP/SHP coalition government, after the October 1991 elections, initially made overtures to the Alevis. Prime Minister Demirel's 'social peace' had two factors: peace between the centre-left and centre-right; and also between Sunnis and Alevis. The latter not unreasonably pointed out that they paid taxes like other citizens; while some of these taxes helped pay the budget for the Sunni oriented Directorate of Religious Affairs (which among other things helped finance the teaching of Sunnism in the school curriculum), Alevism received no such state support. Twenty-two Alevi associations petitioned the government to reshape the religious department to include the cultural and religious rights of Alevis.[11] However, nothing came of these overtures. On 2 July 1993, a Sunni mob attacked and burnt down the hotel in Sivas where the novelist and publisher of Salman Rushdie's *The Satanic Verses*, Aziz Nesin, was staying. This resulted in the deaths of thirty-seven people, mainly Alevi poets and writer/delegates for a conference on the Alevi rebel Pir Sultan Abdal, who was executed in the sixteen century for leading a rebellion. The Alevis were further outraged when Prime Minister Çiller, Interior Minister Mehmet Gazioğlu and even SHP leader and Deputy Prime Minister Erdal İnönü blamed the terrible events on Nesin for 'provoking' the mob.[12] The vacillations of

[7] *Briefing*, no. 1,007, 19 September 1994.

[8] *Ibid.*

[9] I am indebted to Jochen Blaschke, Berliner Institute für Vergleichende Sozialforschung, for this.

[10] *Turkey Briefing*, vol. 5, no. 5, 1990.

[11] *The Month in Turkey*, no. 15, March 1992.

[12] *Briefing*, no. 946, 12 July 1993, which also reported that even some of the police and firemen rescuing Nesin from the fire had beaten him, that shots of the events on Mehmet Ali Birand's popular TV programme '32nd Day' clearly

the government over the Sivas outrage saw a loss of the traditional Alevi support for the SHP, and the message from SHP leader Murat Karayalçin at the 1994 Ankara festival was booed.[13]

The Thirty-first Traditional and Fifth International Hacı Bektaş Veli Festival

Every year from 16-18 August in Hacıbektaş town there is a festival for his followers. In 1990 the government, as part of a move to acknowledge Alevis, took over the running of the annual festival and Erdal İnönü spoke praising Alevi support for Atatürk. However, Minister of Culture Namık Kemal Zeybek also said the government would build a large town mosque in Hacıbektaş (the only mosque is that in the Bektaşi *tekke* monastery complex) and try and bring in tourists – both moves unpopular with the listening Alevis.[14] Next to the monastery complex the foundations of a large building are being laid by the Culture Ministry. Whether this will be a mosque or merely an office to facilitate tourism remains to be seen. Due to the terrible events in Sivas, the 1993 festival was only a small affair, without the customarily large numbers of participants. Because of this, the 1994 event was especially interesting. Who would come to speak from the government? How would participants react?

Understandably, the events in Sivas were never far from people's minds. There were cassettes of songs accompanied by the *bağlama*

---

showed Islamist councillor Cafer Erçakmak inciting the mob, and that the security forces were tardy in dealing with the crisis. The latter was blamed on İnönü himself. Nesin was later threatened with prosecution for provoking the incidents – see *Turkey Briefing*, vol. 8, no. 3, 1994. *Turkish Daily News*, 5 July 1993, reported that an unnamed senior security official stated that the security forces had expected violence by Sunnis against Alevis at this conference (which was organised by the Ministry of Culture) and that soldiers called in had been confronted by 'a believer crowd' challenging an 'infidel': they had hence become confused. He also stated that Nesin's presence was just an excuse to attack Alevis. He claimed that Çiller, during her campaign to become DYP chair, had frequently voiced her desire to 'hear the Islamic call for prayers in every neighbourhood in Turkey' and made continuous references to Allah, which, he alleged, sent the Sunni majority the wrong message and gave tacit official backing to such outrages.

[13] *Briefing*, no. 1,007, 19 September 1994.

[14] Shankland, Ph.D. thesis, *op. cit.* 176-7.

(the long-necked Anatolian lute which is the favoured Alevi instrument) about the outrage, and T-shirts with inscriptions about
the 'immortal martyrs of democracy'. At Çilehane on a hill over-
looking the town where there are a number of Bektaşi monuments
including a huge statue of Hacı Bektaş, the Ulusoy family cemetery,
and a 'birthing stone',[15] there is now a huge statue of two *bağlama*
players, called *Ozanlar*, dedicated to the Sivas dead. In the town
itself, petitions about the lack of will by the authorities to prosecute
those responsible for the attack circulated freely. Copies of a
statement to the same effect in the name of seventeen leading
Alevi organisations were also widely distributed. In the main square
a sign read 'We have not forgotten Sivas'. The official programme
itself explicitly referred to the dead.

Despite the apparent decline in *cems*, many participants at the
festival assured me that regular *cems* remained a way of life and
were held in Alevi quarters in cities with migrants like Istanbul
as well as in more traditional Alevi areas in Anatolia. At the
festival itself *cems* were openly performed. This is probably explained
by the fact that the participants at the festival would naturally be
more likely to keep to the traditional ways than many other
Alevis. Kurdish Alevis were also present at the festival; they spoke
of the problems of being a 'minority within a minority' and of
official discrimination against them. They also told of occasionally
having *cems* in Kurdish despite the oft-repeated Alevi claim that
cems are only conducted in Turkish. However, they saw no separation between themselves and Alevi mother-tongue Turkish
speakers.[16]

[15] A large rock where one can climb in though a side hole and emerge from
a narrow central orifice (symbolising rebirth), and where Bektaşis make small
stone cairns.

[16] The Alevi Kurds live mainly in inhospitable mountainous regions of Tunceli
or in reclaimed marshland near Maraş. McDowall states that a number of Turkish
Alevis claim a Kurdish identity. Some of these embraced Kurdish culture centuries
ago, at a time when some nomadic Sunni Kurdish tribes intermingled with
Turkoman Alevis. The former adopted the Alevi system of beliefs while the
latter adopted Kurdish culture. They now speak Kurdish but sing old Turkoman
songs. McDowall also states, somewhat contentiously, that other Turks very
recently adopted Kurdish identity as a symbol of their underclass and rejected
status (McDowall, *op. cit.*, p. 59). As well as Alevi Kurds, there is also in Turkey
an unorthodox religious community of Kurds known as the Yezidis. They live
predominantly on the Iraqi/Syrian border, southwest and east of Mosul. They

Given the increasingly ambivalent attitude of the state to the Alevi population due to the penetration of Sunnism, as well as the beginning of the end of the Alevis' traditional left-wing political allegiance, it was especially interesting to see how the visiting dignitaries, who included President Demirel and Deputy Prime Minister and SHP leader Murat Karayalçin, spoke to the Alevis, and how their speeches were received by the crowd. On the day of the opening ceremonies, before the speeches began, the CHP bus ploughed its way through the heart of the throng with Deniz Baykal waving from the roof panoply and loud Alevi *bağlama* music blaring. Its loudspeakers proclaimed the CHP as Atatürk's party and Baykal as its leader – an obvious attempt to inherit Atatürk's mantle.

The first speaker was Lütfi Kalele, a right-wing writer who, while condemning the Sivas events, appeared somewhat equivocal about them. He was resolutely booed. He was followed by local dignitaries who welcomed everybody and stressed Hacı Bektaş's well-known dictums on education for all and women. Culture Minister Savaş followed and stressed the line that all should live peacefully together. He was fairly warmly received despite the fact the sound system temporarily broke down. He was followed by Minister Esat Kıratoğlu from the DYP who was one of Prime Minister Çiller's aides. He made an impassioned speech to strong applause from a vocal minority, but boos from others.

Given the Alevis' traditional alignment with the left, it was especially interesting to see how two of the main rivals on the left – the third main rival, Ecevit's DSP, was conspicuous by its absence[17] – spoke and were received. The next speaker was CHP leader Baykal, who was greeted with chants of '*Birleşin!*' ('unify!') and some boos. He repeated the anecdote of how Alevis had

are estimated to number some 20,000 in Turkey (or as Turkish citizens working in Germany), and have traditionally been persecuted, mainly by fellow (Muslim) Kurds who referred to them, mistakenly, as 'Devil Worshippers'. The Yezidis practise a syncretic religion with strong Zoroastrian elements; see John Guest, *Survival among the Kurds: A History of the Yezidis* (London: Kegan Paul, 1993) and Martin van Bruinessen, *Agha, Shaikh and State* (Utrecht: Rijswijck, 1978), pp. 32-33.

[17] Given the traditional left-wing stance of Alevis and the disillusionment with the SHP over the Sivas events, the DSP could be seen as offering a natural home for Alevi support: thus its absence was noteworthy. Perhaps the reason was that Ecevit's power base is outside traditional Alevi areas.

helped Atatürk in the Liberation War to some applause. He then referred to what he would do when he took power, which prompted much barracking and boos. Getting into his stride, he then appealed to the legacy of Hasan (Ali's son) for unity behind his party and stressed equality and socialism as basic principles. He promised that Hacıbektaş would remain a laicist town and said that Bektaşism had been one of the most important roots of Turkish culture for the last 700 years. There was no real difference between him and the Bektaşis, he claimed. Turkey was a democracy which respected human rights, and this was essential. Unification of the left was very important, he said to barracking, but that unity would be achieved through democratic ideas, and Alevis would be essential supporters of this. His speech was followed by the reading of a friendly message from the Azerbaijan Ministry of Culture, which was applauded.[18] Then the ANAP Deputy General-Secretary Rüstü Kazıkçıoğlu came to the podium to some booing. He spoke of the necessity of freedom for Bektaşis and read out a statement from Mesut Yılmaz, but few paid such attention.

Then came Murat Karayalçın. He, like Baykal, was met with chants of '*Birleşin*'. He gave a somewhat lack-lustre speech (his voice sounded rather hoarse) stressing Hacı Bektaş's legacy of a plurality of people and ideas as opposed to a hegemonic culture. Getting up steam he referred to 'forty-four years of democracy' and then brought up the latest government 'democracy package' to little enthusiasm from the crowd. He, like Baykal, stressed that in Turkey there was democracy and respect for human rights. He then turned to local issues, saying how shocked he was that when he came the previous evening the water supply had failed, promising that next year the town's infrastructure would be developed so that such occurrences would not happen again. He ended with appeals to Atatürk's legacy and support for democracy and the left. He was followed by the reading out of lengthy messages from Albania and again from Azerbaijan, as well as one from Tansu Çiller. None of these were well received by the crowd, which, sweltering in the midday heat, was becoming impatient to hear Demirel. He then took the podium to warm applause and made an avuncular speech, saying he had first come

---

[18] The Azeris are also Shiites.

to the town thirty-four years ago and emphasising how happy he was to return there as President. He stressed that all peoples in Turkey should remain calm and should show tolerance to others.

Atatürk's picture and sayings were much in evidence. In the centre of the town is a large arch over the road with sayings by Atatürk and Hacı Bektaş extolling the virtues of knowledge. At Beştaşlar[19] is an eating place with twelve open ovens and a large traditional *cem* house, again with twelve sides referring to the twelve Imams of Alevi belief. Inside this house are posters from newspapers like *Cumhuriyet* about Alevis and huge pictures of the 'trinity' of Ali, Hacı Bektaş and Atatürk. In the evenings there were long concerts by leading performers at the covered sports hall and the amphitheatre. The covered sports hall had a huge picture of Hacı Bektaş on one end facing an equally huge Atatürk on the other, as well as slogans for 'Democracy, Laicism and Peace'.[20] As the mayor of the town, Mustafa Özcivan stated: 'Atatürk has always been loved [by the Alevis], but there is an upsurge of popularity now in reaction to the attacks by [Sunni] Islamic fundamentalists'.[21]

[19] Another place of pilgrimage some 5 or 6 km from the town. Here are large stones standing alone, separated by some distance from a rocky outcrop from which legend has it they flew and landed together to defend Hacı Bektaş against false accusation. On these rocks, people attempted to balance small stones – preferably on as perpendicular a surface as possible. If you are successful you can make a wish. A large single rock, weighing perhaps 1 cwt or more was also an object of interest. If one could lift it cleanly off the ground one was again 'blessed'. Close to the standing stones was a large white rock which symbolises the Devil or the false accuser, and which a small crowd was resolutely stoning – perhaps mirroring aspects of the *hac* to Mecca.

[20] In the past, the performances had often had fairly revolutionary contents. However, this year such radicalism was not much in evidence in the performances I saw, with the partial exception of Muzaffer Özdemier, who finished his set of pyrotechnic virtuoso *bağlama* playing with two solo voice pieces – almost akin to rap music – which contained scathing attacks on Tansu Çiller and the evils of modern society to massive applause.

[21] 'Ataturk, secular hero of the Alawite sect', *The Frontier Post*, Pakistan, 29 March 1995. The same article quotes the town museum caretaker as saying that Atatürk was himself probably an Alevi. He states: 'first of all his father's name was an Alevi name. Secondly he was born in Salonika where there were a lot of Bektaşis ... Of course, he could not declare his religion because he wanted a lay state'. This caretaker also repeated the story that 'Mustafa Kemal

Rising tensions and riots in Istanbul

The Sunni Islamic Welfare Party (RP), which has seen a remarkable growth recently has tried to gain Alevi support with vague promises of Muslim union, but this has not been a success.[22] Tensions rose in September 1994 when an Alevi tomb and place of worship in Karacaahmet in Istanbul was pulled down. Government spokesman Yıldırım Aktuna from the DYP accused the RP, which controlled the mayoralty, of a deliberately anti-Alevi move and called for the Directorate of Religious Affairs to be either scrapped or changed to allow Alevi access to its funds.[23] Tayyıp Erdoğan, RP mayor of Istanbul, denied the accusation.[24] However, there were Sunni-Alevi clashes in the *gecekondular* (squatter settlements) in Istanbul between Alevis and members of the ultra-right Nationalist Action Party (MHP) of Alparslan Türkeş.[25]

Tensions between the Sunni and Alevi communities continued. On 18 February, the Hacı Bektaş Veli Associations in Malatya was attacked by unidentified persons with stones and clubs, and the association's building was damaged.[26] Also in February, the trial began of Alevi leaders accused of incitement after speeches they had made on 2 July 1994 on the anniversary of the 1993 Sivas incidents.[27]

[Atatürk] came here to collect his thoughts in December 1919 before undertaking the National Liberation War against the foreign powers. He asked to be left alone before the tomb of Veli [Hacı Bektaş].' Mayor Ozcivan also insisted that: 'The Alevi community is the most important stone of this secular and democratic republic which Atatürk gave us. If we were not there, the way would lie open for the Islamic fundamentalists.

[22] Professor İzettin Doğan and his followers have had more success but have been accused by more orthodox RP members of betrayal, see *Briefing*, no. 1,007, 19 September 1994.

[23] *Ibid* and TRT, TV, Ankara, 12 September 1994, in SWB EE/2100, B/9, 14/9/94.

[24] TRT, TV, Ankara, 13 September 1994, in SWB EE/2102, B/7, 16/9/94.

[25] *Briefing*, no. 1,0007, 19 September 1994.

[26] *Sabah*, Ankara, 20 February 1995.

[27] The defendants included folk singers Şah Turna Dumlupınar and Ali Ekber Eren, as well as leader of the Pir Sultan Abdal Cultural Association Emel Sungur; *Cumhuriyet*, 22 February 1995. At a meeting to commemorate the anniversary in Istanbul, 6 people were beaten by police and in Izmir a similar meeting was banned by the Governorate on the grounds that the tourism season had started. Meanwhile, a total of 128 people were tried for the incident, but there was

More serious clashes occurred in March 1995 in the Istanbul district of Gaziosmanpaşa after radical Sunni Islamists opened fire on 12 March from a taxi on four coffee houses where many Alevis were watching football on the television. Fifteen Alevis were shot at, of whom two were killed. The Alevi community took to the streets and protested *en masse* later on the same night and over the following days. Demonstrations and marches were held throughout the country. Seventeen policemen and thirteen demonstrators were injured during a violent demonstration in Kızılay, Ankara, and there were similar mass protests in Izmir, Mersin and İzmit provinces.[28] The most dramatic events, however, occurred in Istanbul, notably in the Ümraniye district, with barricades and loss of life.[29] The initial protest left thirty dead after non- uniformed police reportedly opened fire on the demonstrators in the crowd.[30] The rioting in Istanbul lasted several days before the army was called in to restore order.[31] It appears that the

---

much criticism within Turkey that those really responsible would not be brought to justice and that the prosecution was not being rigorously applied; see *Turkey Briefing*, vol. 8, no. 3, 1994. On 26 December, Ankara State Security Court (DGM) sentenced 26 people to 15 years' imprisonment for causing the death of the 37 intellectuals in Sivas. A further 60 were sentenced to 3 years' imprisonment, and 37 suspects were released. After the Court's decision, the accused attacked guards and threw coins and pieces of wood at the judges and at reporters. Outside the court building, the relatives of the 37 victims of the Sivas massacre waited anxiously for the result, and were not satisfied with it. Both sides appealed to a higher court. An important aspect of the verdict was that 5 years would be deducted from each sentence as it was decided that writer Aziz Nesin's speech in Sivas a year before had incited those accused; *Turkey Briefing*, vol. 8, no. 4, 1994.

[28] *Anatolia Agency*, Ankara, 14 March 1995, in SWB EE/2253, B/8, 16/3/95. In Izmir, 17 members of an "illegal leftist organisation" were arrested for organising protests against the DYP, attacking shops, businesses and organisations with molotov cocktails, and occupying the DYP Izmir branch; TRT, radio, Ankara, 22 March 1995, in SWB EE/2260, B/12, 4/3/95.

[29] There were demonstrations and curfews in Üsküdar, Gazi, Zübeyde, Esentepe and Ümraniye districts.

[30] *Turkey Briefing*, vol. 9, no. 1, 1995. As well as the loss of life and injuries, 96 business places, 3 police cars and other cars, 2 tractors and 2 commercial vehicles were destroyed in the riots. The police claimed that they had tried to disperse a crowd marching on Gazi police station by firing into the air but had opened fire on the crowd after there had been some retaliation – TRT, TV, Ankara, 13 March 1995, in SWB EE/2252, B/6 15/3/95.

[31] BBC World Service, 15 March 1995.

Alevis saw the police as being anti-Alevi and sympathetic to radical Sunni elements. The Alevis in Gaziosmanpaşa strongly accused the local police of being extreme nationalists, and the security director of Gaziosmanpaşa district was sacked and all his staff redeployed.[32] Conversely, the demonstrators welcomed the army, which still remains a bastion of secularist Kemalism.

The government and the Turkish press initially put the blame on 'foreign provocateurs', particularly from Greece.[33] However, even while Çiller was blaming 'foreign provocateurs supported from outside',[34] she was also blaming 'intolerant fundamentalists' and hinting that the riots had been provoked so as to try and discredit Turkey and subvert its concurrent attempt to join a customs union with the European Union (EU).[35] As demonstrations continued, Alevi leaders called on their community to stay calm. Two radical Islamic groups claimed responsibility for the initial outrages – the Turkish Revenge Brigade and the Great Eastern Islamic Raiders-Front (İBDA-C). This latter group has claimed responsibility for a number of outrages in recent years and is described by the police as an underground organisation intent on creating a Sunni Kurdish state.[36] Judging from their previous targets, it would seem that this group sees all secularist elements – Turkish or Kurdish – as targets, and as such would view the Alevis, whether they be ethnically Turkish or Kurdish, as 'traitors' to their cause of creating a Sunni state (see Chapter 6).

After the Gaziosmanpaşa incidents, the government attempted

---

[32] TRT, TV, Ankara, 16 March 1995 in SWB EE/2255, B/8, 18/3/95.

[33] For example, *Sabah* referred vaguely to the involvement of the Greek secret service and *Hürriyet* mentioned a report that Prime Minister Çiller said Greek instigation was responsible. President Demirel also said that inter-Turkish confrontation was not responsible (i.e. 'outside' provocation was); EB Radio, Athens, 16 March 1995, in SWB EE/2255, B/6, 18/3/95. Turkish parliament Speaker Hüsamettin Cindoruk also asserted that the perpetrators were 'not Turks nor Turkish citizens ... they must have come from abroad' with the aim of destroying Turkey; TRT, TV, Ankara, 13 March 1995, in SWB EE/2252, B/8, 15/3/95.

[34] TRT, TV, Ankara, 15 March 1995, in SWB EE/2254, B/9, 17/3/95.

[35] TRT, TV, Ankara, 14 March 1995 in SWB EE/2253, B/8, 16/3/95. This connection with the EU customs union was also referred to by Alevi leader İzettin Doğan; TRT, TV, Ankara 13 March 1995 in SWB EE/2252, B/7, 15/3/95.

[36] Jonathan Rugman, *Guardian Weekly*, London, 19 March 1995.

to placate and silence the long-disturbed Alevi community by
giving promises, such as mention of including Alevis in religious
schoolbooks and employing Alevi representatives in the Directorate
of Religious Affairs.

Thus, the left-right conflict of the 1970s, which saw Alevis
targeted as a group by rightist extremists from organisations such
as the MHP, has changed since 1980 into a more religious one,
with Sunni revivalist groups active in attacking Alevis as heretics.
Some Sunni radicals are quite candid in stating that Alevis are
little better than animals and that it is acceptable or even meritorious
for true Muslims to kill them.[37] However, despite this continuing
hostility, Alevism has not yet run its course in Turkey. Maybe
the tragedy in Sivas has helped to bring the community together
and possibly face up to what anthropologists see as a rapid assimilation and loss of separate identity. This was further aided by
the riots in Istanbul in 1995. Talking to an ATV television crew,
one Alevi at the campsite in Hacıbektaş in August 1994 spoke
of the assimilatory policies against Alevis by what is now perceived
as a Sunni state, and how they objected to this; he was soundly
applauded by the crowd of people listening. A purely superficial
look at the mass of Alevi villages between Kayseri and Kahraman
Maraş shows a fair degree of affluence, with new houses and
roofs in evidence (although Shankland's point about the lack of
Alevi towns, excepting Hacı bektaş itself, remains). However, the
central question is still whether an Alevi-Bekta̧is community
centred on the *cems* and the authority of the *dedes* can survive
in a modern state, or whether this element will recede, leaving
only the more purely cultural aspects like the music and dancing.

Other Muslim groups

At this point, it is instructive to look at the attitude of other
Muslim ethnic groups, many of whom came voluntarily to the
Ottoman Empire and Turkey, seeing it as a haven, in contrast
to 'indigenous' groups like the Kurds. As noted in Chapter 2,
in the nineteenth century, many Muslims from the Caucasus fled
to the Ottoman Empire to escape Russian rule. In addition, large
numbers of Muslims, many of whom were not native Turkish

[37] McDowall, *op. cit.* p. 60.

speakers, moved to the Ottoman Empire or Turkey to escape control by the expanding Balkan states. While it has become fashionable to some extent in the new climate for Turks to refer to their own diverse ethnic make-up, the Turkish state still remains concerned at the growth of possible nationalist sentiment among these groups.[38] Nevertheless, the descendants of these non-Turkish immigrants have largely become Turkified under the impact of Kemalist integral nationalism. As in the case of the classic 'melting pot' of the United States, Muslim immigrants have voluntarily subsumed their previous ethnic identity and enthusiastically embraced the Turkish one.[39] This can surely be explained by the concept of Turkey as a kin-state, which is looked at in greater detail in the following chapter. Such people originally came to Turkey, often to escape perceived or outright discrimination, and saw Turkey as a 'mother state'. In such circumstances, it is not surprising that they do not show any antipathy to the variants of Turkish nationalism; on the contrary, they often wholeheartedly embrace it.[40] Moreover, the Islamic variants detailed in Chapter 6 would not have alienated them either; such communities tend to be devout, as the reason for their arrival in the first place was

---

[38] For example, the owner and editor of the magazine *Katdağı*, Aslan Arı, and Murat Özden charged at Ankara DGM on 2 August 1990 with having weakened national sentiment due to an article by Özden on the cultural problems faced by Circassians in Turkey; *Turkey Briefing*, vol. 4, no. 4, September 1990.

[39] This can clearly be observed in the areas of Istanbul where the Albanians have made their home, for example, in the vicinity of the airport where 'Kosova' restaurants are frequent, but where the inhabitants, while proud of their ancestry, see themselves as solidly Turkish. The Muslim Slav immigrants, or the Caucasian Muslims who came to Turkey seeing it as their 'kin-state' (see Chapter 9) are in a similar position. This equates with the US experience, where immigrants from, for example Italy, retain a strong sense of their Italian roots but again see no contradiction with accepting the values and norms of English-speaking US nationalism. This 'melting pot' approach is now under strain within the United States (see Chapter 1).

[40] While this is observable for non-Turkish-speaking Muslim immigrants, for those from Turkic-speaking backgrounds the assimilation is easier still. For example, the Azeri Turks resident in Turkey – most of the Aralık population is Azeri with some 10-15% recent immigrants from Azerbaijan – have little distinct sense of ethnic identity; Jane Howard *The Guardian*, 24 January 1990. The number of Azeris in eastern Turkey is estimated at some 400,000; Jim Bodgener, *The Financial Times*, 24 January 1990.

to remain within the Islamic fold.[41] A possible exception here is the radical ethnic variant detailed in Chapter 5, which might tend to exclude them and view them as 'foreign elements'.

As well as these more recent immigrant Muslim communities, there are others which have been resident in Anatolia for centuries. These include the Laz, who inhabit the Black Sea region beginning some 40 or 50 kilometres east of Rize.[42] They are a Caucasion people speaking a language related to Georgian.[43] Like immigrant Muslim groups, the Laz exhibit a solid Turkish nationalism.[44] This begs the question as to why the Laz are so strongly pro-Turkish while sections of the Kurds are so militantly not. A possible answer may lie in economic factors. As noted in Chapter 1, economic differentiation, especially any perceived backwardness of one's group, often plays an important role in the rise and sustenance of separate nationalist feeling. The Kurds, as noted, inhabit areas in the southeast which are economically under-developed. On the other hand the Laz, before the mass migrations to cities like Istanbul, predominantly resided in communities near the Black Sea and have been very successful in the shipping

---

[41] Immigrant communities from the Balkans, for example, are known for being pious Muslims.

[42] This is the invisible border of 'Lazistan', although many Turks have a habit of referring to anyone living east of Trabzon as being 'Laz'. Many Laz have joined the massive migrations to urban centres like Istanbul. For more on the region see Chris M. Hann, 'Rural Transformation on the East Black Sea Coast: a note on Keyder', *Journal of Peasant Studies*, vol. 12, no. 4, 1985, *Tea and the Domestication of the Turkish State*, Occasional Papers in Modern Turkish Studies, no 1 (Huntingdon: Eothen Press, 1990), and 'Sexual division of labour in Lazistan' in Paul Stirling (ed.), *Culture and Economy: Changes in Turkish Villages* (Huntingdon: Eothen Press, 1993).

[43] Some 100,000 reside in Pazar, Ardeşen, Fındıklı, Arhavi and Hopa, as well as in inland enclaves in the valleys leading down to the Black Sea. They are often distinguished by the aquiline features of the men, who often have reddish hair. They are also famous for their sense of humour and quick wits, in response to which they are often the butt of innumerable jokes made by Turks. Their legendary reputation for quick-wittedness and business acumen is famous throughout Turkey. Paradoxically, there are also jokes about their stupidity and obstinacy, but these seem to be as unfounded as such quasi-racialist humour usually is (for instance, that 'all Scots are mean').

[44] This despite retaining to some extent their own language – there is now a private TV station which broadcastes Laz songs every Friday evening. There is also a Laz journal, *Ogni*, which is published occasionally in Istanbul.

business.[45] The area is also the centre of Turkey's tea growing area and has afforded the local population many advances. Thus, the Laz have, like the Scots in nineteenth-century Britain, taken advantage of economic possibilities and correspondingly refrained from nationalist activity hostile to the Turkish state. Another factor is probably that of terrain and communications. The Kurds live in areas with poor communications and wild mountainous terrain. The Laz, on the other hand, live in areas which are relatively easily accessible to the central authorities. The Laz traditionally saw themselves as defenders of the Muslim state in the mixed Black Sea areas while the Kurds were more tribal and outside the state, tending to view it as hostile. Given this, it is not surprising that the Kemalist state has been much more successful in inculcating its own nationalist values among the Laz than the Kurds, who often remained in traditional pre-national communities.

The situation of the Hemşinlis, who inhabit the upland postures inland from 'Lazistan', is similar.[46] Although they speak Turkish as their mother tongue they have distinct customs and dress. While proudly claiming their separateness, they are staunch Turkish patriots. They have also exploited economic advantages offered by the Turkish state and are prominent in pastry shops in urban centres of the west.[47] Other Muslim minority groups have been less fortunate, especially those who live in the troubled southeast and who have been caught in the struggle between the security forces and the PKK. The Turkish Syriacs who speak a mixture of Kurmanci Kurdish and Arabic and who are descendants of the large Hevkiri tribe are an example. To escape the fighting they

---

[45] Rosie Aycliffe, Marc Dubin and John Gawthrop, *Turkey: The Rough Guide* (London: Penguin, 1994), p. 589.

[46] There is debate over the origin of the Hemşin people. Some say they are an old Turkish tribe descended from the original 10th-century migrations, while others claim that they originally spoke a form of Armenian and were nominally Christian or pagan until the 19th century; this might explain their apparent lack of strong Islamic beliefs; *ibid*, p. 592.

[47] Some 15,000 live permanently in the area; *ibid*. Many others return from their pastry shops and other businesses for the summer *yayla* pastures on the southern slopes of the stunning Kaçkar mountains. One is struck by the way in which 'modern westernised' women with their own shops and cars in places like Izmir return for the whole summer dressed in the traditional leopardskin-patterned turbans and other traditional clothes.

have emigrated *en masse* to Sweden and Germany.[48]

A number of Arabs live in Hatay province and around the border with Syria. In these regions, the population was usually mixed between Arabs, Turks, Turcomen and Cherkez with little intermarriage between the different groups.[49] In recent years the middle class, who were chiefly Cherkez and Turcoman, have assimilated into the Turkish mass. Like the ethnic Turks, they have moved to the cities, leaving the country areas mainly Arab. As Arabic remains the language of the Koran, and the Arabs tend to live in close proximity to Arab states, the small Arab population has remained distinct and not assimilated into the Turkish mass as much as other small Muslim groups. In this, the negative historical legacy between Turks and Arabs has been a factor.[50]

In view of the above, it can be stated that the fears expressed by many Turks that if communal rights are granted to the Kurds, then other groups like the Albanians, Bosnians, Laz and so on will also claim them, leading to a general unravelling of the Turkish ethnic mosaic, are unfounded. There appears to be a qualitative difference between the situation regarding the numerous Kurds who originated in the backward and rugged southeast, and these other smaller Muslim communities who have been apparently successfully assimilated into the majority Turkish identity. While these groups often retain their sense of separateness and consciousness of their different origins and customs, they have no

---

[48] However, reports suggest that even there they cannot escape fully and are pressured, by PKK representatives to support the organisation or have their property left in Turkey destroyed; see *Briefing*, no. 812, 12 November 1990, which reprinted an article on the Turkish Syriacs which first appeared in *İkibine Doğru* in 1987.

[49] A respondent from the area some 40 miles from Hatay told me that she was a Cherkez who had married a Turk but that this was something of an exception. She had recently learned Cherkez but was unable to write it properly. She would like her son to also learn it but he has not, preferring to learn English as a second language instead.

[50] This has ebbed and flowed over time but still remains. Arabs are resentful at perceived 'colonial domination' of them by the Ottoman Turks, to which they ascribe the economic underdevelopment of the Arab lands of the former Ottoman Empire. Hatay province remains a symbol for Arab nationalists and is still shown as part of Syria on Syrian maps. However, there does not seem to be any overt separatist activity in Hatay province – possibly because attachment to Assad's Syria is hardly an enticing prospect at the moment.

problem in accepting the integral Turkish nationalism propagated by the state.

Interestingly, however, there is one other Muslim group which remains to some extent outside the national body: the Roma (the preferred name for Gypsies, known as *Çingene* in Turkish), who are spread out around the country. It is estimated that there are 545,000 Roma in Turkey, with some 25,000 living in quarters of Istanbul where they have dwelt for centuries.[51] Roma especially live in the Trakya (eastern Thrace) region of Turkey, and in the provinces of Samsun, Antalya, Adana, Denizli, Hakkari, Mardin, Cizre, Siirt, Van and Ağrı. They face discrimination throughout Turkey, similar to that experienced by Roma across Europe, and tend to live in ghettos attached to the urban centres.[52] The majority of the Roma are settled, the rest nomadic.[53] Although most of them were originally Christian, many have converted to Islam. Every year they organise large spring festivals and a celebration on 6 May called *Hıdırellez*.

Regarding the attitude of Turks to Roma in modern Turkey, the anthropologist Carol Delaney notes that 'Çingene (Roma) are considered subhuman (by the villagers], because they have no book (Qu'ran or Bible) and are thought to be promiscuous, like

---

[51] *The World Directory of Minorities* (London: Longman/MRG, 1989), p. 214.

[52] The social status of the Roma in Turkey is low and this is reflected in the names they are called. Known usually as *Çingene* the Roma are also known as *Kıptı, Posa* (in the east of Turkey), *Mutrip, Arabacı* (meaning coachmen), *Koçer* (meaning nomads) and *esmer vatandaş* (dark-skinned citizen) in several regions. The very word *Cingene* is a term of contempt. The Oxford Turkish-English dictionary includes 'mean' and 'cunning' as part of its definition (*OUP İnkilap Kitabevi*, 3rd ed, Istanbul 1994). Many popular sayings confirm this prejudice: 'The gypsy is playing and the Kurd is dancing' refers to a noisy and unruly gathering. 'They gave authority to a gypsy man and the first thing he did was to hang his father'. 'Like a gypsy tent' indicates a dirty and miserable place. 'Keep yourself away from the gypsies, they break your arm and leg and make you beg', say many parents to their children; Erol Anar 'The Roma of Samsun province', *Turkey Briefing*, vol. 8, no. 4, 1994. For more on the Roma in Europe see Gratton Puxton, *Roma: Europe's Gypsies* (London: MRG Report, 1987), *passim*, and Hugh Poulton, *The Balkans: Minorities and State in Conflict* (London: MRG Publications, 1993), chapters 7, 9, 13, 14 and 16.

[53] The nomadic Roma earn their living by fortune-telling, making or selling sieves and baskets, copper-work, making tents or tinkering. Many of them traditionally used to migrate across the border to modern Greece. The settled Roma are musicians, florists, grooms, porters or bootblacks.

animals, sharing women in common.'[54] This stigmatisation of Roma due to their alleged lack of faith (having 'no book') appears doubly inconsistent. First, many Roma throughout the empire were or are Muslims (and in the Balkans many were or are also Christians). Second, as Delaney also points out, in the view of the villagers 'not only is humanity unified, but all are essentially Muslim. Humanity is united because all races derive from Adam and Adam was made by God.'[55] Quite why Roma appear to suffer this racism in an Islamic society remains unanswered. Moreover, despite the self-viewed high status of nomadic groups in areas of southeast Anatolia, this did not apply to nomadic Roma. Van Bruinessen states in his classic work on the Kurds[56] that lineages of Roma-type groups were despised by all. Even the lowliest landless peasants looked down on them, and all Kurdish groups deny any inter-marriage with them. The Roma everywhere in the area appeared (and still appear) to be fragmented by occupation, with a strict hierarchy between themselves in terms of intermarriage between different groups – perhaps a continuation of the Indian caste system.[57]

The Roma in Turkey experience a dual oppression from both the government and society. The Roma allege that they are not given jobs in government offices or elsewhere because they are Roma.[58] Many of the nomadic Roma suffer from a lack of citizenship and do not hold identity cards.[59] Settled Roma are dis-

---

[54] Carol Delaney, *The Seed and the Soil: Gender and Cosmology in Turkish Village Society* (Berkeley: University of California Press, 1991) p. 105.

[55] *Ibid*, p. 287.

[56] Martin van Bruinessen, *Agha Shaikh and State* (Utrecht: Rijswijk, 1978), p. 140.

[57] The Roma originated in India; see Donald Kenrick, *Gypsies: from India to the Mediterranean* (Toulose: Gypsy Research Centre, CRDP Midi-Pyrénées, 1993). Many Muslim Roma from the Balkans returned to Anatolia as the Ottoman Empire retreated. For example, the Roma in Samsun came from northern Greece in 1920-1.

[58] Many of them are unemployed, and resort to jobs as bootblacks, porters or musicians. Only 40% of children are said to finish primary school, the drop-out rate being high despite the availability of free schooling. Roma start work and enter marriage early, nearly always to other Roma; Erol Anar, *op. cit.*

[59] In an interview on 13 August 1994 in Ankara, Meryam Erdal of the İHD (The Turkish Human Rights Association) stated that most Roma do not have identity cards. She had studied Roma in Adana where officials refused to give

criminated against in employment. Roma living places receive no municipal services, with dire consequences for their sanitation. If a crime is committed near a Roma settlement then Roma are quickly accused. Roma settlements are also subject to police raids and harassment. Roma claim that they are more exposed to torture than other people when taken into custody. Because they are shunned by society, Roma tend to live collectively, limiting their relations with others as far as possible. Without effective organisation and spokesmen, Roma do not make their grievances heard: they receive little attention from the media or parliament, and are of little interest to political parties. Traditionally, all hangmen had to be Roma.[60]

Thus, the Roma appear not be recognised by the Turkish state or society as real or potential Turkish citizens. Their low social level and lack of political organisation, or any form of intelligentsia to articulate their cause or propagate some form of Roma national consciousness has seen them remain, to a large extent, outside the nationalist discourse. Whether this will continue indefinitely remains to be seen.

The Christian communities

The Christian communities in Turkey have their rights guaranteed by international law under Articles 38-44 of the Lausanne Treaty of 1923. As such, unlike Muslim minorities, they are officially accepted as being minorities within Turkey.[61] However, in the climate of the unitary Kemalist nationalism propagated by the state, members of these communities have, perhaps inevitably,

---

them identity cards as they were seen as nomads or refugees from other countries; other nomadic groups in Turkey have no problems in getting identity cards. A similar situation was reported by Erol Anar, *op. cit.* To the question as to how one recognises a Roma given the diversity of the Turkish population, Erdal replied that locally they are known as being inhabitants of the local Roma ghetto, and that because of their darker skins they are easy to recognise.

[60] I am indebted to Andrew Mango for this last information.

[61] For example, Prime Minister Demirel when submitting his government's 65-page programme to parliament in November 1991, stated: 'No citizen of this country except those accepted under international agreements are in the category of a minority.' Turkish TV, Ankara, 25 November 1991, in SWB ME/1241 A/8, 28 November 1991.

been viewed as potential fifth columnists for external powers and not true 'Turkish citizens'.

This is best illustrated by the situation of Turkey's Greek Orthodox community in Istanbul and the islands of Gökçeada and Bozçaada, who were excluded from the forced population transfers of the early 1920s (see Chapter 4). The community numbered over 100,000 at the time of the Lausanne Treaty. By 1974 the figure had declined to less than 10,000, and today it is estimated to number only a few thousand.[62] In 1922 the Kemalist state attempted to set up a rival Turkish Ottoman Patriarchate under Eftim I in Kayseri to combat the influence of the Patriarchate in the Fener quarter in Istanbul over Orthodox subjects. At the time of the forced population transfers in January 1923 Eftim came to Istanbul, but he was unable to rival the Fener Patriarchate, and the small community with three churches was soon abandoned.[63]

The sorry tale of the 1942 Capital Tax and its impact on non-Muslim communities is detailed in Chapter 4. The Greek community in Turkey also increasingly became victims of Greek-Turkish confrontation over Cyprus and hostages to the situation of the Muslim community of Western Thrace in Greece, which was allowed to remain in exchange for the Orthodox populations exempted from the 1923 population transfers. It appears that regardless of the different governments in Turkey, the policy has remained consistently hostile to the community. In response to perceived persecution of Turks in Cyprus, on 6 and 7 September 1955 a mob, perhaps with government complicity,[64] destroyed much of

[62] The Greek population of the two islands is reported to have fallen from 10,500 in the 1940s to only 1,600 in 1977, while the Greek population in Istanbul similarly declined from 100,000 in 1934 to some 8,000; *The World Directory of Minorities*, p. 193.

[63] This rival Orthodox community nonetheless continued, and on his death Eftim I was succeeded by Turgut Erenerol, who took the title Eftim II. He made his brother, CHP deputy Selçuk Erenerol, who was not a religious man, Patriarchal Deputy; Baskın Oran, 'Lozan'nın "Azınlıkların Korunması" Bölümünü Yeniden Okurken' [forthcoming]. Eftim I is buried in the centre of the Greek Orthodox cemetery in Istanbul with a quotation from Atatürk inscribed on his tomb stating that he was worth a military division. I am indebted to Andrew Mango for this information.

[64] Feroz Ahmad, *The Turkish Experiment in Democracy, 1950-75* (London: Hurst, 1977), p. 54.

the Greek business quarter of Istanbul as well as Greek churches, schools, cemeteries and other historical monuments. The state prohibitions on the establishment of any association based on race, language or religion, which are, in line with the French nationalist model of the unitary state, ostensibly aimed at preventing centripetal forces within society, has been an obstacle. The two islands were declared military zones, and Greek-owned land was compulsorily appropriated and schools were closed. In 1964 the Turkish government expelled *en masse* the 12,000-strong Greek national community (i.e. those having Greek citizenship) in Istanbul.[65] In the same year, Greek Orthodox priests were forbidden to teach religion or perform morning prayers in minority schools. Since then, ethnic Turks have been appointed as teachers in these schools, with the teaching of the Greek language greatly reduced. In 1971 the government closed the Çalki Department of Advanced Religious Studies which prepared appointees for office within the church. Prominent members of the church community were also reported to face restrictions on their travel movements both inside and outside Turkey.[66] Further restrictions were imposed after the Cyprus crises of 1974 when the Turkish government adopted a secret decree which restricted property transactions by Greeks in Turkey and froze their assets.[67]

The legacy of distrust continues to the present day.[68] A number of Byzantine historical monuments were destroyed in the 1980s.[69] When Patriarch Demitrius I returned on 30 July 1990 from a visit to the United States, during which he met President Bush, leading ANAP 'liberal' Mesut Yılmaz called for him to be summoned by the authorities and questioned about his visit.[70] Selçuk

---

[65] *Protocol*, no. 195/91, The Constantinopolitan Society, Athens, 10 June 1991.

[66] *The World Directory of Minorities*, p. 193.

[67] *Ibid.* It appears that this decree was not implemented until after July 1985.

[68] The distrust is mirrored on the Orthodox side. When I visited the Greek churches in 1992, my Turkish companion was refused entry and only allowed in under duress.

[69] This included the Byzantine mosaic floor dating from 1214 in Fatih Camii, which was concreted over, and a number of other Byzantine monuments including the 6th-century church of Saint Constantine at Yeniköy (Eski Andaval) near Niğde. *Turkey Briefing*, vol. 3, no. 6, 1989. Despite this, it must be borne in mind that the number of such monuments in Turkey remains huge, and in some cases they have been restored and re-opened as 'museums'.

Erenerol[71] made accusations that property around the Fener Patriarchate was being purchased by Turkish Greeks (known as 'Rums')
who had renounced Turkish citizenship with the aim of setting
up a mini-state akin to the Vatican in Rome. As a result, officials
from the Patriarchate were taken into custody for questioning
on instructions from the Interior Ministry.[72] There appeared to
be no evidence to support this accusation.[73] On 19 December
1994, Interior Minister Nahit Menteşe called for an investigation
into Patriarch Bartelemos on account of his activities abroad, which
were seen as hostile to Turkey.[74]

The other main Christian minority in Turkey is the Armenian
one, which similarly has rights guaranteed under Articles 38-44
of the Lausanne Treaty. The Armenians suffered particularly heavy
losses in the massacres which took place during the First World
War (see Chapter 3), with relatively few remaining, mostly in
Istanbul and a few other cities. Those who attempted to return
to claim ancestral land were often attacked by local mobs. Some
15,000 Armenians left Hatay district (Alexandretta) in 1939 when
Turkey gained the province from Syria. Armenians also suffered
from the 1942 Capital Tax. According to the Turkish census of
1960, there were 52,756 Armenian speakers in the country, of
whom 37,700 lived in Istanbul.[75] Similarly to the Greek community, they have been viewed with distrust, and they also suffered
in the anti-Greek riots in Istanbul in 1955.

As in the case of the Greeks, the Armenians, who today number
some 30,000-35,000 in Istanbul,[76] suffered educational and other
restrictions in the 1970s, and official harassment in the early 1980s

---

[70] *Turkey Briefing*, vol. 4, no. 4, 1990. Demitrius died on 2 October 1990 and
was succeeded by Metropolitan Bartelemos.

[71] Selçuk Erenerol was the brother of Eftim II (see above). His accusations were
reported by Nilüfer Kars in 'Patrikhane Göz Hapsinde', *Milliyet*, 29 October 1993.

[72] *Milliyet*, 11 November 1993.

[73] Baskin Oran, *op. cit.*, notes that in fact since 1940 there have been very few
house sales involving 'Rums'. Two in the years 1954 and 1989, and 1 in each
of the years 1940, 1941, 1947, 1959, 1964, 1967, 1977, 1979, 1980, 1987,
1988, 1991, 1992 and 1993. In other years there were no sales.

[74] *Info-Türk*, no. 217, December 1994.

[75] *The World Directory of Minorities*, p. 180.

[76] From a widespread poll of Istanbul inhabitants published in *Milliyet*, 1 March
1993.

in response to violent attacks by radical Armenians against Turkish targets abroad.[77]

The Armenian Patriarch Shnork died in March 1990. Under the system codified in 1961 his successor was to be chosen by an electoral college of Armenians in Turkey. However, the Özal government changed this: by only allowing officially recognised Armenian foundations to take part in the election, it put restrictions on candidates. These restrictions included the obligation that the fathers of the candidates be Turkish nationals and raising the age limit from thirty-five to forty years of age for candidates.[78] In 1993, Decision No. 2392 published in *Tebligler Dergisi* stated that from 11 October that year all classes in Armenian minority schools, except those on the Armenian language, would be held in Turkish – in breach of the Lausanne Treaty.[79] Education Minister Nevzat Ayaz replied to criticism of the measure by denying that it was in contradiction of the Lausanne Treaty, but went on to say that the decision had not been made by the Education Ministry and that they were examining the situation.[80] The measure was then revoked and Ayaz announced that, as the Treaty requires, apart from Turkish language and Turkish culture, any language which the school wished could be used as the medium of

[77] *A World Directory of Minorities*, p. 180. A number of extreme Armenian groups have been in operation, ostensibly aiming for an independent Armenian state in eastern Turkey, but in practice apparently operating mainly in revenge for the massacres of 1915/16. One of the main radical extremist Armenian organisations is 'The Secret Army for the Liberation of Armenia' (ASALA), which was founded in the early 1970s and led until 1983 by Hagop Hagopian, who was shot dead in Athens in May 1988. ASALA had been responsible for a number of attacks on Turkish diplomats and other targets. In January 1992 *Milliyet* reported that the Turkish government was investigating reports that ASALA may have been financed from Turkey through organisations like the Ermeni Vakfi, but nothing apparently came of this; *The Month in Turkey* no. 13, January 1992. Since the late 1980s, the ASALA campaign appears to have petered out – possibly through loss of support from the American Armenian community, or (more probably) the death of Hagopian.

[78] *Turkey Briefing*, vol. 4, no. 3, 1990. These measures led to a protest by 33 of the 37 Armenian Church leaders. The age measure was apparently to prevent Bishop Mesrob Mutafyn from standing and instead led to the pliant 64-year-old Bishop Sahan Sivacian, who had no outstanding qualifications, becoming acting Patriarch; Hugh Pope, *The Independent*, London 24 May 1990.

[79] *Cumhuriyet*, 1 December 1993.

[80] *Ibid.*, 3 December 1993.

instruction.[81] However, central authorities' distrust of the Armenian community remained and the government decided to reinforce control over the minority schools. On 27 January 1995, the Armenian directors of the Istanbul Armenian schools and their Turkish vice-directors[82] were summoned to the Education directorate, where the Turkish vice-directors were ordered to inform the authorities of any developments within the schools.[83] There has also been a rise in tension over public perceptions that the Armenians are allegedly in alliance with the PKK in trying to dismember Turkey.[84] At the beginning of 1995 an Armenian Church was bombed.[85] Another factor in relations with the Armenians is the continuing hostilities between Armenia and Azerbaijan over the disputed territory of Nagorno-Karabakh. Turkish official and public opinion strongly supports the Azeris, whom they see as a fellow Turkic people. On the other hand, the Turkish government is keen to reopen trade links with Armenia which

---

[81] *Ibid.*, 10 December 1993.

[82] Despite Article 40 of the Lausanne Treaty, which guarantees autonomy for minority schools, the government appoints a Turkish vice-director of Turkish origin to every minority school. In practice, it is alleged that these vice-directors have unlimited authority over the directors and other teachers – a situation which is very reminiscent of the Soviet one where the nominal leaders of minority Communist Party organisations were members of the relevant minority but the all-powerful First Secretary was always a Russian.

[83] *Info-Türk*, no. 218, January/February 1995.

[84] Despite the history of past bloodshed between Armenians and Kurds, especially in the massacres of 1915/16, the establishment of an Armenian republic, which became fully independent following the USSR's dissolution, has seen past historical competition minimised. Radical Armenians and Kurds have tended to see Turkey as their common enemy, as shown by the press conference in Lebanon on 6 April 1980 when the PKK and ASALA announced their co-operation. *Info-Türk*, no. 216, October 1994, reports that after 16 October, when a right-wing newspaper printed a picture of PKK leader Abdullah Öcalan shaking hands with a man in a religious gown, which the paper claimed was further proof of PKK/Armenian collaboration, a number of threatening letters arrived at Armenian addresses. The letters stated 'Oh you parasites who think yourselves citizens! We nourish you snakes in our bosom and you both eat our bread and will destroy our souls and blood? The time to put a halt to this has long come and gone.' The letters also call on Armenians living in Turkey to leave immediately and end 'This is a last warning to you. Turkey is only for the Turks and not for snakes like you. This is final and don't forget it.'

[85] *Human Rights Yesterday and Today*, 01/013, 10 January 1995, Human Rights Foundation of Turkey, Documentation Centre, Ankara.

would help revitalise transit cities like Kars.[86] If the Nagorno-Karabakh dispute could be settled, then Turkey would almost certainly establish full diplomatic and commercial relations with Armenia, and Armenia would officially renounce irredentist claims on Turkish territory. In principle, this would improve relations between ethnic Turks and Amernians within Turkey, though one cannot be certain that such logic would prevail.

Apart from these two main Christian communities, there were smaller Christian communities in the southeast, who, like the smaller Muslim ones, have become caught in the crossfire between the security forces and the PKK. For example the Assyro-Chaldean Catholic community which before the fighting numbered over 5,000, have now virtually all migrated to Istanbul or Europe.[87] Similar pressures have been brought to bear on the 3,000 estimated Orthodox Assyrians in and around Midyat.[88]

---

[86] This was also stressed recently by the mayor of Kars who, despite being a member of the ultra-nationalist MHP, called for better links with Armenia. Official relations with Armenia have been aided no doubt by Armenian President Ter-Petrossian's opposition and repression of the strongly nationalist Dashnak party in December 1994. In addition, Turkey must be aware of both the pro-Armenian lobby in the US as well as the potential benefits of closer co-operation with Armenia. However, Nagorno-Karabakh remains a stumbling-block.

[87] *Amnesty International*, UA 287/94, 1 August 1994. This document details the plight of the last 5 remaining Assyro-Chaldean families in Kovankaya and Çevizağaci in Beytüşebab in Hakkari province. Kovankaya, which was an Assyro-Chaldean village, was burnt to the ground by security forces in 1990 after villagers refused to join the Village Guard corps. The villagers fled to Istanbul but returned in 1992 and rebuilt some homes. In early June Kovankaya was once more burnt down by the security forces and the villagers moved to Çevizağaçı, another Assyro-Chaldean village, where they were held in arbitrary detention. The UN Special Rapporteur on Religious Intolerance asserted on 5 September 1994 that the Assyro-Chaldeans were subject to 'compulsory Muslim education' and forbidden to practice or build new churches. It also reported severe pressure on them and gave the figure for the minority as over 100,000 in 1975 falling to only some 10,000, UN, E/CN. 4/1995/91.

[88] See *İnfo-Türk*, Brussels, no. 217, December 1994. The Assyrian Democratic Organisation and Human Rights Without Frontiers issued a joint file on 1 June 1994 at a press conference at the Belgian Parliament which listed 200 Assyrian villages destroyed in Turkey in the previous 30 years and a list of 24 Assyrians assassinated in Turkey since 1990 – presumably by Hizbullah death Squads; reported in İnfo-Türk, no. 212, June 1994.

The Jews

As noted in Chapter 3, many Jews viewed the Ottoman Empire as a protector from the intolerance of the Christian European states. Chief Rabbi Haim Bejerano led Turkish Jews into the republican era and turned down overtures from the Greek and Armenian Patriarchs to co-operate against the Turks, publicly denying that Jews were unhappy with the new regime.[89] On 15 September 1925, Bejerano voluntarily renounced the Jewish *millet's* special status as guaranteed under Article 42 of the Lausanne Treaty, and instead opted for ordinary Turkish citizenship. The relationship between the Jewish community and the Turks in republican Turkey has remained relatively successful. Tekin Alp, the Jewish former pan-Turkist and later staunch Kemalist (see Chapter 4) led a campaign for Jews to speak only Turkish and thus fully integrate into Turkish society.[90] Many leading Jewish intellectuals fled Nazi Germany in the 1930s and came to Turkey, where they were given leading academic posts. As noted in Chapter 4, the Jews were subject to discriminatory measures under the 1942 Capital Tax, and there were incidents of anti-Semitism in the media and in Thrace.[91] After the war many Jews emigrated to Israel. In 1927 there were 79,424 Jews in Turkey, of whom 47,035 lived in Istanbul and 17,094 in Izmir. The total rose to

[89] Stanford J. Shaw, *The Jews of the Ottoman Empire and the Turkish Republic,* (London: Macmillan, 1991), p. 244.

[90] Shaw states that this policy was so successful that when Bejerano died in 1931 there was no need to elect a new Chief Rabbi until 1953; *ibid,* pp. 250-1. This must surely be something of an exaggeration.

[91] For example the newspaper *Anadolu* of C.R. Atılhan, which was quickly closed by the authorities. Atılhan went to Nazi Germany and returned in May 1934 to set up another anti-Semitic newspaper, *Milli İnkilap,* which led to an anti-Semitic movement in Thrace; *ibid,* pp. 252-3. Shaw, who goes out of his way to portray the position of Jews in both the Ottoman Empire and the Turkish Republic as entirely harmonious, even goes so far as to state that a positive aspect of the Capital Tax was that by depriving the Jews of their financial support it helped to remove the common prejudice against Jews as being exploiters of ordinary Turks. However, even Shaw admits that this policy was a big mistake, although he still casts doubt on it having had any influence in the subsequent mass emigration of Jews to Israel immediately after the war; *ibid,* p. 256.

an estimated 125,000 in the Second World War as many Jews fled to Turkey to escape the Nazis, but fell immediately afterwards to 76,965 and continued to drop to 45,995 in 1955 and 43,928 in 1960 (of whom 38,267 lived in Istanbul and 4,067 in Izmir.[92] Since then Turkish censuses have not differentiated the population by religion, but the 1993 *Milliyet* poll gave a figure of about 18,000 Jews living in Istanbul.[93] Many of Turkey's Ladino Jews still retain awareness of their Spanish roots and a sense of debt to the Ottoman Empire and Turkey for protecting them.[94] Thus, they combine a primary national identification with the Turkish majority while retaining their Jewish identity and even a sense of distant identification with Spain.

The Jews of Turkey have not been subject to the same official distrust as the Christian communities. One reason for this must surely be that the Jews of both the Ottoman Empire and the Turkish Republic have at no time posed any form of serious territorial threat to the state. On the contrary, as noted in Chapter 3, the Ottoman state was seen by many Jews as one which protected them from the intolerance of Christian Western European states. Regardless of origin, most of Turkey's Jews remain assimilated into Sephardic Jewish culture, but Turkish is now overwhelmingly the first language in place of Ladino.[95] The rise of Islam in Turkey in recent decades has been mirrored by a religious revival among Jews. Despite the waves of emigration to Israel, which have tended to leave behind an aging Jewish population, emigration to Israel now appears to have stopped and assimilation into the Turkish

---

[92] Figures in *ibid*, p. 259.

[93] *Milliyet*, 1 March 1993.

[94] For example, many, like leading businessman Jak Kamhi's mother, retained family names with Spanish connotations: her family name was 'Cordoba', interview with Kamhi in 'The Jews and Islam', *The Open University*, BBC 2 TV, 8/9 June 1995.

[95] In surveys carried out in the 1920s and 1930s, 40% of Jewish men and 10% of the women gave Turkish as their first language. After the 1950s the percentages rose to 100% of both groups. As well as speaking Turkish as their mother tongue, most Turkish Jews now speak a West European language as their second language; 'Judeo-Espanyol Diğer Diller ve Türkçe', *Şalom*, Istanbul, 23 and 30 December 1984. However, attempts to revive Ladino are now being made; these include the establishment of a Ladino folk-song group, which conducts classes among Jewish children in Istanbul; information from Anit Lapidot.

majority seems to be largely complete.[96]

However, the growing emphasis on Sunni Islam as a component of 'Turkishness' has inevitably had a detrimental effect on this assimilation. The rise of the Islamist Welfare Party (RP) has seen a number of anti-Semitic views aired.[97] There have also been some violent incidents against Jews by radical Islamists. On 6 September 1986, twenty-three people were killed when Islamists bombed the Neve Şalom Synagogue in Istanbul, and in the summer of 1989 a small bomb exploded at the Israeli Consulate General in Istanbul.[98] On 2 March 1992 Hizbullah bombed the Neve Şalom Synagogue in Istanbul at a ceremony to commemorate the 500th anniversary of the immigration of the Sephardic Jews from Spain. This was followed on 7 March by a car bomb attack on an Israeli Embassy official at his home in Çankaya district in Ankara.[99] On 27 January 1993, four days after the assassination of Uğur Mumcu (see Chapter 6), leading Jewish businessman Jak Kamhi was attacked by Islamist assailants armed with automatic weapons and a light anti-tank weapon. Kamhi, who it was supposed was targeted due to his prominent position in the Turkish Jewish community, escaped unharmed.[100] Other attacks include the desecration of the largest Jewish Cemetery in Istanbul after the March 1994 elections.[101] These attacks have been strongly condemned by the mainstream parties and press.

[96] Interestingly, Shaw notes that Turkish Jews in Israel remain proud of their Turkish heritage and have a national organisation there, *Türkiyeliler Birliği*, and many still speak Turkish (and Ladino); Shaw, *op. cit.* p. 258.

[97] The most infamous was that of İbrahim Halil Çelik the RP Mayor of Urfa, who praised Hitler for eliminating Jews; *Milliyet*, 14 May 1989. This statement was condemned by both Jews and Turks; *Şalom*, Istanbul, 24 and 31 May 1989, and *Milliyet*, 29 May 1989.

[98] Shaw, *op. cit.* p. 269.

[99] *The Month in Turkey*, no. 15, March 1992. Two members of Hizbullah were later sentenced to 10 years' imprisonment for the bomb attack on the synagogue.

[100] *Turkey Briefing*, vol. 7, no. 1, 1993.

[101] *İnfo-Türk*, no. 213/214, July/August 1994, which also reports Welfare Party (RP) leaders, frequent denunciation of the 'evils' of US imperialism and Zionism and RP leader Erbakan's frequent opposition to the European Union as 'a fifth column of Zionism'. Such views, especially about Turkey being the target of an international Jewish conspiracy organised in Washington, appear to be widespread in Turkey among much of the population; see Adam Smith Albion, 'The Voice of the People', *Institute of Current World Affairs*, ASA-6, 20 March

The foregoing discussion suggests that it is possible to differentiate between the various minority groups outside the Sunni Turkish-speaking majority. The most problematic one has been the Muslim Kurds. While many Muslim Kurds seem to retain the traditional religious loyalty of membership of the Islamic community over any form of overt Kurdish national identity, it seems incontestable that many other Kurds now profess a Kurdish national identity separate from a Turkish one. It seems that the lateness of the penetration of official Kemalist integral Turkish nationalism into the rugged backward southeastern regions allowed modern Kurdish nationalism to be a serious rival. The bloody conflict with the PKK and the heavy state repression - especially in the 1980s – against any form of Kurdish consciousness has seen many Kurds reject state-sponsored nationalism and adopt a Kurdish one in its place. Despite a relaxation in the late 1980s of the more restrictive measures, which attempted to prevent any form of Kurdish cultural identity, the Turkish state and its intellectual elite remain for the most part suspicious of Kurdish aspirations and reluctant to grant any form of real autonomy for the Kurds. On the other hand, other Muslim non-Turkish groups, with the exception of the Roma, who remain to some extent outside the state and society, appear to have adopted integral Turkish nationalism without any real problems. Here, the difference between the many immigrant Muslim communities who viewed the Ottoman Empire and Turkey as a 'kin-state' and the indigenous Kurds is relevant. So, perhaps, is the different economic and geographical positions of groups like the Muslim Laz, who also have adopted Turkish nationalist norms in comparison to the Kurds of the southeast. Given this, the fears of the Turkish establishment that Turkey's ethnic mosaic will unravel if any real rights are granted to the Kurds appear unfounded.[102]

1995, Hanover, PA. The Institute of Jewish Affairs, in its report *Anti-Semitism 1994*, (London: Macmillan, 1994) states that Turkey and Romania were two countries where the Jewish community was under the most severe risk; in Turkey's case, this was due to the rise of RP. Anti-Semitism by the RP and others may partly be explained by Muslim solidarity with the Palestinians, but is unlikely to be the sole explanation.

[102] That the Turkish state is concerned at such an unravelling is shown by the detention of members of the Turkish Human Rights Association (İHD) in May 1994 at the time of a conference on Nationalism and Racism in Europe held

Nonetheless, since Atatürk's time, Turkey has evolved into more of a Sunni state, where Sunni Islam is seen by many as an essential component of 'Turkishness'. This process, as shown in Chapter 6, accelerated in the 1980s, and has left the numerous Turkish- speaking Alevi population in something of a quandary. After being staunch supporters of Kemalist secular Turkish nationalism, they are now faced with the prospect of being seen as an unreliable minority by the Sunni majority, and are subject to actual attack by radical Sunni Islamists. Faced with this growing hostility, the Alevi community has begun to reassert itself and perhaps reverse the decline which many anthropologists had noted in recent years.

The Christian communities have from the outset been seen as suspect and potential tools of outside powers. Even though they and the Jews are still the only officially recognised minorities in Turkey, with their position and rights guaranteed by the Lausanne Treaty, they have been subjected to long-term pressures by successive Turkish administrations. Their numbers have subsequently drastically fallen as many have emigrated. In the troubled southeast, where the government forces have been fighting a bloody war with the PKK, small minority groups, Muslim and Christian, have been caught in the crossfire and have mostly emigrated.

For all of Turkey's minorities, the perception as to whether they pose a threat to the state or not is important, and directly affects both official and public attitudes towards them. Israel is not seen as a threat (except by ardent Islamists) and thus Turkey's Jews are not seen as suspect. Greeks are seen as such mainly because because both Greece and Greek Cyprus are seen as threats – both at the inter-state level and because of actions against Turkish/Muslim communities in both countries. Armenians are also seen as suspect due to the past history of competition over territory, which has seen a massive loss of life. Likewise, the Kurds are seen as a threat which, thanks to the struggle with the

---

in Istanbul. They were detained for distributing leaflets entitled 'Don't touch my friend' which read 'Regardless of his/her ethnic origin, Rum [Greek], Armenian, Kurdish, Laz, Jew, etc., everyone we share the world with is our friend. Without recognising our friends' right to existence with their own identities, we ourselves cannot exist. How happy society would be if everyone could freely state their own identity.' The leaflets were later officially banned for 'spreading separatist propaganda.' *Turkey Briefing*, vol. 8, no. 2, 1994.

PKK, directly threatens the Turkish state. Groups like the Laz and other small Muslim groups have never been seen in this way.

Popular racial or religious prejudice is often quite disconnected from power politics, but international politics do have an important influence on the attitudes of the state, as distinct from society. When the authorities condone or encourage racial or religious prejudice, then violence often ensues. In Turkey this has happened in the case of the Greeks, but, since the Second World War, only marginally with the Armenians, and virtually never with the Jews. The case of the Kurds is more complicated: in recent years the Turkish state has encouraged fierce hostility to the PKK and to the idea of Kurdish nationalism, but not hostility to Kurds as such – probably due to the large numbers of Kurds living in Turkish majority areas, as well as official attachment to the original Kemalist line of 'assimilation' of Anatolia's disparate Muslim population.

Thus, in conclusion, it is possible to state that integral Turkish nationalism has been successful in turning many disparate groups into loyal Turkish citizens imbued with integral Turkish national ideals. The integral nationalism can also be seen as successful in pressuring elements viewed as impossible to assimilate properly into the Turkish whole – that is the Orthodox Christian and Armenian communities – to leave. Thus, perceived foreign elements have been relatively successfully purged and the 'nation' purified. However, the success of integral nationalism has been qualified by the rise of a virulent Kurdish nationalism which has seriously challenged the central organs and which has seen a continuing bloody war. In addition, the increasing Sunni element in the perceived Turkish national psyche has alienated the large Alevi community, as well as alienating the secularised intellectual élites.

9

THOSE OUTSIDE: TURKEY
AS A KIN-STATE

This chapter will look at the situation of Turks outside Turkey and their relation to the 'kin-state',[1] their relationship to Turkish nationalism and their own sense of national identity. Turkey poses an interesting case of the 'kin-state'. We are immediately faced yet again with the questions of who is a Turk, which groups are regarded by Turkey as their 'kin' and which groups view Turkey as their kin-state. As we have seen, the foundation of the Turkish Republic in the 1920s on the ruins of the Ottoman Empire saw large numbers of Turkish speakers who previously had been part of the Ottoman Empire left outside the new state. Those who were Muslims naturally looked to Turkey as their kin-state. In addition, the long imperial past of the Ottoman Empire combined with the heritage of the Islamic Caliphate has resulted in many Muslims who are not ethnic Turks from the former empire, especially the Balkans, looking to Turkey as their kin-state. This is amply reflected in the huge numbers of non-Turkish-speaking Muslims who have immigrated to Turkey (and earlier to the

[1] A 'kin-state' is a state composed of and governed by a majority community, for which groups who reside outside the state's sovereign territory maintain a strong affinity as a result of shared ethnicity, culture, religion, language or perceived history. The role of the 'kin-state' has been a relatively sparsely covered topic. For further discussion see: I.D. Duchacek, *The territorial dimension of politics within, among, and across nations* (Boulder: Westview Press, 1986); I.D. Duchacek and D. Larouche (eds), *Perforated sovereignties and international relations: transsovereign contacts of sub-national governments* (New York: Greenwood Press, 1988); G. Sheffer, 'Ethno-national diasporas and security', *Survival*, vol. 36, no. 2, 1994, pp. 60-79; M. Weiner (ed.), *International migration and security* (Boulder: Westview Press, 1993), chapters 1, 2, and 10; and T. Szayna, *Ethnic conflict in central Europe and the Balkans: a framework and U.S. policy options* (Rand for US Army, 1994).

Ottoman Empire) from Russia, the Caucasus and the Balkans (see Chapter 2).

As shown in Chapters 2 and 3, the Ottoman Empire was ruled by Islamic precepts for most of its existence. In line with these, the empire was, until attempted changes beginning with the *Tanzimat* reforms in the mid-nineteenth century, divided not along ethno-linguistic lines but by religious affiliation – the *millet* system. As such, all Muslims were seen as equal first-class citizens and the élite was multi-ethnic. Until the end of the nineteenth century, the concept of being a 'Turk' as used in modern parlance was alien to the Ottoman élites, who saw themselves as Ottomans (*Osmanlı*) rather than 'Turks', a term which had the connotation of 'uneducated peasants'. The early twentieth century saw the growth of a distinct Turkish nationalism within the empire. Initially led by Turkic-speaking *émigrés* from Russia, this movement gained momentum and become important during the Young Turk regimes of 1908–18. The steady collapse of the Ottoman Empire both fuelled this movement and raised the new ideas of a union of all ethnic Turkic groups in one state – the dream of 'Turan'[2] – stretching from the Balkans to China. The First World War provided a fleeting hope that this dream could be accomplished; however, defeat for the Ottoman Empire put an end to such fantasies. The new rulers led by Mustafa Kemal (Atatürk) resolutely turned their backs on any notions of 'Turan' or expansion from the Anatolian core which was now designated as the indivisible territory of 'the Turkish nation'. But who were 'the Turkish nation'? A shown in Chapter 4, after some ambivalence Kemal (despite himself originating from Macedonia) essentially defined the Turkish nation as being constituted by the Muslim population of Anatolia. Greek Orthodox Christians were expelled *en masse* and exchanged with Muslims from Greece. Religion was the criterion. Turkish-speaking Christians were sent to Greece while non-Turkish-speaking Muslims were sent to Turkey. The Muslim community of Western Thrace and the Orthodox community in Istanbul and two islands were exempted from this population exchange.

Thus, despite the strong territorial model for Kemalist nationalism based on common citizenship (as reflected in Article

---

[2] See footnote 4 of Chapter 5.

66 of the current Constitution which states: 'Everyone bound to the Turkish state through the bond of citizenship is a Turk'), there were from the start also elements of both perceived aliens within and kin outside. The conscious policy of propagating a cohesive sense of national identity and creating a widespread national consciousness in Turkey saw a great emphasis on the ethnic Turks and their language at the expense of other groups like the Kurds, whose separate identity and language were denied. However, despite Atatürk's insistence on abandoning the dream of Turan, summed up in his slogan 'Peace at home, peace in the world', the new state-propagated nationalism strongly stressed Central Asia as the Turks' original fatherland as well as the affinity with other Turkic peoples. This has led to a retention of the sense of 'kin' in Central Asia. As illustrated by school textbooks, the potential ethnic kin of Turks is enormous.[3] Combined with this is the religious factor, which has led many Balkan Muslims who are not ethnic Turks to look to Turkey as a potential kin-state.

The collapse of the Soviet Union created hitherto unknown opportunities for contact with Turkic-speaking groups in Central Asia. Whether such relations can be seen as falling within the current topic of 'kin-states' is debatable. Certainly, the pan-Turkist currents inside and outside Turkey view the Turkic-speaking peoples of Central Asia as kin and look towards ultimate union with them. However, the long years under Soviet rule, which included the deliberate attempt at creating new nations like the Uzbeks and Turcomen, has resulted in these Turkic-speaking peoples having a separate national consciousness. Nationalism is a modern phenomenon, and modern nations can in certain circumstances be created (or similarly can disappear). Turkey sought and seeks to portray itself as a model for the Turkic republics

---

[3] For example, *Sosyal Bilgiler*, printed by the Ministry of Education, 4th ed, 1993 (300,000 copies), gives the numbers of Turks in neighbouring countries as: Greece – 150,000; Bulgaria – 1.5 million; Azerbaijan – the majority of the 7 million population ('the Azerbaijan Turks are connected to the Turks of Turkey by strong bonds'); Georgia – 500,000 'Azeri Turks'; Iran – 18 million Turks; Iraq – 1 million; Syria – 150,000; Northern Cyprus – 700,000 [sic!]; as well as the 'Turkish republics' of Kazakhstan, Uzbekistan, Turkmenistan and Kyrgyzstan and the Turks in Russia (Tatars, Bashkirs, etc.), China (Uigurs), Afghanistan and Yugoslavia. This list does not include the Christian Gaugaz Turkish-speakers, illustrating again that despite Kemal's secularism, which attempted to relegate religion to the private sphere, Islam remains a component of Turkish identity.

and watches events in the Azerbaijan-Armenian conflict with a gaze which reflects strong feelings of kinship for the Azeris.[4]

However, there is acceptance (outside pan-Turkist circles) that while there are many shared cultural values resulting from shared religious, linguistic and historical factors, the Uzbeks, for example, are a separate people from the Turks of Turkey. However, this does not appear to be the case with the Balkan communities.[5] Probably due to their being minorities within the essentially Orthodox Christian states (Albania of course is the exception), which were also remnants of the Ottoman Empire, they continue to be strongly identified on both sides as 'Turks' rather than 'Turkic' peoples. The crucial aspect here appears to be that of a minority. Where the perceived kin outside Turkey constitute a majority, and have built up or been encouraged to build up a separate national consciousness (for example the Uzbeks or the Azeris), then Turkey and Turks perceive their case differently from that of minorities – especially minorities within essentially Christian states. If they were once part of the Ottoman Empire then this is further amplified.[6] However, Muslim minorities within non-

---

[4] The fighting in Nagorno-Karabakh has aided the rise of Turkish nationalism and the fortunes of politicians like Türkeş, Erbakan and Ecevit who play the nationalist card – albeit from different perspectives. Even a 'liberal' like Mesut Yılmaz could state in a press conference that Turkey had some kind of right to protect Azerbaijan under international law (*Briefing*, no. 879, 9 March 1992). There were large-scale demonstrations throughout Turkey and TRNC (northern Cyprus) over the Nagorno-Karabakh war – see Chapter 5 for details on pan-Turkist sentiment towards Azerbaijan. There is, however, a major difference between rhetoric and actual policy (or *realpolitik*) with the latter often overriding the former.

[5] Interestingly, even ethnically non-Turkish students from the Balkans, like Albanians, appear to have less problems adapting to life in Turkey than Azeris, who, both geographically and linguistically, are the closest of the Turkic peoples to the Anatolian Turks (see below).

[6] This view was confirmed to me on 12 August 1994 by İrfan Acar, a senior official at the Turkish Foreign Ministry. Thus, not only the minorities within the Balkans (which are detailed below) fall into this category, but also the Crimean Tatars. Their leader Mustafa Abdul Cemil Karimoglu visited Turkey in February 1992 and met Demirel, who pledged support for their struggle to regain their land, which was taken from them by Stalin as punishment for alleged collaboration with the Nazis in the Second World War. Over 200,000 have returned to their ancestral homeland; almost 500,000 remain in Uzbekistan and Turkmenistan (Turkish TV, Ankara, 7 February 1992, SWB 10/2/92). In August 1994 Demirel stated that the Ukrainian government had agreed that

Muslims states are not the only kin abroad of which Turkey sees itself as a possible protector: Turkic minorities in Iraq, for example, are also felt to fall within the category.[7] Also, of late, the authorities have also come to regard the Christian Turkic people of Moldova – the Gagauz – as falling within this category.[8]

This chapter will concentrate on the communities in Cyprus and the Balkans, both ethnic Turks and other Muslims, who look to Turkey as a 'kin-state', and discuss how Turkey has responded. It will include those in former Yugoslavia and Romania, but will concentrate on those in Cyprus, Greece and Bulgaria, as these make up a 'front line' of groups looking towards the kin-state. It will also look at the situation of the large numbers of Turkish citizens who have settled in Western Europe, especially Germany, for work. They have remained there, and the Turkish Republic is constitutionally bound to take an interest in them.[9]

Turkey could provide material to build houses and other humanitarian aid to help resettle the Crimean Tatars ('Russia' TV channel, Moscow, 24 August 1994, in SWB EE/2088, B/3, 31/8/94). There are many Turkish citizens of Crimean-Tatar origin.

[7] Mosul formed part of the territory claimed in the original 'National Pact', and thus holds a special place in the national psyche. Mümtaz Soysal claims that President Özal canvassed opinion of the Turkish élite on the idea of a federal post-Gulf War Iraq in which Turkey would dominate the Turkoman and Kurdish autonomous provinces. Turkish journalists claimed that Özal was studying government documents on Turkey's claims to oil-rich Mosul; H. Pope, 'Iraq land claim behind Özal's pledge to Kurds', *The Independent* London, 28 January 1991. The Turkish press also takes an interest in the fate of Iraq's Turkic population, for example, *Hürriyet*, 23 January 1991, which reported that Baghdad had executed 25 Iraqi Turks and was pressuring Turks in Kirkuk to migrate to Kurdish regions.

[8] Demirel visited the 150,000 Christian Gagauz community in south-central Moldova during a trip in early June 1994. He underlined Turkish concern for their welfare and for that of the 30,000 or so Gagauz in Romania (mostly in Constanţa); *East European Newsletter*, vol. 8, no. 12, 1994.

[9] These are specifically referred to in the 1982 Constitution by Article 62, which states: 'The State shall take the necessary measures to ensure the family unity, the education of the children, the cultural needs, and the social security of Turkish nationals working abroad, and shall take the necessary measures to safeguard their ties with the country, and to help them on their return home.' In line with this, the Turkish state sends teachers and Imams, and pays for them to work in German schools. Islamic activists in Turkey have recently set up rival organisations in the Diaspora – a feature which is referred to below.

The remnants of the Ottoman Empire in the Balkans

Sizeable Islamic groups – both ethnically and non-ethnically Turkish – remained in all the successor states which emerged from the collapse of Ottoman rule in the Balkans. All the states of the Balkans were new, despite claims to continuity like that of Greece, which looks back to antiquity, or Bulgaria's claim to 1,300 years of existence. All had minorities within their boundaries and perceived kin outside. All tended to perceive themselves as ethnic states based on one dominant nation. They suffered from irredentism on the one hand and internal tensions between majority and minority communities on the other.[10] With the exception of Albania, all the new states were 'Christian' in character, and the presence of sizeable Muslim minorities within the new states was often seen as problematic. These minorities were often viewed as mere remnants of the Ottoman Empire which were expected to disappear.[11]

The Muslim community in Thrace, comprised mainly of ethnic Turks, Islamicised Slavs (Pomaks) and some Roma (Gypsies), remained as a unit looking to Turkey as its kin-state. In Bulgaria, despite large-scale emigration of ethnic Turks and other Muslims, which had been evident and encouraged by the authorities from the outset of the modern state in the nineteenth century, a sizeable

[10] See Hugh Poulton, 'The Rest of the Balkans' in Hugh Miall (ed.), *Minority Rights in Europe: the Scope for a Transnational Regime* (London: RIIA Pinter, 1994, pp. 66-86.

[11] This was especially noticeable in Bulgaria, where at the creation of the modern Bulgarian state ethnic Bulgarians only accounted for perhaps half the total population, with Muslims-Turks and others – accounting for a major percentage. These Muslims were from the start seen as alien and it was presumed that they would leave. Although many did, and have continued to go to the Ottoman Empire/Turkey, many remain and will remain; see W. Höpken, 'From Religious Identity to Ethnic Mobilisation: The Turks of Bulgaria before, during and since Communism', in Hugh Poulton and Suha Taji-Farouki (eds), *Muslim Identity and the Balkan State* (London: Hurst, 1997). A partial exception to this was in Bosnia-Hercegovina, where the Muslim Slav community has remained a major component. Until the recent tragic events it had shown great skill in coming to terms with whatever power controlled the territory – whether it be Austria-Hungary (1878-1918), Royalist Yugoslavia (1918-41) or Communist Yugoslavia (from 1945 to the demise of the old Yugoslav state). See R.J. Donia and J.V.A. Fine, *Bosnia and Hercegovina: A Tradition Betrayed* (London: Hurst, 1994), *passim*.

ethnic Turkish Muslim community remained, as did other Muslim groups. Similarly, in what become Yugoslavia, sizeable Turkish-speaking Muslim groups remained along with other Muslims – most notably in Bosnia. Although an Albanian state had emerged from the Ottoman Empire, many of Yugoslavia's Muslim Albanians saw Turkey as their kin-state instead of Albania, and they moved there taking advantage of emigration agreements between Yugoslavia and Turkey. This was helped by Enver Hoxha's post-war fortress mentality and militant atheism.[12] Similarly, many Slav Muslims from Yugoslavia emigrated to Turkey. While such groups quickly and voluntarily assimilated into the Turkish majority in Turkey,[13] the scale of their numbers has led to feelings of kinship with fellow group members who remained in the Balkans (as is the case of groups originating from the Caucasus who came to Turkey). The religious link derived from the *millet* system lives on, as illustrated by Turkey's reactions to the Bosnian conflict.[14] On the fringes of the Balkans in Romania some 80,000 Turks and Tatars also remain.

Except in the case of Cyprus, Turkish policy towards these groups has mainly been characterised by caution, in line with Atatürk's dictum of 'peace at home, peace in the world', which is still referred to in the preamble to the 1982 Constitution. The

---

[12] See H. Poulton, *The Balkans: Minorities and States in Conflict* (London: MRG Publications, 1993), p. 92. Much of the information in this chapter is based on the authors first-hand research contained in this publication.

[13] See Chapter 8.

[14] An example of this 'solidarity' was the conference on Bosnia-Hercegovina in Ankara on 20-23 October 1994. This included speeches from leading dignitaries and high officials from Sarajevo and Turkey, and began with a recitation of the Koran followed by the Bosnian and Turkish national anthems. More concretely, it was announced by the former Turkish Chief of General Staff, General Doğan Güreş, that Turkey had been breaking the UN arms embargo on former Yugoslavia by supplying arms to the beleaguered Bosnian government (BBC World Service, 4 December 1994). These allegations receved only 'lukewarm' denials, see *The Independent*, London, 6 December 1994. Similarly, Sandžak Muslim politicians in opposition to Belgrade held a widely publicised meeting in Ankara on 27-30 July 1994. During the conflict, the official Turkish role in Bosnia-Hercegovina was restricted to the contribution of a detachment of 1,500 troops to UNPROFOR (the United Nations force there), and participation in the NATO air detachment based in Italy which enforced the no-fly zone. Turkish ground forces are also expected to participate in the enlarged NATO peace keeping force after the Dayton treaty of December 1995.

general line was that although emigration was allowed at various times, and Turkey should remain as a potential home for kin-groups if times were extremely hard, it would be better if they remained as citizens of their respective countries and acted as a link to Turkey.[15] It is possible that military circles in Turkey also viewed the Turkish minorities – especially those in southern Bulgaria and Western Thrace – as potential buffers which could be militarily useful.[16] Until the last ten years or so, while Turkish public opinion was influential at times – especially during the campaign against ethnic Turks in Bulgaria in the late 1980s (see below) – the only effective determinant on the Turkish side was the official line. The growth of Islamic movements within Turkey and the new possibilities afforded by the collapse of the cold-war blocs has to some extent changed this. Official policy has varied according to changing conditions.

Cyprus

In Cyprus, Turkey was guarantor power, and public opinion in Turkey was outraged at what were perceived as Greek threats against the Turkish population on the island during the 1960s.[17] Finally, in 1974, using Article 4 of the Cyprus Treaty of Guarantee as a justification for unilateral intervention, the Ecevit government sent the Turkish army in and effected massive population transfers. This had massive popular backing in Turkey. The invasion eventually resulted in the setting up in 1983 of the ethnically

[15] The two sides of this policy were well illustrated by reactions to the riots in Komotini in early 1990 (see below): Foreign Minister Mesut Yılmaz argued that ethnic Turks should stay in the country of their residence while being granted full citizenship rights, with Ankara helping to protect their interests; Prime Minister Akbulut said Turkey's borders were open and invited the ethnic Turks from Greece to come to Turkey and 'share our soup' (*Mideast Mirror*, 20 February 1990).

[16] A Turkish observer at the BBC, when mentioning this to the author in 1989, poured scorn on such thinking. Nonetheless, the events in the Yugoslav war, where the JNA/Serb army performed badly in areas where Serbs were not present (especially Slovenia) as compared to those where they were able to operate in tandem with local Serbs, have shown that such an 'old fashioned' military view does have some substance.

[17] See Frank Tachau, 'The Face of Turkish Nationalism (as Reflected in the Cyprus Dispute),', *Middle East Journal*, vol. 13, 1959, pp. 262-72.

homogeneous 'Turkish Republic of Northern Cyprus' (TRNC), which is unrecognised by the international community. Since then a number of Turks from Turkey have moved to the area, while a large number of Turkish troops are stationed there to protect the TRNC.[18] This action ran counter to Turkey's general foreign policy and gave rise to fears, especially in Greece, of similar action in areas like Western Thrace.[19]

Cyprus has remained partitioned, and despite repeated efforts by the international community there has been little progress towards a settlement. In June 1994, former Prime Minister Ecevit suggested that the TRNC be internally autonomous but integrated with Turkey for matters of defence and foreign policy. This view was supported by TRNC leader Rauf Denktaş.[20] Mümtaz Soysal, who became Turkish Foreign Minister in August 1994, besides being an advisor to TRNC President Denktaş and something of a 'nationalist hawk', also moved closer to this line. On a visit to the TRNC in August 1994 he backed the TRNC rejection of a federalist solution. While ruling out formal annexation or

---

[18] The figures remain contentious. While the 1992 census gave the TRNC total population as 176, 127, there were and are no official figures for immigrants from Turkey. Greek Cypriots claim there are 60-70,000, while Turkish sources say 15-16,000. Turkish newspapers say there are 46,000. In view of these differing figures a safe estimate is perhaps 30,000. The forced population transfers of 1974 saw some 180,000 Greek-speaking Cypriots flee the north, while some 60,000 Turkish-speaking Cypriots moved there from the south. For further details see Behrooz Morvaridi, 'Demographic Change, Resettlement and Resource use' in C.H. Dodd (ed.), *The Political Social and Economic Development of Northern Cyprus* (Huntingdon: Eothen Press, 1993). In 1988 the UN stated that there were 29,000 Turkish soldiers in the TRNC, but TRNC leader Denktaş claimed the actual figure was 21-22,000; see A. Foreman in *The Guardian*, 10 June 1988, who also alleged that the Turkish Cypriots had grown weary of the special ties with Turkey and looked forward to reunification. According to Foreman, there was little contact between the two communities – '... [the mainland Turks] have little in common with us. ... They're Asians; they don't know our European way of life.' While the standard of living is far higher in the south, and there are differences between the two groups (for instance mainlanders ten to look down on Cypriots as descendants of those sent there by the Sultans), other observers contradict this view.

[19] Huge billboards in Western Thrace showed a bleeding partitioned Cyprus with appropriate captions for both domestic and foreign consumption.

[20] *Briefing*, 5 October 1994, no. 1,005, Ankara.

unification, he nevertheless referred to 'autonomous ties'.[21] These statements were backed by the Turkish Foreign Ministry and the Turkish Ministry of National Defence, which stated that: 'South Cyprus has moved to integrate with Greece. Naturally, the Turkish Cypriots wish to establish similar co-operation and integration with Turkey.' It appeared that Soysal, whose appointment heralded a more aggressive approach by Turkey in foreign policy issues, had cleared this policy with both Prime Minister Çiller and President Demirel, despite objections from Western ambassadors.[22] The Islamic Welfare Party (RP), which has made spectacular gains in Turkey in recent years, adopted a yet more aggressive stance and called for outright annexation.[23] Soysal resigned at the end of November 1994, apparently due to intense disagreements with Çiller on a number of issues. He was replaced by Deputy Prime Minister Murat Karayalçın, who appeared less nationalistic than his predecessor. But while Ankara reverted to a more cautious role, the annexation of the TRNC continued to be threatened by Turkey if Cyprus joined the European Union before a settlement on Cyprus had been agreed by Turkey and the TRNC.[24] It is worth noting that TRNC politicians like Denktaş enjoy considerable influence in Ankara: for example, Denktaş has made several addresses to the Turkish parliament to rapturous approval. This illustrates that in spite of reports of alienation between the two communities mentioned earlier, there remains a strong feeling of 'kin-ship' among Turks in Turkey towards Cypriot Turks.

Greece

The Muslim community in Western Thrace amply illustrates the problems of trying to differentiate groups who look to Turkey

[21] Radio Bayrak Lefkoşa (Nicosia), and Anatolia Agency, Ankara, 31 August 1994, in SWB EE/2090, B/4, 2/9/94.

[22] See *Hürriyet*, Istanbul, 31 August 1994.

[23] RP Secretary-General Asıltürk said that the TRNC decision to withdraw from negotiations must be supported and the TRNC must be annexed to Turkey. He argued that Southern Cyprus will be annexed by Greece; in the case of any confrontation between the TRNC and the south the TRNC would be faced by Greece and the entire EU, and Turkey would lose its status as guarantor TRT TV, Ankara, 30 August 1994 in SWB EE/2089, B/6, 1/9/94).

[24] See *Turkey Briefing*, vol. 9, no. 1, 1995.

as a kin-state by ethnicity or religion alone. In the population exchanges in the 1920s, religion rather than ethnicity or language was the criterion. As a result, many Muslim Slavs (Pomaks) and Roma (Gypsies) went to Turkey. However, those in Western Thrace remained, especially in villages in the Rhodope mountains. Since the 1920s there has been a steady and continuing emigration of Turkish speakers to Turkey, in which some 250,000 have left. A result of this has been that while the number of 'Muslims' in Western Thrace has remained fairly consistent at about 120,000, the share of Turkish speakers as opposed to Bulgarian speakers (Pomaks) has declined. In the 1920s perhaps 10 per cent were Pomaks, while their share is now estimated to be about 25 per cent, or 30,000 people.

The rights of the Muslim community of Western Thrace continue in theory to be guaranteed under Article 45 of the Lausanne Treaty of 24 July 1923. As such, Turkey has seen itself as having some say over the community affairs – more than, for example, in Bulgaria where no such specific treaty exists, but less than Cyprus, where Turkey was a guarantor power. In the initial post-treaty period, a number of anti-Kemalist Turks, predominantly religious leaders, moved to Western Thrace. However, Greece bowed to Turkish pressure and eventually expelled some 150 religious conservatives.

In the initial post-war period there was a rare rapprochement between Greece and Turkey, the traditional enemy, then seen as an ally in NATO against what was perceived as a more serious threat from communist Bulgaria. It was feared that the latter might try to use the Bulgarian-speaking Pomaks as a fifth column. As a result, the Pomaks were actively encouraged to become Turks and compulsory Turkish education was introduced for them. However, the authorities soon reverted to their traditional anti-Turkish line and denial of any ethnic minorities within Greece. In recent times they have gone so far as to prosecute those who try to organise on an explicit Turkish platform even if they are members of parliament.[25] Worried at the rise of ethnic Turkish assertiveness in the region, which has seen serious intercommunal

---

[25] For example, the prosecutions of Sadik Ahmet and İbrahim Şerif. Greece remains obdurate in its denial of any minorities within the country except religious ones.

rioting, the Greek authorities now appear to be trying to reverse this.[26]

A slight relaxation of some of the more petty measures against the Muslim population has occurred. This upturn appears to be the result of an agreement in January 1990 between Prime Minister Mitsotakis and opposition leader Andreas Papandreou shortly after the initial disturbances in Komotini. This agreement foresaw an economic improvement in the area with some concessions to the minority, along with a greater state presence and the settlement of Greeks from the former USSR to strengthen the Greek presence.[27] The agreement also included attempts to split the Muslim community into its component parts and divide the Pomaks and Roma from the ethnic Turks. This policy, which has included attempts to portray the Pomaks as the pre-Slav inhabitants of Thrace who, as such, are 'closer' to the Greeks than the Turks,[28] has been an abject failure. The Pomak community continues to

---

[26] Signs of this assertiveness are the reported statements by the former müftü of Xanthi that 'Muslim Turks ... in Western Thrace are autonomous' (on 21 January 1982) and on 16 December 1983 'the declaration of the Turkish Republic of Northern Cyprus for us means that one more star has been added to the Islamic flag'. His son, Aga Mehmet, a local Turkish politician, reportedly said on 12 March 1984 that if Greece was not able to solve the minority's problem 'we will resort to the mother country Turkey in order to give a satisfactory solution.' All quotes from A. Alexandris, 'Political Expediency and Human Rights: Minority Issues between Greece and Turkey', paper given at the conference' Minority Rights – Policies and Practice in South-East Europe' (Copenhagen, 30 March-April 1990, p. 9).

[27] 'Nea politiki gia tous mousoulmanous', *Eleiferotipia*, Athens, 2 March 1990. I am indebted to R. Meinardus of *Deutsche Welle* for this information. Greek Foreign Minister Andonios Samaras said in 1989 that till then some 5,000 Pontic Greeks had been settled and that the number would increase in 1990 (Greek Radio, Athens, 18 December 1989). However, others claim that these immigrants from the USSR are often shocked at conditions in Western Thrace and do not settle there easily (personal communications) – raising similar issues of kin and Greece as a kin-state.

[28] Attempts to 'prove' this particular thesis has even followed lines reminiscent of Nazi Germany's, with Greek attempts to show that the Pomaks have (literally) Greek rather than Turkish blood. See N.I. Xirotiri *Findings on the Classification of the Frequency of Blood Groups Among Pomaks* (Ph. D. Thesis, Thessalonika, 1971), and P. Hidiroglou, *Hellenic Pomaks and their Relations with Turkey* (Athens: Hirodotos Publications, 2nd ed, 1989) pp. 15-16. Both these works are in Greek and I am indebted to Baskın Oran for this information.

strongly identify itself with the Turkish community and is in the process of becoming solidly Turkicised.[29]

A consistent feature in the relations between Greece and Turkey and the Muslims of Western Thrace has been the Greek government's policy since the early 1960s of reciprocating treatment meted out by the Turkish authorities against Greeks who remained in Istanbul under the Lausanne Treaty. This community has drastically declined in numbers in the face of the Turkish government's similar policies of denial and distrust of minorities.[30] Thus, the legacy of the homogeneous nation-state ideology has severely hampered relations between the two countries. In 1964 the Greek government implemented a secret decision to hinder the purchase of land by Turks in retaliation to the forcing out of ethnic Greeks living in Istanbul.[31] This policy of reciprocation became open during the Colonels' regime from 1967 to 1974.

While the Muslims complain of a number of repressive measures,[32] for the purposes of our discussion the education system in crucial, due to its role in propagating shared cultural values. In 1968 a special teacher training centre for Turks was set up in Thessalonika, whereas before teachers had come from Turkey. The Greek authorities appear to have tried to keep contacts with the kin-state as limited as possible. One aspect of this is the insistence on calling them 'Muslims', not 'Turks'. The training of 'native' teachers, who, the Turks claim, teach an outdated backward curriculum with little contact with developments in Turkey, appears to have been a key part of this. Despite the 1968 Greek-Turkish protocol on education, severe problems of adequate textbooks for the Turks in Western Thrace remain, with accusations that the Greek authorities deliberately hold back books sent from Turkey.[33] The implementation in 1985 of the

[29] It is noticeable that older Pomaks, especially women, speak Bulgarian, but more and more young Pomaks, while able to freely understand Bulgarian, speak Turkish as their first language. For more information on the Pomaks in Greece see *The Pomaks of Greece* [forthcoming report by Euromosaic, Barcelona].

[30] Initially some 100,000, there were less than 10,000 by 1974, and the figure has declined further since – see Chapter 7.

[31] I am indebted to R. Meinardus of *Deutsche Welle* for this information.

[32] See Poulton, *Balkans*, pp. 182-8.

[33] This was reiterated by Turkish Foreign Minister spokeswoman Filiz Dincmen (Turkish TV, Ankara, 1 February 1993 in SWB ME/1604, C/1, 4/2/93)

May 1984 law that the entrance exams to the two secondary
Turkish minority schools in Komotini and Xanthi – there are some
300 primary schools – as well as graduation exams have to be in
Greek resulted in a dramatic decline in numbers of pupils from
227 in Xanthi and 305 in Komotini in 1983-4, to 85 and 42
respectively in 1986-7.

A recent development came in the nationwide municipal elections in Greece on 16 October 1994, when nomarchs or prefects
were elected for the first time as a gradual step in the devolution
of power from the centre. However, whereas in the rest of the
country (save the capital Athens) each prefecture elected one
nomarch, in Thrace (and Athens) there will be 'super nomarchs'
who will preside over the activities of local ones. Thus, the three
prefectures of Western Thrace (where the ethnic Turks
predominate) and the two of Eastern Thrace (where the Pomaks
predominate) will be subordinated to a supernomarch.[34] While
the authorities claim that this structure is established in Thrace
due to the need to co-ordinate badly needed development policy,
it appears rather to illustrate their distrust of the Muslim population.

The Turkish authorities responded to the deterioration of the
situation and corresponding rise in inter-communal tension in
Western Thrace with the traditional openings for those who wanted
to leave. Like the local leaders, the Turkish authorities view the
Pomaks as Turks.[35] They also attempted, by the use of textbooks,
to integrate the education of the minority into that of mainstream
Turkish education.[36] However, this has remained blocked. On

---

[34] Following adverse press comment on this move, the Greek authorities claimed
that supernomarchs were to be introduced all over the country and not just in
Thrace and Athens. However, it appears that the only other area where this
was to happen was in the Aegean, where a group of islands were to have an
assembly of nomarchs. I am indebted to Robert McDonald of The Economist
Intelligence Unit (London) for this information.

[35] Interestingly, the Muslim Roma appear to be seen as different and looked
down upon by all groups. While the Pomaks tended to be seen as lower than
the ethnic Turks, there was and is intermarriage between them, especially in
mixed areas north and northwest of Komotini. Intermarriage by either group
with Roma appears to be almost non-existent. Despite the common bond of
Islam, which is so strong, the stigma against Roma appears to be stronger.

[36] For a full discussion on history textbooks in Greece and Turkey see Hercules
Millas, 'History Textbooks in Greece and Turkey', *History Workshop*, Spring
1991, pp 21-33.

the other hand, the traditional policy of caution has been evident, and there were reports that the Özal government viewed the pre-eminence of Sadik Ahmet among the Muslims of Western Thrace, and the general rise in tension there, with some alarm, even contemplating a deal with then Greek Prime Minister Mitsotakis to remove Ahmet from the political scene.[37]

Tensions between the two countries again rose in early 1995 when the elected Xanthi mufti, Mehmet Emin Aga, was sentenced to ten months' imprisonment by the Larissa court for usurping the title of mufti. This drew sharp criticism from Turkey. The Turkish Foreign Ministry accused the Greek authorities of hindering the Xanthi and Komotini muftis in performing their duties, despite their being elected by the community as laid down by the 1913 Athens agreement and the 1923 Lausanne Treaty. Foreign Minister Karayalçın warned that, unless he was immediately released, Turkey would 'take steps' over this issue.[38]

Bulgaria

In Bulgaria, emigration of Turks to Turkey continued in the inter-war period. During the 1920s and 1930s, Turkish schools, especially primary schools, were closed. The advent of dictatorship in 1934 saw a further deterioration, with bans on the use of the new Latin script and the reinstatement of the Arabic script for all Turkish publications. This was an apparent attempt to dissuade mother-tongue expression – the Arabic script being both difficult to learn and inappropriate for Turkish – and to hinder links with Atatürk's Turkey. The latter had changed its script, and did not actively portray itself as a protector of ethnic Turkish minorities outside the country, being preoccupied with nation-building within the new state.

The post-war period saw a change. The traditional pattern of emigration to Turkey resumed in 1950-1. However, beginning in the 1950s, the Zhivkov regime, over a long period, pursued a repressive forced assimilatory policy, which was progressively applied to all the country's major minority populations with the

---

[37] *Dateline*, (London), 28 October 1989. Ahmet died in a car crash on 24 July 1995.

[38] TRT TV, Ankara, 24 January 1995, in SWB EE/2211, B/1, 26/1/95.

exceptions, for propaganda reasons, of the small Jewish and Armenian minorities. This policy came to a head with the massive violent campaign against the ethnic Turkish minority – some 10 per cent of the population – in late 1984. The Turkish state and public reacted with outrage. Mass rallies were allowed for the first time since the military coup. Huge crowds filled Taksim Square in Istanbul and cheered Özal's empty threats of marching on Sofia. More concretely, Turkey declared willingness to open her borders. In 1989 the Zhivkov regime, panicking at the rising tide of organised discontent among the Turks, allowed them to leave. Some 300,000 fled the country, of whom half subsequently returned.[39] On arrival in Turkey they were issued with refugee cards valid for one year. After this they were able, if they so wished, to acquire Turkish nationality and enjoy the same rights as Turkish citizens, including the right to vote. This accelerated procedure was made possible only due to the Turkish Parliament's adopting amendments to the existing nationality legislation, showing the strength of feeling for these 'fellow Turks'.[40]

In contrast to much of the Balkans, post-Zhivkov Bulgaria has, in the main, remained a beacon of hope in the field of inter-ethnic relations (excepting those relating to Roma). In the October 1991 elections the ethnic Turkish party, the Movement For Rights and Freedoms (DPS) gained twenty-four members of parliament, over 650 village mayors, 1,000 councillors and twenty municipal mayors. It held the balance of power between the former communists and the Union of Democratic Forces (SDS).

---

[39] The emotional response of Turks to these events is well illustrated by Bilal Şimşir, author and diplomat, who wrote: 'They [the Bulgarian Turks] were taken to Bulgaria from Anatolia, now they want to return there, where most of their close relatives have already returned. It is their right to return to Anatolia. And it is Turkey's duty to make this return possible by accepting all the Turks in Bulgaria; it is a historical duty, a contractual duty, a duty owed to Turkishness, and a humanitarian duty. The Turk in Bulgaria suffered a lot in the hands of the Bulgarian. Let this suffering end.' B. Şimşir, *The Turks of Bulgaria (1878-1985)* (London: K. Rüstem, 1988), p. 316. More widespread reactions were the mass rallies in Istanbul and Bursa led by the BAL-GÖÇ emigrant associations, at one of which then Prime Minister Özal threatened action similar to that taken by Turkey in Cyprus in 1974; Poulton, *Balkans*, p. 161.

[40] *Council of Europe Provisional Report on the reception and resettlement of refugees in Turkey* ADOC6267. PROV 1403-10/7/90-2-3. 12 July 1990, para 17 p. 10.

As such, the DPS has played a crucial role in supporting various governments, both inside and outside formal coalitions.

However, despite the return of perhaps half of the original great exodus of 1989, emigration to Turkey continued, spurred on by a severe decline in the economy of many minority regions, especially tobacco-growing ones in the south. Again, the question of 'who is Turk' cropped up, as the Bulgarian Pomak community is experiencing similar pressures to the Pomaks in Greece. The cold war period resulted in the militarisation of the mountainous frontier region inhabited by the two communities, and severe limitations on their freedom of movement. As a result, these communities continued to uphold patterns of pre-modern traditional society, where the modern notion of belonging to a national group is not as strong as that of belonging to a religious community. Since the end of the cold war this has been changing. Whereas in Greece the entire Pomak community appears to be becoming rapidly Turkicised, in Bulgaria, where the Pomaks' mother tongue is that of the majority (that is, Bulgarian), the Pomaks are mainly identifying as Bulgarians, with a minority declaring themselves to be Turks and demanding Turkish education for their children. In early 1990 the Turkish Embassy in Sofia was giving out about 6,000 visas a month; the criterion for obtaining one was the ability to speak Turkish, although in rare cases the consulate did give visas to Pomaks if it was convinced that the person in question was so determined to emigrate that he or she would come to Turkey via another country if necessary. It seems that the ethnic Turks were experiencing a country-to-town shift similar to the Slav Bulgarians in the 1950s and 60s. However, now, with the greater freedom of movement internationally, they were choosing if possible to move to cities in Turkey rather than to Bulgarian ones like Sofia.

In October 1992 Turkey announced tougher immigration measures to try to stem the flood.[41] In 1993 people were allowed to emigrate to Turkey in only some 70–80 cases of divided families.[42] Many continued to come on tourist visas, and the societies for emigrants from the Balkans petitioned the Turkish government to allow children of these 'tourists' (many of whom came to stay)

---

[41] BTA, 28 September 1992 in SWB EE/1499, i, 30/9/92
[42] Figures from Turkish Foreign Ministry, August 1994.

to attend Turkish schools. Agreement with the Turkish Education Ministry on this was reported in September 1993.[43] However, in December 1993 this was reversed.[44]

The DPS is currently faced with serious problems of splits and erosion of support, due in part to emigration and in part to its having supported unpopular economic policies in the last coalition government. It seemed possible that in the late 1994 elections the DPS would not even clear the 4 per cent electoral hurdle, and hence would not be represented in parliament. This could have led to radicalisation among Turks and possibly a deterioration in inter-communal relations. However, in the event the DPS won 5.4 per cent of the vote, which translated into fifteen seats in parliament.[45]

The Balkans generally

The Ottoman legacy has resulted in affinity between Turkey and many non-Turkish Muslims groups in the Balkans. The presence of large Muslim minorities in Bulgaria and the Former Yugoslav Republic of Macedonia (FYROM), as well as the fact that the majority of ethnic Albanians are Muslims, has led to a belt of Turkish influence extending across the south-central Balkans. The concrete expression of this is the proposed East-West Balkan route – the new *Via Egnatia* – linking Dürres, Skopje, Sofia and Istanbul.[46] This sphere of influence extends northwards through the Serbo-

---

[43] *Bizim İnegöl*, İnegöl, 17 September 1993.

[44] Personal communication from Professor Mustafa Kahramanyol, advisor on Balkan affairs to Turkish Prime Minister Tansu Çiller.

[45] Despite its past record of partnership in coalition governments, the DPS's possible participation in a cabinet led by Zhan Videnov of the BSP – the Bulgarian Socialist (formerly Communist) Party – seemed unlikely, due to the nomination of Ilcho Dimitrov as Minister of Education, Science and Technology. He had been Minister of Education and chair of the co-ordinating committee on the 'rebirth process' – the official euphemism for the brutal forced assimilation of the ethnic Turks by the Zhivkov regime – operating with the Bulgarian Academy of Sciences in 1986-9 (*BTA*, Sofia, 24 January 1995, in SWB EE/2211, B/1, 26/1/95).

[46] A protocol between Albania, Macedonia and Bulgaria over this road-rail link was signed with Turkey and Italy on 9 May 1993 (*BTA*, Sofia, 10 May 1993 in SWB EE/WO282, A/9, 20/5/93). Also see H. Poulton, *Who Are The Macedonians?* (London: Hurst, 1995) p. 198.

Croat-speaking Muslims of the Sandžak and on to the Muslim Bosnians. Another expression of this is the setting up under the Turkish aegis of schools in various Balkan countries. While there are at present no schools sponsored directly by the Turkish government, there is a religious school in Skopje, as well as three in Bulgaria (Sofia, Shumen and Momchilgrad) and one each in Albania and Romania. These are sponsored by private foundations in Turkey.[47]

This raises the question of 'kin-state' actors. Until recently, the main actor was the Turkish government, with a subsidiary role played by emigrant associations concentrated mainly in Istanbul and Bursa. However, these latter have tended to be short of money as well as political muscle. Recently, the growth of Islamic groups which have taken great advantage of the opportunities opened up by Özal's privatisation has added another factor. Well financed and politically emerging Islamic groups are now major 'kin-state' actors with their own agenda, which is often at odds with the government line.[48] There are indications that the Turkish government is likewise wary of a growth of Islamic Turkism which it cannot control in the Balkans.

As well as these schools in the Balkans financed by Turkish private foundations – whether Islamic organisations or not – there have in the last three years been a number of stipends paid by the authorities for students from the Balkans to come to study in Turkey. This was set up by Demirel, and students from Bos-

---

[47] Information from Kahramanyol, September 1994. Correspondingly, in Central Asia there are 55 such schools; figures from Turkish Foreign Ministry August 1994.

[48] 'The government line' here applies more to the traditional Kemalist view, although it can be argued that Islamic penetration into Key ministries in the 1980s has seen this 'traditional' approach radically altered; see Chapter 6. Despite this, there remains a sizeable difference between the aims of the Turkish government, and for example, those of the powerful *Zaman* group, which propagates its distinctly Islamic vision to perceived 'kin' outside Turkey in Europe and Central Asia. *Zaman* publishes daily in Azerbaijan and Bulgaria, and is distributed free of charge; E. Gökalp of TDN in *Mideast Mirror*, 1 March 1993. Gökalp also details the plethora of private Islamic radio stations and the like. These unauthorised broadcasting companies operate widely in Bulgaria, and the Bulgarian government has repeatedly sought a solution to these Turkish radio and TV broadcasts; see *BTA*, Sofia 7 September 1994 in SWB EE/2097, B/3, 10/9/94.

nia-Hercegovina, Greece, Bulgaria, Macedonia, and rump Yugoslavia (FRY), have entered various levels of the Turkish education system. In all, in the three years since the programme began, there have been 300 students at religious schools, 250 in high schools and technical high schools, 12,000 at universities and 20 postgraduates. Students have also come to theological schools. For students from Bosnia-Hercegovina, the Bosnian government decides who is to come, but for the others the local community organisations decide.[49] As it is estimated that there are 2 million descendants of Slav Muslims from the Balkans living in Turkey, a number of refugees from the Bosnian tragedy have come to Turkey. Officially there are 7,000, with estimates of up to 30,000, as many more are staying with relatives and have not registered. The Turkish government is attempting to continue with the education of Bosnian refugee children in their own language.

The Turkish Gastarbeiter of Germany and other West European states

The conflict for control over the 'hearts and minds' of the 'Outer Turks' between the Kemalist bureaucracy and the new Islamic challengers is especially noticeable among the Turks in Western Europe. By far the largest number, about 2 million, live in Germany, and the Turkish community there is arguably the most important of such groups of Turkish citizens abroad. There have been a number of studies of this and other Turkish 'guestworker' communities abroad.[50] All these studies look at the problems of national

---

[49] Information from Kahramanyol, who interestingly points out that these students have had less problems in adapting to life in Turkey than the 7,000 or so who have similarly come from the Turkic Central Asian republics.

[50] For example see: İ. Boşgöz and N. Furniss (eds), *Turkish Workers in Europe: An Interdisciplinary Study* (Indiana University Turkish Studies, 1985); P. Antes and K. Kreiser, *Muslims in Germany – German Muslims? Questions of Identity*, Muslims in Europe, Research paper No. 28 (Birmingham: Centre for the Study of Islam and Christian Muslim Relations, Selly Oak Colleges, December 1985), and by the same publisher, J. Slomp, G. Speelman and W. de Wit, *Muslims in the Netherlands* (Muslims in Europe, Research Paper No. 37, March 1988); S. Köksal, 'A Ghetto in a Welfare Society: Turks in Rinkeby', and R. Kastoryano, 'Ethnic Differentiation in France: Turks and Muslims', both in M. Kiray (ed.), *Structural Change in Turkish Society* (Indiana, Indiana University Press, 1991); Y. Soysal, 'Workers in Europe: Interactions with the host society', in M. Heper,

identity of the Turkish guestworkers when they settle permanently in the host country. This is especially problematic in Germany – the classic model for 'ethnic' nationalism – as the state jealously guards what it considers as 'pure' German culture from perceived alien penetration.[51] It is further amplified in the cases of children born in Germany (or in other host countries) of Turkish parents residing there.[52] Half of the Turks in Germany have lived there for almost twenty years. Unlike other immigrant groups (Spaniards, Greeks, etc.), they show little sign of wanting to return to their original homeland.[53] Studies confirm that while Islam is of crucial importance to Turkish immigrants in retaining their 'otherness' in host countries, there is little inter-Islamic solidarity with other Muslim groups.[54] For Turks abroad, Islam is primarily a badge of their Turkish national identity. Despite this, there appeared to be little sign that either first generation or second generation Turks would take advantage of opportunities for naturalisation.[55] It would appear that for the Turks, giving up their 'Turkishness' and completely adopting German culture was and remains a block.

A. Öncü and H. Kramer (eds), *Turkey and the West* (London: I.B. Tauris, 1993). See also N. Landman, 'The Role of the Diyanet in West Europe: Turkish Ethnicity versus European Nationality', in H. Poulton and S. Taji-Farouki (eds), *Muslim Identity and the Balkan State* (London: Hurst, 1997).

[51] This was clearly spelt out in October 1994 at a meeting of experts at the CSCE High Commission for Minorities in the Hague on matters relating to the concept of the 'kin-state' in Europe, by Rolf Gossman, head of the German federal body overseeing immigration matters. He confirmed that immigrants are only accepted if they abandon their own cultures and wholeheartedly accept 'German' Culture. As a result, Germany has so far refused Turkey's attempts to introduce dual citizenship for Turkish guestworkers who have settled in Germany. (Another aspect of this is that it seems likely that if dual citizenship was given to the Turks, they would probably not vote for the ruling Christian Democratic Union).

[52] See especially N. Abandon-Unat, 'Identity Crisis of Turkish Migrants: First and Second Generation' in Başgöz and Furniss, *op . cit.*

[53] A survey conducted by the Federal Ministry for Employment and Social Services showed that 40% of all Turks in Germany want to stay there – Antes and Kreiser, *op. cit.*, p. 14.

[54] E.g. 'Turks in France, despite some Islamic solidarity, assert their national-religious identity in a Turkish Islam that differentiates them from other immigrant groups in France' – R. Kastoryano, *op. cit.*, p. 112. See also references in footnote 50.

[55] *Ibid.*

However, this remains a complex issue. Some who are born in Germany are losing their Turkish identity, but others – especially those who are deliberately taken to stay for lengths of time in Turkey – are not. If the latter remain too long outside the 'mother country' the problems of fully re-integrating into Turkish culture in Turkey become greater.[56]

A crucial development in the strengthening of Turkish identity in Germany has been the rise of radical German nationalism and consequent attacks on immigrants, most notably the firebomb attacks on Turkish hostels in Moen and Solingen in November 1992 and April 1993 respectively. As noted in Chapter 1, nationalisms often thrive in situations where they are faced with a virulently hostile rival nationalism. Following these outrages, numbers of Turks took to the streets of Germany chanting slogans like '*Turkey Turkey über alles*' and 'Allah is great', and a number of clashes occurred between Turks and Germans.[57]

Of course many of these immigrants are not ethnically Turkish but of Kurdish origin, and many of these are politically active Kurdish nationalists who are unable to operate openly in Turkey itself. There are perhaps 400,000 Kurds from Turkey in Germany, of whom it is estimated that over 90 per cent either support or are intimidated into supporting the PKK.[58] Similarly, in Britain, the main Turkish centre in London the *Halk Evi* in Stoke Newington – was taken over by PKK militants in the late 1980s.[59]

---

[56] Typically, such people are described as 'not knowing how to behave the way Turks should' as well as not being fully conversant with the language – T. Mansell, 'The Turkish Diaspora', BBC World Service, 31 October 1994.

[57] *Ibid.*

[58] *Ibid.* The German federal internal security service gave a lower figure in its mid-1993 report, which stated that: 'Of the 1.8 million Turks and Kurds living in Germany, only 34,000 are members of political or ideological organisations. Some 5,000 are believed to be followers of the PKK. Another 6,700 count as Turkish nationalists, including Grey Wolves, while fewer than 5,000 are leftist, extremists. As many as 17,000 belong to Turkish Islamic groups.' – quoted in *İnfo-Türk*, E.200 – 10, June 1993. However these figures relate only to activists and do not count the large numbers of passive supporters.

[59] Personal communication from a then worker at the *Halk Evi*. It is interesting to note that in the British case there was a large influx of politically active Kurdish militants from Turkey in the late 1980s, along with other Turks from Turkey, mainland immigrants replacing those from Cyprus as the largest component of London's Turkish community. Many (perhaps most) of these

In Germany there have been rival demonstrations between Kurds and Turks over the treatment of Kurds in Turkey.[60] In common with other groups, nationalism appears to be strong in the Kurdish diaspora and the conflict within Turkey is mirrored outside. The 'massacres in Kurdistan' appear to be playing a crucial role in reinforcing Kurdish identity among Turkey's Kurds abroad.[61] While this can perhaps be over-stressed, there does appear to be a difference between the greater solidarity and political activism of the Kurds abroad compared with the Turks.[62]

The 'communications revolution' has also had profound effects. On the one hand it has meant that a country like Greece or Bulgaria is no longer able to isolate itself from the outside world and pursue policies of forced assimilation against minorities, which include Turks and other Muslims. On the other hand, Turkish citizens in Western Europe can now easily tune into domestic Turkish television.[63] This has greatly aided a retention of national identity. For men, especially, the role of football, supporting Turkish football teams and watching the matches on television, plays an important role.[64] This again shows how the 'global revolution', far from

---

new arrivals were 'illegal' immigrants. Especially interesting is the fact that, in the periodic sweeps of 'sweatshops' and cheap restaurants in the area by the authorities, while ethnic Turks tended to be deported, ethnic Kurds were allowed to remain. This has occurred despite Britain's notoriously restrictive immigration policies and the British government's refusal to publicly condemn Turkey's handling of its Kurdish population.

[60] Local teachers inform me there is acute antagonism between Kurds and Turks in London classrooms – more so than is apparent in Turkey itself among the general population.

[61] While the ethnic Turkish community in Germany looks primarily for the economic benefits, it seems that many Kurds feel for the 'national struggle' first. Selim Ferat, an academic living in Berlin states 'a Kurd in Germany is still living his life in Kurdistan.' Events in 'Kurdistan' are felt and reflected upon immediately by the Kurdish community in Germany (Mansell, BBC World Service, 31 October 1994).

[62] In line with the argument that oppression creates activism, it is noteworthy that the militant Turkish left organisations, who like the Kurds, have been subject to heavy persecution in Turkey, are by far the most visible and active groups in the West – the others being more economically minded.

[63] Similarly, sections of 'domestic Turkish television' are actually produced in Western Europe and beamed into Turkey itself.

[64] For example, Stoke Newington in London is full of 'members only' Turkish football supporters clubs. In the ubiquitous tea rooms for men the television

creating a unified 'world culture' (see Chapter 1) can actually play a crucial role in preserving and strengthening cultural differences.

While private television plays a similar role for women, 'traditional' Turkish attitudes towards women remain. Indeed, the claim that second-generation Turks in Germany do not know how to behave correctly usually refers to attitudes of and towards women. As one observer put it,[65] many Turkish women abroad live in Europe and the twentieth century in the morning when they go out, but when they return home they revert back to traditional modes of strict male control. This dual role puts a great deal of strain on many women, as well as on their menfolk; the latter feel constrained to act in 'traditional' modes even though they are living in societies where these modes do not apply.[66]

Like Muslims living in Orthodox Christian states in the Balkans, Islam has been and continues to be a crucial element of identification for many Turkish citizens in Western Europe. In many host countries the Islamic organisation of Turkish migrants functions as an ethnic interest group, making claims and demands which transcend purely religious ones.[67] Here, the situation varies from country to country. Although Turkish guestworkers began to arrive in Germany at the beginning of the 1960s, there were already a large number of mosques in the country,[68] and this feature is replicated in many other places where Turks came as guestworkers; Europe had had Islamic contact and small scale symbiosis well before the arrival of the Turkish workforce. The organisation of the religious life of Turkish citizens abroad, as foreseen in Article 62 of the Turkish Constitution, is mainly channelled through the Turkish Directorate of Religious Affairs (*Diyanet İşleri Başkanlığı* or *Diyanet* for short). As noted in Chapter 6, the *Diyanet* advocates a unity which is primarily Turkish, with nationalist ideals like patriotism, love of the fatherland and mar-

---

showing Turkish programmes is the focal point.

[65] Mansell, BBC World Service, 31 October 1994.

[66] See T. Kocturk, *A Matter of Honour: Experiences of Turkish women immigrants* (London: Zed, 1992), and the poignant true story of 'Aynur' which was serialised in Cumhuriyet, 8, 9 and 10 May 1984 by reporter M. Yasin, and reprinted in İ. Boşgöz and N. Furniss, *op. cit.*, pp. 175-91.

[67] Y. Soysal, *op. cit.*, p. 235.

[68] See Antes and Kreiser, *op. cit.*, pp. 9-10, for the 'pre-history' of Islam in Germany before the arrival of the modern immigrants from Turkey.

tyrdom propagated as Islamic values. Atatürk's secular state-building nationalism is dressed up in Islamic clothes – a position akin to the so-called Turkish Islamic Synthesis (see Chapter 6). However, in the 1970s oppositional Muslim groups began to be active in setting up mosques and prayer rooms and expounding a competing Islamic ideology. Followers of Nakşibendi Sheikh Süleyman Hilmi Tunahan (who died in 1960) set up a network of Turkish Islamic centres in Western Europe. In the late 1970s and early 1980s, the '*Milli Görüş*' movement, set up by radical Islamists against the official *Diyanet* position, also gained strong support among migrants. A radical wing split off in 1983 and openly attacked the secular Republic of Turkey as well as the *Diyanet*, which was portrayed as the 'Directorate of Treachery Affairs' (*Hiyanet İşleri Başkanlığı*).[69]

Faced with this challenge, the *Diyanet* responded by greatly expanding its own network. The number of *Diyanet*-controlled Imams in Western Europe grew from eighty in 1961 to over 600 in 1989. In addition, the Turkish authorities set up semi-official representatives of the *Diyanet* in various European countries to administer many mosques for Turks. For example, the Islamic Foundation in the Netherlands, which is formally linked to the *Diyanet* in its statutes, runs some 70 per cent of the 160 Turkish mosques in the Netherlands. In Germany there is the *Diyanet İşleri Türk-İslam Birliği* (DİTB) which similarly controls between half and two-thirds of Germany's Turkish mosques. Similar organisations exist in Belgium and other West European countries. The *Diyanet* linked organisation has controlled the majority of mosques in Germany and the Netherlands, where Turks are the dominant Islamic community. In Belgium their influence is somewhat checked by the position of the Islamic Cultural Centre in Brussels, which is controlled by the World Muslim League.[70]

Thus, the *Diyanet* is a major force among Turkish Muslims in Western Europe. However, the rival Islamic organisations are serious competitors. In the late 1970s and early 1980s, the *Diyanet* attacked the Islamic Cultural Centres of the Süleymanlcıs in Ger-

[69] N. Landman, 'The Present Position and Future Prospects for the *Diyanet* in Europe', paper given at conference, 'Muslim Minorities in Post-Bipolar Europe', (Amman, Jordan, September 1994). Interestingly, '*Milli Görüş*' means 'national viewpoint', which again shows how radical Islamism is competing in the nationalist arena.
[70] *Ibid.*

many and the Netherlands for being extremist and illegal. The latter countered by accusing the *Diyanet* of attempting to stifle independent development of Turkish Islamic communities, and of intervention by Turkey in the internal affairs of other states.[71] Some form of *modus vivendi* appears to have arisen between the *Diyanet* and most other Turkish Muslim groups, although tensions remain. The rise in Turkey of a radical Islam critical of the official *Diyanet* line is mirrored in Turkish communities abroad. Criticism has also come from non-Muslims who view the strong 'official' Turkish nationalist content in the *Diyanet* – such as loyalty to the Turkish flag and deep emotion at the Turkish national anthem – as hindering integration into the European host society and running counter to perceived ideas of a European Islam.

Of course, these considerations only apply to Turkish Sunni Muslims. The Alevis are estimated to have made up a disproportionally high percentage of guestworkers in the 1960s and 1970s.[72] In addition, as noted in Chapters 4 and 8, Alevis have since the birth of the republic traditionally tended to support parties of the left, and there was a sizeable emigration of radical leftwingers from Turkey following the military coup of 1980. Such people, fleeing severe persecution within Turkey by the military rulers, were also unsympathetic to Sunni Islamic models of Turkish identity, preferring radical Marxist models based on class rather than national issues;[73] Alevis were also prominent among these groups.[74] Despite the claims of former leading Marxist Riza

[71] See 'Süleyman Hilmi Tunahan en de Islam in Turkije', *Qiblah* 7/4, Nether-lands 1983, p. 30, and its German equivalent, N. Dinçer., 'Wer ist Süleyman Efendi, was ist Süleymancılık?' (unpubl. MS. Dinçer was a Süleymancı leader in Germany in the early 1980s). These are referred to in Landman, *op. cit.*

[72] *Briefing*, no. 1,007, 19 September 1994.

[73] However, as our original definition of nationalism was as an activist political movement aiming at a cultural hegemony for the perceived national group, this would also include radical Marxist groups who, while their claims are based on class rather than nation, aimed at imposing a unified 'proletarian' culture and values on Turkish society – see Chapter 10.

[74] The best example is the case of Riza Rüstü Yürükoğlu, a noted leftwinger and author of a number of Marxist works on Turkey who became Turkish Communist Party (TKP) General Secretary at the 5th Congress in 1985. He is also a leading member of the Alevi community abroad and author of *Okunacak En Büyük Kitap İnsandır: Tarihte Ve Günümüzde Alevilik* (Istanbul: Alev Yayınevi, 3rd edn 1992). Although as noted in Chapter 8, Alevism has some traits of communal decision-making and egalitarianism which are not incompatible with

Yürükoğlu about the essentially irreligious aspects of Alevism, there has, similarly to the rise of Sunnism, been something of an Alevi revival, including the religious aspect. This has occurred both within Turkey and among the guestworkers in Western Europe, with a growth of Alevi associations in cities like Berlin.[75]

There are a variety of groups in the Balkans and elsewhere who look towards Turkey as a kin-state in some form or other. This has been reflected in the continual waves of emigration to Turkey of ethnic Turks and other Muslims, as well as the waves of emotion and feelings of solidarity with, for example, the Bosnian Muslims. Turkish policy in the Balkans towards the 'front-line' groups in Cyprus, Greece and Bulgaria has varied from direct military involvement in Cyprus to attempts to use agreements on education in Greece and declarations regarding oppression of Turks in Bulgaria. The post-communist environment has seen great changes and created new opportunities for Turkey, which is now a major regional power faced with weaker and smaller countries like Bulgaria, FYROM, and Albania. In addition, there are large numbers of Turkish citizens now living permanently or semi-permanently in Western Europe whose attitude towards the 'mother country' is complex. It varies from generation to generation, as well as from group to group, with the 'Kurdish Question' often to the fore.

---

left-wing ideology, there are fundamental contradictions between revolutionary Marxism and Alevism. In an interview with Yürükoğlu in *Pazar*, no. 278, London, 6 November 1994, p. 6, these contradictions become clearer. He tries to 'square the circle' by pointing out that Marxism was only born in the 19th century and hence implies that it can be grafted onto traditional Alevism. To the question 'Do you believe in God' he replied 'Of course not. I do not believe in Allah, I am a communist.' Such attempts to marry Alevi and Marxist ideology have at times strange results, with pictures of hereditary sheikhs side-by-side with those of Karl Marx. Adherents of this view like to portray Alevism as essentially non-religious — more of a philosophy than a faith. This point was made to me strongly at the Alevi centre in east London, where the poem '*Bir Şah Olsam*' ('If I were King') by Halil Öztoprak Dede in *Kervan*, no. 32, November/December 1993, p. 14, was held up as a classic Alevi view which also correlates with the communist one. It calls for the abolition of all *tarikats*, and states that there is no real difference between states and religions and that all should live under one flag of the world.

[75] I am indebted to Jochen Blaschke, Berliner Institut für Vergleichende Sozialforschung, for this information.

What is noticeable from the above discussion is how the struggle of the different ideologies competing for the totality of 'the Turkish Nation' (or in the case of the Kurds for part of it) is reflected in the Turkish communities abroad. In the Balkans, a similar struggle continues between those who see Islam as the primary focus of 'Turkishness' in those societies and those who look more to 'ethnic' traits. In both the Balkans and Western Europe there is a struggle between the official state Islam propagated by the *Diyanet* and the more radically Islamic rival of the *Milli Görüş* movement which directly relates to the similar struggle within Turkey. In Western Europe, Turkey's internal struggle with the PKK is mirrored in competing street demonstrations and generalised antagonism on a wide scale, which stretches right down to the classroom. In the Balkans, while there are no indigenous Kurdish populations to clash with indigenous Turkish or perceived Turkish/Muslim ones, the PKK factor is still present.[76] However, the lack of sizeable Kurdish communities make this 'Kurdish issue' a secondary factor there.

A major difference is evident in the feelings of national attachment between those groups in the Balkans and the groups of Turkish guestworkers living in Western Europe. The former communities appear in little danger of becoming assimilated into the (Christian) majority. On the contrary, policies pursued by Greece, and by Zhivkov's Bulgaria, of attempted assimilation by force if necessary, have proved counterproductive in the case of the Muslims. Here, the *millet* heritage of the Ottoman Empire lives on. While the Balkan states have had considerable success in assimilating fellow Orthodox Christian groups into the majority, the Muslims have proved far harder to assimilate. It appears that the harder the Christian Balkan states like Bulgaria and Greece tried to forcibly assimilate the ethnic Turks, the more resistance, in the form of Turkish nationalism, appeared.[77] Moreover, in

[76] For example, the Turkish government has over a long period accused the Greek government of allowing the PKK to openly run offices and plan anti-Turkish actions from Athens. Anti-Turkish Bulgarian nationalists also held an international Kurdish conference in Sofia in September 1994 at which a PKK representative spoke (TRT TV, Ankara, 28 September 1994, in SWB EE/2114, B/7, 30/9/94, and BTA, 21 September 1994, in SWB EE/2110, B/6, 26/9/94).

[77] In Bulgaria, while the Turks always appeared to view themselves as separate despite years of steady 'silent' assimilatory pressures from the communist authorities,

many parts of the Balkans there is a process of attraction towards the majority Muslim group of smaller Muslim groups like the Pomaks. In the eastern Balkans, the ethnic-Turkish mass is the main group exerting this attraction, while in the west there is also the Muslim Albanian one as a rival. Thus, far from appearing endangered in terms of national identity, the Turks in the Balkans seem to be becoming more assertive and actually assimilating other groups themselves. In all, most Muslims in the Balkans look towards Turkey as a kin-state with varying degrees of intensity, and this process appears to be continuing. The main exception is that of the Albanians, who have their own state and quasi-state of Kosovo. However, even in this case, many Muslim Albanians have emigrated to Turkey in recent times.

In Western Europe this process is not so marked. Many second-generation Turks are becoming assimilated into the host society. They are looking less and less to Turkey as a 'kin-state' and more to their own role in the states in which they reside. The difference may have two main causes. First, the ethnic Turks and Muslims in the Balkans are long-standing populations who have been in-digenous to the area for centuries. Such populations have tended to resort to Turkish nationalism as a means of defence against overt assimilatory pressures form the successor states of the Ottoman Empire. That these successor states (with the exception of Albania) saw themselves as essentially Christian made the position of Muslim Turkish and non-Turkish minorities especially problematic. In Western Europe the situation is different. Here, the Turkish minorities are essentially composed of people who have voluntarily moved to a foreign country where, whether for economic reasons or for reasons of political asylum, they feel life – or at least some aspects of it – is preferable to that in Turkey. Thus, the feeling of loss of identity over the generations is not seen as so much of a danger.

The second cause relates to the nature of the dominant nationalism in Western Europe, and the contrast between the actual national ideologies of Balkan states and those of Western Europe. While the Western European countries are, like those

---

the severely repressive 'rebirth' campaign of late 1984 onwards saw a definite rise of assertive Turkish nationalism in defence; see Höpken *op. cit.* The situation is similar in Greece and in Cyprus, where the rise of aspirations for *enosis* (union) with Greece and outrages by Colonel Grivas led to a corresponding rise of assertive Turkish defensive nationalism.

of the Balkans, essentially Christian states, there is, in Western Europe generally, a less overt nationalism and a greater appreciation of multi-cultural and multi-denominational societies.[78] Even in Western Europe, however, Germany pursues a policy under which its would-be citizens have to accept a perceived 'pure' German culture. In today's Germany, especially in what was formerly the German Democratic Republic, overt extreme nationalist or racist attitudes and actions are evident, resulting in nationalist reactions by Turkish immigrants. Nevertheless, the overall position is best illustrated by comparing France with Greece. Both states refuse to accept that ethnic minorities exist within their borders.[79] However, while French citizens are not persecuted in the courts for claiming to be, or for claiming the existence of, minorities within the country, Greek citizens are currently treated in this way.

This difference between indigenous populations who react against an aggressive state nationalism by propagating their own nationalism, and communities who seek refuge in another state and appear more willing to submerge their national identity within the dominant one, also has parallells to the internal Turkish situation. In this case, the Kurds have, in the main, stubbornly resisted attempts to assimilate them. On the other hand, other groups who migrated to the Ottoman Empire or Turkey for refuge – like Circassians, Slav Muslims or Albanians – have shown themselves far more willing to lose their original identities. Instead, they have adopted a Turkish identity – whether that be the 'official' Kemalist concept or one of its competitors.

---

[78] Of course, in the past Western Europe has shown as much intolerance as any other region. Whether the Balkan Christian model is a product of the Orthodox nature of the state religion is arguable. Some, like S.P. Huntington, suggest that this is so; see his 'The Clash of Civilizations?', *Foreign Affairs*, vol. 72, no. 3, 1993, and A. Pollis, 'Eastern Orthodoxy and Human Rights', *Human Rights Quarterly*, 1993. All countries experience reactions against multi-culturalism from xenophobic segments of society. The point here is how far such reactions are merely reactions and not essential components of the actual state national ideology.

[79] France declared itself unwilling to accept Article 27 of the International Covenant on Civil and Political Rights (ICCPR – the UN human rights bill which entered into force on 23 March 1976), which deals with minorities, arguing that there were none in France. Similar attitudes are apparent in Greece, which has not even ratified the ICCPR. Naturally, France is the 'civic' nationalist model *par excellence*, and was widely copied by countries like Greece and Turkey.

10

NATIONALIST SCHIZOPHRENIA:
THE STRUGGLE CONTINUES

From the above discussion, we can highlight certain key issues and draw the following conclusions. The nineteenth century saw the penetration of nationalism into the Ottoman Empire, which tried to accommodate to the new ideas. Initially, the *Tanzimat* reforms attempted to change the way it classified its subjects by religion – the *millet* system – and create instead an 'Ottoman citizen' regardless of religious affiliation. This was resisted both by sections of the governing Muslim élite and by Christian groups who increasingly fell under the sway of the new ideas. Faced with this failure, and with the potential defection of Muslim populations like the Muslim Albanians and Arabs, Abdülhamid II stressed Islam and the role of the Sultan as Caliph to hold the empire together. However, while this policy had some initial success, he was unable to prevent the continuing Ottoman decline and the penetration of nationalist ideas among his subjects.

In the late nineteenth and early twentieth century the beginnings of an ethnic Turkish nationalism arose in the empire. Turkic *émigrés* from Russia, who themselves had been subject to Russification in the Russian Empire, were in the forefront of this new movement. However, the competing claims of the Islamic community as the 'imagined community' of Anderson's terminology remained. The ideologues of the new Turkism in the Ottoman Empire continued to show an ambivalence towards the three essentially contradictory programmes of: 'Ottomanism', which attempted to appeal to all the peoples of the empire; 'Islamism', which looked to Islamic union with fellow Muslims; and 'Turkism', which looked to fellow Turks. Thus there was a confusion between a territorial, an ethnic or a religious basis for the 'nation'.

The Young Turk regimes, following the revolution of 1908,

315

saw the new doctrine of Turkism move from being a hidden agenda into an openly espoused ideology in the First World War. This included the aim of creating a huge ethnic state which would include all the Muslim Turkic peoples of the Russian Empire. Thus, in this period the ethnic variant came to the fore. However, defeat in the First World War brought an end to this chimera. Instead, the Ottoman state faced the real possibility of almost total dismemberment. The threat of foreign Christian rule, initially in the east, and then, following the Greek invasion, in the west of the country, galvanised the Muslim population of Anatolia into a war of resistance against the perceived invaders. As is often the case, war and foreign invasion greatly helped the spread of nationalist ideas of the resistance groups, headed by Mustafa Kemal, which sprang up all over the country.

The resistance war saw an initial alliance between Muslim groups in Anatolia, of which the Kurds were the most numerous after the Turks – an alliance which Kemal initially recognised. He even went so far as to promise some form of autonomy for the Kurds. This alliance, which was by no means adhered to either by all the Turkish-speaking Muslims or by all the Kurdish speakers, was essentially based on common Islamic bonds amplified by the common threat from rival Christians. Kemal, the practical soldier, based his concept of the national territory on Anatolia, which he saw as a basically defensible unit. As such, he turned his back on all ideas of either attempting to regain lost territories of the Ottoman Empire outside the Anatolian heartland territories, which included his own birthplace in Macedonia, or on uniting with fellow Turkic Muslims in the Caucasus or Central Asia. As such, his concept of the nation was essentially 'territorial'. However, there was also a strong religious component to it. Initially, he appeared to countenance including non-Muslims in the new Turkey, but faced with their continuing actions, he decided that they could not be included in the new nation, and they were expelled or had fled *en masse* (with the exception of communities in Istanbul and two islands). Thus, his concept of the 'nation' also initially had a religious basis.

Following the victory, the Turkish republic was established and Kemal introduced a number of sweeping reforms. Included in these reforms was an attempt to relegate Islam to the private sphere and remove it as a potential political force – this despite

Kemal's use of it in this manner in the resistance war. There was a strong reaction in the east, where Sunni Kurds led by Sheikh Said rose in mass revolt in 1925 even before the bulk of the reforms came about. Although this revolt appears to have been essentially religious rather than ethnically Kurdish, Kemal backtracked on previous hints at including the Kurds as a separate component of the new state. Instead, a conscious attempt was made to inculcate Turkish nationalism as the primary focus of political loyalty for all citizens. To achieve this, the central institutions of the state, including the educational system and the army, were used. As Islam was now relegated to the private sphere, the new state's nationalism began to exhibit a strong 'ethnic' component. The entire Ottoman period was effectively negated. Instead, the state ideologues looked back, in classic nationalist fashion, to a mythologised pre-Islamic Turkish history. Strong social and other pressure was brought to bear to make all citizens speak Turkish as their mother tongue. Non-Turks were viewed with distrust – a distrust which came to the fore in the Second World War with the notorious Capital Tax of 1942.

Thus, classic Kemalist nationalism exhibited many of the key features discussed in Chapter 1. The 'imagined community' of Anderson's terminology, which in the pre-nationalist era had been the religious community was to be replaced by the nation. Using Smith's classification of 'territorial' and 'ethnic' nationalisms, Kemalist nationalism can be seen as strongly territorial in its espousal of Anatolia as the territory and in its repudiation of possible claims on Turks or fellow Muslims from the Ottoman Empire or elsewhere left outside the new state. On the other hand, it also exhibited marked 'ethnic' strains. The latter strains can initially be seen in the expulsion of Christian minorities, who were viewed as potentially disloyal to the state. Although this was primarily a religious rather than an ethnic measure, it can still be seen to fall within Smith's 'ethnic' rubric. Additionally, while the denial of any ethnic minorities within the Anatolian Muslim community (primarily the numerous Kurds of the southeast) can be seen as an aspect of the strict enforcement of the territorial model,[1] the

---

[1] For example, France, the territorial archetype, similarly refuses to recognise any minorities within the French state and instead officially views all as (equal) Frenchmen.

emphasis on Turkish, and the state repression of all expressions of a separate Kurdish national consciousness, can be seen as having 'ethnic' components. This is more clearly shown in the discriminatory measures against non-Turks and non-Turkish Muslims in the Second World War. Kemalist nationalism also strongly viewed itself as a modernising force along the lines of Gellner's paradigm, and set about constructing a high Turkish culture constructed and propagated by a centralised education system and the central state organs.

The state-propagated nationalism brooked no rival variants. However, despite the full weight of the new state's central apparatus propagating the new ideology, and the one-party system, the Kemalist state was not totalitarian in the way that Stalin's USSR or Hitler's Germany were. It did not exhibit the same ruthless application of total control over society. While the new ideology was adopted and espoused by the new élites in the urban centres, the mass of the population living in the villages remained relatively immune to it until the 1950s. They continued to live lives bound by traditional Islamic precepts. This was especially so in the rugged mountainous southeast, where the Kurds predominated. This lack of penetration by the Kemalist state into the periphery allowed large sections of the population to remain relatively untouched by the new ideology.

When the one-party system was dismantled in the late-1940s and the 1950s, and democratic practices began to take root, the continuing Islamic sensibilities of the large majority of the population began to make themselves evident. To win elections, politicians needed to take this into account. The classic Kemalist élite attitude of ignoring religious sensibilities and dictating cultural norms to the masses became increasingly untenable. At the same time, mass migration from the periphery to the urban centres began to change traditional attitudes for the first time. This process had two contradictory sides: On the one hand, the mass of the population began to truly be subjected to the centre's nationalist ideology. On the other, the centre itself had to take into account the (Sunni) Islamic wishes of the majority.

Thus, in the decades after 1950, Sunni Islam increasingly became integrated into the state nationalist ideology. This was especially evident after the military coup of 1980. The previous decade had seen increasing anarchy and street violence. The military authorities, despite seeing themselves as the bastions of Kemalist orthodoxy, deliberately propagated Islam as a form of social cement. In this they tried to ensure that the Islamic values they were now deliberately espousing were always to be subordinated to Kemalist ideals. Islam was to be used as a prop for Turkish nationalism, not as a rival to it.

This policy (which had historical echoes with Abdülhamid's use of Islam in the late nineteenth century) was similar to the so-called Turkish Islamic Synthesis espoused by those on the radical right. The pan-Turkist ethnic variant of Turkish nationalism, discredited by defeat in the First World War and proscribed by Kemal, had never entirely disappeared. It resurfaced in the Second World War when again the traditional Russian enemy seemed to be weak. In the 1960s, this pan-Turkic variant adopted Sunni Islam as one of its perceived bases of Turkism – apparently in an attempt to widen its mass appeal. However, it has remained peripheral, despite playing an important role in the street violence of the 1970s, when its membership in weak coalition governments lent it an importance its electoral strength never warranted. The collapse of the USSR saw pan-Turkism again appear on the agenda, with the possibility of Turkey being the dominant member of some form of economic union with the new Turkic states of Central Asia. However, the initial euphoria appears to have subsided somewhat. The radical ethnic variant, however, has continued to be a relevant factor – especially in the eastern areas where Sunni and Alevi communities, and Turks and Kurds cohabit, and it has benefited by the continuing tensions between these groups. There are also widespread feelings of kinship between Turkey and Turkish and even non-Turkish Muslim groups in the Balkans, illustrating a continuing 'ethnic' facet of Turkish nationalism.

More successful than the pan-Turks have been those appealing to Islamic solidarity as the primary focus of identity. They have garnered support from the discontented and uprooted villagers who moved to the squatter settlements of the big cities. Despite being proscribed by the state in both successive constitutions and penal codes, the Islamic political movement has continued. Under the leadership of Necmettin Erbakan – himself a member of the technocratic élite – the Islamic movement has managed, in the main, to remain just inside the law. Despite membership in weak coalitions in the 1970s, it appeared to remain electorally a small party until the 1980s. The 1980s saw a fundamental change due to the opportunities for greater openness in public expression which were ushered in by the Özal governments. Özal himself was a devout Muslim as well as being of part Kurdish descent, and allowed greater opportunities for expounding Islamicist ideas. The old central state and Kemalist monopoly of the means of expression was broken. At the same time, a new generation of university-educated Islamic intellectuals appeared who were adept at taking advantage of the new situation. They were also adept at arguing their views in opposition to the old secular Kemalist élites. As a result, the Islamic Welfare Party (RP) managed to break out of its seeming electoral prison and become a truly mass party challenging the main political groupings.

This growth in Islamic political influence saw the old secular élites experience something akin to panic. This was compounded by the appearance of radical Islamic groups willing to murder those they saw as enemies of their vision as to what constitutes the Turkish nation. The old élites were long used to dictating their vision of Turkish identity and culture unopposed. Now they were faced with an adversary which they had thought that modernisation would sweep away, but which, on the contrary, was both growing, and adept at using the new technological opportunities afforded by this modernisation. The Sunni Islamic forces also have strong appeal to the Sunni Kurds, a factor which to some extent cuts across the ethnic barrier.

The increase in political influence of Sunni Islam has severely upset the large Alevi minority which traditionally supported the Kemalist reforms. The Alevis welcomed Kemal's attempts to relegate Islam to the private sphere, as this would remove the threat posed to them by any form of Sunni Islamic state. Recent anthropological studies purported to show that Alevism as a way of life was on the decline in the modern Turkish state. However, in reaction to the growth of Sunni Islamism, both in the central state bureaucracy and in the shape of the RP, the Alevis have recently begun to reassert their identity. This has been aided by a number of outrages perpetrated against Alevis by radical Sunnis. However, the Kurds remain the most problematic minority for Kemalist Turkish nationalism. The above-noted lack of penetration of Kemalism into the periphery in the rugged southeast allowed a rival Kurdish nationalism to emerge. This nationalism was based on linguistic ties, and this, as shown in Chapter 1, made it a powerful rival. The central state responded with a blanket denial that the Kurds of Turkey are a separate people and continued with the Kemalist solutions of brute military force to subjugate any opposition. This policy appears to have played into the hands of the extremist PKK by outlawing all moderate Kurdish voices, leaving the radical PKK to claim to speak for the entire Kurdish minority. This organisation, until recently ostensibly Marxist-Leninist but basically Kurdish nationalist, has shown itself to be ruthless in its methods, as well as unconcerned at state reprisals which it (correctly) saw as beneficial to its recruitment. While the government understandably could not tolerate an armed op-position group operating within the country, the ongoing hostilities in the southeast have seriously damaged Turkey's economy, as well as its international reputation. The denial of the Kurds as a separate people became increasingly untenable. Eventually, the Turkish authorities have been forced to acknowledge the existence of a separate Kurdish national consciousness in Turkey. Thus, the Kemalist integral nationalism which effectively denied the existence of any minorities apart from the small religious ones recognised by the Treaty of Lausanne has changed. An aspect of this is a new found interest in the Turkish ethnic mosaic as well as a new interest in the historical roots of the nation – roots which include the neglected Ottoman period.[2] However, influential figures in the establishment remain obdurate over the Kurdish issue, and it remains one of Turkey's biggest problems.

It could be argued that, given the premise of Chapter 1, defining nationalism as an activist political movement aiming at cultural hegemony over the whole nation (however defined), this study has neglected the radical Marxist left. It is true that they, despite espousing proletarian internationalism, also aimed at political and cultural hegemony over the nation. In this it is also perhaps relevant that many who supported Marxist groups in the 1970s, switched to the Islamic movement in the 1980s when it seemed that Marxism as an ideology was on the defensive. On the other hand, the Marxist left officially negates any form of 'narrow' nationalism,

---

[2] See for instance Bozkurt Güvenç, *Türk Kimliği: Kültür Tarihinin Kaynakları* (Ankara, Kültür Bakanlığı, 1993). This book, written by an advisor to President Demirel, bemoans the fact that Turks are unable to really answer questions as to their identity as they do not not know their cultural history; p 338.

and the PKK – until recently ostensibly a Marxist-Leninist organisation – which is undoubtedly nationalist in ideology and practice has been covered. Moreover, the extreme left, like the extreme
right, has remained a peripheral force. While the extreme right
has remained as something of an electoral constant in Turkish
politics – albeit a permanent minority one – by contrast, the left
in general has severely suffered in recent years. Violent left-wing
groups continue to have gun battles with the police and indulge
in killings. The mass of the population, however, in recent elections
seems to have continued to move to the right. The centre-right
parties or the Islamic RP, at the present time appear to dominate.
The centre-left parties, who claim the Kemalist mantle and espouse
the classic Kemalist secular nationalism, are suffering severe electoral
erosion, while the radical left has faded to the periphery of the
periphery. Given all this, and restrictions on space, the radical
Marxists, apart from the PKK, have not been covered.

Turkey today exhibits a form of nationalist schizophrenia with
a number of competing nationalisms vying for hegemony over
possession of the whole or parts of the population. In retrospect,
it is possible to conclude that the two weakest points in Kemal's
nationalism relate to his attempt to remove Islam as a component,
and his denial of the Kurds as a separate people. Both these issues
have returned in recent years to dominate Turkish politics. While
the ethnic nationalist variant of pan-Turkism seems destined to
remain peripheral, the Islamic variants appear to still be growing
– although it seems unlikely that they will increase much beyond
their present electoral level of 20% or so. The classic secular
Kemalist nationalism appears to be on the defensive, despite large
scale manifestations of support in the cities like that at Uğur
Mumcu's funeral. The centre-right, which espouses Sunni Islam
as a key component of Turkish identity, but one which is subordinated to Kemalist norms, remains the strongest factor at present.
The struggle for hegemony continues.

BIBLIOGRAPHY AND MAIN SOURCES

Newspapers and magazines

Briefing (Ankara, weekly).
BBC Summary of World Broadcasts (SWB) (daily).
Cumhuriyet (Istanbul, daily).
The Financial Times (London, daily).
The Guardian (London, daily).
Human Rights, Yesterday and Today (Human Rights Foundation of Turkey, Documentation Centre, Ankara, daily).
Hürriyet (Istanbul, daily).
The Independent (London, daily).
Info-Türk (Brussels, monthly).
Mideast Mirror (London, daily).
Middle East International (London, monthly).
Milliyet (Istanbul, daily).
Le Monde (Paris, daily).
The Month in Turkey (London, monthly: discontinued).
Nokta (Istanbul, weekly).
Sabah (Ankara, daily).
The Times (London, daily).
Turkey Briefing (London, bi-monthly/quarterly).
Turkey Confidential (London, monthly).
Turkish Daily News (Ankara, daily).
Turkish Probe (Ankara, weekly).
Urgent Actions on Turkey (Amnesty International, London).

Books and articles

Vermund Aarbakke, 'Ethnic Rivalry and the Quest for Macedonia' (unpublished M.A. thesis, University of Copenhagen, 1992).
Nermin Abandon-Unat, 'Identity Crisis of Turkish Migrants: First and

Second Generation' in İlhan Başgöz and Norman Furniss (eds), *Turkish Workers in Europe: An Interdisciplinary Study* (Bloomington: Indiana University Turkish Studies, 1985.)

Feride Acar, 'Women in the Ideology of Islamic Revivalism in Turkey: Three Islamic Women's Journals' in R. Tapper (ed.), *Islam in Turkey* (London: I.B. Tauris, 1991).

İrfan Acar, *Dış Politika* (Ankara: Sevinç Maatbası, 1993).

Admiralty, *The Turkish and the Pan-Turkish Ideal* (London: London War Staff Intelligence Division, Admiralty, 1917).

Mehmet Ali Ağaoğulları, 'The Ultranationalist Right' in I.C. Schick and E.A. Tonak (eds), *Turkey in Transition – New Perspectives* (Oxford University Press, 1987).

Feroz Ahmad, *The Turkish Experiment in Democracy 1950-75* (London: Hurst, 1977).

——, *The Young Turks: The Committee of Union and Progress in Turkish Politics 1908-1914* (Oxford: Clarendon Press, 1969).

——, 'The Political Economy of Kemalism' in A. Kazancıgil and E. Özbudun (eds), *Ataturk: Founder of a Modern State* (London: Hurst, 1981).

Taner Akçam, *Türk Ulusal Kimlığı ve Ermeni Sorunu* (Istanbul: İletişim, 1992).

Yusuf Akçura, *Üç Tarz-i Siyaset* (Ankara: Türk Tarih Kurumu, 1976).

——, *Türkçülük*, (Istanbul: Toker, 1990).

Sina Akşin, *Jön Türkler ve İttihat ve Terakki* (Istanbul: Remzi Kitabevi, 1987).

——, 'Turkish Nationalism Today', in *Turkish Yearbook of International Relations 1976*, vol. 16, 1977.

Adam Smith Albion, 'The Voice of the People', *Institute of Current World Affairs*, ASA-6, Hanover, 20 March 1995.

Alexis Alexandris, *The Greek Minority in Istanbul and Greek-Turkish Relations 1918-1974* (Athens: Center for Asia Minor Studies, 1983).

——, 'Political Expediency and Human Rights: Minority Issues between Greece and Turkey', paper given at conference 'Minority Rights Policies and Practice in South-East Europe', Copenhagen, 30 March–1 April 1990.

Arnold J. Toynbee A.J.T. *Report on the Pan-Turanian Movement* (London: Intelligence Bureau Department of Information, Admiralty, L/MIL/17/16/23, 1917).

Türker Alkan, *The Political Integration of Europe: A Content Analysis of the Turkish, French, German and Italian History Textbooks* (Ankara: METU Publications, 1982).

Tekin Alp (Moise Cohen), *Le Kemalisme* (Paris: Alcan, 1937).

——, *The Turkish and the Pan-Turkish Ideal* (London: transl. London War Staff Intelligence Division, Admiralty, 1917).

Şahin Alpay, 'The Turkish Press and the Kurdish Problem', paper given at 'The Turkish Media Today' workshop, SOAS, London University, London, 21 May 1992.

——, 'Journalists: Cautious Democrats' in M. Heper, A. Öncü and H. Kramer (eds), *Turkey and the West* (London: I.B. Tauris, 1993).

Türker Altan, 'The National Salvation Party in Turkey' in Metin Heper and Raphael Israeli (eds), *Islam and Politics in the Modern Middle East*, (New York: Croom Helm, 1984).

Amnesty International, *Turkey: A policy of denial*, AI EUR 44/01/95 (London: Amnesty International, February 1995).

Benedict Anderson, *Imagined Communities: Reflections on the Origin and Spread of Nationalism* (London: Verso, rev. edn, 1991).

Peter Alford Andrews, *Ethnic Groups in The Republic of Turkey* (Wiesbaden: Dr Ludwig Reichert Verlag, 1989).

Musa Anter, *Hatıralarım* (Istanbul: Yönayıncılık, 1991).

Peter Antes and Klaus Kreiser, *Muslims in Germany – German Muslims? Questions of Identity*, Muslims in Europe, Research Paper no. 28 (Birmingham: Centre for the Study of Islam and Christian Muslim Relations, Selly Oak Colleges December 1985).

Masami Arai, *Turkish Nationalism in the Young Turk Era* (Leiden: E.J. Brill, 1992).

Harold C. Armstrong, *Grey Wolf: Mustafa Kemal – An Intimate Study of a Dictator* (London: Arthur Barker, 1932).

John Armstrong, *Nations Before Nationalism*, (Chapel Hill: University of North Carolina Press, 1982).

Mustafa Kemal Atatürk, *Nutuk* (Ankara: Kültür Bakanlığı Yayınları, 1980).

——, *Atatürk'ün Tamim, Telgraf ve Beyannmeleri, 1917-1938*, vol. 4 (Ankara: Türk Inkilap Tarihi Enstitütü, 1964).

Rosie Aycliffe, Marc Dubin and John Gawthrop, *Turkey: The Rough Guide* (London: Penguin, 1994).

Abdulkadır Aygan, *PKK'nın İçinden* (Ankara: Yeni Forum Yayınları, no. 3, 1987).

Elizabeth Bacon, *Central Asia under Russian Rule: A Study in Culture Change*, (Ithaca, NY: Cornell University Press, 1966).

Frank E. Bailey, *British Policy and the Turkish Reform Movement: A study in Anglo-Turkish relations 1826-1853*, (New York: Howard Fertig, 1970).

İlhan Başgöz and Norman Furniss (eds), *Turkish Workers in Europe: An Interdisciplinary Study* (Bloomington: Indiana University Turkish Studies, 1985).

Daniel G. Bates, *Nomads and Farmers*, (Ann Arbor: Michingan University Press, 1973).

——, 'Differential access to pasture in a nomadic society: the Yörük of southeastern Turkey' in W. Irons and N. Dyson-Hudson (eds), *Perspectives on Nomadism* (Leiden: E.J. Brill, 1972).

Mehmet Bayrak, *Kürtler ve Ulusal-Demokratik Mücadeleleri*, (Ankara: Öz-Ge, 1993).

Alexandre Benningsen and S. Enders Wimbush, *Mystics and Commissars: Sufism in the Soviet Union* (London: Hurst, 1985).

Niyazi Berkes, 'Ziya Gökalp; His contribution to Turkish Nationalism', *Middle East Journal*, vol. 8, 1954.

——, *Development of Secularism in Turkey* (Montreal: McGill University Press, 1964).

Ismail Kemal Bey, *Memoirs* (London: Constable, 1920).

Faruk Bilici, 'Acteurs de développement des relations entre la Turquie et le monde turc: les vaktı(s)', *CEMOTI (Cahiers d'Études sur la Méditerranée Oriental et le Monde Turco-Iranian)*, no. 13, 1992.

Mehmet Ali Birand, *Shirts of Steel: an anatomy of the Turkish armed forces* (London: I.B. Tauris, 1991).

——, *Apo ve PKK* (Istanbul: Milliyet Yayinlari, 1992).

John Kinglsey Birge, *The Bektashi order of Dervishes* (London: Hartford, 1937).

Birinci Türk Tarih Kongresi: Konferanslar Müzakere zabıtalan (Istanbul: T.C. Maarif Vekâletii, 1932).

Benjamin Braude and Bernard Lewis, *Christians and Jews in the Ottoman Empire* (New York: Holmes and Meier, 1982).

Marie Benningsen Broxup *et al.*, *The North Caucasus Barrier: The Russian Advance towards the Muslim World* (London: Hurst, 1992).

David Brown, 'Foreword' to Faik Ökte, *The Tragedy of the Turkish Capital Tax*, (London: Croom Helm, 1964).

Martin M. van Bruinessen, *Agha, Shaikh and State* (Utrecht: Rijswijk, University, 1978).

——, 'Between guerrilla war and political murder: The Workers' Party of Kurdistan', *Middle East Report*, no. 152, 1988.

Ali Bulaç, *Din ve Modernizm* (Istanbul: n. p., 1991).

Ayşe N. Çağlar, 'The Greywolves as Metaphor' in A. Finkel and N. Sirmen (eds), *Turkish State, Turkish Society* (London: Routledge 1990).

Gerard Chaliand, (ed.), *People Without a Country: The Kurds and Kurdistan* (London: Zed, 1980).

Bruce Chatwin, *The Songlines*, (London: Picador, 1988).

Richard Clogg, 'The Greeks' in Benjamin Braude and Bernard Lewis (eds), *Christians and Jews in the Ottoman empire: the functioning of a plural society*, vol. 1 (New York: Holmes and Meier, 1982).

Linda Colley, *Britons: Forging the Nation 1707-1837* (London: Pimlico, 1994).

The Constantinopolitan Society, *Protocol*, no. 195/91, Athens, 10 June 1991.

Council of Europe Provisional Report on the reception and resettlement of *refugees in Turkey* ADOC6267. PROV 1403-10/7/90-2-3, 12 July 1990.

Bülent Dâver, 'Secularism in Turkey', *SBFD*, vol. 22, no. 1, 1967.

Roderic H. Davison, *Reform in the Ottoman Empire 1856-1876* (Princeton University Press, 1963).

C. Ernest Dawn, *From Ottomanism to Arabism*, (Urbana: University of Illinois, 1973).

Carol Delaney, *The Seed and the Soil: Gender and Cosmology in Turkish Village Society*, (Berkeley: University of California Press, 1991).

——, 'Traditional Modes of Authority and Co-operation' in Paul Stirling (ed.) *Culture and Economy: Changes in Turkish Villages* (Huntingdon: Eothen Press, 1993).

Selim Deringil, 'The Ottoman Empire and Pan-Islam in Turkic Russia', paper delivered at 'Change in Modern Turkey: Politics, Society, Economy' Manchester University, 5-6 May 1993.

——, 'The Ottoman Empire and Russian Muslims: brothers or rivals?', *Central Asian Survey*, vol. 13, no. 3, 1994.

——, 'The Invention of Tradition as Public Image in the late Ottoman Empire', *Comparative Studies in Society and History*, vol. 3, no. 1, 1993.

——, 'The Ottoman response to the Egyptian Crisis of 1881-1882' *Middle Eastern Studies*, vol. 24, 1988.

Robert Devereux, *The First Ottoman Constitutional Period: a study of the Midhat Constitution and Parliament* (Baltimore: Johns Hopkins University Press, 1963).

Clement H. Dodd, *Democracy and Development in Turkey* (Huntingdon: Eothen Press, 1979).

——, *The Crisis of Turkish Democracy* (Huntingon: Eothen Press, 2nd edn, 1990).

D. Mehmet Doğan, *Kemalizm* (Istanbul: Alternatif Üniversite, 1992).

Doğruyol Partisi – Cumhuriyet Halk Partisi Hükümetinin Uygulamı Programı (Ankara: 21 March 1995).

Robert J. Donia and John V.A. Fine, *Bosnia and Hercegovina: A Tradition Betrayed* (London: Hurst, 1994).

Ivo D. Duchacek, *The territorial dimension of politics within, among, and across nations* (Boulder, CO: Westview Press, 1986).

—— and Daniel Larouche (eds), *Perforated sovereignties and international relations: transsovereign contacts of sub-national governments* (New York: Greenwood Press, 1988).

Paul Dumont, 'Disciples of the Light: The Nurcu Movement in Turkey', *Central Asian Survey*, vol. 5, no. 2, 1986.

Edith Durham, *High Albania* (London: Edward Arnold, 1909).

Halidé Edib (Adıvar), *Memoirs of Halidé Edib* (London: John Murray, 1926).

Charles Eliot, *Turkey in Europe* (London: Frank Cass, 2nd edn, 1965).

Shmuel N. Eisenstadt, *Modernization: Protest and Change* (Englewood Cliffs, NJ: Prentice-Hall, 1966).

Necmettin Erbakan, *Millî Görüş* (Istanbul: Dergâh Yayinlari, 1975).

Üstün Ergüder, 'The Motherland Party, 1983-1989' in M. Heper and H. Landau (eds), *Political parties and democracy in Turkey* (London: I.B. Tauris, 1991).

Hamza Eroğlu, 'Atatürk's Conception of Nation and Nationalism' in Turhan Feyzioğlu (ed), *Atatürk's Way*, (Istanbul: Qtomarsan, 1982).

Büşra Ersanlı-Behar, *The Turkish History Thesis: A Cultural Dimension of the Kemalist Revolution* (unpubl. Ph. D. thesis, Boğaziçi University, 1989).

Euromosaic, *The Pomaks of Greece* (Barcelona, forthcoming).

European Parliament Working Document, A Series A 2-160/85, *Committee of Inquiry into the rise of fascism in Europe*, December 1985.

Ahmet Ferid [Tek], *Bir Mektup*, in Yusuf Akçura, *Üç Tarz-i Siyaset*, (Ankara: Türk Tarih Kurumu, 1976).

F.W. Fernau, 'Le Retour des "Quartorze" en Turquie', *Orient*, vol. 7, no. 25, 1963.

Turhan Feyzioğlu, 'Secularism: Cornerstone of the Turkish Republic' in Turhan Feyzioğlu (ed.), *Atatürk's Way*, (Istanbul: Otomarsan, 1982).

H.G.R. Field, 'Religious commitment and work orientations of Turkish students', in *Human Organisation*, Lexington, vol. 27, no. 2, 1969.

Ernest Gellner, *Nations and Nationalism* (Oxford: Blackwell, 1983).

François Georgeon, *Aux Origines du Nationalisme Turc. Yusuf Akçura (1876-1935)* (Paris: Institut d'Études Anatoliennes, 1980).

——, 'Les Foyeurs Turcs à L'Epoque Kemaliste', *Turcica*, vol. 14, 1982.

Haluk Gerger, 'The Plight of the Kurds', in *Balkan War Report: Bulletin of the Institute for War and Peace Reporting*, no. 24, 1994.

E. Ghareeb, *The Kurdish Question in Iraq* (New York: Syracuse University Press, 1981).

Hamilton A.R. Gibb and Harold Bowen, *Islamic Society and the West*, vol. 2 (Oxford University Press, 1950).

İsmet Giritli, 'The Ideology of Kemalism' in Turhan Feyzioğlu (ed.), *Atatürk's Way* (Istanbul: Otomarsan, 1982).

Erdogan Göger, *Türk Tabiiyet Hukuku* (Ankara: n.p., 3rd ed, 1975).

Altan Gökalp, *Têtes Rouges et Bouches Noires* (Paris: Société d'Ethnographie, 1980).

Ziya Gökalp, *Turkish Nationalism and Western Civilisation*, selected essays translated by Niyazi Berkes (London: Geo. Allen and Unwin, 1959).

——, *The Principles of Turkism* (Leiden: E.J. Brill, 1968)

Ayvaz Gökdemir, *Türk Kimliği* (Ankara: Ecdad, 1990).

Nilülfer Göle, 'The Quest for the Islamic Self within the context of Modernity', paper presented at the MIT conference 'Rethinking the Project of Modernity in Turkey', Massachusetts Institute of Technology, March 1994.

Ergün Göze, *Türklük Kavgası (Istanbul: Boúgaziçi, 1990)*.

Ronald Grigor, *Looking towards Ararat* (Bloomington: Indiana University Press, 1993).

Sarah Graham-Brown, *Education Rights and Minorities* (London: Minority Rights Group, June 1994).

John Guest, *Survival among the Kurds: A History of the Yezidis* (London: Kegan Paul International, 1993).

Haldun Gülalp, 'Modernisation Policies and Islamist Politics', paper presented at the MIT conference 'Rethinking the Project of Modernity in Turkey', Massachusetts Institute of Technology, March 1994.

Ersin Gündoğan, *Teknolojinin Ötesi* (Istanbul, n.p. 1991).

Bozkurt Güvenç, *Türk Kimliği: Kültür Tarihinin Kaynakları* (Ankara: Kültür Bakanlığı, 1993).

—, Gencay Saylan, İlhan Tekeli and Şerafettin Turan, *Türk-Islam Sentezi Dosyası* (Istanbul: Sarmal, 1991).

Sylvia Haim (ed.), *Arab Nationalism: an Anthology* (Berkeley: University of California Press, 1962).

William Hale, 'The Turkish Army in Politics 1960-73' in A. Finkel and N. Sirman (eds), *Turkish State, Turkish Society* (London: Routledge, 1990).

—, 'Ideology and Economic Development in Turkey, 1930-1945', *British Society for Middle Eastern Studies Bulletin*, vol. 7, 1980.

Besir Hamitoğulları, 'İktisadi Vahşi Büyümenin Bunalımları ve İslam Kalkınma Modelinin Vaadettikleri' in Ahmet Tabakoğlu and İsmail Kurt (eds), *İktisadı Kalkınma ve İslam* (Istanbul, n.p., 1987).

Şükrü Hanioğlu, *Bir Siyasal örgüt olarak Osmanlı İttihad ve Terrakki Cemiyeti ve Jön Türklük*, vol. 1 (Istanbul: Iletişim, 1985).

Chris M. Hann, 'Rural Transformation on the East Black Sea Coast: a note on Keyder', *Journal of Peasant Studies*, vol. 12, no. 4, 1985.

—, *Tea and the Domestication of the Turkish State*, Occasional Papers in Modern Turkish Studies 1 (Huntingdon: Eothen Press, 1990).

—, 'Sexual division of labour in Lazistan' in Paul Stirling (ed.), *Culture and Economy: Changes in Turkish Villages* (Huntingdon. Eothen Press, 1993).

Baymirza Hayit, *Sovyetler Birligi'ndeki Türklügün ve İslamın Bazı Meseleleri* (Istanbul: Türk Dünyası Araştırmaları Vakfi Yayını, 1987).

Helsinki Watch, *Turkey: New Restrictive Anti-Terror Law* (New York: Helsinki Watch, 10 June 1991).

—, *Forced Displacement of Ethnic Kurds from Southeastern Turkey* (New York: Helsinki Watch, October 1994).

Paul B. Henze, 'Circassian Resistance to Russia' in Marie Broxup *et al.*, *The North Caucasus Barrier: The Russian Advance towards the Muslim World* (London: Hurst, 1992).

Metin Heper, 'Political Culture as a Dimension of Compatibility' in M. Heper, Ayşe Öncü and H. Kramer (eds), *Turkey and the West: Changing Political and Cultural Identities* (London: I.B. Tauris, 1993).

Uriel Heyd, *Foundations of Turkish Nationalism – the Life and Teachings of Ziya Gökalp* (London: Harvill Press, 1950).

——, 'Islam in Modern Turkey', *Royal Central Asian Journal*, vol. 34, 1947.

——, *Language Reform in Modern Turkey* (Jerusalem: Israel Oriental Society, 1954).

Eric Hobsbawm, *Nations and Nationalism since 1780: Programme, Myth, Reality* (Cambridge University Press, 1990).

——, and T. Ranger (eds), *The Invention of Tradition* (Cambridge University Press, 1983).

Wolfgang Höpken, 'From Religious Identity to Ethnic Mobilisation: The Turks of Bulgaria before, during and since Communism' in Hugh Poulton and Suha Taji-Farouki (eds), *Muslim Identity and the Balkan State* (London: Hurst, 1997).

Charles W. Hostler, *Turkism and the Soviets: the Turks of the world and their political objectives* (London: Geo. Allen and Unwin, 1957).

The Human Rights Foundation of Turkey, *The Story of DEP* Ankara: The Human Rights Foundation of Turkey, Documentation Centre, n.d.).

S.T. Hunter, 'Will Azerbaijan's new rulers safeguard Western interests?', *Middle East International*, 24 July 1992.

Samuel P. Huntington, 'The Clash of Civilizations?' in *Foreign Affairs*, vol. 72, no. 3, 1993.

İkinci Türk Kongresi, 20-25 Eylul, 1937: Kongrenin çalışmaları ve Kongreye Sunulan Tebliğler (Istanbul: Kenan Matbaasi, 1943).

Ismet G. Imset, *The PKK: A report on Separatist Violence in Turkey (1973-1992)* (Ankara: Turkish Daily News Publications, 1992).

A. Afet İnan, Medeni Bilgiler ve Atatürk'ün El Yazıları (Ankara: Türk Tarih Kurumu, 1969).

——, 'Atatürk ve Tarih Tezi', *Belleten*, vol. 3, 1939.

The Institute of Jewish Affairs, *Anti-Semitism 1994* (London: Macmillan, 1994).

W. Irons and N. Dyson-Hudson (eds), *Perspectives on Nomadism* (Leiden: E.J. Brill, 1972).

Cemal Kafader, 'The New Visibility of Sufism in Turkish Studies and Cultural Life' in Raymond Litchez (ed.), *The Dervish Lodge; Architecture, Art and Sufism in Ottoman Turkey* (Berkeley: University of California Press, 1992).

Enver Ziya Karal, 'Önsöz' in Yusuf Akçura, *Üç Tarz-i Siyaset* (Ankara: Türk Tarih Kurumu, 1976).

——, 'Osmanli Tarihinde Türk Dili Sorunu (Tarih Açısından bir Açıklama)' in *Bilim Kültür ve Öğretim Dili Olararak Türkçe* (Ankara: Türk Tarihi Kurumu, 1978).

Yakup Kadri Karaosmanoğlu, 'Atatürk ve Türk Dili' in *Atatürk ve Türk Dili* (Ankara: Türk Dil Kurumu, 1963).

Kemal H. Karpat (ed.), *Political and Social Thought in the Contemporary Middle East* (London: Pall Mall, 1968).

——, *An Inquiry into the Social Foundation of Nationalism in the Ottoman State: From Social Estates to Classes, from Millets to Nations* (Princeton University Press, 1973).

——, 'The Turkish Left', *Journal of Contemporary History*, vol. 1, no. 2, 1966.

——, 'Socialism and the Labor Party of Turkey', *Middle East Journal*, vol. 21, 1967.

——, *The Gecekondu – Rural Migration and Urbanisation* (Cambridge University Press, 1976).

Kemal Kartal, *Kentleşme ve İnsan* (Ankara: n.p., 1978).

Riva Kastoryano, 'Ethnic Differentiation in France: Turks and Muslims' in M. Kiray (ed.), *Structural Change in Turkish Society* (Bloomington: Indiana University Press, 1991).

Elie Kedourie, *Nationalism* (London: Hutchinson, 1966)

——, *Nationalism in Asia and Africa* (New York: Meridian, 1970).

Ruşen Keleş and Artun Ünsal, *Kent ve Siyasal Siddet* (Ankara: Ankara Üniverisitesi: Siyasal Bilgiler Fakültesi Yayınları, 1982).

Ali Kemal, *Cevabımız* in Yusuf Akçura, *Üç Tarzi-i Siyaset* (Ankara: Türk Tarih Kurumu, 1976).

Kendal [sic], 'Kurdistan in Turkey' in G. Chaliand (ed.), *People Without a Country: The Kurds and Kurdistan* (London: Zed, 1980).

Donald Kenrick, *Gypsies: from India to the Mediterranean* (Toulouse: Gypsy Research Centre, CRDP Midi-Pyrénées, 1993).

Suna Kili, *Turkish Constitutional Developments and Assembly Debates on the Constitutions of 1924 and 1961* (Istanbul: Robert College Research Centre, 1971).

——, *Kemalism*, (Istanbul: Robert College Research Centre, 1969).

——, 'Kemalism in Contemporary Turkey', *International Political Science Review*, vol. 1, no. 3, 1980.

Lord Kinross, *Atatürk: The Rebirth of a Nation* (London: Weidenfeld and Nicolson, 1964).

Tahire Kocturk, *A Matter of Honour: Experiences of Turkish women immigrants* (London: Zed, 1992).

Hans Kohn, *The Idea of Nationalism: A study in its Origins and Background* (New York: Macmillan, 1967).

Sema Köksal, 'A Ghetto in a Welfare Society: Turks in Rinkeby' in Mübeccel Kiray (ed.), *Structural Change in Turkish Society* (Bloomington: Indiana University Press, 1991)

Kurdish Human Rights Project, *Final Resolution of the international conference on North-West Kurdistan (South-East Turkey)* (London: Kurdish Human Rights Project, June 1994).

David Kushner, *The Rise of Turkish Nationalism 1976-1908* (London: Frank Cass, 1977).

Jacob M. Landau, *Pan-Turkism: From Irredentism to Cooperation* (London: Hurst, 1995).

——, *Radical Politics in Modern Turkey* (Leiden: E.J. Brill, 1974).

——, 'The First Turkish Language Congress' in Joshua A. Fishman (ed.), *The Earliest Stage of Language Planning: The 'First Congress' Phenomenom* (Berlin: Mouton de Gruyter, 1993).

——, *Tekinalp, Turkish Patriot 1883-1961* (Amsterdam: Nederlands Historisch-Archeologisch Institut te Istanbul, 1984).

Nico Landman, 'The Role of the Diyanet in West Europe: Turkish Ethnicity versus European Nationality' in Hugh Poulton and Suha Taji-Farouki (eds), *Muslim Identity and the Balkan State* (London, Hurst, 1997.

——, 'The Present Position and Future Prospects for the *Diyanet* in Europe', paper given at conference, 'Muslim Minorities in Post-Bipolar Europe', Amman, Jordan, September 1994.

David M. Lang and Christopher J. Walker, *The Armenians* (London: Minority Rights group, 1987).

Daniel Lerner, *The Passing of Traditional Society: Modernizing the Middle East* (New York: Free Press, 1964).

Agâh S. Leverend, *Türk Dilinde Gelişme ve Sadeleşme Evreleri* (Ankara: Türk Dil Kurumu, 1949).

Ned Levine, 'Value Orientations among Migrants in Ankara, Turkey: Case studies', *Journal of Asian and African Studies*, vol. 8, 1983.

Bernard Lewis, *The Emergence of Modern Turkey* (Oxford University Press, 1961).

——, 'History-writing and National Revival in Turkey', *Middle Eastern Affairs*, vol. 4, 1953.

——, 'Ali Pasha on Nationalism', *Middle Eastern Studies*, vol. 10, 1974.

Geoffrey L. Lewis, *Turkey* (London: Ernest Benn, 3rd edn, 1966). 'Atatürk's Language Reform as an Aspect of Modernisation in the Republic of Turkey' in Jacob M. Landau (ed.), *Atatürk and the Modernisation of Turkey* (Boulder, CO: Westview Press 1984).

Arend Lijphart, *Democracies: Patterns of majoritarian and consensus government in twenty-one countries* (New Haven: Yale University Press, 1984).

Lilo Linke, *Allah Dethroned: A Journey through Modern Turkey* (London: Constable, 1937).

Juan J. Linz, 'Some Notes Towards a Comparative Study of Fascism in Sociological Historical Perspective' in Walter Laqueur (ed.) *Fascism: A Readers Guide* (London: Pelican, 1982).

Igor Lipovsky, *The Socialist Movement in Turkey 1960-1980* (Leiden: E.J. Brill, 1992).

——, 'The Legal Socialist Parties of Turkey 1960-1980', *Middle Eastern Studies*, vol, 27, 1991.

Mahmut Makal, *A Village in Anatolia* (London: Vallentine Mitchell, 1954).

Andrew Mango, 'Remembering the Minorities', *Middle Eastern Studies*, vol. 21, 1985.

——, 'Turkey: The Emergence of a Modern Problem' in W. Hale (ed.), *Aspects of Modern Turkey?* (London: Bowker, 1976).

——, 'Turks and Kurds', *Middle East Studies*, vol. 30, no. 4 (Oct. 1994), pp. 975-96.

Şerif Mardin, *The Genesis of Young Ottoman Thought* (Princeton University Press, 1962).

——, 'Religion and Secularism in Turkey' in Kazancıgil and Özbudun (eds), *Atatürk: Founder of a Modern State* (London: Hurst, 1981).

——, *Religion and Social Change in Modern Turkey: The Case of Bediüzzaman Said Nursi* (Albany: State University of New York Press, 1989).

——, *Jön Türklerin Siyası Fikirleri 1895-1905*, (Ankara: Iletişim, 1964.

——, 'The Nakşibendi Order in Turkish History' in R. Tapper (ed.), *Islam in Modern Turkey* (London: I.B. Tauris, 1991).

——, 'Religion in Modern Turkey', *International Social Science Journal*, 1977.

——, 'Ideology and Religion in the Turkish Revolution', *International Journal of Middle Eastern Studies*, vol. 2, 1971.

Guiseppe Mazzini, *The Duties of Man and other Essays* (New York: Everyman Library, 1966).

Edward Mortimer, *Faith and Power: The Politics of Islam* (London: Faber and Faber, 1982).

Justin McCarthy, 'Foundation of the Turkish Republic: Social and Economic Change', *Middle Eastern Studies*, vol. 19, 1983.

——, *Muslims and Minorities: The Population of Ottoman Anatolia and the End of the Empire* (New York University Press, 1983).

Michael E. Meeker, 'Once there was, once there wasn't: National Monuments and Interpersonal Exchange', paper presented at the MIT conference *Rethinking the Project of Modernity in Turkey*, Massachusetts Institute of Technology, March 1994.

——, 'The New Muslim Intellectuals in the Republic of Turkey', in R. Tapper (ed.), *Islam in Modern Turkey* (London: I.B. Tauris, 1991).

Minority Rights Group, *The World Directory of Minorities* (London, Longmans/MRG, 1989).

Hercules Milas, 'History Textbooks in Greece and Turkey', *History Workshop*, 1991.

Milliyetçi Çalışma Partisi Programı (Ankara: 27 December 1988).

——, *M.Ç.P. Genel Merkezi Eğitim Programı* (Ankara: n.d. [probably 1988]).

——, *Körfez Krizi ve M.Ç.P* (Ankara: September 1990).

Behrooz Morvaridi, 'Demographic Change, Resettlement and Resource use' in Clement Dodd (ed.), *The Political Social and Economic Development of Northern Cyprus* (Huntingdon: Eothen Press, 1993).

Nadir Nad, *Perde Arkalarından* (Istanbul, n.p., 1964).

Tom Nairn, *The Break-up of Britain* (London: Verso, 1981).

Roger Ness, 'Being an Alevi Muslim in S.W. Anatolia and Norway: The impact of migration on a heterodox Turkish community' in Tomas Gerholm and Yngve G. Lithman (eds), *The New Islamic Presence in Western Europe* (London: Mansell, 1988).

Mehmet Ümit Necef, 'New conceptions on the Kurdish Question in the Turkish political establishment', MS. partly reprinted in *Turkey Briefing*, vol. 6, no. 5, 1992.

Harry T. Norris, *Islam in the Balkans: Religion and Society between Europe and the Arab World* (London: Hurst, 1993).

John D. Norton, 'Bektaşhis in Turkey' in D. MacEoin and A. al-Shahi (eds), *Islam in the Modern World* (London: Croom Helm, 1983).

Faik Ökte, *The Tragedy of the Turkish Capital Tax* (London: Croom Helm, 1987).

Emelie A. Olson, 'Türbe and Evliye: Saints' Shrines as Environments that Facititate Communication and Innovation' in Mübeccel Kiray (ed.), *Structural Change in Turkish Society* (Bloomington: Indiana University Press, 1991).

Robert T. Olson *The Emergence of Kurdish Nationalism and the Sheikh Said Rebellion, 1880-1925* (Austin: University of Texas Press, 1989).

Ayşe Öncü, 'Academics: The West in the Discourse of University Reform' in Metin Heper, Ayşe Öncü and Heinz Kramer (eds), *Turkey and the West: Changing Political and Cultural Identities* (London: I.B. Tauris, 1993).

Baskın Oran, *Atatürk Milliyetçiliği: Resmi İdeoloji Dışı Bir İnceleme* (Ankara: Bilgi Yayınevi, Ankara, 3rd edn, 1993).

İrfan Orga, *Portrait of a Turkish Family* (London: Victor Gollancz, 1950).

İsmet Özel, *Üç Mesele: Teknik, Medeniyet ve Yabancılaşma* (Istanbul, n.p., 1992).

——, 'Kalkınma? İlerleme? Varolma?' in Ahmet Tabakoğlu and İsmaii Kurt (eds), *İktisadi Kalkınma ve İslam* (Istanbul, n. p., 1987).

Meral Özbek, 'Arabesk Culture: A Case of Modernisation and Popular Identity', paper presented at the MIT conference 'Rethinking the

Project of Modernity in Turkey', Massachusetts Institute of Technology, March 1994.

Ergun Özbudun, 'The Nature of the Kemalist Political Regime' in A. Kazancıgil and E. Özbudun (eds), *Ataturk: Founder of a Modern State* (London: Hurst, 1981).

Hikmet Özdemir, *Rejim ve Asker* (Istanbul: Afa Yayınları, 1986).

Taha Parla, *The Social and Political Thought of Ziya Gökalp, 1876-1924* (Leiden: E.J. Brill, 1985).

Adamantia Pollis, 'Eastern Orthodoxy and Human Rights', *Human Rights Quarterly*, 1993.

Hugh Poulton, *The Balkans: Minorities and States in Conflict* (London: MRG Publications, 1993.

——, *Who are the Macedonians?* (London: Hurst, 1995).

——, 'The Rest of the Balkans' in H. Miall (ed.), *Minority Rights in Europe: the Scope for a Transnational Regime* (London: RIIA, Pinter, 1994).

Gratton Puxton, *Roma: Europe's Gypsies* (London: MRG Report, 1987).

Ernest E. Ramsaur Jr., *The Young Turks – Prelude to the Revolution of 1908* (Princeton University Press, 1957).

Howard A. Reed, 'Secularism and Islam in Turkish Politics', *Current History*, vol. 32, no. 190, 1957.

Ernest Renan, 'What is a Nation?' in A. Zimmern, *Modern Political Doctrines* (Oxford University Press, 1939).

Dankwart A. Rustow, 'Atatürk as Founder of a State' in Nermin Abadan (ed.), *Yavuz Abadan'a Armağan* (Ankara: Sevinç Matbaası, 1969).

——, 'Atatürk as an Institution Builder' in A. Kazancıgil and E. Özbudun (eds), *Atatürk: Founder of a Modern State* (London: Hurst, 1981).

——, 'The Founding of a Nation State: Atatürk's historical achievement', in *Papers and Discussion: Türkiye İş Bankası International Symposium* on Atatürk (17-22 May 1981) (Ankara: TİSA Matbaacılık Sanayi, 1984).

——, Jeremy Salt, *Imperialism, Evangelism and the Ottoman Armenians 1878-1896* (London: Frank Cass, 1993).

——, 'Nationalism and the Rise of Muslim Sentiment in Turkey', *Middle Eastern Studies*, vol. 31, no. 1, 1995.

Mehmet Saray, *Azerbaycan Türkleri Tarihi* (Istanbul: Yeni Türk Cumhuriyetleri Tarihihi Serisi – 1, 1993).

Cemal Sener, *Atatürk ve Aleviler* (Istanbul: Alev Yayınevi, 1991).

Hugh Seton-Watson, *Nations and States: An Enquiry into the Origins of Nations and the Politics of Nationalism* (London: Methuen, 1977).

Ömer Seyfettin, *Türklük Ülküsü (Mefkûresi)* (Istanbul: Toker, 1990).

Bilal Şimşir, *The Turks of Bulgaria (1878-1985)* (London: K. Rüstem, 1988).

David Shankland, 'Alevi and Sunni in Rural Turkey: Diverse Paths of Change' (unpubl. Ph. D. thesis, Cambridge, Darwin College, 1993).

336 *Bibliography and Main Sources*

——, 'Alevi and Sunni in Rural Anatolia: Diverse Paths of Change' in Paul Stirling (ed.), *Culture and Economy: Changes in Turkish Villages* (Huntingdon: Eothen Press, 1993).

Stanford J. Shaw, *The Jews of the Ottoman Empire and the Turkish Republic* (London: Macmillan, 1991).

Gabriel Sheffer, 'Ethno-national diasporas and security', *Survival*, vol. 36, no. 2, 1994.

Stavro Skendi, *The Albanian National Awakening 1878-1912* (Princeton University Press, 1967).

Jan Slomp, Ge Speelman and Willem de Wit, *Muslims in the Netherlands*, Research Paper no. 37 Muslims in Europe (Birmingham: Centre for the Study of Islam and Christian Muslim Relations, Selly Oak Colleges, March 1988).

Neil J. Smelser, 'Towards a Theory of Modernization' in Neil Smelser, *Essays in Sociological Behaviour* (Englewood Cliffs, NJ: Prentice-Hall, 1968).

Anthony Smith, *Nationalism in the Twentieth Century* (Oxford University Press, 1979).

——, *Theories of Nationalism* (London: Duckworth, 1971).

——, 'The Formation of Nationalist Movements' in Anthony Smith (ed.), *Nationalist Movements* (London: Macmillian, 1976).

James Sowerwine, 'Nation-Building in Central Asia: The Turkish Connection', *Journal of South Asian and Middle Eastern Studies*, vol. 18, 1993.

Yasemin Soysal, 'Workers in Europe: Interactions with the host society' in M. Heper, A. Öncü and H. Kramer (eds), *Turkey and the West*, (London: I.B. Tauris, 1993).

Paul Stirling *Turkish Village* (London: Weidenfeld and Nicolson, 1965).

——, 'Social Change and Social Control in Republican Turkey', in *Papers and Discussion, Türkiye İş Bankası International Symposium on Atatürk (17-22 May 1981)* (Ankara: TİSA Matbaacılık Sanayı, 1981).

Martin Stokes, *The Arabesk Debate: Music and Musicians in Modern Turkey* (Oxford: Clarendon, 1992).

T.C. Devlet, *Milli Kültür Raporu* (Ankara: Devlet Planlama Teşkilatı Yayını, 1983).

——, 'Terörizm ile Mücadele Kanunu', *T.C Resmi Gazete*, no. 20, 843, Ankara, 12 April 1991.

T.C. Eğitim Bakanlığı, *Türkiye Tarihi* (Ankara: 1924).

——, *Türk Tarihinin Anahatlarına Medhal* (Istanbul: 1931).

——, *Ortamektep İçin Tarih* vol 1, 3rd reprint (Istanbul: 1936).

——, *Tarih*, vol. 4 (Istanbul: 1931).

——, *İlkokullar için Sosyal Bilgiler 5* (Ankara: 4th edn, 1993).

——, *Ortaokullar İcin Din Kültürü ve Ahlâk Bilgisi III* (Ankara, n.d.)

——, *Temel Eğitim ve Ortaöğretim Din ve Ahlak Dersi Programı* (Ankara, n.d. [prepared in 1982]).

——, *Milli Eğtim Bakanlığı Din Bilgisi Öğretimi* (Ankara, September 1981).

——, *İmam-Hatip Liseleri Öğretim Programları* (Ankara, 1985).

——, *Sosyal Bilgiler* (Ankara, 1993).

Ahmet Tabakoğlu, 'İslam İktisadi Açısından 'Kalkınma'" in Ahmet Tabakoğlu and Ismail kurt (eds), *Iktisadi Kalkinma ve Islam* (Istanbul, n.p. 1987).

Frank Tachau, 'The Face of Turkish Nationalism (as Reflected in the Cyprus Dispute)', *Middle East Journal*, vol. 13, 1959.

——, 'The Search for National Identity among the Turks', *Welt des Islams*, vol. 8, 1963.

Richard Tapper, 'Introduction' in R. Tapper (ed.), *Islam in Modern Turkey* (London: I.B. Tauris, 1991).

Richard and Nancy Tapper, 'Religion, Education and Continuity in a Provincial Town' in R. Tapper (ed.), *Islam in Modern Turkey* (London: I.B. Tauris, 1991).

——, ' "Thank God we're secular!" Aspects of fundamentalism in a Turkish town' in Lionel Caplan (ed.), *Aspects of Religious Fundamentalism* (London: Macmillan, 1987).

Nurhan Tezcan (ed.) *Atatürk ün Yazdığı Yurttaşlık Bilgileri* (Istanbul: Çağdaş, 1989).

——, *Atatürk'un Söyelv ve Demeleri* (Ankara: Atatürk Kültür, Dil ve Tarih Yuksel Kurumu, Atatürk Araştırma Merkezi, 1989).

Lewis V. Thomas, 'Recent Developments in Turkish Islam', *Middle Eastern Journal* vol. 6, 1952.

Bassam Tibi, *Arab Nationalism* (London: Macmillan, 2nd edn, 1990).

Ferdinand Tönnies, *Community and Association* (London: Routledge, 1955).

Binnaz Toprak, *Islam and Political Development in Turkey* (Leiden: E.J. Brill, 1981).

——, 'The Religious Right' in I.C. Schik and A.E. Tonak (eds), *Turkey in Transition*, Oxford University Press, 1984).

——, 'Islamist Intellectuals: Revolt against Industry and Technology' in Metin Heper, Ayşe Öncü and Heinz Kramer (eds), *Turkey and the West: Changing Political and Cultural Identities* (London: I.B. Tauris, 1993).

Zafer Toprak, *Türkiye'de 'Milli İktisad' (1908-1918)* (Ankara: Yurt, 1982).

J. Spencer Trimingham, *The Sufi Orders of Islam* (Oxford: Clarendon Press, 1971).

William Tucker, 'The Shaikh Said Rebellion in Turkey in 1925', *Die Welt des Islam*, vol. 18, 1977-8.

Hüseyin Tunce, *Türk Yurdu – üzerine bir inceleme* (Ankara: Kültür Bakanligi, 1990).

Mete Tunçay, *Türkiye Cumhuriyet'inde Tek-Parti Yönetiminin Kurulması,* 1923-1931 (Ankara: Yurt, 1981).

İlter Turan, 'Religion and Political Culture in Turkey' in R. Tapper (ed.), *Islam in Modern Turkey* (London: I.B. Tauris, 1991).

Türk Ocakları, *Güney-Doğu Anadolu'nun Tarihi Kültürel Ekonomik Jeo-Politik ve Sosyal Durumu* (Ankara: Türk Ocakları Merkez İdare Heyeti, 1992).

——, *Türk Ocakları Merkez İdare Heyeti: Yeni Devre IV Olağan Kurultay Raporu* (Ankara: Türk Ocakları Merkez İdare Heyeti, 1992).

Alparslan Türkeş, *Yeni Ufaklara Doğru* (Istanbul: Kutluğ, 1973).

——, 'SSCB'ndeki Türk Cumhuriyetleri ve Muhtar Bülgeleri ile İlişkiler, Konusunda meclis konuşmaları', *Birleşim TBMM Tutanakları,* 12 and 17 December 1991.

Turkish Human Rights Association (İHD), *Training and Education in the Emergency State Region* (Ankara: İHD, November 1994).

——, *The Report by the Delegation for Human Rights on Immigration* (Ankara: İHD, July 1994).

R. Tuzmuhamedov, *How the National Question Was Solved in Soviet Central Asia (A Reply to Falsifiers)* (Moscow: Progress, 1973).

United Nations, *UN Declaration on the Rights of Persons Belonging to National or Ethnic, Religious and Linguistic Minorities* (adopted by the UN General Assembly; Resolution 47/135, 18 December 1992).

——, *The International Bill of Human Rights* (New York: United Nations, 1978).

Füsun Üstel, 'Les "Foyers Turcs" et les "Turcs de l'Exterieur"', *CEMOTI,* no. 16, 1993.

Vamık D. Volkan and Norman Itzkowitz, *Turks and Greeks: Neighbours in Conflict* (Huntingdon: Eothen Press, 1994).

Wayne S. Vucinich, *Serbia between East and West* (Stanford University Press, 1968).

Walter F. Weiker, *Political Tutelage and Democracy in Turkey – The Free Party and its Aftermath* (Leiden: E.J. Brill, 1973).

M. Weiner (ed.), *International Migration and Security* (Boulder, CO: Westview Press, 1993).

Lale Yalçın-Heckmenn, 'Kurdish tribal organization and local political processes' in A. Finkel and N. Sirman (eds), *Turkish State, Turkish Society* (London: Routledge, 1990).

——, 'Ethnic Islam and nationalism among Kurds in Turkey' in Richard Tapper (ed.), *Islam in Modern Turkey* (London: I.B. Tauris, 1991).

——, 'Global Ideologies, Local Strategies: Notes on the recent history of a Kurdish village in Hakkari', paper given at SOAS, London University, 8 December 1994.

Ahmet Emin Yalman, *Turkey in My Time* (Norman: University of Oklahoma Press, 1956).

Nur Yalman, 'Islamic reform and the mystic tradition in Eastern Turkey', *Archives Européens de Sociologie*, vol. 10, 1969.

Feroz A.K. Yasamee, 'Abdülhamid II and the Ottoman Defence Problem', *Diplomacy and Statecraft*, vol. 4, no. 1, 1993.

——, 'The Ottoman Empire, the Sudan and the Red Sea Coast, 1883–1889' in S. Deringil and S. Kuneralp (eds), *The Ottomans in Africa: Studies in Ottoman Diplomatic History* (Istanbul: Isis, 1990).

Riza Yürükoğlu, *Okunacak En Büyük Kitap insandir: Tarih te ve Günümüzde Alevilik* (Istanbul: Alev Yayinevi, 1990).

Thomas Szayna, *Ethnic conflict in central Europe and the Balkans: a framework and U.S. policy options* (RAND for US Army, 1994).

Zeine N. Zeine,. *Arab-Turkish Relations and the Emergence of Arab Nationalism* (Beirut: Khayat, 1958).

Erik J. Zürcher, *Turkey: A Modern History* (London: I.B. Tauris, 1993).

——, *The Unionist Factor – The role of the CUP in the Turkish National Movement 1905-1926* (Leiden: E.J. Brill, 1984).

——, *Political Opposition in the Early Turkish Republic: the Progressive Republican Party 1924-1925* (Leiden: E.J. Brill, 1991).

INDEX

Abdülhamid II: 33, 45; use of Islam and Caliphate, 58-62, 315, 319; overthrow, 65, 69; 68
Abdülmecid, 51
Abkhaz, 245
Afghanistan, 148
Africa, 13, 17, 18
African National Congress, 237
Aga, M., 299
Ağaoğlu, A., 103, 107, 132, 133
Ağaoğulları M.A., 135, 147, 152
Ağralı, F., 119
Ahmet, S., 299
Akçura, Y.: 62; life and ideolgy 72-5; Turanism and *Türk Ocağı*, 82-3, 103, 105; at first History Congress 107; 132, 133, 168
Aktuna, Y., 262
Albania and Albanians: 33, 37, 39, 43, 44, 59; rise of Albanian nationalism, 64-7; 78, 86, 95, 122, 153, 291, 311, 313, 315
Alevis: 9, 36ff; in Kemalist state 125-7; attacks on by rightists 162; RP view 187; attacks on by Sunni radicals 189; 203; Alevi Kurds, 98, 207-8, 258; structures of community, 252-4; Sivas outrage, 256-7; 31st HacıBektaş Veli Festival, 257-61; rising tension and riots in Istanbul, 262-5; 283-4; among *Gastarbeiter*, 310-1; 320; *see also* Bektaşis and Shias
Algeria, 29
Ali, 35, 255, 261
Ali Paşa, 51, 55
Ali Suavi, 55, 57

Alican, E., 138
Alp Tekin (Moise Cohen), 83ff, 123-4, 279
Altan, Ç., 227
ANAP (Motherland Party): 140, 180; 'Holy Alliance' and lifting head-scarf ban 195; 204, 255, 260, 274
Anatolia (as *patrie*): 25, 40, 41, 128, 317; in tandem with Turkism, 62-4; 86, 97
Anderson, B., 17, 39, 85, 315
Anter, M., 155
AO (Hearth of the Enlightened), 179-80, 184
AP (Justice Party) *see* Demirel
Arabesk, 145
Arabs and Arabia: 33; nationalism 35ff, 60; 39, 59, 86, 95, 98, 233, 315; in Turkey, 269;
Armenia and Armenians: 42, 52, 63, 123, 124, 288; massacres 59-60ff, 81, 114, 152; ASALA (Secret Army for the Liberation of Armenia) and hostility from right 153-4; community in Turkey, 275-8, 283-4
ASALA (Secret Army for the Liberation of Armenia), 153
Asım, N., (Yazıksız), 61ff, 63
Association of Hearths of Ideals, 143
Association of Idealistic Youth, 143
Atatürk (Mustafa Kemal): 8; part in CUP revolution, 70; Independence War and great reforms, 87-92, 126; ideology of

341